The Southerner
A Romance of the Real Lincoln

Thomas Dixon

Contents

THE SOUTHERNER 8
PROLOGUE 8
I 8
II 12
III 15
IV 17
V 21
VI 26
VII 32
VIII 36
IX 41
X 50
XI 53
XII 58
XIII 62
The Story 70
  CHAPTER I THE MAN OF THE HOUR 70
  CHAPTER II JANGLING VOICES 89
  CHAPTER III IN BETTY'S GARDEN 94
  CHAPTER IV A PAIR OF YOUNG EYES 98
  CHAPTER V THE FIRST SHOT 101
  CHAPTER VI THE PARTING OF THE WAYS 104
  CHAPTER VII LOVE AND DUTY 110
  CHAPTER VIII THE TRIAL BY FIRE 116
  CHAPTER IX VICTORY IN DEFEAT 128
  CHAPTER X THE AWAKENING 132
  CHAPTER XI THE MAN ON HORSEBACK 137
  CHAPTER XII LOVE AND PRIDE 144
  CHAPTER XIII THE SPIRES OF RICHMOND 152
  CHAPTER XIV THE RETREAT 168
  CHAPTER XV TANGLED THREADS 171
  CHAPTER XVI THE CHALLENGE 180
  CHAPTER XVII THE DAY'S WORK 191
  CHAPTER XVIII DIPLOMACY 204
  CHAPTER XIX THE REBEL 210
  CHAPTER XX THE INSULT 222
  CHAPTER XXI THE BLOODIEST DAY 225
  CHAPTER XXII BENEATH THE SKIN 228
  CHAPTER XXIII THE USURPER 231
  CHAPTER XXIV THE CONSPIRACY 237
  CHAPTER XXV THE TUG OF WAR 241
  CHAPTER XXVI THE REST HOUR 257
  CHAPTER XXVII DEEPENING SHADOWS 263
  CHAPTER XXVIII THE MOONLIT RIVER 282
  CHAPTER XXIX THE PANIC 288
  CHAPTER XXX SUNSHINE AND STORM 297
  CHAPTER XXXI BETWEEN THE LINES 308
  CHAPTER XXXII THE WHIRLWIND 311
  CHAPTER XXXIII THE BROTHERS MEET 321
  CHAPTER XXXIV LOVE'S PLEDGE 328
  CHAPTER XXXV THE DARKEST HOUR 332

CHAPTER XXXVI THE ASSASSIN 347
CHAPTER XXXVII MR. DAVIS SPEAKS 356
CHAPTER XXXVIII THE STOLEN MARCH 360
CHAPTER XXXIX VICTORY 365
CHAPTER XL WITH MALICE TOWARD NONE 369

THE SOUTHERNER

A ROMANCE OF THE REAL LINCOLN

BY

Thomas Dixon

LEADING CHARACTERS OF THE STORY

1809-1818

Scene: A Cabin in the Woods

TOM, A Man of the Forest and Stream. NANCY, The Woman Who Saw a Vision. THE BOY, Her Son. DENNIS, His Cousin. BONEY, A Fighting Coon Dog.

1861-1865

Scene: The White House

SENATOR GILBERT WINTER, The Radical Leader. BETTY, His Daughter. JOHN VAUGHAN, A Union Soldier. NED VAUGHAN, His Brother, a Rebel. ABRAHAM LINCOLN, The President. MRS. LINCOLN, His Wife. PHOEBE, Her Maid. JULIUS CAESAR THORNTON, Who Was Volunteered. COLONEL NICOLAY, The President's Secretary. MAJOR JOHN HAY, Assistant Secretary. WILLIAM TECUMSEH SHERMAN, Who Stole a March. GEORGE B. MCCLELLAN, The Man on Horseback. ROBERT E. LEE, The Southern Commander.

THE SOUTHERNER

PROLOGUE
I

Tom seated himself at the table and looked into his wife's face with a smile:
"Nancy, it's a meal fit for a king!"

The supper over, he smoked his pipe before the cabin fire of blazing logs, while she cleared the wooden dishes. He watched her get the paper, goose-quill pen and ink as a prisoner sees the scaffold building for his execution.

"Now we're all ready," she said cheerfully.

The man laid his pipe down with a helpless look. A brief respite flashed through his mind. Maybe he could sidestep the lessons before she pinned him down.

"Lord, Nancy, I forgot my gun. I must grease her right away," he cried.

He rose with a quick decisive movement and took his rifle from the rack. She knew it was useless to protest and let him have his way.

Over every inch of its heavy barrel and polished walnut stock he rubbed a piece of greased linen with loving care, drew back the flint-lock and greased carefully every nook and turn of its mechanism, lifted the gun finally to his shoulder and drew an imaginary bead on the head of a turkey gobbler two hundred yards away. A glowing coal of hickory wood in the fire served for his game.

He lowered the gun and held it before him with pride:

"Nancy, she's the dandiest piece o' iron that wuz ever twisted inter the shape of a weepon. Old 'Speakeasy's her name! She's got the softest voice that ever whispered death to a varmint or an Injun--hit ain't much louder'n the crack of a whip, but, man alive, when she talks she says somethin'. 'Kerpeow!' she whispers soft an' low! She's got a voice like yourn, Nancy--kinder sighs when she speaks----"

"Well," the wife broke in with a shake of her dark head, "has mother's little boy played long enough with his toy?"

"I reckon so," Tom laughed.

"Then it's time for school." She gently took the rifle from his hands, placed it on the buck horns and took her seat at the table.

The man looked ruefully at the stool, suddenly straightened his massive frame, lifted his hand above his head and cocked his eye inquiringly:

"May I git er drink er water fust?"

The teacher laughed in spite of herself:

"Yes, you big lubber, and hurry up."

Tom seized the water bucket and started for the door.

"Where are you going?" she cried in dismay.

"I'll jest run down to the spring fer a fresh bucket----"

"O Tom!" she exclaimed.

"I'll be right back in a minute, Honey," he protested softly. "Hit's goin' ter be powerful hot--I'll need a whole bucket time I'm through."

Before she could answer he was gone.

He managed to stay nearly a half hour. She put the baby to sleep and sat waiting with her pensive young eyes gazing at the leaping flames. She heard him stop and answer the call of an owl from the woods. A whip-poor-will was softly singing from the bushes nearby. He stopped to call him also, and then found an excuse to linger ten minutes more fooling with his dogs.

The laggard came at last and dropped on his stool by her side. He sat for five minutes staring helplessly at the copy she had set. Big beads of perspiration stood on his forehead when he took the pen. He held it awkwardly and timidly as if it were a live reptile. She took his clumsy hand in hers and showed him how to hold it.

"My, but yo' hand's soft an' sweet, Nancy,--jest lemme hold that a while----"

She rapped his knuckles.

"All right, teacher, I'll be good," he protested, and bent his huge shoulders low over his task. He bore so hard on the frail quill pen the ink ran in a big blot.

"Not so hard, Tom!" she cried.

"But I got so much strenk in my right arm I jist can't hold it back."

"You must try again."

He tried again and made a heavy tremulous line. His arm moved at a snail's gait and wobbled frightfully.

"Make the line quicker," she urged encouragingly. "Begin at the top and come down----"

"Here, you show me how!"

She took his rough hand quietly in hers, and guided it swiftly from right to left in straight smooth lines until a dozen were made, when he suddenly drew her close, kissed her lips, and held the slender fingers in a grip of iron. She lay still in his embrace for a moment, released herself and turned from him with a sigh. He drew her quickly to the light of the fire and saw the unshed tears in her eyes.

"What's the use ter worry, Nancy gal?" he said. "Give it up ez a bad job. I wouldn't fool with no sech scholar ef I wuz you. Ye can't teach an old dog new tricks----"

"I won't give up!" she cried with sudden energy. "I can teach you and I will. I won't give up and be nobody. O Tom, you promised me before we were married to let me teach you--didn't you promise?"

"Yes, Honey, I did----" he paused and his fine teeth gleamed through the black beard--"but ye know a feller'll promise any thing ter git his gal----"

"Didn't you mean to keep your word?" She broke in sharply.

"Of course I did, Nancy, I never wuz more earnest in my life--'ceptin when I got religion. But I had no idee larnin' come so hard. I'd ruther fight Injuns an' wil' cats or rob a bee tree any day than ter tackle them pot hooks you're sickin' after me----"

"Well, I won't give up," she interrupted impatiently, "and you'd just as well make up your mind to stick to it. You can do what other men have done. You're good, honest and true, you're kindhearted and popular. They've already made you the road supervisor of this township. Learn to read and write and you can make a good speech and go to the Legislature."

"Ah, Nancy, what do ye want me ter do that fur, anyhow, gal? I'd be the happiest man in the world right here in this cabin by the woods ef you'd jest be happy with me. Can't ye quit hankerin' after them things, Honey?"

She shook her dark head firmly.

"You know, Nancy, we wuz neighbors to Dan'l Boone. We thought he wuz about the biggest man that ever lived. Somehow the love o' the woods an' fields is always singin' in my heart. Them still shinin' stars up in the sky out thar to-night keep a callin' me. I could hear the music o' my hounds in my soul ez I stood by the spring a while ago. Ye know what scares me most ter death sometimes, gal?" He paused and looked into her eyes intently.

"No, what?" she asked.

"That you'll make a carpenter outen me yit ef I don't mind."

Again a smile broke through the cloud in her eyes: "I don't think there's much danger of *that*, Tom----"

"Yes ther is, too," he laughed. "Ye see, I love you so and try ter make ye happy, an' ef there wuz ter come er time that there wuz plenty o' work an' real money in it, I'd stick to it jist ter please you, an' be a lost an' ruined soul! Yessir, they'd carve on my headstone jest one line:

"BORN A MAN--AND DIED A JACKLEG CARPENTER.

"Wouldn't that be awful?"

The momentary smile on the woman's sensitive face faded into a look of pain. She tried to make a good-natured reply, but her lips refused to move.

The man pressed on eagerly:

"O Nancy, why can't ye be happy here? We've a snug little cabin nest, we've enough to eat and enough to wear. The baby's laughin' at yer heels all day and snugglin' in her little bed at night. The birds make music fur ye in the trees. The creek down thar's laughin' an' singing' winter an' summer. The world's too purty an' life's too short ter throw hit away fightin' an' scramblin' fur nothin'."

"For something--Tom--something big----"

"Don't keer how big 'tis--what of it? All turns ter ashes in yer hands bye an' bye an' yer life's gone. We can't live these young days over again, can we? Ye know the preacher says: 'What shall hit profit a man ef he gain the whole world an' lose his life?' Let me off'n these lessons, Honey? I'm too old; ye can't larn me new tricks now. Let me off fer good an' all, won't ye?"

"No," was the firm answer. "It means too much. I won't give up and let the man I love sign his name forever with a cross mark."

"I ain't goin' ter sign no more papers nohow!" Tom broke in.

"I signed our marriage bond with a mark, Tom," she went on evenly, "just because you couldn't write your name. You've got to learn, I won't give up!"

"Well, it's too late to-night fur any more lessons, now *ain't* it?"

"Yes, we'll make up for it next time."

The tired hunter was soon sound asleep dreaming of the life that was the breath of his nostrils.

Through the still winter's night the young wife lay with wide staring eyes. Over and over again she weighed her chances in the grim struggle begun for the mastery of his mind. The longer she asked herself the question of success or failure the more doubtful seemed the outcome. How still the world!

The new life within her strong young body suddenly stirred, and a feeling of awe thrilled her heart. God had suddenly signalled from the shores of Eternity.

When her husband waked at dawn he stared at her smiling face in surprise.

"What ye laughin' about, Nancy?" he cried.

She turned toward him with a startled look:

"I had a vision, Tom!"

"A dream, I reckon."

"God had answered the prayer of my heart," she went on breathlessly, "and sent me a son. I saw him a strong, brave, patient, wise, gentle man. Thousands hung on his words and great men came to do him homage. With bowed head he led me into a beautiful home that had shining white pillars. He bowed low and whispered in my ear: 'This is yours, my angel mother. I bought it for you with my life. All that I am I owe to you.'"

She paused a moment and whispered:

"O Tom, man, a new song is singing in my soul!"

II

The woman rose quietly and went the rounds of her daily work. She made her bed to-day in trance-like silence. It was no gilded couch, but it had been built by the hand of her lover and was sacred. It filled the space in one corner of the cabin farthest from the fire. A single post of straight cedar securely fixed in the ground held the poles in place which formed the side and foot rail. The walls of the cabin formed the other side and head. Across from the pole were fixed the slender hickory sticks that formed the springy hammock on which the first mattress of moss and grass rested. On this was placed a feather bed made from the wild fowl Tom had killed during the past two years. The pillows were of the finest feathers from the breasts of ducks. A single quilt of ample size covered all, and over this was thrown a huge counterpane of bear skins. Two enormous bear rugs almost completely covered the dirt floor, and a carpet of oak leaves filled out the spaces.

The feather bed beaten smooth, the fur covering drawn in place and the pillows set upright against the cabin wall, she turned to the two bunks in the opposite corner and carefully re-arranged them. They might be used soon. This was the corner of her home set aside for guests. Tom had skillfully built two berths boat fashion, one above the other, in this corner, and a curtain drawn over a smooth wooden rod cut this space off from the rest of the room when occupied at night by visitors.

The master of this cabin never allowed a stranger to pass without urging him to stop and in a way that took no denial.

A savory dish of stewed squirrel and corn dumplings served for lunch. The baby's face was one glorious smear of joy and grease at its finish.

The mother took the bucket from its shelf and walked leisurely to the spring, whose limpid waters gushed from a rock at the foot of the hill. The child toddled after her, the little moccasined feet stepping gingerly over the sharp gravel of the rough places.

Before filling the bucket she listened again for the crack of Tom's rifle, and could hear nothing. A death-like stillness brooded over the woods and fields. He was probably watching for muskrat under the bluff of the creek. He had promised to stay within call to-day.

The afternoon dragged wearily. She tried to read the one book she possessed, the Bible. The pages seemed to fade and the eyes refused to see.

"O Man, Man, why don't you come home!" she cried at last.

She rose, walked to the door, looked and listened--only the distant rattle of a woodpecker's beak on a dead tree in the woods. The snow began to fall in little fitful dabs. It was two miles to the nearest cabin, and her soul rose in fierce rebellion at her loneliness. It was easy for a man who loved the woods, the fields and running waters, this life, but for the woman who must wait and long and eat her heart out alone--she vowed anew that she would not endure it. By the sheer pull of her will she would lift this man from his drifting life and make him take his place in the real battle of the world. If her new baby were only a boy, he could help her and she would win. Again she stood dreaming of the vision she had seen at dawn.

The dark young face suddenly went white and her hand gripped the facing of the door.

She waited half doubting, half amused at her fears. It was only the twinge of a muscle perhaps. She smiled at her sudden panic. The thought had scarcely formed before she blanched the second time and the firm lips came together with sudden energy as she glanced at the child playing on the rug at her feet.

She seized the horn that hung beside the door and blew the pioneer's long call of danger. Its shrill note rang through the woods against the hills in cadences that seemed half muffled by the falling snow.

Again her anxious eyes looked from the doorway. Would he never come! The trembling slender hand once more lifted the horn, a single wild note rang out and broke suddenly into silence. The horn fell from her limp grasp and she lifted her eyes to the darkening sky in prayer, as Tom's voice from the edge of the woods came strong and full:

"Yes, Honey, I'm comin'!"

There was no question of doctor or nurse. The young pioneer mother only asked for her mate.

For two fearful hours she gripped his rough hands until at last her nails brought the blood, but the man didn't know or care. Every smothered cry that came from her lips began to tear the heart out of his body at last. He could hold the long pent agony no longer without words.

"My God, Nancy, what can I do for ye, Honey?"

Her breath came in gasps and her eyes were shining with a strange intensity.

"Nothing, Tom, nothing now--I'm looking Death in the face and I'm not afraid----"

"Please lemme give ye some whiskey," he pleaded, pressing the glass to her lips.

"No--no, take it away--I hate it. My baby shall be clean and strong or I want to die."

The decision seemed to brace her spirit for the last test when the trembling feet entered the shadows of the dim valley that lies between Life and Death.

The dark, slender figure lay still and white at last. A sharp cry from lusty lungs, and the grey eyes slowly opened, with a timid wondering look.

"Tom!" she cried with quick eager tones.

"Yes, Nancy, yes!"

"A boy?"

"Of course--and a buster he is, too."

"Give him to me--quick!"

The stalwart figure bent over the bed and laid the little red bundle in her arms. She pressed him tenderly to her heart, felt his breath on her breast and the joyous tears slowly poured down her cheeks.

III

Before the first year of the boy's life had passed the task of teaching his good-natured, stubborn father became impossible. The best the wife could do was to make him trace his name in sprawling letters that resembled writing and painfully spell his way through the simplest passages in the Bible.

The day she gave up was one of dumb despair. She resolved at last to live in her boy. All she had hoped and dreamed of life should be his and he would be hers. Her hands could make him good or bad, brave or cowardly, noble or ignoble.

He was a remarkable child physically, and grew out of his clothes faster than she could make them. It was easy to see from his second year that he would be a man of extraordinary stature. Both mother and father were above the average height, but he would overtop them both. When he tumbled over the bear rugs on the cabin floor his father would roar with laughter:

"For the Lord's sake, Nancy, look at them legs! They're windin' blades. Ef he ever gits grown, he won't have ter ax fer a blessin', he kin jest reach up an' hand it down hisself!"

He was four years old when he got the first vision of his mother that time should never blot out. His father was away on a carpenter job of four days. Sleeping in the lower bunk in the corner, he waked with a start to hear the chickens cackling loudly. His mother was quietly dressing. He leaped to his feet shivering in the dark and whispered:

"What is it, Ma?"

"Something's after the chickens."

"Not a hawk?"

"No, nor an owl, or fox, or weasel--or they'd squall--they're cackling."

The rooster cackled louder than ever and the Boy recognized the voice of his speckled hen accompanying him. How weird it sounded in the darkness of the still spring night! The cold chills ran down his back and he caught his mother's dress as she reached for the rifle that stood beside her bed.

"You're not goin' out there, Ma?" the Boy protested.

"Yes. It's a dirty thief after our horse."

Her voice was low and steady and her hand was without tremor as she grasped his.

"Get back in bed. I won't be gone a minute."

She left the cabin and noiselessly walked toward the low shed in which the horse was stabled.

The Boy was at her heels. She knew and rejoiced in the love that made him brave for her sake.

She paused a moment, listened, and then lifted her tall, slim form and advanced steadily. Her bare feet made no noise. The waning moon was shining with soft radiance. The Boy's heart was in his throat as he watched her slender neck and head outlined against the sky. Never had he seen anything so calm and utterly brave.

There was a slight noise at the stable. The chickens cackled with louder call. Five minutes passed and they were silent. A shadowy figure appeared at the corner of the stable. She raised the rifle and flashed a dagger-like flame into the darkness.

A smothered cry, the shadow leaped the fence and the beat of swift feet could be heard in the distance.

The Boy clung close to her side and his voice was husky as he spoke:

"Ain't you afraid, Ma?"

The calm answer rang forever through his memory:

"I don't know what fear means, my Boy. It's not the first time I've caught these prowling scoundrels."

Next morning he saw the dark blood marks on the trail over which the thief had fled, and looked into his mother's wistful grey eyes with a new reverence and awe.

IV

The Boy was quick to know and love the birds of hedge and field and woods. The martins that built in his gourds on the tall pole had opened his eyes. The red and bluebirds, the thrush, the wren, the robin, the catbird, and song sparrows were his daily companions.

A mocking-bird came at last to build her nest in a bush beside the garden, and her mate began to make the sky ring with his song. The puzzle of the feathered tribe whose habits he couldn't fathom was the whip-poor-will. His mother seemed to dislike his ominous sound. But the soft mournful notes appealed to the Boy's fancy. Often at night he sat in the doorway of the cabin watching the gathering shadows and the flicker of the fire when supper was cooking, listening to the tireless song within a few feet of the house.

"Why don't you like 'em, Ma?" he asked, while one was singing with unusually deep and haunting voice so near the cabin that its echo seemed to come from the chimney jamb.

It was some time before she replied:

"They say it's a sign of death for them to come so close to the house."

The Boy laughed:

"You don't believe it?"

"I don't know."

"Well, I like 'em," he stoutly declared. "I like to feel the cold shivers when they sing right under my feet. You're not afraid of a little whip-poor-will?"

He looked up into her sombre face with a smile.

"No," was the gentle answer, "but I want to live to see my Boy a fine strong man," she paused, stooped, and drew him into her arms.

There was something in her tones that brought a lump into his throat. The moon was shining in the full white glory of the Southern spring. A night of marvellous beauty enfolded the little cabin. He looked into her eyes and they were shining with tears.

"What's the matter?" he asked tenderly.

"Nothing, Boy, I'm just dreaming of you!"

* * * * *

The first day of the fall in his sixth year he asked his mother to let him go to the next corn-shucking.

"You're too little a boy."

"I can shuck corn," he stoutly argued.

"You'll be good, if I let you go?" she asked.

"What's to hurt me there?"

"Nothing, unless you let it. The men drink whiskey, the girls dance. Sometimes there's a quarrel or fight."

"It won't hurt me ef I 'tend to my own business, will it?"

"Nothing will ever hurt you, if you'll just do that, Boy," the father broke in.

"May I go?"

"Yes, we're invited next week to a quilting and corn-shucking. I'll go with you."

The Boy shouted for joy and counted the days until the wonderful event. They left home at two o'clock in the wagon. The quilting began at three, the corn-shucking at sundown.

The house was a marvellous structure to the Boy's excited imagination. It was the first home he had ever seen not built of logs.

"Why, Ma," he cried in open-eyed wonder, "there ain't no logs in the house! How did they ever put it together?"

"With bricks and mortar."

The Boy couldn't keep his eyes off this building. It was a simple, one-story square structure of four rooms and an attic, with little dormer windows peeping from the four sides of the pointed roof. McDonald, the thrifty Scotch-Irishman, from the old world, had built it of bricks he had ground and burnt on his own place.

The dormer windows peeping from the roof caught the Boy's fancy.

"Do you reckon his boys sleep up there and peep out of them holes?"

The mother smiled.

"Maybe so."

"Why don't we build a house like that?" he asked at last. "Don't you want it?"

The mother squeezed his little hand:

"When you're a man will you build your mother one?"

He looked into her eyes a moment, caught the pensive longing and answered:

"Yes. I will."

She stooped and kissed the firm mouth and was about to lead him into the large work-room where the women were gathering around the quilts stretched on their frames, when a negro slave suddenly appeared to take her horse to the stable. He was fat, jolly and coal black. His yellow teeth gleamed in their blue gums with a jovial welcome.

The Boy stood rooted to the spot and watched until the negro disappeared. It was the first black man he had ever seen. He had heard of negroes and that they were slaves. But he had no idea that one human being could be so different from another.

In breathless awe he asked:

"Is he folks?"

"Of course, Boy," his mother answered, smiling.

"What made him so black?"

"The sun in Africa."

"What made his nose so flat and his lips so thick?"

"He was born that way."

"What made him come here?"

"He didn't. The slave traders put him in chains and brought him across the sea and sold him into slavery."

The little body suddenly stiffened:

"Why didn't he kill 'em?"

"He didn't know how to defend himself."

"Why don't he run away?"

"He hasn't sense enough, I reckon. He's got a home, plenty to eat and plenty to wear, and he's afraid he'll be caught and whipped."

The mother had to pull the Boy with her into the quilting room. His eyes followed the negro to the stable with a strange fascination. The thing that puzzled him beyond all comprehension was why a big strong man like that, if he were a man, would submit. Why didn't he fight and die? A curious feeling of contempt filled his mind. This black thing that looked like a man, walked like a man and talked like a man couldn't be one! No real man would grin and laugh and be a slave. The black fool seemed to be happy. He had not only grinned and laughed, but he went away whistling and singing.

In three hours the quilts were finished and the men had gathered for the cornshucking.

Before eight o'clock the last ear was shucked, and a long white pile of clean husked corn lay glistening in the moonlight where the dark pyramid had stood at sunset.

With a shout the men rose, stretched their legs and washed their hands in the troughs filled with water, provided for the occasion. They sat down to supper at four long tables placed in the kitchen and work room, where the quilts had been stretched.

Never had the Boy seen such a feast--barbecued shoat, turkeys, ducks, chickens, venison, bear meat, sweet potatoes, wild honey, corn dodgers, wheat biscuit, stickies and pound cake--pound cake until you couldn't eat another mouthful and still they brought more!

After the supper the young folks sang and danced before the big fires until ten o'clock, and then the crowd began to thin, and by eleven the last man was gone and the harvest festival was over.

It was nearly twelve before the Boy knelt at his mother's knee to say his prayers.

When the last words were spoken he still knelt, his eyes gazing into the flickering fire.

The mother bent low:

"What are you thinking about, Boy? The house you're going to build for me?"

"No."

"What?"

"That nigger--wasn't he funny? You don't want me to get you any niggers with the house do you?"

"No."

"I didn't think you would," he went on thoughtfully, "because you said General Washington set his slaves free and wanted everybody else to do it too."

He paused and shook his head thoughtfully. "But he was funny--he was laughin' and whistlin' and singin'!"

V

The air of the Southern autumn was like wine. The Boy's heart beat with new life. The scarlet and purple glory of the woods fired his imagination. He found himself whistling and singing at his tasks. He proudly showed a bee tree to his mother, the honey was gathered and safely stored. A barrel of walnuts, a barrel of hickorynuts and two bushels of chestnuts were piled near his bed in the loft.

But the day his martins left, he came near breaking down. He saw them circle high in graceful sweeping curves over the gourds, chattering and laughing with a strange new note in their cries.

He watched them wistfully. His mother found him looking with shining eyes far up into the still autumn sky. His voice was weak and unsteady when he spoke:

"I--can--hardly--hear--'em--now; they're so high!"

A slender hand touched his tangled hair:

"Don't worry, Boy, they'll come again."

"You're sure, Ma?" he asked, pathetically.

"Sure."

"Will they know when it's time?"

"Some one always tells them."

"Who?"

"God. That's what the Bible means when it says, 'the stork knoweth her appointed time.' I read that to you the other night, don't you remember?"

"But maybe God'll be so busy he'll forget my birds?"

"He never forgets, he counts the beat of a sparrow's wing."

The mother's faith was contagious. The drooping spirit caught the flash of light from her eyes and smiled.

"We'll watch for 'em next spring, won't we? And I'll put up new gourds long before they come!"

Comforted at last, he went to the woods to gather chinquapins. The squirrels were scampering in all directions and he asked his father that night to let him go hunting with him next day.

"All right, Boy!" was the hearty answer. "We'll have some fun this winter."

He paused as he saw the mother's lips suddenly close and a shadow pass over her dark, sensitive face.

"Hit's no use ter worry, Nancy," he went on good-naturedly. "I promised you not ter take him 'less he wanted ter go. But hit's in the blood, and hit's got ter come out."

Tom picked the Boy up and placed him on his knee and stroked his dark head. Sarah crouched at his feet and smiled. He was going to tell about the Indians again. She could tell by the look in his eye as he watched the flames leap over the logs.

"Did ye know, Boy," he began slowly, "that we come out to Kaintuck with Daniel Boone?"

"Did we?"

"Yes sirree, with old Dan'l hisself. It wuz thirty years ago. I wuz a little shaver no bigger'n you, but I remember jest as well ez ef it wuz yistiddy. Lordy, Boy, thar wuz er man that wuz er man! Ye couldn't a made no jackleg carpenter outen him----" He paused and cast a sly wink at Nancy as she bent over her knitting.

"Tell me about him?" the Boy cried.

"Yessir, Dan'l Boone wuz a man an' no mistake. The Indians would ketch 'im an' keep er ketchin' 'im an' he'd slip through their fingers slicker'n a eel. The very fust trip he tuck out here he wuz captured by the Redskins. Dan'l wuz with his friend John Stuart.

"They left their camp one day an' set out on a big hunt, and all of a sudden they wuz grabbed by the Injuns."

"Why didn't they shoot 'em?" the Boy asked.

"They wuz too many of 'em an' they wuz too quick for Dan'l. He didn't have no show at all. The Injuns robbed 'em of everything they had an' kept 'em prisoners.

"But ole Dan'l wuz a slick un. He'd been studyin' Injuns all his life an' he knowed 'em frum a ter izard. They didn't have nothin' but bows an' arrers then an' he had a rifle thes like mine. He never got flustered or riled by the way they wuz treatin' him, but let on like he wuz happy ez er June bug. Dan'l would raise his rifle, put a bullet twixt a buffalo's eyes an' he'd drap in his tracks. The Injuns wuz tickled ter death an' thought him the greatest man that ever lived--an' he wuz, too. So they got ter likin' him an' treatin' 'im better. For seven days an' nights him an' Stuart helped 'em hunt an' showed 'em how ter work er rifle. The Injuns was plum fooled by Dan'l's friendly ways an' didn't watch 'im so close.

"So one night Dan'l helped 'em ter eat a bigger supper than ever. They wuz all full enough ter bust, an' went ter sleep an' slept like logs. Hit wuz a dark night an' the fire burned low, an' long 'bout midnight Dan'l made up his mind ter give 'em the slip.

"Hit wuz er dangerous job. Ef he failed hit wuz death shore-nuff, for nothin' makes a Injun so pizen mad ez fer anybody ter be treated nice by 'em an' then try ter get away. The Redskins wuz all sleepin' round the fire. They wuz used ter jumpin' in the middle o' the night or any minute. Mebbe they wuz all ersleep, an' mebbe they wasn't.

"Old Dan'l he pertended ter be sleepin' the sleep er the dead, an' I tell ye he riz mighty keerful, shuck Stuart easy, waked him up an' motioned him ter foller. Talk about sneakin' up on a wild duck er a turkey--ole Dan'l done some slick business gettin' away frum that fire! Man, ef they'd rustled a leaf er broke a twig, them savages would a all been up an' on 'em in a minute. Holdin' tight to their guns--you kin bet they didn't leave them--and a steppin' light ez feathers they crept away from the fire an' out into the deep dark o' the woods. They stopped an' stood as still ez death an' watched till they see the Injuns hadn't waked----"

The pioneer paused and his white teeth shone through his black beard as he cocked his shaggy head to one side and looked into the Boy's wide eyes.

"And then what do you reckon Dan'l Boone done, sir?"

"What?"

"Waal, ye seed the way them bees made fer their trees, didn't ye, when they got a load er honey?"

"Yes, that's the way I found their home."

"But you had the daylight, mind ye! And Dan'l was in pitch black night, but, sir, he made a bee-line through them dark woods straight for his camp he'd left seven days afore. And, man, yer kin bet they made tracks when they got clear o' the Redskins! Hit wuz six hours till day an' when the Injuns waked they didn't know which way ter look----"

Tom paused and the Boy cried eagerly:

"Did they get there?"

"Git whar?" the father asked dreamily.

"Get back to their own camp?"

"Straight ez a bee-line I tell ye. But the camp had been busted and robbed and the other men wuz gone."

"Gone where?"

Tom shook his shaggy head.

"Nobody never knowed ter this day--reckon the Injuns scalped 'em----"

He paused again and a dreamy look overspread his rugged face.

"Like they scalped your own grandpa that day."

"Did they scalp my grandpa?" the Boy asked in an awed whisper.

"That they did. Your Uncle Mordecai an' me was workin' with him in the new ground, cleanin' it fur corn when all of a sudden the Injuns riz right up outen the ground. Your grandpa drapped dead the fust shot, an' Mordecai flew ter the cabin fer the rifle. A big Redskin jumped over a log an' scalped my own daddy before my eyes! He grabbed me an' started pullin' me ter the woods, an' then, Sonny, somethin' happened----"

Tom looked at the long rifle in its buck's horn rest and smiled:

"Old 'Speakeasy' up thar stretched her long neck through a chink in the logs an' said somethin' ter Mr. Redskin. She didn't raise her voice much louder'n a whisper. She jist kinder sighed:

"*Kerpeow!*"

"I kin hear hit echoin' through them woods yit. That Injun drapped my hands before I heerd the gun, an' she hadn't more'n sung out afore he wuz lyin' in a heap at my feet. The ball had gone clean through him----"

Tom paused again and looked for a long time in silence into the glowing coals.

The little cabin was very still. The Boy lifted his face to his mother's curiously:

"Ma, you said God counted the beat of a sparrow's wing?"

"Yes."

"Well, what was He doin' when that Indian scalped my grandpa?"

The mother threw a startled look at the bold little questioner and answered reverently:

"Keeping watch in Heaven, my Boy. The hairs of your head are numbered and not one falls without his knowledge. We had to pay the price of blood for this beautiful country. Nothing is ever worth having that doesn't cost precious lives."

Again the cabin was still. An owl's deep cry boomed from the woods and a solitary wolf answered in the distance. The Boy's brow was wrinkled for a moment and then he suddenly looked up to his father's rugged face:

"And what became of Dan'l Boone?"

"Oh, he lit on his feet all right. He always did. He moved on with Stuart, built him another camp in the deepest woods he could find and hunted there all winter--jest think, Boy, all winter--every day--thar wuz a man that wuz a man shore nuff!"

"Yes, sirree!" the listener agreed.

The mother lifted her head and thoughtfully watched the sparkling eyes.

"And do you want to know why Daniel Boone was great, my son?" she quietly asked.

"Yes, why?" was the quick response.

"Because he used his mind and his hands, while the other men around him just used their hands. He learned to read and write when he was a little boy. He mixed brains with his powder and shot."

"Did he, Pa?" the questioner cried.

The father smiled. He could afford to be generous. The Boy looked to him as the authority on Daniel Boone.

"Yes, I reckon he did. He wuz smart. I didn't have no chance when I wuz little."

"Then I'm going to learn, too. Ma can teach me." He leaped from his father's lap and climbed into hers. "You will, won't you, Ma?"

The mother smiled us she slowly answered:

"Yes, Honey, I'll begin to-morrow night when you get back from hunting."

VI

Slowly but surely the indomitable will within the Boy's breast conquered the cries of aching muscles, and he went about his daily farm tasks with the dogged persistence of habit. He had learned to whistle at his work and his eager mind began to look for new worlds to conquer.

At the right moment the tempter appeared. It rained on Saturday and Austin, his neighbor, came over to see him. They cracked walnuts and hickory-nuts in the loft while the rain pattered noisily on the board roof. Austin had a definite suggestion for Sunday that would break the monotony of life.

"Let's me an' you not go ter meetin' ter-morrow?" the neighbor ventured for a starter.

"All right!" the Boy agreed. "Preachin' makes me tired anyhow."

"Me, too, an' I tell ye what I'll do. I'll get my Ma ter let me come ter your house to stay all day, an' when your folks go off ter meetin', me an' you'll have some fun!"

"What?"

"We'll stay all day on the creek banks, find duck nests, turkey and quail nests, an',----" Austin paused and dropped his voice, "go in swimmin' if we take a notion----"

The Boy slowly shook his head.

"No, less don't do that."

"Why?"

"'Cause Ma don't 'low me to go in the creek till June--says I might ketch my death o' cold."

"Shucks! I've been in twice already!"

"Have ye?"

"Yep!"

"And ye didn't get sick?"

"Do I *look* sick?"

"Not a bit."

"Well, then?"

"All right--we'll go."

The spirit of freedom born of the fields and woods had grown into something more than an attitude of mind. He was ready for the deed--the positive act of adventure. He didn't like to disobey his mother. But he couldn't afford to let Austin think that he was a molly-coddle, a mere babe hanging to her skirts. He was doing a man's work. It was time he took a few of man's privileges.

He revelled in the situation of adventure that night and saw himself the hero of stirring scenes.

Next morning on Austin's arrival he asked his mother to let him stay at home and play.

"Don't you want to go to meeting and hear the new preacher?" she asked persuasively.

"No, I'm tired."

The mother smiled indulgently. He was young--far too young yet to know the meaning of true religion. She was a Baptist, and the first principle of her religion was personal faith and direct relations of the individual soul with God. She remembered her own hours of torture in childhood.

"All right, Boy," she said graciously. "Be good now, while we're gone."

His big toe was digging in the dirt while he murmured:

"Yes'm."

The wagon had no sooner disappeared than he and Austin were flying with swift bare feet along the path that led to the creek. It was the hottest day of the spring--a close air and broiling sun to be remembered longer than the hottest day of August.

They ran for a mile without a pause, rolled in the sand on the banks of the creek and shouted their joy in perfect freedom. They explored the deep cane brakes and stalked imaginary buffaloes and bears without number, encountering nothing bigger than a grey fox and a couple of muskrats.

"Let's cross over!" Austin cried. "I saw a bear track on that side one day. We can trail him to his den and show him to your Pap when he comes home. Here's a log!"

The Boy looked dubiously, measured it with his eye, and shook his head.

"Nope--it's too little and too high in the air--it'll wobble," he declared.

"But we can coon it over!" Austin urged. "We can grab hold of a limb over there and slide down--it's easy--come on!"

Before he could make further objection, the young adventurer quickly straddled the swaying pole, and, with the agility of a cat, hopped across, grasped one of the limbs and slipped to the sand.

"Come on!" he shouted. "See how easy it is!"

The Boy looked doubtfully at the swaying sapling and wished he had gone to hear that preacher after all. It would never do to say he was afraid. The other fellow had done it so quickly. And it was no use to argue with Austin that his legs were shorter, his body more compact and so much easier to hold his balance. The idea of cowardice was something too vile for thought. The Boy felt that he was doomed to fall before he moved but he waved a brave little hand in answer:

"All right, I'm comin'!"

Half way across the pole began to tear its roots from the bluff. He felt it sinking, stopped and held his breath as it suddenly broke with a crash and fell.

"Look out! Hold tight!" Austin yelled.

He did his best, but lost his balance and toppled head downward into the deep still water.

His mouth flew open at the first touch of the chill stream; he gasped for breath and drew into his lungs a strangling flood. The blood rushed to his brain in a wild explosion of terror. He struck out madly with his long arms and legs, fighting with desperation for breath and drinking in only the agony and fear of death. His mother's voice came low and faint and far away in some other world, saying softly:

"Be good now, while we're gone!"

Again he struck out blindly, fiercely, madly into the darkness that was slowly swallowing him body and soul.

His hand touched something as he sank, he grasped it with instinctive terror and knew no more until he waked in the infernal regions with the Devil sitting on his stomach glaring into his eyes and holding him by the throat trying to choke him to death. His head was down a steep hill.

With a mighty effort he threw the Devil off, loosed his hold and sucked in a tiny breath of air, and then another and another, coughing and spluttering and wheezing foam and water from his mouth and ears and nose and eyes.

At last a voice gasped:

"Is--that--you--Austin?"

"You bet it's me! I got ye a breathin' all right now--who'd ye think it wuz?"

The Boy coughed again and squeezed his lungs clear of water.

"Why--I was afraid I was dead and you was the Old Scratch and had me."

"Well, I thought you was a goner shore nuff till yer hand grabbed the pole I stuck after ye. Man alive, but you did hold onto it! I lakened ter never got yer hand loose so's I could pull ye up on the bank and turn ye upside down and squeeze the water outen ye."

"Did you sit on my stomach and choke me?" the Boy asked.

"I set on yer and mashed the water out, but I didn't choke you."

"I thought the Old Scratch had me!"

For an hour they talked in awed whispers of Sin and Death and Trouble and then the blood of youth shook off the nightmare.

They were alive and unhurt. They were all right and it was a good joke. They swore eternal secrecy. The day was yet young and it was a glorious one. Their clothes were wet and they had to be dried before night. That settled it. They would strip, hang their clothes in the hot sun and wallow in the sand and play in the shallow water until sundown.

"And besides," Austin urged, "this here's a warnin' straight from the Lord--me and you must learn ter swim."

"That's so, ain't it?" the Boy agreed.

"It's what I calls a sign from on high--and it pints right into the creek!"

They agreed that the thing to do was to heed at once this divine revelation and devote the whole Sabbath day to the solemn work--in the creek.

They found a beautifully sunny spot with an immense sand bar and wide shallow safe waters. They carefully placed their clothes to dry and basked in the bright sun. They practiced swimming in water waist deep and Austin learned to make three strokes and reach the length of his body before sinking.

They rolled in the sun again and ate their lunch. They ran naked through the woods to a branch that flowed into the creek, followed it to the source and drank at a beautiful spring.

Through the long afternoon they lived in a fairy world of freedom, of dreams and make-believe. They talked of great hunters and discussed the best methods of attacking all manner of wild beasts.

The sun was sinking toward the western hills when they hastily picked up their clothes and found a safe ford across which they could wade, holding their things above their heads.

The Boy reached the house just as the wagon drove up to the door. He hurried to help his father with the horse. A sense of elation filled his mind that he was shrewd enough to keep his own secrets. Of course, his mother needn't know what had happened. He was none the worse for it.

In answer to her question of how he had spent the day he vaguely answered:

"In the woods. They're awfully pretty now with the dogwood all in bloom."

He talked incessantly at supper, teasing Sarah about her jolly time at the meeting. Toward the end of the meal he grew silent. A curious sensation began on his back and shoulders and arms. He paid no attention to it at first, but it rapidly grew worse. The more he tried to shake off the feeling the more distinct and sharp it grew. At last every inch of his body seemed to be on fire.

He rose slowly from the table and walked to his stool in the corner wondering--wondering and fearing. He sat in dead silence for half an hour. The perspiration began to stand out on his forehead. It was no use longer to try to fool himself, there was something the matter--something big--something terrible! A fierce and scorching fever was burning him to death. He dared not move. Every muscle quivered with agony when he tried.

The mother's keen eye saw the tears he couldn't keep back.

"What's the matter, Boy?" she tenderly asked while his father was at the stable putting the wagon under the shed.

"I don't know 'm," he choked. "I'm all on fire--I'm burnin' up----"

She touched his forehead and slipped her arm around his shoulders.

He screamed with pain.

The mother looked into his face with a sudden start.

"Why, what on earth, child? What have you been doing to-day?"

He hesitated and tried to be brave, but it was no use. He felt that he would drop dead the next moment unless relief came. He buried his face in her lap and sobbed his bitter confession.

"Do you think I'm going to die?" he asked.

She smiled:

"No, my Boy, you're only sunburned. How long were you naked in the sun?"

"From 'bout ten o'clock till nearly sundown----"

He moved again and screamed with agony.

The mother tenderly undressed the little, red, swollen body. The rough clothes had stuck to the blistered skin in one place and the pain was so frightful he nearly fainted before they were finally removed.

For two days and nights she never left his side, holding his hand to give him courage when he was compelled to move. Almost his entire body, inch by inch, was blistered. She covered it with cream and allowed only two greased linen cloths to touch him.

On the second day as he lay panting for breath and holding her hand with feverish grasp he looked into her pensive grey eyes through his own bleared and bloodshot with pain and said softly:

"I'm sorry, Ma."

She pressed his hand:

"It's all right, my Boy; your mother loves you."

"I'm not sorry for the pain," he gasped. "What hurts me worse is that you're so sweet to me!"

The dark face bent and kissed his trembling lips:

"It's all for the best. You couldn't have understood the preacher Sunday when he took the text: 'The stars in their courses fought against Sisera.' You learned it for yourself the only way we really learn anything. God's in the wind and rain, the sun, the storm. All nature works with him. You can easily fool your mother. It's not what you seem to others; it's what you are that counts. God sees and knows. You see and know in your little heart. I want you to be a great man--only a good man can ever be great."

And so for an hour she poured into his heart her faith in God and His glory until He became the one power fixed forever in the child's imagination.

VII

The Boy lost his skin but grew another and incidentally absorbed some ideas he never forgot.

On the day he was able to put on his clothes, it poured down rain and work in the fields was impossible. A sense of delicious joy filled him. He worked because he had to, not because he liked it. He was too proud to shirk, too brave to cry when every nerve and muscle of his little body ached with mortal weariness, but he hated it.

The sun rose bright and warm and shone clear in the Southern sky next morning before he was called. He climbed down the ladder from his loft wondering what marvellous thing had happened that he should be sleeping with the sun already high in the heavens.

"What's the matter, Ma?" he asked anxiously. "Why didn't you call me?"

"It's too wet to plow. Your father's going to chop wood in the clearing. He wanted you to pile brush after him, but I asked him to let you off to go fishing for me."

He ate breakfast with his heart beating a tattoo, rushed into the garden, dug a gourd full of worms, drew his long cane rod from the eaves of the cabin, and with old Boney trotting at his heels was soon on his way to a deep pool in the bend of the creek.

Fishing for *her*! His mother understood. He wondered why he had ever been fool enough to disobey her that Sunday. He could die for her without a moment's hesitation.

It was glorious to have this marvellous day of spring all his own. The birds were singing on every field and hedge. The trees flashed their polished new leaves. The sweet languor of the South was in the air and he drew it in with deep breaths that sent the joy of life tingling through every vein.

Four joyous hours flew on tireless wings. He had caught five catfish and a big eel--more than enough for a good meal for the whole family.

He held them up proudly. How his mother's eyes would sparkle! He could see

Sarah's admiring gaze and hear his father's good-natured approval.

He had just struck the path for home when the forlorn figure of a rough bearded man came limping to meet him.

He stepped aside in the grass to let him pass. But the man stopped and gazed at the fish.

"My, my, Sonny, but you've got a fine string there!" he exclaimed.

"Pretty good for one day," the Boy proudly answered.

"An' just ter think I ain't had nothin' ter eat in 'most two days."

"Don't you live nowhere?" the youngster asked in surprise.

"I used ter have a home afore the war, but my folks thought I wuz dead an' moved away. I'm tryin' ter find 'em. Hit's a hard job with a Britisher's bullet still a-pinchin' me in the leg."

"Did you fight with General Washington?"

"Lordy, no, I ain't that old, ef I do look like a scarecrow. No, I fit under Old Hickory at New Orleans. I tell ye, Sonny, them Britishers burnt out Washington fur us but we give 'em a taste o' fire at New Orleans they ain't goin' ter fergit."

"Did we lick 'em good?"

"Boy, ye ain't never heard tell er sich a scrimmage--we thrashed 'em till they warn't no fight in 'em, an' they scrambled back aboard them ships an' skeddaddled home. Britishers can't fight nohow. We've licked 'em twice an' we kin lick 'em agin. But the old soldier that does the fightin'--everybody fergits him!"

The Boy looked longingly at his string of fish for a moment with the pride of his heart, and then held up his treasure.

"You can have my fish if ye want 'em; they'll make you a nice supper."

The old soldier stroked the tangled hair and took his string of fish.

"You're a fine boy! I won't fergit you, Sonny!"

The words comforted him until he neared the house. And then a sense of bitter loss welled up in spite of all.

"Did I do right, Ma?" he asked wistfully.

She placed her hand on his forehead:

"Yes--I'm proud of you. I know what that gift cost a boy's heart. It was big because it was all you had and the pride of your soul was in it."

The sense of loss was gone and he was rich and happy again.

When the supper was over and they sat before the flickering firelight he asked her a question over which his mind had puzzled since he left the old soldier.

"Why is it," he said thoughtfully, "British soldiers can't fight?"

The mother smiled:

"Who said they couldn't fight?"

"The old soldier I gave my fish to. He said we just made hash out o' them. We've licked 'em twice and we can do it again!"

The last sentence he didn't quote. He gave it as a personal opinion based on established facts.

"We didn't win because the British couldn't fight," the mother gravely responded.

"Then why?" he persisted.

"The Lord was good to us."

"How?"

The question came with an accent of indignation. Sometimes he couldn't help getting cross with his mother when she began to give the Lord credit for everything. If the Lord did it all why should he give his string of fish to an old soldier!

The grey eyes looked into his with wistful tenderness. She had been shocked once before by the fear that there was something in this child's eternal why that would keep him out of the church. The one deep desire of her heart was that he should be good.

"Would you like to hear," she began softly, "something about the Revolution which my old school teacher told me in Virginia?"

"Yes, tell me!" he answered eagerly.

"He said that we could never have won our independence but for God. We didn't win because British soldiers couldn't fight. We held out for ten years because we outran them. We ran quicker, covered more ground, got further into the woods and stayed there longer than any fighters the British had ever met before. That's why we got the best of them. Our men who fought and ran away lived to fight another day. General Washington was always great in retreat. He never fought unless he was ready and could choose his own field. He waited until his enemies were in snug quarters drinking and gambling, and then on a dark night, so dark and cold that some of his own men would freeze to death, he pushed across a river, fell on them, cut them to pieces and retreated.

"The number of men he commanded was so small he could not face his foes in the open if he could avoid it. His men were poorly armed, poorly drilled, half-clothed and half-starved at times. The British troops were the best drilled and finest fighting men of the world in their day, armed with good guns, well fed, well clothed, and well paid."

She paused and smiled at the memory of her teacher's narrative.

"What do you suppose happened on one of our battlefields?"

"I dunno--what?"

"When the Red-coats charged, our boys ran at the first crack of a gun. They ran so well that they all got away except one little fellow who had a game leg. He stumbled and fell in a hole. A big British soldier raised a musket to brain him. The little fellow looked up and cried: 'All right. Kill away, ding ye--ye won't get much!'

"The Britisher laughed, picked him up, brushed his clothes and told him to go home."

The Boy laughed again and again.

"He was a spunky one anyhow, wasn't he?"

"Yes," the mother nodded, "that's why the Red-coat let him go. And we never could have endured if God hadn't inspired one man to hold fast when other hearts had failed."

"And who was he?" the Boy broke in.

"General Washington. At Valley Forge our cause was lost but for him. Our men were not paid. They could get no clothes, they were freezing and starving. They quit and went home in hundreds and gave up in despair. And then, Boy----"

Her voice dropped to a tense whisper:

"General Washington fell on his knees and prayed until he saw the shining face of God and got his answer. Next day he called his ragged, hungry men together and said:

"'Soldiers, though all my armies desert, the war shall go on. If I must, I'll gather my faithful followers in Virginia, retreat to the mountains and fight until our country is free!'

"His words cheered the despairing men and they stood by him. We were saved at last because help came in time. Lord Cornwallis had laid the South in ashes, and camped at Yorktown, his army of veterans laden with spoils. He was only waiting for the transports from New York to take his victorious men North, join the army there and end the war, and then----"

She drew a deep breath and her eyes sparkled:

"And then, Boy, it happened--the miracle! Into the Chesapeake Bay in Virginia, three big ships dropped anchor at the mouth of the York River. Our people on the shore thought they were the transports and that the end had come. But the ships were too far away to make out their flags, and so they sent swift couriers across the Peninsula, to see if there were any signs in the roadstead at Hampton. There--Glory to God! lay a great fleet flying the flag of France. The French had loaned us twenty millions of dollars, and sent their navy and their army to help us. Had the Lord sent down a host from the sky we couldn't have been more surprised. They landed, joined with General Washington's ragged men, and closed in on Cornwallis. Surprised and trapped he surrendered and we won.

"But there never was a year before that, my Boy, that we were strong enough to resist the British army had the mother country sent a real general here to command her troops."

"Why didn't she?" the Boy interrupted.

Again the mother's voice dropped low:

"Because God wouldn't let her--that's the only reason. If Lord Clive had ever landed on our shores, Washington might now be sleeping in a traitor's grave."

The voice again became soft and dreamy--almost inaudible.

"And he didn't come?" the Boy whispered.

"No. On the day he was to sail he put the papers in his pocket, went into his room, locked the door and blew his own brains out. This is God's country, my son. He gave us freedom. He has great plans for us."

The fire flickered low and the Boy's eyes glowed with a strange intensity.

VIII

A barbecue, with political speaking, was held at the village ten miles away. The family started at sunrise. The day was an event in the lives of every man, woman and child within a radius of twenty miles. Many came as far as thirty miles and walked the whole distance. Before nine o'clock a crowd of two thousand had gathered.

The dark, lithe young mother who led her boy by the hand down the crowded aisle of the improvised brush arbor that day performed a deed which was destined to change the history of the world.

The speaker who held the crowd spellbound for two hours was Henry Clay. The Boy not only heard an eloquent orator. His spirit entered for all time into fellowship with a great human soul.

In words that throbbed with passion, he pictured the coming glory of a mighty nation whose shores would be washed by two oceans, whose wealth and manhood would be the hope and inspiration of the world. Never before had words been given such wings. The ringing tones found the Boy's soul and set his brain on fire. A big idea was born within his breast. This was his country. His feet pressed its soil. Its hills and plains, its rivers and seas were his. His hands would help to build this vision of a great spirit into the living thing. He breathed softly and his eyes sparkled. When the crowd cheered, he leaped to his feet, swung his little cap into the air and shouted with all his might. When the last glowing picture of the peroration faded into a silence that could be felt, and the tumult had died away, he saw men and women crowding around the orator to shake his hand.

"Take me, Ma!" he whispered. "I want to see him close!"

The mother lifted him in her arms above the crowd, pressed forward, and the Boy's shining eyes caught those of the brilliant statesman. Over the heads of the men by his side the orator extended his hand and grasped the trembling outstretched fingers.

He smiled and nodded, that was all. The Boy understood. From that moment he had an ideal leader whose words were inspired.

The mother's dark face was lit for a moment with tender pride. She made no effort to reach the orator's side. It was enough that she had seen the flash from her Boy's eyes. She was content. The day was filled with a great joy.

The summer camp meetings began the following week. The grounds were located a mile from the straggling little village which was the center of the county's activities. All religious denominations used the spacious auditorium for their services. The Methodists camped there an entire month. The Baptists stayed but two weeks. The Baptist temperament frowned on the social frivolities which were inseparable from these long intimate associations at close quarters. The more volatile temperament of the Methodists revelled in them, and Methodism grew with astounding rapidity under the system.

The auditorium was simply a huge quadrangular shed with board roof uphold by cedar posts. At one end of the shed stood the platform on which was built the pulpit, a square box-like structure about four feet high. The seats were made of rough-hewn half logs set on pegs driven in augur holes. There were no backs to them. A single wide aisle led from the end facing the pulpit, and two narrow ones intersected the main aisle at the centre.

In front of the pulpit were placed the mourner's benches facing the three sides of the space left for the free movement of the mourners under the stress of religious emotion.

The Boy's mother and father were devout members of the Baptist Church, but they were not demonstrative. They modestly and reverently took their seats in an inconspicuous position about midway the building, entering from one of the small aisles on the side. The Boy had often been to a regular church service before, but this was his first camp meeting.

Four preachers sat in grim silence behind the pulpit's solid box front. The Boy could just see the tops of their heads over the board that held the big gilt-edged Bible.

The entire first two days and nights were given to a series of terrific sermons on Death, Hell, and the Judgment, with a brief glimpse of the pearly gates of Heaven and a few strains from the golden harps inside for the damned to hear by way of contrast. The first purpose of the preachers was to arouse a deep under-current of religious emotional excitement that at the proper moment would explode and sweep the crowd with resistless fire. Usually the fuse was timed to explode on the morning of the third day. Sometimes, when sermons of extraordinary power had followed each other in rapid succession, the fire broke out by a sort of spontaneous combustion on the night of the second day.

It did so this time. The mother had no trouble in keeping the Boy by her side through these first two days. He felt instinctively the growing emotional tension about him, and knew in his bones that something would break loose soon. He was keyed to a high pitch of interest to see just what it would be like.

The storm broke in the middle of the second sermon on the second night. The preacher had worked himself into a frenzy of emotional excitement. His arms were waving over his head, his eyes blazing, his feet stamping, his voice screaming in anguish as he described the agony of a soul lost forever in the seething cauldron of eternal hell fire!

A tremulous startled moan, half-wail, half-scream came from a girl just in front of the Boy, as she dropped her head in her hands.

"What's the matter with her?" he whispered. "Has she got a pain?"

His mother pressed his hand:

"Sh!"

And then the storm broke. From every direction came the startled cries of long pent terror and anguish. The girl staggered to her feet and started stumbling down the aisle to the mourners' bench without invitation, and from every row of seats they tumbled, crowding on her heels, sobbing, wailing, screaming, groaning.

The preacher ceased to talk and, in a high tremulous voice, that rang through the excited crowd as the peal of the Archangel's trumpet, began to sing:

"Come humble sinners in whose breasts   A thousand thoughts revolve!"

The crowd rose instinctively and all who were not mourning, joined in the half-savage, terror-stricken wail of the song. The sinners that hadn't given up at the first break of the storm could not resist the thrill of this wild music. One by one they pushed their way through the crowd, found the aisle and staggered blindly to the front.

The Boy noticed curiously that it seemed to be the rule for them to completely cover their streaming eyes with a handkerchief or with the bare hands and go it blindly for the mourners' benches. If they missed the way and butted into anything, a church member kindly took them by the arm and guided them to a vacant place where they dropped on their knees.

The Boy had leaped on the bench and stood beside his mother to get a better view of the turmoil. He couldn't keep his eyes off a tall, red-headed, thick-bearded man just across the aisle three rows behind who kept twitching his face, looking toward the door and struggling against the impulse to follow the mourners. Presently he broke down with a loud cry:

"Lord, have mercy!"

He placed his hands over his face and started on a run to the front.

The Boy giggled, and his mother pinched him.

"Did ye see that red-headed feller, Ma," he whispered. "He didn't do fair. He peeked through his fingers--I saw his eyes!"

"Sh!"

The preachers had come down from the pulpit now and stood over the wailing prostrated mourners and exhorted them to repent and believe before it was forever and eternally too late. Three of them were talking at the same time to different groups of mourners. The louder they exhorted the louder the sinners cried. The fourth preacher walked down the aisle searching for those who were yet hardening their hearts and stiffening their necks. He paused beside a prim little old maid who had lately arrived from Tidewater Virginia. Her bright eyes were dry.

"Dear lady, are you a child of God?" the preacher cried.

The prim figured stiffened indignantly:

"No, sir! I'm an Episcopalian!"

The preacher groaned and passed on and the Boy stuffed his fist in his mouth.

For half an hour the roar of the conflict was incessant, and its violence indescribable. It was broken now and then by a kindly soul among the elderly women raising a sweet old-fashioned hymn.

Suddenly an exhorter threw his hands above his head and, in a voice that soared above the roar of mourners and their attendants, cried:

"Behold the Lamb of God that taketh away the sins of the world!"

Quick as a flash came an answering shout from the red-headed man who leaped to his feet and with wide staring eyes looked up at the roof.

"I see him! I see Jesus up a tree!"

A fat woman lifted her head and shouted:

"Hold him till I get there!"

And she started for the red-headed man. There was a single moment of strange silence and the Boy laughed aloud.

His mother caught and shook him violently. He crammed his little fist again into his mouth, but the stopper wouldn't hold.

He dropped to his seat to keep the people from seeing him, buried his face in his hands and laughed in smothered giggles in spite of all his mother could do.

At last he whispered:

"Take me out quick! I'm goin' to bust--I'll bust wide open I tell ye!"

She rose sternly, seized his arm and led him a half mile into the woods. He kept looking back and laughing softly.

She gazed at him sorrowfully:

"I'm ashamed of you, Boy! How could you do such a thing!"

"I just couldn't help it!"

He sat down on a stone and laughed again.

"What makes the fools holler so?" he asked through his tears.

"They are praying God to forgive their sins."

"But why holler so loud? He ain't deaf--is He? You said that God's in the sun and wind and dew and rain--in the breath we breathe. Ain't He everywhere then? Why do they holler at Him?"

The mother turned away to hide a smile she couldn't keep back, and a cloud overspread her dark face. Surely this was an evil sign--this spirit of irreverent levity in the mind of a child so young. What could it mean? She had forgotten that she had been teaching him to think, and didn't know, perhaps, that he who thinks must laugh or die.

After that she let him spend long hours at the spring playing with boys and girls of his age. He didn't go into the meetings again. But he enjoyed the season. The watermelons, muskmelons, and ginger cakes were the best he had ever eaten.

IX

During the Christmas holidays the father got ready for a coon hunt in which the Boy should see his first battle royal in the world of sport.

Dennis came over and brought four extra dogs, two of his own and two which he had borrowed for the holidays.

A sudden change came over the spirit of old Boney--short for Napoleon Bonaparte. He understood the talk about coons as clearly as if he could speak the English language. He was in a quiver of eager excitement. He knew from the Boy's talk that he was going, too. He wagged his tail, pushed his warm nose under his little friend's arm, whining and trembling while he tried to explain what it meant to strike a coon's trail in the deep night, chase him over miles of woods and swamps and field, tree him and fight it out, a battle to the death between dog and beast!

At two o'clock, before day, his father's voice called and in a jiffy he was down the ladder, his eyes shining. He had gone to sleep with his clothes on and lost no time in dressing.

Without delay the start was made. Down the dim pathway to the creek and then along its banks for two miles, its laughing waters rippling soft music amid the shadows, or gleaming white and mirror-like in the starlit open spaces.

In half an hour the stars were obscured by a thin veil of fleecy clouds, and, striking no trail in the bottoms, they turned to the big tract of woods on the hills and plunged straight into their depths for two miles.

"Hush!"

Tom suddenly stopped:

Far off to the right came the bark of a dog on the run.

"Ain't that old Boney's voice?" the father asked.

"I don't think so," the Boy answered.

The note of wild savage music was one he had never heard before.

"Yes it was, too," was the emphatic decision. He squared his broad shoulders and gave the hunter's shout of answer-joy to the dog's call.

Never had the Boy heard such a shout from human lips. It sent shivers down his spine.

The dog heard and louder came the answering note, a deep tremulous boom through the woods that meant to the older man's trained ear that he was on the run.

"That's old Boney shore's yer born!" the father cried, "an' he ain't got no doubts 'bout hit nother. He's got his head in the air. The trail's so hot he don't have ter nose the ground. You'll hear somethin' in a minute when the younger pups git to him."

Two hounds suddenly opened with long quivering wails.

"Thar's my dogs--they've hit it now!" Dennis cried excitedly.

Another hound joined the procession, then another and another, and in two minutes the whole pack of eight were in full cry.

Again the hunter's deep voice rang his wild cheer through the woods and every dog raised his answering cry a note higher.

"Ain't that music!" Tom cried in ecstacy.

They stood and listened. The dogs were still in the woods and with each yelp were coming nearer. Evidently the trail led toward them, but in the rear and almost toward the exact spot at which they had entered the forest.

"Just listen at old Boney!" the Boy cried. "I can tell him now. He can beat 'em all!"

Loud and clear above the chorus of the others rang the long savage boom of Boney's voice, quivering with passion, defiant, daring, sure of victory! It came at regular intervals as if to measure the miles that separated him from the battle he smelled afar. He was far in the lead. He was past-master of this sport. The others were not in his class.

The Boy's heart swelled with pride.

"Old Boney's showin' 'em all the way!" he exclaimed triumphantly.

"Yer can bet he always does that, Sonny!" the father answered. "That's a hot trail. Nigh ez I can figger we're goin' ter have some fun. There's more'n one coon travelin' over that ground."

"How can you tell?" Dennis asked incredulously.

"Hit's too easy fer the other pups--they'd lose the scent now an' then ef they weren't but one. They ain't lost it a minute since they struck it--Lord, jest listen!"

He paused and held his breath.

"Did ye ever hear anything like hit on this yearth!" Dennis cried.

Every dog was opening now at the top of his voice at regular intervals, the swing and leap of their bodies over the brush and around the trees registering in each stirring note.

Again Tom gave a shout of approval.

The sound of the leader's voice suddenly flattened and faded.

"By Gum!" the old hunter cried, "they've left the woods, struck that field an' makin' for the creek! Ye won't need that axe ter-night, Dennis."

"Why?"

"Wait an' see!" was the short answer.

They hurried from the woods and had scarcely reached the edge of the field when suddenly old Boney's cry stopped short and in a moment the others were silent.

"Good Lord, they've lost it!" Dennis groaned.

And then came the quick, sharp, fierce bark of the leader announcing that the quarry had been located.

Tom gave a yell of triumph and started on a run for the spot.

"Up one o' them big sycamores in the edge o' that water I'll bet!" Dennis wailed.

"You'll need no axe," was the older man's short comment.

They pushed their way rapidly through the cane to the banks of the creek and found the dogs scratching with might and main straight down into the sand about ten feet from the water's edge.

"Well, I'll be doggoned," Dennis cried, "if I ever seed anything like that afore! They've gone plum crazy. They ain't no hole here. A coon can't jist drap inter the ground without a hole."

The old hunter laughed:

"No, but a coon mought learn somethin' from a beaver now an' then an' locate the door to his house under the water line an' climb up here ter find a safe place, couldn't he?"

"I don't believe it!" Dennis sneered.

"You'll have ter go to the house an' git a spade," Tom said finally. "It'll take one ter dig a hole big enough ter ever persuade one er these dogs ter put his nose in that den. Hit ain't more'n a mile ter the house--hurry back."

Dennis started on a run.

"Don't yer let 'em out an' start that fight afore I git here!" he called.

"You'll see it all," Tom reassured him.

He made the dogs stop scratching and lie down to rest.

"Jest save yer strenk, boys," Tom cried. "Yer'll need it presently."

They sat down, the father lit his pipe and told the Boy the story of a great fight he had witnessed on such a creek bank once before in his life.

Day was dawning and the eastern sky reddening.

The Boy stamped on the solid ground and couldn't believe it possible that any dog could smell game through six feet of earth.

He lifted Boney's long nose and looked at it curiously. His wonderful nostrils were widely distended and though he lay quite still in the sand on the edge of the hole his muscles were quivering with excitement and his wistful hound eyes had in them now the red glare of coming battle.

It was quick work when Dennis arrived to throw the sand and soft earth away and open a hole five feet in depth and of sufficient width to allow all the dogs to get foothold inside.

Suddenly the spade crashed through an opening below and the rasp of sharp desperate teeth and claws rang against its polished surface.

"Did you hear that?" Tom laughed.

Another spadeful out and they could be plainly seen. How many it was impossible to tell, but three pairs of glowing bloodshot eyes in the shadows showed plainly.

Tom straightened his massive figure and gave a shout to the dogs. They all danced around the upper rim of the hole and barked with fierce boastful yelps, but not one would venture his nose within two feet of those grim shining eyes.

"Well, Dennis," Tom sighed, "I reckon I'll have ter shove you down thar an' hold ye by the heels while yer pull one of 'em out!"

"I'll be doggoned ef yer do!" he remarked with emphasis.

Tom laughed. "You wuz afeared ye wouldn't git here in time ye know."

"Oh, I'm in time all right!"

The hunter put his hands in his pockets and gazed at the warriors below.

"Waal, we'll try ter git a dog ter yank one of 'em out an' then they'll all come. But I have my doubts. I don't believe that Godamighty ever yet built a dog that'll stick his nose in that hole. Hit takes three dogs ter kill one coon in a fair fight. Old Boney's the only pup I ever seed do it by hisself. But it's askin' too much o' him ter stick his nose in a place like that with three of 'em lookin' right at him ready ter tear his eyes out. But they ain't nothin' like tryin'----"

He paused and looked at the old warrior of a hundred bloody fields, pointed at the bottom of the hole and in stern command shouted:

"Fetch 'em out, Bone!"

With a deep growl the faithful old soldier sprang to the front. With teeth shining in white gleaming rows he scrambled within a foot of the opening of the den, circled it twice, his eyes fixed on the flashing lights below. They followed his every move. He tried the stratagem of right and left flank movements, but the space was too narrow. He dashed straight toward the opening once with a loud angry cry, hoping to get the flash of a coward's back. He met three double rows of white needle-like teeth daring him to come on.

He squatted flat on his belly and growled with desperate fury, but he wouldn't go closer. The hunter urged in vain.

"Hit's no use!" he cried at last. "Jest ez well axe er dog ter walk into a den er lions. I don't blame him."

The Boy's pride was hurt.

"I can make him bring one out," he said.

Tom shook his head:

"Not much. Less see ye?"

The Boy stepped down to the dog's side.

"Look out, ye fool, don't let yer foot slip in thar!" his father warned.

The Boy knelt beside the dog, patted his back and began to talk to him in low tense tones:

"Fetch 'im out, Bone! Go after 'm! Sick 'em, boy, sick 'em!"

Closer and closer the brave old fighter edged his way, only a low mad growl answering to the Boy's urging. His eyes were blazing now in the red rays of the rising sun like two balls of fire. With a sudden savage plunge he hurled himself into the den and quick as a flash of lightning his short hairy neck gave a flirt, and a coon as large as one of the hounds whizzed ten feet into the air, and, with his white teeth shining, struck the ground, lighting squarely on his feet. A hound dashed for him and one slap from the long sharp claws sent him howling and bleeding into the canes.

But old Boney had watched him in the air, and, circling the pack that faced the coon, with a quick leap had downed him. Then every dog was with him and the battle was on. Eight dogs to one coon and yet so sharp were his claws, so keen the steel-like points of his teeth, he sometimes had four dogs rolling in agony beside the growling mass of fur and teeth and nails.

The fight had scarcely begun when one of the remaining coons leaped out of the den. Tom's watchful eye had seen him. He pulled three dogs from the first battle group and hurled them on the new fighter. He had scarcely started this struggle when the third sprang to the top of the earthen breastwork, surveyed the field and with sullen deliberation, trotted to the water's edge, jumped in and, placing two paws on a swaying limb, dared any dog to come.

Here was work for the veteran! Boney was the only dog in the pack who would dare accept that challenge. Tom choked him off the first coon, pulled him to the bank and showed him his enemy in the water. He looked just a moment at the snarling, daring mouth and made the plunge.

The boy had followed the dog and watched with bated breath. He circled the coon twice, swimming in swift graceful curves. But his enemy was too shrewd. A flank movement was impossible. The coon's fierce mouth was squarely facing him at every turn and the dog plunged straight on his foe.

To his horror the Boy saw the fangs sink into his friend's head, four sets of sharp claws circle his neck, a tense grey ball of fur hanging its dead weight below. The water ran red for a moment as both slowly sank to the bottom.

Eyes wide with anguish he heard his father cry:

"By the Lord, he'll kill that dog shore--he's a goner!"

"No, he won't neither!" the Boy shouted, leaping into the water where he saw them go down.

Before his father could warn him of the danger his head disappeared in the deep still eddy.

"Look out for us, Dennis, with a pole I'm goin' ter dive fer 'em!"

In a moment they came to the surface, the man holding the Boy, the Boy grasping his dog, the coon fastened to the dog's head.

"Well, don't that beat the devil!" Tom laughed, as he carried them to a little rocky island in the middle of the creek.

The Boy intent on saving his dog had held his breath and was not even strangled. The dog had buried his nose in the coon's throat and was chewing and choking with savage determination.

Tom stood over them now on the little island with its smooth stone-paved battle arena ringed with the music of laughing waters. He threw both hands above his shaggy head and yelled himself hoarse--the wild cry of the hunter's soul in delirious joy.

"*Yaaaiih! Yaaaiih!*"

A moment's pause, and then the low snarl and growl and clash of tooth and claw! Again the hunter's gnarled hands flew over his head.

"*Yaaaiih! Yaaaaiiih! Yaaiih! Yaaaaiiiihhh!!*"

On the shore Dennis stood first over one group of swirling, rolling, snarling brutes, and then over the other, yelling and cheering.

The coon on the island suddenly broke his assailant's death-like grip, and, with a quick leap, reached the water. Boney was on him in a moment and down they went beneath the surface again.

The Boy sprang to the rescue.

His father brushed him roughly aside:

"Keep out! I'll git 'em!"

Three times the coon made the dash for deep water and three times Tom carried both dog and coon back to the little island yelling his battle cry anew.

The smooth stones began to show red. Fur and dog hair flew in little tufts and struck the ground, sometimes with the flat splash of red flesh.

The Boy frowned and his lips quivered. At last he could hold in no longer. Through chattering teeth he moaned:

"He'll kill Boney, Pa!"

"Let him alone!" was the sharp command. "I never see sich a dog in my life. He'll kill that coon by hisself, I tell ye!"

Again his enemy broke Boney's grim hold on his throat, sprang back four feet and, to the dog's surprise, made no effort to reach the water. Instead he stood straight and quivering on his hind legs and faced his enemy, his white needle-like fangs gleaming in two rows and his savage fore-claws opening and closing with deadly threat.

The old warrior, taken completely by surprise by this new stratagem of his foe, circled in a vain effort to reach the flank or rear. Each turn only brought them again face to face, and at last he plunged straight on the centre line of attack. With a quick side leap the coon struck the dog's head a blow with his claw that split his ear for three inches as cleanly and evenly as if a surgeon's knife had been used.

With a low growl of rage and pain, Boney wheeled and repeated his assault with the same results for the other ear. He turned in silence and deliberately crept toward his foe. There would be no chance for a side blow. He wouldn't plunge or spring. He might get another bloody gash, but he wouldn't miss again.

This time he found the body, they closed and rolled over and over in close blood-stained grip. For the first time Tom's face showed doubts, and he called to Dennis:

"Choke off two dogs from that fust coon an' throw 'em in here!"

They came in a moment and clinched with Boney's enemy. The charge of two new troopers drove the coon to desperation. The sharp claws flew like lightning. The new dogs ran back into the water with howls of pain and scrambled up the bank to their old job.

Boney paid no attention either to the unexpected assault of his friends or their ignoble desertion. Every ounce of his dog-manhood was up now. It was a battle to the death and he had no wish to live if he couldn't whip any coon that ever made a track in his path.

The Boy's pride was roused now and the fighting instinct that slumbers in every human soul flashed through his excited eyes. He drew near and watched with increasing excitement and joined with his father at last in shouts and cheers.

"Did ye ever see such a dog!" he cried through his tears.

"He beats creation!" was the admiring answer.

The Boy bent low over the squirming pair and his voice was in perfect tune with his dog's low growl:

"Eat him up, Bone! Eat him alive!"

"Don't touch 'em!" Tom warned. "Let 'im have a fair fight--ef he don't kill that coon I'll eat 'im raw, hide an' hair!"

Boney had succeeded at last in fastening his teeth in a firm grip on the coon's throat. He held it without a cry of pain while the claws ripped his ears and gashed his head. Deeper and deeper sank his teeth until at last the razor claws that were cutting relaxed slowly and the long lean body with its beautiful fur lay full length on the red-marked stones.

The dog loosed his hold instantly. His work was done. He scorned to strike a fallen foe. He started to the water's edge to quench his thirst and staggered in a circle. The blood had blinded him.

The Boy sprang to his side, lifted him tenderly in his arms, carried him to the water and bathed his eyes and head.

"He's cut all to pieces!" he sobbed at last. "He'll die--I just know it!"

"Na!" his father answered scornfully. "Be all right in two or three days."

The Boy went back and looked at the slim body of the dead coon with wonder.

"Why did this one fight so much harder than the ones on the bank?" he asked thoughtfully.

"'Cause she's their mother," Tom said casually, "an' them's her two children."

Something hurt deep down in the Boy's soul as he looked at the graceful nose and the red-stained fur at her throat. He saw his mother's straight neck and head outlined again against the starlit sky the night she stood before him rifle in hand and shot at that midnight prowler.

His mouth closed firmly and he spoke with bitter decision:

"I don't like coon hunting. I'm not coming any more."

"Good Lord, Boy, we got ter have skins h'ain't we?" was the hearty answer.

"I reckon so," he sorrowfully admitted. But all the way home he walked in brooding silence.

X

The following winter brought the event for which the mother had planned and about which she had dreamed since her boy was born--a school!

The men gathered on the appointed day, cut the logs and split the boards for the house. Another day and it was raised and the roof in place.

Tom volunteered to make the teacher's table and chair and benches for the scholars. He had the best set of tools in the county and he wished to do it because he knew it would please his wife. There was no money in it but his life was swiftly passing in that sort of work. He was too big-hearted and generous to complain. Besides the world in which he lived--the world of field and wood, of dog and gun, of game and the open road was too beautiful and interesting to complain about it. He was glad to be alive and tried to make his neighbors think as he did about it.

When the great day dawned the young mother eagerly prepared breakfast for her children. She wouldn't allow Sarah to help this morning. It must be a perfect day in her life. She washed the Boy's face and hands with scrupulous care when the breakfast things were cleared away, and her grey eyes were shining with a joy he had never seen before. He caught her excitement and the spirit of it took possession of his imagination.

"What'll school be like, Ma?" he asked in a tense whisper.

"Oh, this one won't be very exciting; maybe in a little room built of logs. But it's the beginning, Boy, of greater things. Just spelling, reading, writing and arithmetic now--but you're starting on the way that leads out of these silent, lonely woods into the big world where great men fight and make history. Your father has never known this way. He's good and kind and gentle and generous, but he's just a child, because he doesn't know. You're going to be a man among men for your mother's sake, aren't you?"

She seized his arms and gripped them in her eagerness until he felt the pain.

"Won't you, Boy?" she repeated tensely.

He looked up steadily and then slowly said:

"Yes, I will."

She clasped him impulsively in her arms and hurried from the cabin leading the children by the hand. The Boy could feel her slender fingers trembling.

When they drew near the cross roads where the little log house had been built, she stopped, nervously fixed their clothes, took off the Boy's cap and brushed his thick black hair.

They were the first to arrive, but in a few minutes others came, and by nine o'clock more than thirty scholars were in their seats. The mother's heart sank within her when she met the teacher and heard him talk. It was only too evident that he was poorly equipped for his work. He could barely read and could neither write nor teach arithmetic. The one qualification about which there was absolute certainty, was that he could lick the biggest boy in school whenever the occasion demanded it. He conveyed this interesting bit of information to the assemblage in no uncertain language.

The mother could scarcely keep back her tears. By the end of the week it was plain that her children knew as much as their teacher.

"What's the use?" Tom asked in disgust. "Hit's a waste o' time an' money. Let 'em quit!"

"No, I can't take them out!" was the firm reply. "They may not learn much, but if the school keeps going, don't you see, a better man will come bye and bye, and then it will be worth while."

Tom shook his head, but let her have her own way.

"Besides," she went on, "he'll learn something being with the other children."

"Learn to fight, mebbe," the husband laughed.

He did, too, and the way it came about was as big a surprise to the Boy as it was to the youngster he fought.

The small bully of the school lived in the same direction as the Boy and Sarah. They frequently walked together for a mile going or coming and grew to know one another well. The Boy disliked this tow-head urchin from the moment they met. But he was quiet, unobtrusive and modest and generally allowed the loud-mouthed one to have his way. The tow-head took the Boy's quiet ways for submission and insisted on patronizing his friend. The Boy good-naturedly submitted when it cost him nothing of self-respect.

At the close of school, the tow-head whispered:

"Come by the spring with me, I want to show you somethin'!"

"No, I don't want to," he replied.

"Let Sarah go on an' we'll catch her--I got a funny trick ter show you. You'll kill yourself a-laughin'."

The Boy's curiosity was aroused and he consented.

They hastened to the spring where the embers of a fire at which the scholars were accustomed to warm their lunch, were still smouldering. The tow-headed one drew from the corner of the fence a turtle which he had captured and tied, scooped a red-hot coal from the fire with a piece of board and placed it on the turtle's back.

The poor creature, tortured by the burning coal, started in a scramble trying to run from the fire. The tow-head roared with laughter.

The Boy flushed with sudden rage, sprang forward and knocked the coal off.

The two faced each other.

"You do that again an' I'll knock you down!" shouted the bully.

"You do it again and I'll knock you down," was the sturdy answer.

"You will, will you?" the tow-head cried with scorn. "Well, I'll show you."

With a bound he replaced the coal.

The Boy knocked it off and pounced on him.

The fight was brief. They had scarcely touched the ground before the Boy was on top pounding with both his little, clinched fists.

"Stop it--you're killin' me!" the under one screamed.

"Will you let him alone?" the Boy hissed.

"You're killin' me, I tell ye!" the tow-head yelled in terror. "Stop it I say--would you kill a feller just for a doggoned old cooter?"

"Will you let him alone?"

"Yes, if ye won't kill me."

The Boy slowly rose. The tow-head leaped to his feet and with a look of terror started on a run.

"You needn't run, I won't hit ye again!" the Boy cried.

But the legs only moved faster. Never since he was born did the Boy see a pair of legs get over the ground like that. He sat down and laughed and then hurried on to join Sarah.

He didn't tell his sister what had happened. His mother mustn't know that he had been in a fight. But when he felt the touch of her hand on his forehead that night as he rose from her knee he couldn't bear the thought of deceiving her again and so he confessed.

"It wasn't wrong, was it, to fight for a thing like that?" he asked wistfully.

"No," came the answer. "He needed a thrashing--the little scoundrel, and I'm glad you did it."

XI

The school flickered out in five weeks and the following summer another lasted for six weeks.

And then they moved to the land Tom had staked off in the heart of the great forest fifteen miles from the northern banks of the Ohio. He would still be in sight of the soil of Kentucky.

The Boy's heart beat with new wonder as they slowly floated across the broad surface of the river. He could conceive of no greater one.

"There *is* a bigger one!" his father said. "The Mississippi is the daddy of 'em all--the Ohio's lost when it rolls into her banks--stretchin' for a thousand miles an' more from the mountains in the north way down to the Gulf of Mexico at New Orleans."

"And it's all ours?" he asked in wonder.

"Yes, and plenty more big ones that pour into hit from the West."

The Boy saw again the impassioned face of the orator telling the glories of his country, and his heart swelled with pride.

They left the river and plunged into the trackless forest. No roads had yet scarred its virgin soil. Only the blazed trail for the first ten miles--the trail Tom had marked with his own hatchet--and then the magnificent woods without a mark. Five miles further they penetrated, cutting down the brush and trees to make way for the wagon.

They stopped at last on a beautiful densely wooded hill near a stream of limpid water. A rough camp was quickly built Indian fashion and covered with bear skins.

The next day the father put into the Boy's hand the new axe he had bought for him.

"You're not quite eight years old, Boy," he said, encouragingly, "but you're big as a twelve-year-old an' you're spunky. Do you think you can swing an axe that's a man's size?"

"Yes," was the sturdy answer.

And from that day he did it with a song on his lips no matter how heavy the heart that beat in his little breast.

At first they cut the small poles and built a half-faced camp, and made it strong enough to stand the storms of winter in case a cabin could not be finished before spring. This half-faced camp was made of small logs built on three sides, with the fourth open to the south. In front of this opening the log fire was built and its flame never died day or night.

To the soul of the Boy this half-faced camp with its blazing logs in the shadow of giant trees was the most wonderful dwelling he had ever seen. The stars that twinkled in the sky beyond the lacing boughs were set in his ceiling. No king in his palace could ask for more.

But into the young mother's heart slowly crept the first shadows of a nameless dread. Fifteen miles from a human habitation in the depths of an unmarked wilderness with only a hunter's camp for her home, and she had dreamed of schools! To her children her face always gave good cheer. But at night she lay awake for long, pitiful hours watching the stars and fighting the battle alone with despair.

Yet there was never a thought of surrender. God lived and her faith was in Him. The same stars were shining above that sparkled in old Virginia and Kentucky. Something within sang for joy at the sight of her Boy--strong of limb and dauntless of soul. He was God's answer to her cry, and always she went the even tenor of her way singing softly that he might hear.

His father set him to the task of clearing the first acre of ground for the crop next spring. It seemed a joke to send a child with an axe into that huge forest and tell him to clear the way for civilization. And yet he went with firm, eager steps.

He chose the biggest tree in sight for his first task--a giant oak three feet in diameter, its straight trunk rising a hundred feet without a limb or knot to mar its perfect beauty.

The Boy leaped on the fallen monarch of the woods with a new sense of power. Far above gleamed a tiny space in the sky. His hand had made it. He was a force to be reckoned with now. He was doing things that counted in a man's world.

Day after day his axe rang in the woods until a big white patch of sky showed with gleaming piles of clouds. And shimmering sunbeams were warming the earth for the seed of the coming spring. His tall thin body ached with mortal weariness, but the spirit within was too proud to whine or complain. He had taken a man's place. His mother needed him and he'd play the part.

The winter was the hardest and busiest he had ever known. He shot his first wild turkey from the door of their log camp the second week after arrival. Proud of his marksmanship he talked of it for a week, and yet he didn't make a good hunter. He allowed his father to go alone oftener than he would accompany him. There was a queer little voice somewhere within that protested against the killing. He wouldn't acknowledge it to himself but half the joy of his shot at his turkey was destroyed by the sight of the blood-stained broken wing when he picked it up.

The mother watched this trait with deepening pride. His practice at writing and reading was sheer joy now. Her interest was so keen he always tried his best that he might see her smile.

It was time to begin the spring planting before the heavy logs were rolled and burned and the smaller ones made ready for the cabin. The corn couldn't wait. The cabin must remain unfinished until the crop was laid by.

It had been a long, lonely winter for the mother. But with the coming of spring, the wooded world was clothed in beauty so fresh and marvellous, she forgot the loneliness in new hopes and joys.

Settlers were moving in now. Every week Tom brought the news of another neighbor. Her aunt came in midsummer bringing Dennis and his dogs with fun and companionship for the Boy.

The new cabin was not quite finished, but they moved in and gave their kin their old camp for a home, all ready without the stroke of an axe.

Dennis was wild over the hunting and proposed to the Boy a deer hunt all by themselves.

"Let's just me and you go, Boy, an' show Tom what we can do with a rifle without him. You can take the first shot with old 'Speakeasy' an' then I'll try her. The deer'll be ez thick ez bees around that Salt Lick now."

The Boy consented. Boney went with him for company. As a self-respecting coon dog he scorned to hunt any animal that couldn't fight with an even chance for his life. As for a deer--he'd as lief chase a calf!

Dennis placed the Boy at a choice stand behind a steep hill in which the deer would be sure to plunge in their final rush to escape the dogs when close pressed in the valley.

"Now the minute you see him jump that ridge let him have it!" Dennis said. "He'll come straight down the hill right inter your face."

The Boy took his place and began to feel the savage excitement of his older companion. He threw the gun in place and drew a bead on an imaginary bounding deer.

"All right. I'll crack him!" he promised.

"Now, for the Lord's sake, don't you miss 'im!" Dennis warned. "I don't want Tom ter have the laugh on us."

The Boy promised, and Dennis called his dogs and hurried into the bottoms toward the Salt Lick. In half an hour the dogs opened on a hot trail that grew fainter and fainter in the distance until they could scarcely be heard. They stopped altogether for a moment and then took up the cry gradually growing clearer and clearer. The deer had run the limit of his first impulse and taken the back track, returning directly over the same trail.

Nearer and nearer the pack drew, the trail growing hotter and hotter with each leap of the hounds.

The Boy was trembling with excitement. He cocked his gun and stood ready. Boney lay on a pile of leaves ten feet away quietly dozing. Louder and louder rang the cry of the hounds. They seemed to be right back of the hill now. The deer should leap over its crest at any moment. His gun was half lifted and his eyes flaming with excitement when a beautiful half grown fawn sprang over the hill and stood for a moment staring with wide startled eyes straight into his.

The savage yelp of the hounds close behind rang clear, sharp and piercing as they reared the summit. The panting, trembling fawn glanced despairingly behind, looked again into the Boy's eyes, and as the first dog leaped the hill crest made his choice. Staggering and panting with terror, he dropped on his knees by the Boy's side, the bloodshot eyes begging piteously for help.

The Boy dropped his gun and gathered the trembling thing in his arms. In a moment the hounds were on him leaping and tearing at the fawn. He kicked them right and left and yelled with all his might:

"Down, I tell you! Down or I'll kill you!"

The hounds continued to leap and snap in spite of his kicks and cries until Boney saw the struggle, and stepped between his master and his tormenters. One low growl and not another hound came near.

When Dennis arrived panting for breath he couldn't believe his eyes. The Boy was holding the exhausted fawn in his lap with a glazed look in his eyes.

"Well, of all the dam-fool things I ever see sence God made me, this takes the cake!" he cried in disgust. "Why didn't ye shoot him?"

"Because he ran to me for help--how could I shoot him?"

Dennis sat down and roared:

"Well, of all the deer huntin', this beats me!"

The Boy rose, still holding the fawn in his arms.

"You can take the gun and go on. Boney and me'll go back home----"

"You ain't goin' ter carry that thing clean home, are you?"

"Yes, I am," was the quiet answer. "And I'll kill any dog that tries to hurt him."

Dennis was still laughing when he disappeared, Boney walking slowly at his heels.

He showed the fawn to his mother and told Sarah she could have him for a pet. The mother watched him with shining eyes while he built a pen and then lifted the still trembling wild thing inside.

Next morning the pen was down and the captive gone. The Boy didn't seem much surprised or appear to care. When he was alone with his mother she whispered:

"Didn't you go out there last night and let it loose when the dogs were asleep?"

He was still a moment and then nodded his head.

His mother clasped him to her heart.

"O my Boy! My own--I love you!"

XII

The second winter in the wilderness was not so hard. The heavy work of clearing the timber for the corn fields was done and the new cabin and its furniture had been finished except the door, for which there was little use.

The new neighbors had brought cheer to the mother's heart.

An early spring broke the winter of 1818 and clothed the wilderness world in robes of matchless beauty.

The Boy's gourds were placed beside the new garden and the noise of chattering martins echoed over the cabin. The toughened muscles of his strong, slim body no longer ached in rebellion at his tasks. Work had become a part of the rhythm of life. He could sing at his hardest task. The freedom and strength of the woods had gotten into his blood. In this world of waving trees, of birds and beasts, of laughing sky and rippling waters, there were no masters, no slaves. Millions in gold were of no value in its elemental struggle. Character, skill, strength and manhood only counted. Poverty was teaching him the first great lesson of human life, that man shall eat his bread in the sweat of his brow and that industry is the only foundation on which the moral and material universe has ever rested or can rest.

Solitude and the stimulus of his mother's mind were slowly teaching him to think--to think deeply and fearlessly, and think for himself.

Entering now in his ninth year, he was shy, reticent, over-grown, consciously awkward, homely and ill clad--he grew so rapidly it was impossible to make his clothes fit. But in the depths of his hazel-grey eyes there were slumbering fires that set him apart from the boys of his age. His mother saw and understood.

A child in years and yet he had already learned the secrets of the toil necessary to meet the needs of life. He swung a woodman's axe with any man. He could plow and plant a field, make its crop, harvest and store its fruits and cook them for the table. He could run, jump, wrestle, swim and fight when manhood called. He knew the language of the winds and clouds, and spoke the tongues of woods and field.

And he could read and write. His mother's passionate yearning and quenchless enthusiasm had placed in his hand the key to books and the secrets of the ages were his for the asking.

He would never see the walls of a college, but he had already taken his degree in Industry, Patience, Caution, Courage, Pity and Gentleness.

The beauty and glory of this remarkable spring brought him into still closer communion with his mother's spirit. They had read every story of the Bible, some of them twice or three times, and his stubborn mind had fought with her many a friendly battle over their teachings. Always too wise and patient to command his faith, she waited its growth in the fulness of time. He had read every tale in "AEsop's Fables" and brought a thousand smiles to his mother's dark face by his quaint comments. She was dreaming now of new books to place in his eager hands. Corn was ten cents a bushel, wheat twenty-five, and a cow was only worth six dollars. Whiskey, hams and tobacco were legal tender and used instead of money. She had ceased to dream of wealth in goods and chattels until conditions were changed. Her one aim in life was to train the minds of her children and to this joyous task she gave her soul and body. It was the only thing worth while. That God would give her strength for this was all she asked.

And then the great shadow fell.

The mother and children were walking home from the woods through the glory of the Southern spring morning in awed silence. The path was hedged with violets and buttercups. The sweet odor of grapevine, blackberry and dewberry blossoms filled the air. Dogwood and black-haw lit with white flame the farthest shadows of the forest and the music of birds seemed part of the mingled perfume of flowers.

The boy's keen ear caught the drone of bees and his sharp eye watched them climb slowly toward their storehouse in a towering tree. All nature was laughing in the madness of joy.

The Boy silently took his mother's hand and asked in subdued tones:

"What is the pest, Ma, and what makes it?"

"Nobody knows," she answered softly. "It comes like a thief in the night and stays for months and sometimes for years. They call it the 'milk-sick' because the cows die, too--and sometimes the horses. The old Indian women say it starts from the cows eating a poison flower in the woods. The doctors know nothing about it. It just comes and kills, that's all."

The little hand suddenly gripped hers with trembling hold:

"O Ma, if it kills you!"

A tender smile lighted her dark face as the warmth of his love ran like fire through her veins.

"It can't harm me, my son, unless God wills it. When he calls I shall be ready."

All the way home he clung to her hand and sometimes when they paused stroked it tenderly with both his.

"What's it like?" he asked at last. "Can't you take bitters for it in time to stop it? How do you know when it's come?"

"You begin to feel drowsy, a whitish coating is on the tongue, a burning in the stomach, the feet and legs get cold. You're restless and the pulse grows weak."

"How long does it last?"

"Sometimes it kills in three days, sometimes two weeks. Sometimes it's chronic and hangs on for years and then kills."

Every morning through the long black summer of the scourge he asked her with wistful tenderness if she were well. Her cheerful answers at last brought peace to his anxious heart and he gradually ceased to fear. She was too sweet and loving and God too good that she should die. Besides, both his father and mother had given him a lesson in quiet, simple heroism that steadied his nerves.

He looked at the rugged figure of his father with a new sense of admiration. He was no more afraid of Death than of Life. He was giving himself without a question in an utterly unselfish devotion to the stricken community. There were no doctors within thirty miles, and if one came he could but shake his head and advise simple remedies that did no good. Only careful nursing counted for anything. Without money, without price, without a murmur the father gave his life to this work. No neighbor within five miles was stricken that he did not find a place by that bedside in fearless, loving, unselfish service.

And when Death came, this simple friend went for his tools, cut down a tree, ripped the boards from its trunk, made the coffin, and with tender reverence dug a grave and lowered the loved one. He was doctor, nurse, casket-maker, grave-digger, comforter and priest. His reverent lips had long known the language of prayer.

With tireless zeal the mother joined in this ministry of love, and the Boy saw her slender dark figure walk so often beside trembling feet as they entered the valley of the great shadow, that he grew to believe that she led a charmed life. Nor did he fear when Dennis came one morning and in choking tones said that both his uncle and aunt were stricken in the little half-faced camp but a few hundred yards away. He was sorry for Dennis. He had never known father or mother--only this uncle and aunt.

"Don't you worry, Dennis," the Boy said tenderly. "You'll live with us if they die."

They both died within a few days. The night after the last burial, Dennis crawled into the loft with the Boy to be his companion for many a year.

And then the blow fell, swift, terrible and utterly unexpected. He had long ago made up his mind that God had flung about his mother's form the spell of his Almighty power and the pestilence that walked in the night dared not draw near. An angel with flaming sword stood beside their cabin door.

Last night in the soft moonlight a whip-poor-will was singing nearby and he fancied he saw the white winged sentinel, and laughed for joy.

When he climbed down from his loft next morning his mother was in bed and

Sarah was alone over the fire cooking breakfast.

His heart stood still. He walked with unsteady step to her bedside and whispered:

"Are you sick, Ma?"

"Yes, dear, it has come."

He grasped her hot outstretched hand and fell on his knees in sobbing anguish. He knew now--it was the angel of Death he had seen.

XIII

Death stood at the door with drawn sword to slay not to defend, but the Boy resolved to fight. She should not give up--she should not die. He would fight for her with all the hosts of hell and single-handed if he must.

He rose from his knees still holding her hand, his first hopeless burst of despair over, his heart beating with desperate resolution.

"You won't give up, will you, Ma?" he whispered.

She smiled wanly and he rushed on with breathless intensity: "I'm not going to let you die. I won't--I tell you I won't. I'll fight this thing--and you've got to help me--won't you?"

"I'm ready for God's will, my Boy," she said simply.

"I don't want you to say that!" he pleaded. "I want you to fight and never give up. Why you can't die, Ma--you just can't. You're my only teacher now. There ain't no schools here. How can I learn books without you to help me? Say you'll get well. Please say it for me--please, just say it----"

He paused and couldn't go on for a moment, "Say you'll try then--just for me--please say it!"

"I'll try, Boy," she said tenderly at last.

He flew to the creek bank and in two hours came home with an armful of fresh sarsaparilla roots. He cut and pounded them into a soft pulp and made a poultice. Sarah helped him put it in place. He made his mother drink the bitters every hour. He got stones ready and had them hot to wrap in cloths and put to her feet the moment they felt cold. He wouldn't take her word for it either. He kept slipping his little hands under the cover to feel.

The mother smiled at his tender, eager touch.

"Now, Boy," she said softly. "I'm feeling comfortable, will you do something for me?"

"What is it?" he cried eagerly.

She smiled again:

"Read to me. I want to hear your voice."

"All right--what?"

"The Bible, of course."

"What story?"

"Not a story this time--the twenty-third Psalm."

The Boy took the worn Bible from the shelf, sat down on the edge of the bed, opened, and began in low tones to read:

"The Lord is my Shepherd, I shall not want----"

His voice choked and he stopped:

"O, Ma, I just can't read that now--why--why did he let this come to you if He's your Shepherd--why--why--why!"

He buried his face in his hands and her slender fingers touched his hair:

"He knows best, my son--read on--the words are sweet to my soul from your lips."

With an effort he opened the Book again:

"He maketh me to lie down in green pastures;

"He leadeth me beside the still waters.

"He restoreth my soul:

"He leadeth me in the paths of righteousness for His name's sake.

"Yea, though I walk through the valley of the shadow of death,

"I will fear no evil; for thou art with me----"

Again the voice choked into silence and he closed the Book.

"I can't--I can't read it. I'm afraid you're going to give up!" he sobbed. "O Ma, you won't, will you? Please say you won't?"

"No, no, I won't give up, my Boy," she said soothingly. "I'm just ready for anything He sends----"

"But I don't want you to say that!" he broke in passionately. "You must fight.

You mustn't be ready. You mustn't think about dying. I won't let you die--I tell you!"

She stroked his forehead with gentle touch:

"I won't give up for your sake----"

"It's a promise now?" he cried.

"Yes, I promise----"

"Then I'm going for a doctor right away----"

"You can't find him, Boy," his father said. "It's thirty miles across the Ohio into Kentucky where he lives. An' in all this sickness he ain't at home. Hit's foolishness ter go----"

"I'll find him," was the firm response.

The father made no further protest. He helped him saddle the horse, buckled the stirrups to fit his little bare legs and gave him as clear directions as he could.

"The moon'll be shinin' all night, Boy," were his last words. "Yer can cross the river before eight o'clock. Ef ye git lost on t'other side ax yer way frum the fust house ye come to----"

The Boy nodded, and when had fixed his bare toes in the stirrups he leaned low and whispered:

"You won't give up, Pa, will ye? You'll fight for her till I get back?"

The big gnarled fist closed over the little hand on the pommel of the saddle, and the father's voice was husky:

"As long as there's breath in her body--hurry now."

The last command was not needed. The horse felt the quiver of tense suffering in the low voice and the nervous touch of the switch on his side. With a quick bound he was off at a full gallop down the trail toward the river.

The sun had set before they reached the open country beyond the great forest, but by seven o'clock the Boy saw from the hill top the shining mirror of the river in the calm moonlit valley. Before night he had succeeded in rousing the ferryman and reached the opposite shore.

He lost the way once about nine o'clock and a settler whose light he saw in the woods called sharply from the door with his rifle in hand:

"Who are you?"

"I'm just a little boy," the voice faltered. "I'm trying to find the doctor's house.

My mother's about to die and I'm lost. I want you to show me the road."

The rifle was lowered and the cabin stirred. The man dropped back and a woman appeared in the door way.

"Won't ye come in, Honey, and rest a minute and me give ye somethin' to eat while Pa's gettin' ready to go with ye a piece?"

"No'm I can't eat nuthin'----"

He didn't dare go near that tender voice that spoke so clearly its sympathy in the night. He would be crying in a minute if he did and he couldn't afford that.

The settler caught a horse and rode with him an hour to make sure he wouldn't miss the way again.

He reached the doctor's house by eleven o'clock, and to his joy found him at home. The rough old man refused to move an inch until he had fed his horse and eaten a hearty meal.

The Boy tried to eat, but couldn't. The food stuck squarely in his throat. It was no use.

He went outside and waited beside his horse until the doctor was ready. It seemed an eternity, the awful wait. How serene the still beauty of the autumn night! Not a breath of wind stirred. The full moon hung in the sky straight overhead, flooding the earth with silver radiance, marking in clear and vivid lines the shadows of the trees on the ground.

Bitter wonder and rebellion filled his young soul. How could God sit unmoved among those shining stars and leave his mother to die!

The doctor came at last and they started.

In vain he urged that they gallop.

"I won't do it, sir!" the old man snapped. "Your horse has come thirty miles. I'll not let you kill him and I'm not going to kill myself plunging over a rough road at night."

They reached the cabin at daylight. The Boy saw the glow of the flame in the big fireplace through the woods and his heart beat high with new hope. Now that the doctor was here he felt sure her life could be saved.

The Boy stood close by his side when he felt her pulse, and looked at the strange whitish-brown coating on her tongue.

"You can do something, Doctor?" he asked anxiously.

"Yes," was the short answer.

He asked for a towel and bowl and opened his saddlebags. He examined the point of his lancet and bared the slender arm.

"What are ye goin' ter do?" Tom asked with a frown.

"Bleed her, of course. It's the only thing to do----"

The Boy suddenly pushed himself between the doctor and the bed and looked up into his stern face with a resolute stare:

"You shan't do it. I don't know nothin' much about doctorin' but I got sense enough to know that'll kill her--and you shan't do it!"

The doctor looked angrily at the father.

"I say so, too," Tom replied. "She's too weak for that."

With a snort of anger, the old man threw the lancet into his saddlebags, snapped them together and strode through the cabin door.

The Boy followed him wistfully to the stable, and when he seized the bridle to put on the horse, caught his hand and looked up:

"Please don't go," he begged. "I'm mighty sorry I made you mad. I didn't go to do it. You see----" his voice faltered--"I love her so I just couldn't let you cut her arm open and see her bleed. I didn't mean to hurt your feelings. Won't you stay and help us? Can't ye do somethin' else for her? I'll pay ye. I'll go work for ye a whole year or five years if ye want me--if you'll just save her--just save her, that's all--don't go--please don't!"

Something in the child's anguish found the rough old man's heart. His eyes grew misty for a moment, he slipped one arm about the Boy's shoulders and drew him close.

"God knows I'd stay and do something if I could, Sonny, but I don't know what to do. I'm not sure I'm right about the bleeding or I'd stay and make you help me do it. But I'm not sure--I'm not sure--and I can do no good by staying. Keep her warm, give her all the good food her stomach will retain. That's all I can tell you. She's in God's hands."

With a heavy heart the Boy watched him ride away as the sun rose over the eastern hills. The doctor's last words sank into his soul. She was in God's hands! Well, he would go to God and beg Him to save her. He went into the woods, knelt behind a great oak and in the simple words of a child asked for the desire of his heart. Three times every day and every night he prayed.

For four days no change was apparent. She was very weak and tired, but suffered no pain. His prayer was heard and would be answered!

The first symptom of failure in circulation, he promptly met by placing the hot stones to her feet. And for hours he and Sarah would rub her until the cold disappeared.

On the morning of the seventh day she was unusually bright.

"Why, you're better, Ma, aren't you?" he cried with joy.

Her eyes were shining with a strange excitement:

"Yes. I'm a lot better. I'm going to sit up awhile. I'm tired lying down."

She threw herself quickly on the side of the bed and her feet touched the bearskin rug. She rose trembling and smiling and took a step. She tottered a bit, but the Boy was laughing and holding her arm. She reached the chair by the fire and he wrapped a great skin about her feet and limbs.

"Look, Pa, she's getting well!" the Boy shouted.

Tom watched her gravely without reply.

She took the Boy's hand, still smiling:

"I had such a wonderful dream," she began slowly--"the same one I had before you were born, my Boy. God had answered my prayer and sent me a son. I watched him grow to be a strong, brave, patient, wise and gentle man. Thousands hung on his words and the great from the ends of the earth came to do him homage. With uncovered head he led me into a beautiful home with white pillars. And then he bowed low and whispered in my ear: 'This is yours, my angel mother. I bought it for you with my life. All that I am I owe to you'----"

Her voice sank to a whisper that was half a sob and half a laugh.

"See how she's smiling, Pa," the Boy cried. "She's getting well!"

"Don't ye understand!" the father whispered. "Look--at her eyes--she's not tellin' you a dream--she's looking through the white gates of heaven--it's Death, Boy--it's come--Lord God, have mercy!"

With a groan he dropped by her side and her thin hand rested gently on his shaggy head.

The Boy stared at her in agonizing wonder as she felt for his hand and feebly held it. She was gazing now into the depths of his soul with her pensive hungry eyes.

"He good to your father, my son----" she paused for breath and looked at him tenderly. She knew the father was the child of the future--this Boy, the man.

"Yes!" he whispered.

"And love your sister----"

"Yes."

"Be a man among men, for your mother's sake----"

"Yes, Ma, I will!"

The little head bent low and the voice was silent.

They went to work to make her coffin at noon. An unused walnut log of burled fibre had been lying in the sun and drying for two years, since Tom had built the furniture for the cabin. Dennis helped him rip the boards from this dark, rich wood, shape and plane it for the pieces he would need.

The Boy sat with dry eyes and aching heart, making the wooden nails to fasten these boards together.

He stopped suddenly, walked to the bench at which his father was working and laid by his side the first pins he had whittled.

"I can't do it, Pa," he gasped. "I just can't make the nails for her coffin. I feel like somebody's drivin' 'em through my heart!"

The rugged face was lighted with tenderness as he slowly answered:

"Why, we must make it, Boy--hit's the last thing we kin do ter show our love fur her--ter make it all smooth an' purty outen this fine dark wood. Yer wouldn't put her in the ground an' throw the cold dirt right on her face, would you?"

The slim figure shivered:

"No--no--I wouldn't do that! Yes, I'll help--we must make it beautiful, mustn't we?"

And then he went back to the pitiful task.

They dug her grave, these loving hands, father and son and orphan waif, on a gentle hill in the deep woods. As the sun sank in a sea of scarlet clouds next day, they lowered the coffin. The father lifted his voice in a simple prayer and the Boy took his sister's hand and led her in silence back to the lonely cabin. He couldn't stay to see them throw the dirt over her. He couldn't endure it.

He had heard of ghosts in graveyards, and he wondered vaguely if such things could be true. He hoped it was. When the others were asleep, just before day, he slipped noiselessly from his bed and made his way to her grave.

The waning moon was shining in cold white splendor. The woods were silent. He watched and waited and hoped with half-faith and half-fear that he might see her radiant form rise from the dead.

A leaf rustled behind him and he turned with a thrill of awful joy. He wasn't afraid. He'd clasp her in his arms if he could. With firm step and head erect, eyes wide and nostrils dilated, he walked straight into the shadows to see and know.

And there, standing in a spot of pale moonlight, stood his dog looking up into his eyes with patient, loving sympathy. He hadn't shed a tear since her death. Now the flood tide broke the barriers. He sank to the ground, slipped his arm around the dog's neck, and sobbed aloud.

He wrote a tear stained letter to the only parson he knew. It was his first historic record and he signed his name in bold, well rounded letters--"A. LINCOLN." Three months later the faithful old man came in answer to his request and preached her funeral sermon. Something in the lad's wistful eyes that day fired him with eloquence. Through all life the words rang with strange solemn power in the Boy's heart:

"O Death, where is thy sting! O grave, where is thy victory! Blessed are they that die in the Lord! Death is not the chill shadow of the night--but the grey light of the dawn--the dawn of a new eternal day. Lift up your eyes and see its beauty. Open your ears and hear the stir of its wondrous life!"

When the last friend had gone, the forlorn little figure stood beside the grave alone. There was a wistful smile on his lips as he slowly whispered:

"I'll not forget, Ma, dear--I'll not forget. I'll live for you."

Nor did he forget. In her slender figure a new force had appeared in human history. The peasant woman of the old world has ever taught her child contentment with his lot. And patient millions beyond the seas bend their backs without a murmur to the task their fathers bore three thousand years ago.

Free America has given the race a new peasant woman. Born among the lowliest of her kind, she walks earth's way with her feet in the dust, her head among the stars.

This one died young in the cabin beside the deep woods, but not before her hand had kindled a fire of divine discontent in the soul of her son that only God could extinguish.

The Story

CHAPTER I
THE MAN OF THE HOUR

"It's positively uncanny----"

Betty Winter paused on the top step of the Capitol and gazed over the great silent crowd with a shiver.

"The silence--yes," Ned Vaughan answered slowly. "I wondered if you had felt it, too."

"It's more like a funeral than an Inauguration."

The young reporter smiled:

"If you believe General Scott there may be several funerals in Washington before the day's work is done."

"And you *don't* believe him?" the girl asked seriously.

"Nonsense! All this feverish preparation for violence----"

Betty laughed:

"I'm afraid you're not a good judge of the needs of the incoming administration. As an avowed Secessionist--you're hardly in their confidence."

"Thank God, I'm not."

"What are those horses doing over there by the trees?"

"Masked battery of artillery."

"Don't be silly!"

"It's true. Old Scott's going to save the Capital on Inauguration Day any how! The Avenue's lined with soldiers--sharpshooters posted in the windows along the whole route of the Inaugural procession, a company of troops in each end of the Capitol. He has built a wooden tunnel from the street into the north end of the building and that's lined with guards. A squad of fifty soldiers are under the platform where we're going to sit----"

"No!"

"Look through the cracks and see for yourself!" Vaughan cried with scorn.

The sparkling brown eyes were focused on the board platform.

"I do see them moving," she said slowly, as a look of deep seriousness swept the fair young face. "Perhaps General Scott's right after all. Father says we're walking on a volcano----"

"But not that kind of a volcano, Miss Betty," Vaughan interrupted. "Senator Winter's an Abolitionist. He hates the South with every breath he breathes."

Betty nodded:

"And prays God night and morning to give him greater strength with which to hate it harder--yes----"

"But you're not so blind?"

"There must be a little fire where there's so much smoke. A crazy fool might try to kill the new President."

Ned Vaughan's slender figure stiffened:

"The South won't fight that way. If they begin war it will be the most solemn act of life. It will be for God and country, and what they believe to be right. The Southern people are not assassins. When they take Washington it will be with the bayonet."

"And yet your brother had a taste of Southern feeling here the night of the election when a mob broke in and smashed the office of the **Republican**."

"A gang of hoodlums," he protested. "Anything may happen on election night to an opposition newspaper. The Southern men who formed that mob will never give this administration trouble----"

"I'm so anxious to meet your brother," Betty interrupted. "Why doesn't he come?"

"He's in the Senate Chamber for the ceremonies. He'll join us before the procession gets here."

"He's as handsome as everybody says?" she asked naively.

"I'll admit he's a good-looking fellow if he is my brother."

"And vain?"

"As a peacock----"

"Conceited?"

"Very."

"And a woman hater!"

"Far from it--he's easy. He may not think so, but between us he's an easy mark. I've always been afraid he'll make a fool of himself and marry without the consent of his younger brother. He's a great care to me."

The brown eyes twinkled:

"You love him very much?"

Ned Vaughan nodded his dark head slowly:

"Yes. We've quarrelled every day since the election."

"Over politics?"

"What else?"

"Love, perhaps."

The dark eyes met hers.

"No, he hasn't seen you yet----"

Betty's laugh was genial and contagious.

He had meant to be serious and hoped that she would give him the opening he'd been sparring for. But she refused the challenge with such amusement he was piqued.

"You're from Missouri, but you're a true Southerner, Mr. Vaughan."

"And you're a heartless Puritan," he answered with a frown.

She shook her golden brown curls:

"No--no--no! My name's an accident. My father was born in Maine on the Canada line. But my mother was French. I'm her daughter. I love sunlight and flowers, music and foolishness--and dream of troubadours who sing under my window. I hate long faces and gloom. But my father has ambition. I love him, and so I endure things."

Ned Vaughan looked at her timidly. For the life of him he couldn't make her out. Was she laughing at him? He half suspected it, and yet there was something sweet and appealing in the way she gazed into his eyes. He gave it up and changed the subject.

He had promised to bring John to-day and introduce him. He had been prattling like a fool about this older brother. He wished to God now something would keep him. The pangs of jealousy had already began to gnaw at the thought of her hand resting in his.

From the way Betty Winter had laughed she was quite capable of flying two strings to her bow. And with all the keener interest because they happened to be brothers. Why had she asked him so pointedly about John? He had excited her curiosity, of course, by his silly brother--hero-worship. He had told her of his brilliant career in New York under Horace Greeley on the *Tribune*--of Greeley's personal interest, and the flattering letter he had written to Colonel Forney, which had made him the city editor of the New Party organ in Washington--of his cool heroism the night the mob had attacked the *Republican* office--and last he had hinted of an affair over a woman in New York that had led to a challenge and a bloodless duel--bloodless because his opponent failed to appear. It was his own fault, of course, if Betty was keeping him at arm's length to-day. No girl could fail to be interested in such a man--no matter who her father might be--Puritan or Cavalier.

His arm trembled in spite of his effort at self-control as he led her down the stately steps of the eastern facade toward the Inaugural platform. He paused on the edge of the boards and pointed to the huge bronze figure of the statue of Liberty which had been cast to crown the dome of the Capitol. It lay prostrate in the mud and the crowds were climbing over it.

"I wonder if Miss Liberty will ever be lifted to her place on high?" he said musingly.

"If they do finish the dome," Betty replied, "and crown it with that bronze, my father should sue for damages. One of his most eloquent figures of speech will be ruined. That prostrate work of art lying in the mud has given thousands of votes to the Republicans. I've caught myself crying over his eloquence at times myself."

Ned Vaughan smiled:

"A queer superstition has grown up in Washington that the dome of the Capitol will never be completed----"

"Do you believe it?"

"No. It will be finished. But I'm not sure whether Abraham Lincoln or Jefferson Davis will preside on that occasion."

"And I haven't the slightest doubt on that point," Betty said with quick emphasis.

"I thought you were not a student of politics?" he dryly observed.

"I'm not. It's just a feeling. Women know things by intuition."

The young man glanced upward at the huge crane which swung from the unfinished structure of the dome.

"Anyhow, Miss Betty," he said smilingly, "your Black Republican President has a beautiful day for the Inaugural."

"We'll hope it's a sign for the future--shall we?"

"I hope so," was the serious answer. "God knows there haven't been many happy signs lately. It was dark and threatening at dawn this morning and a few drops of rain fell up to eight o'clock."

"You were up at dawn?" the girl asked in surprise.

"Yes. The Senate has been in session all night over the new amendment to the Constitution guaranteeing to the South security in the possession of their slaves."

"And they passed it?"

"Yes----"

"Over my father's prostrate form?"

"Yes--an administrative measure, too. I've an idea from the 'moderation' of your father's remarks that there'll be some fun between the White House and the Senate Chamber during the next four years. For my part I share his scorn for such eleventh hour repentance. It's too late. The mischief has been done. Secession is a fact and we've got to face it."

"But we haven't heard from the new President yet," Betty ventured.

"No. That's why this crowd's so still. For the first time since the foundation of the government, the thousands banked in front of this platform really wish to hear what a President-elect has to say."

"Isn't that a tremendous tribute to the man?"

"Possibly so--possibly not. He has been silent since his election. Not a word has fallen from his lips to indicate his policy. He has more real power from the moment he takes the oath of office than any crowned head of Europe. From his lips to-day will fall the word that means peace or war. That's why this crowd's so still."

"It's weird," Betty whispered. "You can feel their very hearts beat. Do you suppose the new President realizes the meaning of such a moment?"

"I don't think this one will. I interviewed Stanton, the retiring Attorney General of Buchanan's Cabinet, yesterday. He knows Lincoln personally--was with him in a lawsuit once before the United States Court. Stanton says he's a coward and a fool and the ugliest white man who ever appeared on this planet. He has already christened him 'The Original Gorilla,' or 'The Illinois Ape'----"

"I wonder," Betty broke in with petulance, "if such a man could be elected President? I'm morbidly curious to see him. My father, as an Abolitionist, had to vote for him and he must support his administration as a Republican Senator. But his favorite name for the new Chief Magistrate is, 'The Illinois Slave Hound.' I've a growing feeling that his enemies have overdone their work. I'm going to judge him fairly."

Vaughan's lips slightly curved.

"They say he's a good stump speaker--a little shy on grammar, perhaps, but good on jokes--of the coarser kind. He ought to get one or two good guffaws even out of this sober crowd to-day."

"You think he'll stoop to coarse jokes?"

"Of course----"

"Is that your brother?" Betty asked with a quick intake of breath, lifting her head toward a stalwart figure rapidly coming down the wide marble steps.

Ned Vaughan looked up with a frown:

"How did you recognize him?"

"By his resemblance to you, of course."

"Thanks."

"You're as much alike as two black-eyed peas--except that you're more slender and boyish."

"And not quite so good-looking?"

A low mischievous laugh was her answer as John lifted his hat and stood smiling before them.

"Miss Winter, this is my brother, whose praises I've long been chanting. I've a little work to do in the crowd--I'll be back in a few minutes."

There was just a touch of irony in the smile with which the younger man spoke as he hurried away, but the girl was too much absorbed in the striking picture John Vaughan made to notice. The sparkling brown eyes took him in from head to foot in a quick comprehending flash. The fame of his personal appearance was more than justified. He was the most strikingly good-looking man she had ever seen, and to her surprise there was not the slightest trace of self-consciousness or conceit about him. His high intellectual forehead, thick black hair inclined to curl at the ends and straight heavy eyebrows suggested at once a man of brains and power. He looked older than he was--at least thirty, though he had just turned twenty-six. The square strong jaw and large chin were eloquent of reserve force. Two rows of white, perfect teeth smiled behind the black drooping moustache and invited friendship. The one disquieting feature about him was the look from the depths of his dark brown eyes--so dark they were black in shadow. He had been a dreamer when very young and followed Charles A. Dana to Brook Farm for a brief stay.

Before he had spoken a dozen words the girl felt the charm of his singular and powerful personality.

"I needn't say that I'm glad to see you, Miss Winter," he began, with a friendly smile. "Ned has told me so much about you the past month I'd made up my mind to join the Abolitionists, and apply for a secretaryship to the Senator if I couldn't manage it any other way."

"And you'll be content to resume a normal life after to-day?"

She looked into his eyes with mischievous challenge. She had recovered her poise.

He laughed, and a shadow suddenly swept his face:

"I wonder, Miss Winter, if any of us will live a normal life after to-day?"

"You've seen the Rail-splitter, our new President?"

"No, I didn't wait in the Senate Chamber. I came out here to make sure of my seat beside you----"

"To hear every word of the Inaugural, of course," Betty broke in.

"Yes, of course----" he paused and the faintest suggestion of a smile flickered about the corners of his eyes. "Ned told me you had three good seats. I am anxious to hear what he says--but more anxious to see him when he says it. I can read his Inaugural, but I want to see the soul of the man behind its conventional phrases----"

"He'll use conventional phrases?"

"Certainly. They all do. But no man ever came to the Presidential chair with as little confidence back of him. The Abolitionists have already begun to denounce him before he has taken the oath of office. The rank and file of the party that elected him are not Abolitionists and never for a moment believed that the Southern people were in earnest when they threatened Secession during the campaign. We thought it bluff. To say that the whole North and West is panic-stricken is the simple truth.

"Horace Greeley and the ***Tribune*** are for Secession.

"'Let our erring sisters go!' the editor tells the millions who hang on his words as the oracle of heaven.

"The North has been talking Secession for thirty years, and now that the South is doing what they've been threatening, we wake up and try to persuade ourselves that no such right exists in a sovereign state. Yet we all know that Great Britain surrendered to the thirteen colonies as sovereign states and named each one of them in her articles of surrender and our treaty of peace. We know that there never would have been a Constitution or a Union if the men who drew it and created the Union had dared to question the right of either of these sovereign states to withdraw when they wished. They didn't dare to raise the question. They left it for their children to settle. Now we're facing it with a vengeance.

"Our fathers only dreamed a Union. They never lived to see it. This country has always been an aggregation of jangling, discordant, antagonistic sections. How is this man who comes into power to-day, this humble rail-splitter, this County Court advocate, to achieve what our greatest statesmen have tried for nearly a hundred years and failed to do? Seward, the man he has called to be Secretary of State, has been here for two months, juggling with his enemies. He's a Secessionist at heart and expects the Union to be divided----"

"Surely," Betty interrupted, "you can't believe that."

"It's true. We don't dare say this in our paper, but we know it. So sure is Seward of the collapse of the Lincoln administration that he withdrew his acceptance of the post of Secretary of State, only day before yesterday. It's uncertain at this hour whether he'll be in the cabinet----"

"Why?" Betty asked in breathless surprise.

The young editor was silent a moment and spoke in low tones:

"You can keep a secret?"

"State secrets--easily."

"Mr. Seward expects to be called to a position of greater power than President----"

"You mean?"

"The Dictatorship. That's the talk in the inner circles. Nobody in the North expects war or wants war----"

"Except my father," Betty laughed.

"The Abolitionists don't count. If we have war there are not enough of them to form a corporal's guard--to say nothing of an army. The North is hopelessly divided and confused. If the South unites--if North Carolina, Virginia, Tennessee, Kentucky, Arkansas, Missouri and Maryland join the Confederacy under Davis, the Union is lost. What's going to hinder them from uniting? They are all Slave States. They believe the new President is a Black Abolitionist Republican. He isn't, of course, but they believe it. How can he reassure them? The States that have already plunged into Secession have hauled the flag down from every fort and arsenal except Sumter and Pickens. The new President can only retake these forts by force. The first shot fired will sweep every Slave State out of the Union and arraign the millions of Democratic voters in the North solidly against the Government. God pity the man who takes the oath to-day to preserve, protect and defend the Constitution!"

When John Vaughan's voice died away at last into a passionate whisper, Betty stood looking at him in a spell. She recovered herself with a start and a smile.

"You've mistaken your calling, Mr. Vaughan," she said with emotion.

"Why do you say that?"

"You're a statesman--not an editor--you should be in the Cabinet."

"Much obliged, Miss Betty--but I'm not in this one, thank you. Besides, you're mistaken. I'm only an intelligent observer and reporter of events. I've never had the will to do creative things."

"Why?"

"The responsibility is too great. Fools rush in where angels fear to tread. Only God Almighty can save this Nation to-day. It's too much to expect of one man."

"Yet God must use man, mustn't He?"

"Yes. That's why my soul goes out in sympathy to the lonely figure who steps out of obscurity and poverty to-day to do this impossible thing. No such responsibility was ever before laid on the shoulders of one man. In all the history of the world he has no precedent, no guide----"

Ned interrupted the flow of John's impassioned speech by suddenly appearing with uplifted hand.

"Never such a crowd as this!"

"Why, they say it's smaller than usual!" Betty exclaimed.

"I don't mean size," Ned went on rapidly. "It's their temper that's remarkable. An Inauguration crowd should support the administration. The Lord help the Railsplitter if that sullen dumb mob are his constituents! Half of them are downright hostile----"

"Washington's a Southern town," John remarked.

"They are not Washington folks--not one in a hundred. And the only honest backers old Abe seems to have are about a thousand serious young fellows from the West, whom General Scott has armed as a special guard to circle the crowd."

He paused and pointed to a group of a dozen Westerners standing beside a bush in the outer rim of the throng.

"There's a bunch of them--and there's one stationed every ten yards. The artillery in position, the infantry in line, the sharpshooters masked in windows, the guard under the platform with muskets cocked, and a thousand volunteers to threaten the crowd from without, I think the new President should get a respectful hearing! The procession is coming up the Avenue now with a guard of sappers and miners packed so closely around the open carriage you can't even see the top of old Abe's head----"

"Let's get our seats!" Betty cried.

They had scarcely taken them when a ripple of excitement swept the crowd as every head was turned toward the aisle that led down the centre of the platform.

"Oh, it's Mrs. Lincoln and the children and her sisters!" Betty exclaimed. "What perfect taste in her dress! She knows how to wear it, too. What a typical, plump, self-poised Southern matron she looks. And, oh, those darling little boys--aren't they dears! She's a Kentuckian, too--the irony of Fate! A Southerner with a Southern wife entering the White House and eight great Southern States seceding from the Union because of it. It's a funny world, isn't it?"

"The South hardly claims Mr. Lincoln as a Southerner," Ned remarked dryly.

"Claim it or not, he is," John declared, nodding toward Betty, "as truly a Southerner as Jefferson Davis. They were both born in Kentucky almost on the same day----"

Another ripple of excitement and the Diplomatic Corps entered with measured stately tread, their gorgeous uniforms flashing in the sun. They took their seats on the left of the canopy, Lord Lyons, the British minister, seated beside the representative of the Court of France, two men destined to play their parts in the drama of Life and Death on whose first act the curtain of history was slowly rising.

The black-robed Supreme Court of the Republic, in cap and gown, slowly followed and took their places on the right, opposite the Diplomatic Corps.

The Marine band struck the first notes of the National Hymn amid a silence whose oppressiveness could be felt. The tension of a great fear had gripped the hearts of the crowd with icy fingers. The stoutest soul felt its spell and was powerless to shake it off.

Was it the end of the Republic? Or the storm clouded dawn of a new and more wonderful life? God only could tell, and there were few men present who dared to venture a prediction.

A wave of subdued excitement rippled the throng and every eye was focused on the procession from the Senate Chamber.

"They're coming!" Betty whispered excitedly.

The contrast between the retiring President, James Buchanan, and Abraham Lincoln was startling even at the distance of the first view from the platform. The man of the old era was heavy and awkward in his movements, far advanced in years, with thin snow white hair, his pallid full face seamed and wrinkled and his head curiously inclined to the left shoulder. An immense white cravat like a poultice pushed his high standing collar up to the ears. The sharp contrast of the black swallow-tailed coat, with the dead white of cravat, collar, face and hair, suggested the uncanny idea of a moving corpse.

With his eyes fixed on Buchanan, John suddenly exclaimed:

"A man who's dead and don't know it!"

Only for a moment did the actual President hold the eye. The man of the hour loomed large at the head of the procession and instantly fixed the attention of every man and woman within the range of vision. His giant figure seemed to tower more than a foot above his surroundings. Everything about him was large--an immense head, crowned with thick shock of coarse black hair, his strong jaws rimmed with bristling new whiskers, long arms and longer legs, large hands, big features, every movement quick and powerful. The first impression was one of enormous strength. He looked every inch the stalwart backwoods athlete, capable of all the feats of physical strength campaign stories had credited to his record. One glance at his magnificent frame and no one doubted the boast of his admirers that he could lift a thousand pounds, five hundred in each hand, or bend an iron poker by striking it across the muscle of his arm.

As he reached the speaker's stand beneath the crowded canopy, there was an instant's awkward pause. In his new immaculate dress suit with black satin vest, shining silk hat and gold-headed cane, he seemed a little ill at ease. He looked in vain for a place to put his hat and cane and finally found a corner of the railing against which to lean the stick, but there seemed no place left for his new hat. Senator Stephen A. Douglas, his defeated Northern opponent for the Presidency, with a friendly smile, took it from his hands.

As Douglas slipped gracefully back to his seat, he whispered to the lady beside him:

"If I can't be President, at least I can hold his hat!"

The simple, but significant, act of courtesy from the great leader of the Northern Democracy was not lost on the new Chief Magistrate. He could hardly believe what his eyes had seen at first, and then he smiled. Instantly the rugged features were transformed and his whole being was lighted with a strange soft radiance whose warmth was contagious.

Betty's eyes were dancing with excitement.

"He's not ugly at all!" she whispered.

Ned softly laughed:

"He certainly is not a beauty?"

"Who expects beauty in a real man?" she answered, with a touch of scorn. And Ned shot a look of inquiry at John's handsome face. But the older brother was too intent on the drama before him to notice. The editor's eyes were riveted on the new President, studying every detail of his impressive personality. He had never seen him before and was trying to form a just and accurate judgment of his character. Beyond a doubt he was big physically--this impression was overwhelming--everything large--the head with its high crown of skull and thick, bushy hair, deep cavernous eyes, heavy eyebrows which moved in quick sympathy with every emotion, large nose, large ears, large mouth, large, thick under lip, very high cheek bones, massive jaw bones with upturned chin, a sinewy long neck, long arms, and large hands, long legs, and big feet. A giant physically--and yet somehow he gave the impression of excessive gauntness and about his face there dwelt a strange impression of sadness and spiritual anguish. The hollowness of his cheeks accented by his swarthy complexion emphasized this.

The crowd had recognized him instantly, but without the slightest applause. The silence was intense, oppressive, painful. John glanced up and saw the huge figure of Senator Wigfall, of Texas, looking down on the scene from the base of one of the white columns of the central facade. He waved his arm defiantly and laughed. His presence in the Senate after all his associates had withdrawn was the subject of keen speculation. He was believed to be a spy of the Confederate Government. He had asked General Scott, half in jest, if he would dare to arrest a Senator of the United States for treason. The answer was significant of the times. Looking the Senator straight in the eye the old hero slowly said:

"No--I'd blow him to hell!"

Evidently the Senator was not as yet unduly alarmed. His expression of triumphant contempt for the evident lack of enthusiasm could not be mistaken. When John Vaughan recalled the confusion in the ranks of the triumphant party he knew that the Senator's scorn would he redoubled if he but knew half the truth. Again he turned toward the tall, lonely man with sinking heart.

The ceremony moved swiftly. The silence was too oppressive to admit delay. Senator Baker, of Oregon, the warm personal friend of Lincoln, stepped quickly to the edge of the platform. With hand outstretched in an easy graceful gesture, he said:

"Fellow Citizens: I introduce to you Abraham Lincoln, the President-elect of the United States of America."

Again the silence of death, as the once ragged, lonely, barefoot boy from a Kentucky cabin stepped forward into the fiercest light that ever beat on human head.

He quickly adjusted his glasses, drew his tall figure to its full height, and began to read his address, his face suddenly radiant with the poise of conscious reserve power, oblivious of crowd, ceremony, hostility or friendship. His voice was strong, high pitched, clear, ringing, and his articulation singularly and beautifully perfect.

His words carried to the outer edge of the vast silent throng.

Betty watched his mobile features with increasing fascination. His bushy eyebrows and the muscles of his sensitive face moved and flashed in sympathy with every emotion. In a countenance of such large and rugged lines every movement spoke unusual power. The lift of an eyebrow, the curve of the lip, the flash of the eye were gestures more eloquent than the impassioned sweep of the ordinary orator's arm. He made no gesture with hand or arm or the mass of his towering body. No portrait of this man had ever been made. She had seen many pictures and not one of them had suggested the deep, subtle, indirect expression of his face--something that seemed to link him with the big forces of nature.

The crowd was feeling this now and men were leaning forward from their seats on the platform. The venerable Chief Justice of the Supreme Court, Roger B. Taney, whose clear, accurate and mercilessly logical decision on Slavery had created the storm which swept Lincoln into power, was watching him with bated breath, and not for an instant during the Inaugural address did he lower his sombre eyes from the face of the speaker.

John C. Breckenridge, the retiring Vice-President, his defeated opponent from the Southern States, the proud Kentucky chevalier, was listening with keen and painful intensity, his handsome cultured features pale with the consciousness of coming tragedy.

His opening words had been reassuring to the South, but woke no response from the silent thousands who stood before him as he went on:

"I have no purpose directly or indirectly to interfere with the institution of Slavery in the States where it exists. I believe I have no lawful right to do so, and I have no inclination to do so."

The simplicity, directness and clearness of this statement could find no parallel in the pompous words of his predecessors. The man was talking in the language of the people. It was something new under the sun.

And then, with the clear ring of a trumpet, each syllable falling clean cut and sharp with marvellous distinctness, he continued:

"I hold that the Union of these States is perpetual----"

He paused for an instant, his voice suddenly failing from deep emotion and then, as if stung by the silence with which this thrilling thought was received, he uttered the only words not written in his manuscript, and made the only gesture of his entire address. His great fist came down with a resounding smash on the table and in tones heard by the last man who hung on the edge of the throng, he said:

"No State has the right to secede!"

And still no cheer came from the strangely silent crowd--only a vague shiver swept the hearts of the Southern people before him. If the North loved the Union they were giving no tokens to the tall, lonely figure on that platform.

At last the sentences, big with the fate of millions, were slowly and tenderly spoken:

"I shall take care that the laws of the Union be faithfully executed in all the States. Doing this I deem to be a simple duty on my part, and I shall perform it----"

At last he had touched the hidden powder magazine with an electric spark, and a cheer swept the crowd. It died away at last--rose with new power and rose a third time before it subsided, and the clear voice went on:

"I trust this will not be regarded as a menace, but only as the declared purpose of the Union that it will constitutionally defend and maintain itself. In doing this there needs be no bloodshed or violence; and there shall be none unless it be forced upon the National authority. The power confided in me will be used to hold and occupy and possess the property and places belonging to the Government."

Again the powder mine exploded, and a cheer rose. The grim walls of Fort Sumter and Pickens, in far off Southern waters, flashed red before every eye.

The applause suddenly died away into the old silence, and a man in the crowd before the platform yelled:

"We're for Jefferson Davis!"

There was no answer and no disorder--only the shrill cry of the Southerner through the silence, and the speaker continued his address. Senator Douglas looked uneasily over the crowd toward the spot from whence came the cry. His brow wrinkled with a frown.

John Vaughan leaned toward Betty and whispered half to himself:

"I wonder if those cheers were defiance after all?"

But the girl was too intent on the words of the speaker to answer. His next sentence brought a smile and a nod of approval from Senator Douglas.

"But beyond what may be necessary for those objects, there will be no invasion, no using of force against or among the people anywhere----"

Again and again Douglas nodded his approval and spoke it in low tones:

"Good! Good! That means no coercion."

And then, followed in solemn tones, the fateful sentences:

"In *your* hands, my dissatisfied fellow countrymen, and not in *mine* is the momentous issue of civil war. The Government will not assail *you* unless you *first* assail *it*. You can have no conflict without yourselves being the aggressors. *You* have no oath registered in Heaven to destroy the Government, while *I* shall have the most solemn one to 'preserve, protect and defend' it. *You* can forbear the *assault* upon it; *I* can *not* shrink from the *defense* of it----"

Again he paused, and the crowd hung spellbound as he began his closing paragraph in tender persuasive accents throbbing with emotion, his clear voice breaking for the first time:

"I am loath to close. We are not enemies, but friends. We must not be enemies. Though passion may have strained, it must not break our bonds of affection. The mystic chords of memory stretching from every battlefield and patriot grave to every living heart and hearthstone all over this broad land will yet swell the chorus of the Union when again touched, as surely they will be, by the better angels of our nature."

The closing words fell from his sensitive lips with the sad dreamy eyes blinded by tears.

At last he had touched the hearts of all. The sincerity and beauty of the simple appeal for the moment hushed bitterness and passion and the cheer was universal.

The black-robed figure of the venerable Chief Justice stepped forward with extended open Bible. His bony, trembling fingers and cadaverous intellectual face gave the last touch of dramatic contrast between the old and new regimes.

The tall, dark man reverently laid his left hand on the open Book, raised his right arm, and slowly repeated the words of the oath:

"I do solemnly swear that I will faithfully execute the office of President of the United States, and will, to the best of my ability, preserve, protect and defend the Constitution of the United States, so help me God!"

The words had scarcely died on his lips when the distant boom of cannon proclaimed the new President. The crowd on the platform rose and stood with uncovered heads, while the procession formed in the same order as at its entrance and returned to the White House.

"What do you think of it?" Betty asked breathlessly, turning to Ned.

The firm young lips came together with sudden passion:

"The argument has ended. To your tents, O Israel! It means war----"

"Nonsense," John broke in impetuously. "It means anything or nothing. It's hot and cold--a straddle, a contradiction----"

He paused and turned to Betty:

"What do you think?"

"Of the President?" she asked dreamily.

"Of his Inaugural," John corrected.

"I don't know whether it means peace or war, not being a statesman, but of one thing I'm sure----"

She paused and Ned leaned close:

"Yes?"

"That a great man has appeared on the scene----"

Both men laughed and she went on with deep earnestness:

"I mean it--he's splendid--he's wonderful! He's a poet--a dreamer--and so typically Southern, Mr. Ned Vaughan. I could easily picture him fighting a duel over a fine point of honor, as he did once. He's patient, careful, wise, cautious--very tender and very strong. To me he's inspired----"

Again both men laughed.

"I honestly believe that God has sent him into the Kingdom for such a time as this."

"You get that impression from his rambling address with its obvious effort to straddle the Universe?" John asked incredulously.

"Not from what he said," Betty persisted, "so much as the way he said it--though I got the very clear idea that his purpose is to save the Union. He made that thought ring through my mind over all others."

"You really like him?" Ned asked with a cold smile.

"I love him," was the eager answer. "He's adorable. He's genuine--a man of the people. We've had many Presidents who wore purple and fine linen and professed democracy--now we've the real thing. I wonder if they'll crucify him. All through his address I could see the little ragged forlorn boy standing beside his mother's grave crying his heart out in despair and loneliness. He's wonderful. And he's not overawed by these big white pillars above us, either. The man who tries to set up for a Dictator while he's in the White House will find trouble----"

"The two leading men he has called to his cabinet," John broke in musingly, "hold him in contempt."

"There's a surprise in store for Mr. Seward and Mr. Chase," Betty ventured.

"I'm afraid your father will not agree with you, Miss Betty," Ned laughed, glancing toward Senator Winter. "I foresee trouble for you."

"No danger. My father never quarrels with me over politics. He just pities my ignorance and lets it go at that. He never condescends to my level----"

She stopped suddenly and waved her hand toward the group of excited men who had gathered around Senator Winter.

A smile of recognition lighted the sombre Puritan face, as he pushed his friends aside and rapidly approached.

"How's my little girl?" he cried tenderly. "Enjoy the show?"

"Yes, dear, immensely--you know Mr. John Vaughan, Father, don't you?"

The old man smiled grimly as he extended his hand:

"I know who he is--though I haven't had the honor of an introduction. I'm glad to see you, Mr. Vaughan--though I don't agree with many of your editorials."

"We'll hope for better things in the future, Senator," John laughed.

"What's your impression of the Inaugural, Senator?" Ned asked, with a twinkle of mischief in his eye.

"You are asking me that as a reporter, young man, or as a friend of my daughter?"

"Both, sir."

"Then I'll give you two answers. One for the public and one for you. I've an idea you're going to be a rebel, sir----"

"We hope not, Senator," John protested.

"I've my suspicions from an interview we had once. But you're a good reporter, sir. I trust your ability and honesty however deeply I suspect your patriotism. As a Republican Senator I say to you for publication: The President couldn't well have said less. It might have been unwise to say more. To you, as a budding young rebel and a friend of my daughter, I say, with the utmost frankness, that I have no power to express my contempt for that address. From the lips of the man we elected to strangle Slavery fell the cowardly words:

"'I have no purpose directly or indirectly to interfere with the institution of Slavery in the States where it exists'----"

The grim blue-grey eyes flashed with rage, he paused for breath and then, livid with suppressed emotion, continued:

"For fifty years every man who has stood on this platform to take the oath as President has turned his face to the South and bowed the knee to Baal. We hoped for better things to-day----" He paused a moment and his eyes filled with angry tears:

"How long, O Lord! How long!"

"But you mustn't forget, Senator, that he didn't run and we didn't win on an Abolition platform. We only raised the issue of the extension of Slavery into the new territories----"

"Yes!" the old man sneered. "But you didn't fool the South! They are past masters in the art of politics. The South is seceding because they know that the Republican Party was organized to destroy Slavery--and that its triumph is a challenge to a life and death fight on that issue. It's a waste of time to beat the devil round the stump. We've got to face it. I hate a trimmer and a coward!--But don't you dare print that for a while, young man----"

"Hardly, sir," Ned answered with a smile.

"I've got to support my own administration for a few days at least--and then!--well, we won't cross any bridges till we come to them."

He stopped abruptly and turned to John:

"Come to see us, Mr. Vaughan. Your paper should be a power before the end of the coming four years. I know Forney, your chief. I'd like to know you better----"

"Thank you, Senator," the young editor responded cordially.

"Can't you dine with us to-morrow night, Mr. Vaughan?" Betty asked, unconsciously bending toward his straight, well poised figure. Ned observed her with a frown, and heard John's answer in a sudden surge of anger.

"Certainly, Miss Betty, with pleasure."

To Ned's certain knowledge it was the first invitation of the kind he had accepted since his advent in Washington. Again he cursed himself for a fool for introducing them.

Betty beamed her friendliest look straight into his eyes and softly said:

"You'll come, of course, Mr. Ned?"

For the life of him he couldn't get back his conventional tones for an answer. His voice trembled in spite of his effort.

"Thank you," he said slowly, "it will not be possible. I've an assignment at the White House for that evening."

He turned abruptly and left them.

CHAPTER II
JANGLING VOICES

The roar of the Inauguration passed, and Washington was itself again--an old-fashioned Southern town of sixty thousand inhabitants, no longer asleep perhaps, but still aristocratic, skeptical, sneering in its attitude toward the new administration.

Behind the scenes in his Cabinet reigned confusion incredible. The tall dark backwoodsman who presided over these wrangling giants appeared at first to their superior wisdom a dazed spectator.

He had called them because they were indispensable. Now that the issues were to be faced, Mr. Seward, Mr. Chase, Mr. Cameron and Mr. Bates realized that the country lawyer who had won the Presidency over their superior claims knew his weakness and relied on their strength, training, and long experience in public affairs.

Certainly it had not occurred to one of them that his act in calling the greatest men of his party, and the party of opposition as well, into his Cabinet was a deed of such intellectual audacity that it scarcely had a parallel in history.

Mr. Seward, the Secretary of State, had reluctantly consented to enter the Cabinet at the last moment as an act of patriotism to save the country from impending ruin too great for any other man to face. His attitude was a reasonable one. He was the undoubted leader of the triumphant party.

Without a moment's hesitation on the first day of his service as Secretary of State he assumed the position of a Prime Minister, whose duties included a general supervision of all the Departments of Government, as well as a Regent's supervision over the Executive.

Salmon P. Chase, the Secretary of the Treasury, at once took up the gauntlet thrown down by his rival. He not only regarded the President with contempt, but he extended it to the political trickster who dared to assume the airs of Premiership in a Democratic Republic.

To these Cabinet meetings came no voices of comfort from the country. The Abolitionist press, which represented the aggressive conscience of the North, continued to ridicule and denounce the Inaugural address in unmeasured terms.

The simple truth was soon apparent to the sombre eyes of the President. He was facing the gravest problem that ever confronted a statesman without an organized party on which he could depend for support. But two of his Cabinet had any confidence in his ability or genuine loyalty--Gideon Welles, a Northern Democrat, and Montgomery Blair, a Southern aristocrat.

The problem before him was bigger than faction, bigger than party, bigger than Slavery. Could a government founded on the genuine principles of Democracy live? Could such a Union be held together composed of warring sections with vast territories extending over thousands of miles, washed by two oceans extending from the frozen mountains of Canada to the endless summers of the tropics?

If the Southern people should unite in a slave-holding Confederacy, it was not only a question as to whether he could shape an army mighty enough to conquer them, the more urgent and by far the graver problem was whether he could mould into unity the warring factions of the turbulent, passion-torn North. These people who had elected him--could he ever hope to bind them into a solid fighting unit? If their representatives in his Cabinet were truly representatives the task was beyond human power.

And yet the tall, lonely figure calmly faced it without a tremor. In the depths of his cavernous eyes there burned a steady flame but few of the men about him saw, or understood if they saw--that flame was something new in the history of the race--a faith in the common man which dared to give a new valuation to the individual and set new standards for the Democracy of the world. He believed that the heart of the masses of the people North, South, East and West was sound at the core and that as their Chief Magistrate he could ultimately appeal to them over the heads of all traditions--all factions, and all accepted leaders.

He was the most advised man and the worst advised man in history. It became necessary to think for himself or cease to think at all.

General Scott, the venerable hero of Lundy Lane, in command of the army, had suggested as a solution of the turmoil the division of the country into four separate Confederacies and had roughly drawn their outlines!

Horace Greeley had made the *Tribune* the most powerful newspaper in the history of America. The Republicans throughout the country had been educated by its teachings and held its authority second only to the Word of God. And yet from the moment of Lincoln's election the chief occupation of this powerful paper was to criticize and condemn the measures and policies of the President.

Over and over he repeated the deadly advice to the Nation:

"If the Cotton States shall decide that they can do better out of the Union than in it, we insist on letting them go in peace."

He serenely insisted:

"If eight Southern States, having five millions of people, choose to separate from us, they cannot be permanently withheld from doing so by Federal cannon. The South has as good right to secede from the Union as the Colonies had to secede from Great Britain. If they choose to form an independent Nation they have a clear moral right to do so, and we will do our best to forward their views."

Is it to be wondered at that the Southern people were absolutely clear in their conception of the right to secede if such doctrines were taught in the North by the highest authority within the party which had elected Abraham Lincoln?

If his own party leaders were boldly proclaiming such treason to the Union how could he hope to stem the tide that had set in for its ruin?

The thousands of conservative men North and South who voted for Bell and Everett demanded peace at any price. An orator in New York at a great mass meeting dared to say:

"If a revolution of force is to begin it shall be inaugurated at home! It will be just as brutal to send men to butcher our brothers of the South as it will be to massacre them in the Northern States."

The business interests of the Northern cities were bitterly and unanimously arrayed against any attempt to use force against the South. The city of New York was thoroughly imbued with Secession sentiment, and its Mayor, through Daniel E. Sickles, one of the members of Congress, demanded the establishment of a free and independent Municipal State on the island of Manhattan.

Seward had just written to Charles F. Adams, our minister to England:

"Only an imperial and despotic government could subjugate thoroughly disaffected and insurrectionary members of the State. This Federal Republican country of ours is, of all forms of Government, the very one which is the most unfitted for such a labor."

This letter could only mean one of two things, either that the first member of the Cabinet was a Secessionist and meant to allow the South to go unmolested, or he planned to change our form of Government by a *coup d'etat* in the crisis and assume the Dictatorship. In either event his attitude boded ill for the new President and his future.

Wendell Phillips, the eloquent friend of Senator Winter, declared in Boston in a public address:

"Here are a series of states who think their peculiar institutions require that they should have a separate government. They have the right to decide that question without appealing to you or me. Standing with the principles of '76 behind us, who can deny them the right? Abraham Lincoln has no right to a soldier in Fort Sumter. There is no longer a Union. You can not go through Massachusetts and recruit men to bombard Charleston or New Orleans. Nothing but madness can provoke a war with the Gulf States."

The last member of his distracted, divided, passion-ridden Cabinet had gone at the close of its first eventful sitting. The dark figure of the President stood beside the window looking over the mirror-like surface of the Potomac to the hills of Virginia.

The shadow of a great sorrow shrouded his face and form. The shoulders drooped. But the light in the depths of his sombre eyes was growing steadily in intensity.

Old Edward, the veteran hallman, appeared at the door with his endless effort to wash his hands without water.

"A young gentleman wishes to see you, sir, a reporter I think--Mr. Ned Vaughan, of the **Daily Republican**."

Without lifting his eyes from the Virginia hills, the quiet voice said:

"Let him in."

In vain the wily diplomat of the press sought to obtain a declaration of policy on the question of the relief of Fort Sumter. In his easy, friendly way the President made him welcome, but only smiled and slowly shook his head in answer to each pointed question, or laughed aloud at the skillful traps he was invited to enter.

"It's no use, my boy," he said at last, with a weary gesture. "I'm not going to tell you anything to-day----" he paused, and the light suddenly flashed from beneath his shaggy brows, "----except this--you can say to your readers that my course is as plain as a turnpike road. It is marked out by the Constitution. I am in no doubt which way to go. I am going to try to save the Union."

"In short," Ned laughed, "you propose to stand by your Inaugural?"

"That's a pretty good guess, young man! I'm surprised that you paid such close attention to my address."

"Perhaps I had an interpreter?"

"Did you?"

"Yes."

"Who?"

"A very beautiful young woman, Mr. President," Ned answered serenely.

The hazel-grey eyes twinkled:

"What's her name, sir?"

"Miss Betty Winter."

"Not the daughter of that old grizzly bear who's always camping on my trail?"

"The same, sir."

The swarthy face lighted with a radiant smile:

"What did she say about my Inaugural?"

"That it was the utterance of a wise, patient, great man."

Two big hands suddenly closed on Ned's and the tall figure bent low.

"Thank you for telling me that, my boy. It helps me after a hard day!"

"She said many other things, too, sir," Ned added.

"Did she?"

"With enthusiasm."

"Tell her to come to me," the President said slowly. "I want to talk to her."

He paused, turned to his desk and seized a pen:

"I'll send a subpoena for her--that's better."

On one of his cards he quickly wrote:

"MY DEAR MISS WINTER:

"You are hereby summoned to immediately appear before the Chief Magistrate to testify concerning grave matters of State.

A. LINCOLN."

He slipped his long arm around Ned's shoulder and walked with him to the door:

"Serve that on her for me, will you, right away?"

With a nod and a smile, the reporter bowed and turned his steps toward the Senator's house.

CHAPTER III
IN BETTY'S GARDEN

Ned Vaughan paused with a moment of indecision before the plain, old-fashioned, brick house in which Senator Winter lived on the Capitol Hill. It was a confession of abject weakness to decline her invitation to dinner with his brother and jump at the first chance to butt in before the dinner hour.

Why should he worry? She was too serious and honest to play with any man, to say nothing of an attempt to flirt with two at the same time.

He refused to believe in the seriousness of any impression she had made on his brother's conceited fancy. His light love affairs had become notorious in his set. He was only amusing himself with Betty and she was too simple and pure to understand. Yet to warn her at this stage of the game against his own brother was obviously impossible.

He suddenly turned on his heel:

"I'm a fool. I'll wait till to-morrow!"

He walked rapidly to the corner, stopped abruptly, turned back to the door and rang the bell.

"Anyhow, I'm not a coward!" he muttered.

The pretty Irish maid who opened the door smiled graciously and knowingly. It made him furious. She mistook his rage for blushes and giggled insinuatingly.

"Miss Betty's in the garden, sor; she says to come right out there----"

"What?" Ned gasped.

"Yiss-sor; she saw you come up to the door just now and told me to tell you."

Again the girl giggled and again he flushed with rage.

He found her in the garden, busy with her flowers. The border of tall jonquils were in full bloom, a gorgeous yellow flame leaping from both sides of the narrow walkway which circled the high brick wall covered with a mass of honeysuckle. She held a huge pair of pruning shears, clipping the honeysuckle away from the budding violet beds.

She lifted her laughing brown eyes to his.

"Do help me!" she cried. "This honeysuckle vine is going to cover the whole garden and smother the house itself, I'm afraid."

He took the shears from her pink fingers and felt the thrill of their touch for just a moment.

His eyes lingered on the beautiful picture she made with flushed face and tangled ringlets of golden brown hair falling over forehead and cheeks and white rounded throat. The blue gingham apron was infinitely more becoming than the most elaborate ball costume. It suggested home and the sweet intimacy of comradeship.

"You're lovely in that blue apron, Miss Betty," he said with earnestness.

"Then I'm forgiven for making home folks of you?"

"I'm very happy in it."

"Well, you see I had no choice," she hastened to add. "I just had to finish these flowers before dressing for dinner. I'm expecting that handsome brother of yours directly and I must look my best for him, now mustn't I?"

She smiled into his eyes with such charming audacity he had to laugh.

"Of course, you must!" he agreed, and bent quickly to the task of clearing her violet bed of entangled vines. In ten minutes his strong hand had done the work of an hour for her slender fingers.

"How swiftly and beautifully you work, Ned!" she exclaimed as he rose with face flushed and gazed a moment admiringly on the witchery of her exquisite figure.

"How would you like me for a steady gardener?"

"I hope you're not going to lose your job on your brother's paper?"

"It's possible."

"Why?"

"We don't agree on politics."

"A reporter don't have to agree with an editor. He only obeys orders."

"That's it," Ned answered, with a firm snap of his strong jaw. "I'm not going to take orders from this Government many more days from the present outlook."

Betty looked him straight in the eye in silence and slowly asked:

"You're not really going to join the rebels?"

The slender boyish figure suddenly straightened and his lips quivered:

"Perhaps."

"You can't mean it!" she cried incredulously.

"Would you care?" he asked slowly.

"Very much," was the quick answer. "I should be shocked and disappointed in you. I've never believed for a moment that you meant what you said. I thought you were only debating the question from the Southern side."

"Tell me," Ned broke in, "does your father mean half he says about Lincoln and the South?"

"Every word he says. My father is made of the stuff that kindles martyr fires. He will march to the stake for his principles when the time comes."

"You admire that kind of man?"

"Don't you?"

"Yes. And for that reason I can't understand why you admire a trimmer and a time server."

"You mean?"

"The Rail-splitter in the White House."

"But he's not!" Betty protested. "I can feel the hand of steel beneath his glove--wait and see."

Ned laughed:

"Let Ephraim alone, he's joined to his idols! As our old preacher used to say in Missouri. Your delusion is hopeless. It's well the President is safely married."

Betty's eyes twinkled. Ned paused, blushed, fumbled in his pocket and drew out the card the President had given him to deliver.

"I am ordered by the administration," he gravely continued, "to serve this document on the daughter of Senator Winter."

Betty's eyes danced with amazement as she read the message in the handwriting of the Chief Magistrate.

"He sent this to me?"

"Ordered me to serve it on you at once--my excuse for coming at this unseemly hour."

"But why?"

"I gave him a hint of your opinion of his Inaugural. I think it's a case of a drowning man grasping a straw."

"Well, this is splendid!" she exclaimed.

"You take it seriously?"

"It's a great honor."

"And are you going?"

"I'd go to-night if it were possible--to-morrow sure----"

She looked at the card curiously.

"I've a strange presentiment that something wonderful will come of this meeting."

"No doubt of it. When Senator Winter's daughter becomes the champion of the 'Slave Hound of Illinois' there'll be a sensation in the Capital gossip to say nothing of what may happen at home."

"I'll risk what happens at home, Ned! My father has two great passions, the hatred of Slavery and the love of his frivolous daughter. I can twist him around my little finger----"

She paused, snapped her finger and smiled up into his face sweetly:

"Do you doubt it, sir?"

"No," he answered with a frown, dropping his voice to low tender tones. "But would you mind telling me, Miss Betty, why you called me 'Mr. Ned' the other day when I introduced you to John?"

The faintest tinge of red flashed in her cheeks:

"I must have done it unconsciously."

"Please don't do it again. It hurts. You've called me Ned too long to drop it now, don't you think?"

"Yes."

Her eyes twinkled with mischief as she took his hand in parting.

"Good-bye--Ned!" she breathed softly.

And then he did a foolish thing, but the impulse was resistless. He bent low, reverently kissed the tips of her fingers and fled without daring to look back.

CHAPTER IV
A PAIR OF YOUNG EYES

When Betty's card was sent in at the White House next morning, a smile lighted the sombre face of the President. He waved his long arms impulsively to his Secretaries and the waiting crowd of Congressmen:

"Clear everybody out for a few minutes, boys; I've an appointment at this hour."

The tall figure bowed with courtly deference over the little hand and his voice was touched with deep feeling:

"I want to thank you personally, Miss Betty, for your kind words about my Inaugural. They helped and cheered me in a trying moment."

"I'm glad," was the smiling answer.

"Tell me everything you said about it?" he urged laughingly.

"I'm afraid Mrs. Lincoln might not like it!" she said demurely.

"We'll risk it. I'm going to take you in to see her in a minute. I want her to know you. Tell me, what else did you say?"

He spoke with the eager wistfulness of a boy. It was only too plain that few messages of good cheer had come to lighten the burden his responsibilities had brought.

A smile touched her eyes with tender sympathy:

"You won't be vain if I tell you exactly what I said, Mr. President?"

"After all the brickbats that have been coming my way?" he laughed. No man could laugh with more genuine hearty enjoyment. His laughter convulsed his whole being for the moment and fairly hypnotized his hearer into sympathy with his mood.

"Out with it, Miss Betty, I need it!" he urged.

"I said, Mr. President, that you were very tender and very strong----" she paused and looked straight into his deep set eyes "----and that a great man had appeared in our history."

He was still for a moment and a mist veiled the light at which she gazed. He took her hand in both his, pressed it gently and murmured:

"Thank you, Miss Betty, I shall try to prove worthy of my little champion."

"I think you do things without trying, Mr. President," she answered.

"And you don't want an office, do you?"

"No."

"You have no favors to ask for your friends, have you?"

"None whatever."

"And you're Senator Winter's daughter?"

"Yes."

"The old grizzly bear! He hates me--but I've always liked him----"

"I hope you'll always like him," Betty quickly broke in.

"Of course I will. I've never cherished resentments. Life's too short, and the office I fill is too big for that. Do you know why I've sent for you?"

Betty smiled:

"To have me flatter you, of course. All men are vain. The greater the man, the greater his vanity."

Again he laughed with every muscle of his face and body.

"Honestly--no, that's not the reason," he said confidentially. "I want you to accept a position in my Cabinet."

"I didn't know that women were admitted?"

"They're not, but I've always been in favor of votes for women and I'm going to make a place for you."

Betty's lips trembled with a smile:

"What's the salary?"

"No salary, save the eternal gratitude of your Chief--will you accept?"

"I'll consider it--what duty?"

He looked steadily into her brown eyes:

"You have very bright, clear eyes, Miss Betty, I can see myself in them now more distinctly than in that mirror over the mantel. I'd like to borrow your eyes now and then to see things with. Will you accept the position?"

"If I can be of service, yes."

"The White House is open to you at all hours, and I shall send for you sometimes when I'm blue and puzzled and want a pair of pure, beautiful, young eyes--you understand?"

Betty extended her hand and her voice trembled:

"You have conferred on me a very great honor, Mr. President."

"For instance now," he said dreamily: "You endorse my Inaugural?"

"I'm sure it was wise, firm, friendly, dignified."

"I couldn't have said less than that I must possess and hold the property of the Government, could I? Well, I must now order a fleet to sail for Charleston Harbor to relieve our fort or allow the men who wear our uniform and fly our flag to die of starvation or surrender. Pretty poor Commander-in-Chief of the Army and Navy if I do that, am I not? Suppose I send a fleet to provision our men in Fort Sumter, not reinforce it--mind you, merely provisions for the handful of men who are there,--and suppose the Southern troops manning those land batteries open fire on our flag and force Major Anderson to surrender--what would happen in the North?"

He paused and looked at her steadily. The fine young figure suddenly stiffened:

"Every man, woman and child would say fight!"

The big jaws came together with firm precision and his huge fist struck the table:

"That's what I think. And at the same time something else would be happening over there----" His long arm swept toward the hills of Virginia, dark and threatening on the horizon. "The moment that shot crashes against our fort, North Carolina, Virginia, Arkansas, and Tennessee will join the Confederacy, to say nothing of what may happen in Maryland, Delaware, Kentucky and Missouri--all Slave States. The shock will be felt on both sides with precisely opposite effects. Sometimes we must do our duty and leave the rest to God, mustn't we? Yes--of course we must--and now, I've kept you too long, Miss Betty. It's a bargain, isn't it? You accept the position in my Cabinet?"

"Of course, Mr. President,--but if my duties are no heavier than I find them on this occasion, I fear I shall be of little help."

"You've been of the greatest service to me. You've confirmed my decision on a great problem of State. Come now and see Mother and the children. I want you to know them and like them."

He led her quickly into the family apartment and introduced her to Mrs. Lincoln. He found her in the midst of a grave discussion with Lizzie Garland, her colored dressmaker.

"This is old Grizzly's lovely daughter, Miss Betty Winter, Mother. She has joined the administration, stands squarely with us against the world, the flesh, the devil--and her father! I told her you'd give her the keys to the house----"

With a wave of his big hand he was gone.

Mrs. Lincoln's greeting was simple and hearty. In half an hour Betty had found a place in her heart for life, the boys were claiming her as their own, and a train of influences were set in motion destined to make history.

CHAPTER V
THE FIRST SHOT

The first month of the new administration passed in a strange peace that proved to be the calm before the storm. On the first day of April, All Fool's Day, Mr. Seward decided to bring to a definite issue the question of supreme authority in the government. That Abraham Lincoln was the nominal President was true, of course. Mr. Seward generously decided to allow him to remain nominally at the head of the Nation and assume himself the full responsibilities of a Dictatorship.

The Secretary of State strolled leisurely into the executive office more careless in dress than usual, the knot of his cravat under his left ear, a huge lighted cigar in his hand. He handed the President a folded sheet of official paper, bowed carelessly and retired.

He had drawn up his proclamation under the title:
SOME THOUGHTS FOR THE PRESIDENT'S CONSIDERATION.

In this remarkable document he proposed to assume the Dictatorship and outlined his policy as director of the Nation's affairs.

He would immediately provoke war with Great Britain, Russia, Spain and France!

The dark-visaged giant adjusted his glasses and read this paper with a smile of incredulous amazement. He wiped his glasses and read it again. And then without consultation with a single human being, and without a moment's hesitation he wrote a brief reply to the great man and his generous offer. There was no bluster, no wrath, no demand for an apology to his insulted dignity, but in the simplest and friendliest and most direct language he informed his Secretary that if a dictator were needed to save the country he would undertake the dangerous and difficult job himself inasmuch as he had been called by the people to be their Commander-in-Chief, and that he expected the cooeperation, advice and support of **all** the members of his Cabinet.

He did not even refer to the wild scheme of plunging the country into war with two-thirds of the civilized world. The bare announcement of such a suggestion would have driven the Secretary from public life. The quiet man who presided over the turbulent Cabinet never hinted to one of its members that such a document had reached his hands.

But as the shades of night fell over the Capitol on that first day of April, 1861, there was one distinguished statesman within the city who knew that a real man had been elected President and that he was going to wield the power placed in his hands without a tremor of fear or an instant's hesitation.

It took many months for other members of his Cabinet to learn this--but there was no more trouble with his Secretary of State. He became at once his loyal, earnest and faithful counsellor.

On April the 6th, the fleet was sent to sea under sealed orders to relieve Fort Sumter in the harbor of Charleston, South Carolina. The President had been loath to commit the act which must inevitably provoke war--unless the whole movement of Secession in the South was one of political bluff. The highest military authority of the country had advised him that the fort could not be held by any force at present visible, and that its evacuation was inevitable in any event.

His Cabinet, with two exceptions, were against any attempt to relieve it. The sentiment of the people of the North was bitterly opposed to war on the South.

On April the 7th, the fleet was at sea on its way to the Southern coast, its guns shotted, its great battle flags streaming in the wind.

In accordance with the amenities of war the President notified General Beauregard, Commander of the Southern forces in Charleston Harbor, that he had sent his fleet to put provisions into Sumter, but not at present to put in men, arms or ammunition, *unless the fort should be attacked*.

On the night this message was dispatched Roger A. Pryor, of Virginia, made a speech in Charleston, from the balcony of the Mills Hotel to practically the entire white population of the city. Its message was fierce, direct, electric. It was summed up in a single sentence:

"Strike the first armed blow in defense of Southern rights and within one hour by Shrewsbury clock, old Virginia will stand, her battle flags flying, by your side!"

On the morning of the 11th General Beauregard sent Pryor as a special messenger to Major Anderson demanding the surrender of Fort Sumter, and on his refusal, which was a matter of course, instructed him to go at once to the nearest battery and order its Commander to open fire.

The formalities at Sumter quickly ended, Pryor repaired to Battery Johnson, met the young Captain of artillery in command and presented his order.

With a shout the Captain threw his arms around the messenger and with streaming eyes cried:

"Your wonderful speech last night made this glorious thing possible! You shall have the immortal honor of firing the first gun!"

And then a strange revulsion of fooling--or was it a flash of foreboding from the hell-lit, battle-scorched future! The orator hesitated and turned pale. It was an honor he could not now decline and yet he instinctively shrank from it.

He mopped the perspiration from his brow and looked about in a helpless way. His eye suddenly rested on a grey-haired, stalwart sentinel passing with quick firm tread. He recognized him immediately as a distinguished fellow Virginian, a man of large wealth and uncompromising opinions on Southern rights.

When Virginia had refused to secede, he cursed his countrymen as a set of hesitating cowards, left the State and moved to South Carolina. He had volunteered among the first and carried a musket as a private soldier in spite of his snow-white hairs.

Pryor turned to the Commandant:

"I appreciate, sir, the honor you would do me, but I could not think of taking it from one more worthy than myself. There is the man whose devotion to our cause is greater than mine."

He introduced Edmund Ruffin and gave a brief outline of his career. The boyish Commandant faced him:

"Will you accept the honor of firing the first shot, sir?"

The square jaw closed with a snap:

"By God, I will!"

The old man seized the lanyard and waited for the Captain and messenger to reach the front to witness the effect of the shot.

They had scarcely cleared the enclosure when the first gun of actual civil war thundered its fateful message across the still waters of the beautiful Southern harbor.

They watched the great screaming shell rise into the sky, curve downward and burst with sullen roar squarely over the doomed fort.

The deed was done!

Instantly came the answering cry of fierce, ungovernable wrath from the millions of the North. The four remaining Southern States wheeled into line, flung their battle flags into the sky, and the bloodiest war in the history of the world had begun.

CHAPTER VI
THE PARTING OF THE WAYS

The wave of fiery enthusiasm for the Union which swept the North was precisely what the clear eyes of the President had foreseen. A half million men would have sprung to their arms if there had been any to spring to. The whole country,

North, South, East and West was utterly unprepared for war. The regular army of the United States consisted of only sixteen thousand men scattered over a vast territory.

The President called for seventy-five thousand volunteer militiamen for three months' service to restore order in the Southern States. Even this number was more than the War Department could equip before their terms would expire and the President had no authority to call State troops for a longer service.

On the day following the call, Massachusetts started three fully equipped regiments to the front. The first reached Baltimore on the 19th. On their march through the streets to change cars for Washington, they were attacked by a fierce mob and the first battle of the Civil War was fought. The regiment lost four killed and thirty-six wounded and the mob, twelve killed and a great number wounded. Grimed with blood and dirt the troops reached Washington at five o'clock in the afternoon, the first armed rescuers of the Capital. They were quartered in the magnificent Senate Chamber on the Capitol Hill.

The President was immediately confronted by the gravest crisis. The first blood had stained the soil of the only Slave State, which lay between Washington and the loyal North. If Maryland should join the Confederacy it would be impossible to hold the Capital. The city would be surrounded and isolated in hostile territory.

From the first he had believed that the only conceivable way to save the Union was to prevent the Border Slave States of Maryland, Kentucky and Missouri from joining the South. For the moment it seemed that Maryland was lost, and with it the Capital of the Nation. A storm of fury swept through the city of Baltimore and the whole State over the killing of her unarmed citizens by the "Abolition" troops from Massachusetts!

The Mayor of Baltimore sent a committee to the President who declared in the most solemn tones:

"It is not possible for more soldiers to pass through Baltimore unless they fight their way at every step."

And to make sure that the attempt would not be repeated he burned the railroad bridges connecting the North and cut every telegraph wire completely isolating the Capital.

Gilbert Winter, with his cold blue eyes flashing their slumbering fires of hate, stalked into the White House as the Baltimore committee were passing down the steps. Without announcement he confronted the President.

"In the name of the outraged dignity of this Republic," he thundered, "I demand that these traitors be arrested, tried by drumhead court-martial and hanged as spies!"

The patient giant figure lifted a big hand in a gesture of mild protest:

"Hardly, Senator!"

"And what was your answer?"

"I have written the Governor and the Mayor," the quiet voice went on, "that for the future troops *must* be brought here, but I make no point of bringing them through Baltimore----"

"Indeed!" Winter sneered.

"All I want is to get them here. I have ordered them to march around Baltimore. And in fulfilment of this promise I've sent a regiment back to Philadelphia to come by water----"

"Great God--could cowardice sink to baser crawling!"

The tall man merely smiled--his furious visitor starting for the door, turned and growled:

"It is absolutely useless to discuss this question further?"

"Absolutely, Senator."

"And you will not order our regular troops to take Baltimore immediately at the point of the bayonet?"

"I will not."

"Good day, sir!"

"Good day, Senator."

With a muttered explosion of wrath Gilbert Winter shook the dust of the White House floor from his feet and solemnly promised God it would be many moons before he degraded himself by again entering its portals.

The President had need of all his patience and caution in dealing with Maryland. The next protest demanded that troops should not pass by way of Annapolis or over any other spot of the soil of the State.

He calmly but firmly replied:

"My troops must reach Washington. They can neither fly over the State of

Maryland nor burrow under it: therefore, they must cross it, and your people must learn that there is no piece of American soil too good to be pressed by the foot of a loyal soldier on his march to the defense of the Capital and his country."

During these anxious days while the fate of Maryland hung in the balance the Government was given a startling revelation of what it would mean to have Maryland hostile territory.

For a week the President and his Cabinet were in a state of siege. They got no news. They could send none save by courier. The maddest rumors were daily afloat. The President was supposed to be governing a country from which he was completely isolated.

The tension at last became unbearable. The giant figure stood for hours alone before his window in the White House, his sombre hazel-grey eyes fixed on the hills beyond the Potomac. When the silence could no longer be endured the anguish of his heart broke forth in impassioned protest:

"Great God! Why don't they come? Why don't they come! Is our Nation a myth? Is there no North?"

And then the tide turned and the troops poured into the city.

His patient, careful and friendly treatment of the Marylanders quickly proved its wisdom. A reaction in favor of the Union set in and the State remained loyal to the flag. The importance of this fact could not be exaggerated. Without Maryland, Washington could not have been held. And the moment the Capital should fall Europe would recognize the Confederacy.

The saving of Maryland for the Union, in fact, established Washington as the real seat of Government, though it was destined to remain for years but an armed fortress on the frontiers of a new Nation.

The stirring events at Sumter and Baltimore brought more than one family to the grief and horror of brother against brother and father against son.

John Vaughan stood in his room livid with rage confronting Ned on the first day that communication was opened with the outside world.

"You are not going to do this insane thing I tell you, Ned!"

The boyish figure stiffened:

"I am going home to Missouri on the first train out of Washington, raise a company and fight for the South."

The older man's voice dropped to persuasive tones:

"Isn't there something bigger than fighting for a section? Let's stand by the Nation!"

"That's just what I refuse to do. The United States have never been a Nation. This country is a Republic of Republics--not an Empire. The South is going to fight for the right of local self-government and the liberties our fathers won from the tyrants of the old world. The South is right eternally and forever right. The States of this Union have always been sovereign."

"All right--all right," John growled impatiently, "granted, my boy. Still Secession is impossible. A Nation can't jump out of its own skin once it has grown it. This country has become a Nation. Steam and electricity have made it so. Railroads have bound us together in iron bands. Can't you see that?"

"No, I can't. Right is right."

"But if we have actually grown into a mighty united people with one tongue and one ideal is it right to draw the sword to destroy what God has joined together? Silently, swiftly, surely during the past thirty years we have become one people and the love of the Union has become a deathless passion----"

"You've had a poor way of showing it!" Ned sneered.

"Still, boy, it's true. I didn't realize it myself until that fort was fired on and the flag hauled down. And then it came to me in a blinding flash. Old Webster's voice has been hushed in death, but his soul lives in the hearts of our boys. There's hardly one of us who hasn't repeated at school his immortal words. They came back to me with thrilling power the day I read of that shot. They are ringing in my soul to-day----"

John paused and a rapt look crept into his eyes, as he began slowly to repeat the closing words of Webster's speech:

"'When mine eyes shall be turned to behold for the last time the sun in heaven, may I not see him shining on the broken and dishonored fragments of a once glorious Union; on States dissevered, discordant, belligerent; or a land rent with civil feuds, or drenched, it may be, with fratricidal blood! Let their last feeble and lingering glance rather behold the gracious ensign of the Republic, now known and honored throughout the earth, still full high advanced, its arms and trophies streaming in their original lustre, not a stripe erased or polluted, not a single star obscured, bearing for its motto no such miserable interrogatory as "What is all this worth?" nor those other words of delusion and folly, "Liberty first and Union afterward," but everywhere, spread all over with living light, blazing in all its ample folds, as they float over the sea and over the land and in every wind under the whole heavens, that other sentiment dear to every American heart--"Liberty *and* Union, now and forever, one and inseparable----""

He paused, his voice choking with emotion, as he seized Ned's arm:

"O, Boy, Boy, isn't that a greater ideal? That's all the President is asking to-day--to stand by the Union----"

"He is making war on the South!"

"But only as the South is forcing him reluctantly to defend the Union by force. The South is mad. She will come to her senses after the shock of the first skirmish is over. With the Southern members in their places, they have a majority in Congress against the President. He can move neither hand nor foot. What has the South to gain by Secession? They always controlled the Union and can continue to do so if they stand united with their Northern friends. In the end their defeat is as sure as that twenty millions of free white Americans can whip five millions of equal courage and daring. They have everything to lose and nothing to gain. It's madness--it surpasses belief!"

"That's why I'm going to fight for them!" Ned's answer flashed. "They stand for a principle--their equal rights under the Republic their fathers created. They haven't paused to figure on success or failure. Five million freemen have drawn the sword against twenty millions because their rights have been invaded. Might has never yet made right. The South's daring is sublime and, by God, I stand with them!"

His words had the ring of steel in their finality. The two men faced each other for a moment, tense, earnest, defiant.

The younger extended his hand:

"Good-bye, John."

The handsome face of the older brother went suddenly white and he shook his head:

"No. From to-day we are no longer brothers--we can't be friends!"

Ned smiled, waved his hand and from the door firmly answered:

"As you like--from to-day--foes----"

He closed the door and with swift step turned his face toward the house of Senator Winter.

CHAPTER VII
LOVE AND DUTY

The pretty Irish maid nodded and smiled with such a sympathetic look as she ushered Ned into the cosy back parlor, he wondered if it meant anything. Could she have guessed Betty's secret? She might give him a hint that would lift the fear from his heart.

He smiled back into her laughing eyes and began awkwardly:

"Oh, I say, Peggy----"

She dropped a pretty courtesy:

"Yiss-sor?"

Somehow it wouldn't work. The words refused to come. Love was too big and sweet and sacred. It couldn't be hinted at to a third person. And so he merely stammered:

"Will you--er--please--tell Miss Betty I'm here?"

"Yiss-sor!" Peggy giggled.

He was glad to be rid of her. He drew his handkerchief, mopped the perspiration from his brow and sat down by the open window to wait. His heart was pounding. He looked about the room with vague longing. He had spent many a swift hour of pain and joy in this room. The sight and sound of her had grown into his very life--he couldn't realize how intimately and how hopelessly until this moment of parting perhaps forever.

The portrait of her mother hung over the mantel--a life-size oil painting by a noted French artist, the same brilliant laughing eyes, the same deep golden brown hair, its wayward ringlets playing loosely about her fine forehead and shell-like ears.

Beyond a doubt this pretty mother with the sunshine of France in her blood had known how to flirt in her day--and her beautiful daughter was enough like that picture to have been her twin sister.

On the mantel beneath this portrait sat photographs in solid silver frames, one of Wendell Phillips, one of William Lloyd Garrison and one of John C. Fremont, the first Republican candidate for President. Directly opposite on the wall hung an oil painting of John Brown. Ned caught the flash of the fanatic in the old madman's eye and was startled at the striking resemblance to Senator Winter. He had never thought of it before. Gilbert Winter might have been his brother in the flesh as he undoubtedly was in spirit.

The thought chilled. He looked out the window with a sigh and wondered how far the old tyrant would carry his hatred of the South into his daughter's life. His eye rested for a moment on the row of lilacs in full bloom in the garden and caught the flash of the big new leaves of the magnolia which shadowed the rear wall. The early honeysuckle had begun to blossom on the south side, and the violet beds were a solid mass of gorgeous blue. Through the open window came the rich odor of the long rows of narcissus in full white glory where the jonquils had flamed a month ago.

What a beautiful world to be beaten into a scarred battlefield!

For just a moment the thought wrung the heart of youth and love. It was hard just when the tenderest and sweetest impulses that ever filled his soul wore clamoring for speech, to turn his back on all, say good-bye and go--to war--perhaps to kill his own brother.

And there could be no mistake, war had come. Overhead he caught the steady tramp of Senator Winter's feet, a caged lion walking back and forth with hungry eyes turned toward the South. He could feel his deadly hostility through the very walls.

A battery of artillery suddenly roared through the streets, the dull heavy rattle of its wheels over the cobblestones, and the crack of the driver's whip echoing and reechoing through the house. Behind it came the steady tramp, tramp, of a regiment of infantry, the loud call of their volunteer officers ringing sharply their orders at the turn of the street. Far off on the Capitol Hill he heard the sharp note of a bugle and the rattle of horses' hoofs. Every hour the raw troops were pouring into the city from the North, the East and the West.

He wondered with a strange catch in his throat what difference this was going to make between him and the girl he loved. There was no longer any question about the love. He marvelled that he had been too stupid to realize it and speak before this shadow had fallen between them. She knew that his sympathies were with the South and he knew with equal certainty she had never believed that he would fight to destroy the Union when the test should come. He dreaded the shock when he must tell her.

His heart grew sick with fear. What chance had he with everything against him--her old, fanatical father who loved her with the tender devotion of his strong manhood--her own blind admiration for the new President, whose coming had brought war--and worst of all he must go and leave John by her side! His brother had given no hint of his real feelings, but his deeds had been more eloquent than words. He had seen Betty every week since the day they had met--sometimes twice. This he knew. There may have been times he didn't know.

All the more reason why he must put the thing to the test. Besides he ***must*** speak. His hour had struck. His country was calling, and he must go--to meet Death or Glory. The woman he loved must know.

He heard the soft rustle of her dress on the stairs and sprang to his feet. She paused in the doorway a vision of ravishing beauty in full evening dress, her bare arms and exquisite neck and throat gleaming in the shadows.

She smiled graciously, her brown eyes sparkling with the conscious power which youth and beauty can never conceal.

She held out her soft warm hand and his trembling cold fingers grasped it.

"I'm sorry to have kept you, Ned," she began softly, "but I was dressing for the reception at the White House. I promised Mrs. Lincoln to help her."

"I didn't mind the wait, Miss Betty," he answered soberly. "Come into the garden--I can talk better there among your flowers--I never mind waiting for you."

"Why?"

"I've time to dream."

"Before you must wake?" she laughed.

"I'm afraid it's so this time----"

"Why so serious--what's the matter?"

"I'm going to the front."

"So are thousands of brave men, Ned. I've always known you'd go when the test came."

He bit his lips and was silent. It was hard, but he had to say it:

"I am going to fight for the South, Miss Betty."

The silence was painful. She looked steadily into his dark earnest eyes. There was something too big and fine in them to be met with anger or reproach. He was deadly pale and waited breathlessly for her to speak.

"I'm sorry," she breathed softly.

"You know that it costs me something to say this to you," he stammered.

"Yes, I know----"

"But it must be. It's a question of principle--a question that cuts to the bone of a fellow's life and character. A man must be true to what he believes to be right, mustn't he?"

His voice was tender, wistful, pleading. The sweet, young face upturned to his caught his mood:

"Yes, Ned."

"I couldn't be a real man and do less, could I?"

"No--but I'm sorry"--she paused and suddenly asked, "Your brother agrees with you?"

Ned frowned: "Why do you ask that question?"

"Because I was sure that he was on our side----"

"Is that all?"

"And I've always supposed he was a sort of guardian----"

"Only because he has always been my big brother and I've loved and admired him very much. I cried my eyes out the day he left home out in Missouri and came East to college."

"And you're going to fight him?"

"It's possible."

"It's horrible!"

"And yet, men who are not savages could only do such things drawn by the mightiest forces that move a human soul--you must know that, Miss Betty."

"Yes."

"There's only one thing in life that's bigger----"

"And that?"

"Is love. I've held it too high and holy a word to speak lightly. I shall tell but one woman that I love her----"

She looked at him tenderly:

"You glorious, foolish boy!"

Pale and trembling he took her hand, led her to a seat and sank on his knees by her side.

"I love you, Betty!" he gasped. "I've loved you from the moment we met, tenderly, madly, reverently. I've been afraid to touch your hand lately lest you feel the pounding of my heart and know. And now it's come--this hour when I must say I love you and good-bye in the same breath! Be gentle and sweet to me. I'm afraid to ask if you love me. It's too good to be true. I'm not worthy to even touch your little hand--and yet I'm daring to hold it in mine----"

He paused and bowed his head, overcome with emotion.

Betty gently pressed his trembling fingers. Her voice was low.

"I'm proud of your love, Ned. It's very beautiful----"

"But you don't love me?" he groaned.

"Not as you love me."

He looked searchingly and hungrily into her brown eyes:

"Is it John?"

She shook her head slowly and thoughtfully:

"No."

"And it's no one else?"

"No."

"Then I won't take that answer!" he cried with desperate earnestness. "I'm going to win you. I'll love you with a love so big and true I'll make you love me. Everything's against me now. Your father's against me. I'm going to fight your country and your people. You admire the new President. I despise him. The passions of war have separated us, that's all. But I won't give up. The war can't last long. You'll see things in a different way when it ends."

Betty smiled into his pleading eyes:

"How little you know me, Boy! Nothing on this earth could separate me from the man I love----" she paused and breathed quickly "----I'd follow him blindfold to the bottomless pit once I'd given him my heart!"

Ned rose suddenly to his foot and drew Betty with him. His hand now was hot with the passion that fired his soul.

"Then you're worth fighting for. And I'm going to fight--fight for what I believe to be right and fight for you----"

He stopped suddenly and his slender figure straightened:

"I'm coming back to you, Betty!" he said with clear ringing emphasis. "I'm coming back to Washington. I'll be with an army conquering, triumphant, because they are right. There'll be a new President in the White House and I'll win!"

He bowed and reverently kissed the tips of her fingers.

"You glorious boy!" she sighed. "It's beautiful to be loved like that! I'm proud of it--I'll hold my head a little higher with every thought of you----"

"And you'll think of me sometimes when war has separated us?"

"I'll never forget!"

"And remember that I'm fighting my way back to your side?"

A tender smile played about the corners of her eyes and mouth:

"I'll remember."

With a quick, firm movement he turned, passed through the house, and strode toward the iron gate.

He suddenly confronted John entering.

The two brothers faced each other for a moment angrily and awkwardly, and then the anger slowly melted from the younger man's eyes.

"You are taking dinner with Miss Betty to-night?" Ned asked in friendly tones.

"Yes, I'm going with her to the White House," was the cold reply.

"I'm leaving in an hour. Don't you think it's foolish for two brothers who have been what you and I have been to each other to part like this? We may not see one another again."

John hesitated and then slowly slipped his arm around the younger man, holding him in silence. When his voice was steady he said:

"Forgive me, Boy. I was blind with anger. It meant so much to me. But we'll face it. We'll have to fight it out--as God gives us wisdom to see the right----"

Ned's hand found his, and clasped it firmly:

"As God gives us to see the right, John--Good-bye."

"Good-bye, Boy,--it's hard to say it!"

They clung to each other for a moment and slowly drew apart as the shadows of the soft spring night deepened.

CHAPTER VIII
THE TRIAL BY FIRE

The troops transformed Washington from a lazy Southern town of sixty thousand inhabitants into an armed fortress of the frontier, swarming with a quarter of a million excited men and women. Soldiers thronged the streets and sidewalks and sprawled over every inch of greensward, their uniforms of every cut and color on which the sun of heaven had shone during the past two hundred years of history.

When the tumult and the shouts of departing regiments had died away from the home towns in the North and the flags that were flying from every house had begun to fade under the hot rays of the advancing summer, the patriotic orators and editors began to demand of their President why his grand army of seventy-five thousand lingered at the Capital. When he mildly suggested the necessity of drilling, equipping and properly arming them he was laughed at by the wise, and scoffed at as a coward by the brave.

Mutterings of discontent grew deeper and more threatening. They demanded a short, sharp, decisive campaign. Let the army wheel into line, march straight into Richmond, take Jefferson Davis a prisoner, hang him and a few leaders of the "rebellion," and the trouble would be over. This demand became at length the maddened cry of a mob:

"On to Richmond!"

Every demagogue howled it. Every newspaper repeated it. As city after city, and State after State took up the cry, the pressure on the man at the helm of Government became resistless. It was a political necessity to fight a battle and fight at once or lose control of the people he had been called to lead.

The Abolitionists only sneered at this cry. They demanded an answer to a single insistent question:

"What are you going to fight about?"

A battle which does not settle the question of Slavery they declared to be a waste of blood and treasure. If the slave was not the issue, why fight? The South would return to the Union which they had always ruled if let alone. Why fight them for nothing?

Gilbert Winter, their spokesman at Washington, again confronted the President with his uncompromising demand:

"An immediate proclamation of emancipation!"

And the President with quiet dignity refused to consider it.

"Why?" again thundered the Senator.

His answer was always the same:

"I am not questioning the right or wrong of Slavery. If Slavery is not wrong, nothing is wrong. But the Constitution, which I have sworn to uphold in the Border States of Maryland, Missouri and Kentucky, guarantees to their people the right to hold slaves if they choose. We have already eleven Southern States solidly arrayed against us. Add the Border States by such a proclamation, and the contest is settled before a blow is struck. I know the power of State loyalty in the South. I was born there. Many a mother in Richmond wept the days the stars and stripes were lowered from their Capitol. And well they might--for their sires created this Republic. But they brushed their tears away and sent their sons to the front next day to fight that flag in the name of Virginia. So would thousands of mothers in these remaining Slave States if I put them to the test. I'm going to save them for the Union. In God's own time Slavery will be destroyed."

Against every demand of the heart of the party which had given him power, he stood firm in the position he had taken.

But there was no resisting the universal demand for a march on Richmond. The cry was literally from twenty millions. He must heed it or yield the reins of power to more daring hands.

To add to the President's burden, his Secretary of State was still dreaming of foreign wars. He had drawn up a letter of instruction to our Minister to Great Britain which would have provoked an armed conflict. When the backwoodsman from Southern Illinois read this document he was compelled to lay aside his other duties and practically rewrite it. His work showed a freedom of mind, a balance of judicial temperament, an insight into foreign affairs, a skill in the use of language, a delicacy of criticism, a mastery of the arts of diplomacy which placed him among the foremost statesmen of any age, and all the ages.

He saved the Nation from a second disastrous war, as a mere matter of the routine of his office, and at once turned to the pressing work of the approaching battle.

John Vaughan had joined the army as correspondent for his paper, and Betty had been his companion on many tours of inspection through camp, hospitals and drill grounds. Her quick wit and brilliant mind were an inspiring stimulus. She was cool and self-possessed and it rested him to be near her. She was the only restful woman he had ever encountered at short range. He was delighted that she seemed content without love-making. There was never a moment when he could catch the challenge of sex in a word or attitude. He might have been her older brother, so perfect and even, so free and simple her manner.

Betty had watched him with the keenest caution. The first glance at John's handsome face had convinced her of his boundless vanity and beneath it a streak of something cruel. She would have liked him instantly but for this. His vanity she could forgive. All good-looking men are vain. His character was a study of which she never tired. He strangely distressed and disturbed her--and this kept puzzling and piquing her curiosity. Every time she determined to end their association this everlasting question of the man's inner character came to torment her imagination.

She was a little disappointed at his not volunteering at the first call as his gallant young brother had done. Yet his reasoning was sound.

"What's the use?" he replied to her question. "Five men have already volunteered for every one who can be used. I'm not a soldier by profession or inclination. A campaign of thirty days, one big battle and the war's over. The President has more men than he can arm or equip. My paper needs me----"

The army encamped along the banks of the Potomac received orders to advance for the long expected battle in the hills of Virginia.

Betty stood with the crowds of sweethearts and wives and sisters and mothers and watched them march away through the dust and heat and grime of the Southern summer, drums throbbing, banners streaming, bayonets flashing and bands playing.

John Vaughan was in the ranks of a New York regiment. He pressed Betty's hand with a lingering touch he hadn't intended. She seemed unconscious that he was holding it.

"You are going to march in the ranks?" she asked in surprise.

"Yes. I want to see war as it is. These boys are my friends from New York."

"You will fight with them?"

"No--just see with their eyes--that's all. And then tell you exactly what happened. I can hide behind a barn or a tree without being court-martialed."

She looked at him quickly with a new interest, pressed his hand again and said:

"Good luck!"

"And home again soon!" he cried with a wave of his arms as he hurried to join his marching men.

The army camped at Centreville, seven miles from Beauregard's lines, and spent the 19th and 20th of July resting and girding their loins for the first baptism of fire. The volunteers were eager for the fray. The first touch of the skirmishers had resulted in fifteen or twenty killed. But the action had been too far away to make any serious impression.

Between the two armies crept the silvery thread of the little stream of Bull Run, its clear beautiful waters flashing in the July sun.

Saturday night, the 20th, orders were issued to John's regiment to be in readiness to advance against the enemy at two o'clock before day on Sunday morning. A thrill of fierce excitement swept the camp. They were loaded down with overcoats, haversacks, knapsacks and baggage, baggage, baggage without end. The single New York regiment to which he had attached himself required forty wagons to move its baggage. They had a bakery and cooking establishment that would have done credit to Broadway. They hurriedly packed all they could carry in readiness for the march into battle. What would happen to the rest God only knew, but they hoped for the best. Of course, the battle couldn't last long. It was only necessary for this grand army to make a demonstration with its drums throbbing, its fifes screaming, its bayonets flashing and its magnificent uniforms glittering in the sun--the plumes, the Scotch bonnets, the Turkish fez, the Garibaldi shirts, the blue and grey and gold, the black and yellow, and the red and blue of the fire Zouaves--when the rebel mob saw these things they would take to their heels.

What the boys were really afraid of was that every rebel would escape before they could use their handcuffs and ropes. This would be too bad because the procession through the crowded streets at home would be incomplete without captives as a warning to future traitors. They were going to have a load to carry with their blanket rolls, haversack and knapsack and the full fighting rounds of cartridges, but they were not going to leave the handcuffs. If they had to drop anything on the march they might ease up on a blanket or half their heavy cartridges.

John found sleep impossible, and was ready to move at one o'clock. The dust was rising already in parched clouds from the dry Virginia roads. He walked to the edge of the woods and gazed over the dark moonlit hills around Centreville. A gentle breeze began to stir the leaves overhead but it was hot and lifeless. He caught the smell of sweating horses in a battery of artillery, hitched for the march. It was going to be a day of frightful heat under the clear blazing sun of the South, this Sunday, the 21st of July, 1861. He could see already in his imagination the long lines of sweating half fainting marchers staggering under the strain. Yet not for a moment did he doubt the result.

From a store on the hill at Centreville came the plaintive strains of a negro's voice accompanied by a banjo. A crowd of Congressmen had driven out from Washington on a picnic to see the spectacle of the first and last battle of the "Rebellion." They were drinking good whiskey and making merry.

For the first time a little doubt crept into his mind. Were they all too cocksure? It might be a serious business after all. It was only for a moment and his fears vanished. He was glad Ned was not in those grey lines in front. His company had been formed promptly, and he had been elected first lieutenant, but they were still in Southern Missouri under General Sterling Price. He shouldn't like to come on his brother's body dead or wounded after the battle--the young dare-devil fool!

Promptly at two o'clock the sharp orders rang from the regimental commander:

"Forward march!"

The lines swung carelessly into the powdered dust of the road and moved forward into the fading moonlight, talking, laughing, chatting, joking. War was yet a joke and the contagious fire of patriotism had flung its halo even over this night's work. Except here and there a veteran of the Mexican War, not one of these men had ever seen a battle or had the remotest idea what it was like.

John was marching with Sherman's brigade of Tyler's division. At six o'clock they reached the stone bridge which crossed Bull Run. On the hills beyond stretched a straggling line of grey figures. It couldn't be an army. Only a few skirmishers thrown out to warn off an attempt to cross the bridge. A white puff of smoke flashed on a hill toward the South, and the deep boom of a Confederate cannon echoed over the valley. Tyler's guns answered in grim chorus. The men gripped their muskets and waited the word of command. John's brigade was deployed along the edge of a piece of woods on the right of the Warrenton turnpike and stood for hours. A rumble of disgust swept the lines:

"What t'ell are we waitin' for?"

"Why don't we get at 'em?"

"And this is war!"

And no breakfast either. An hour passed and only an occasional crack of a musket across the shining thread of silver water and the slow sullen echo of the artillery. They seemed to be just practising. The shots all fell short and nobody was hurt.

Another hour--it was eight o'clock and still they stood and looked off into space. Nine o'clock passed and the fierce rays of the climbing July sun drove the men to the shelter of the trees.

"If this is war," yelled a red-breeched, fierce young Zouave, "I'll take firecrackers and a Fourth of July for mine!"

"Keep your shirt on, Sonny," observed a corporal. "We **may** have some fun yet before night."

At ten o'clock something happened.

Suddenly a thousand grey clad men leaped from their cover over the hills and swept up stream at double quick. A solid mass of dust-covered figures were swarming below the stone bridge.

The regiment's battery dashed into position, its guns were trained and their roar shook the earth. The swarming grey lines below the bridge paid no attention. The shots fell short and Sherman sent for heavier guns.

The men in grey had formed a new line of battle and faced the Sudley and

New Market road. Far up this road could now be seen a mighty cloud of dust which marked the approach of the main body of McDowell's Union army. He had made a wide flank movement, crossed Bull Run at Sudley Ford and was attempting to completely turn the Confederate position, while Sherman held the stone bridge with a demonstration of force.

A cheer swept the line as the dust rose higher and denser and nearer.

Banks of storm clouds were rising from the horizon. The air was thick and oppressive, as the two armies drew close in tense battle array. The turning movement had only been partly successful. It had been discovered before complete and a grey line had wheeled, gripped their muskets and stood ready to meet the attack.

The dust, cloud suddenly fell. McDowell's two divisions of eighteen thousand men spread out in the woods and made ready for the shock.

The sun burst through the gathering clouds for a moment and the edge of the woods flashed with polished steel.

A Federal battery dashed into position and placed one of its big black-wheeled guns in the front yard of a little white-washed farmhouse. The farmer's wife faced the commander with indignant fury:

"Take that thing outen my front yard!"

The dust-and sweat-covered men paid no attention. They quickly sunk the wheels into the ground and piled their shells in place for work.

The old woman stamped her foot and shouted again: "Take that thing away I tell you--I won't have it here!"

The captain seized his lanyard, trained his piece and the big black lips roared.

With a scream of terror the woman covered her ears, rushed inside and slammed the door. They found her torn and mangled body there after the battle. An answering shell had crashed through the roof and exploded.

Sherman's men, standing in the woods before the stone bridge waiting orders, saw the white and blue fog of battle rise above the tree tops and felt the earth tremble beneath their feet.

And then came to John's ears the first full crash of musketry fire in close deadly range. As company, regiment and brigade joined in volley after volley, it was like the sound of the continuous ripping of heavy canvas, magnified on the scale of a thousand. As the storm cloud swept over the smoke-choked field the rattle of musketry sounded as if an angry God rode somewhere in their fiery depths, and with giant hand was ripping the heavens open!

An hour passed and a shout of triumph swept the Federal lines. They charged and drove the Confederate forces back a half mile from their first stand. There was a lull--a strange silence brooded over the flaming woods and the guns opened from their new position--the artillery's deep thunder and the ripping crash of muskets. Another hour and another wild shout of victory. They had driven the Southerners three quarters of a mile further.

The shouts suddenly stopped. They had struck something.

The grim dust-covered figure of a Southern Brigadier General on a little sorrel horse had barred the way. His bulging forehead with its sombre blue eyes hung ominously over the pommel of his saddle.

General Bee, of South Carolina, rallying his shattered, broken brigade, pointed his sword to the strange figure and shouted to his men:

"See Jackson standing like a stone wall--rally to the Virginians!"

A bursting shell struck him dead in the next instant, but the world had heard and the name "Stonewall" became immortal.

With the last shout, the cry of victory had swept the field to the farthest line of reserves. John Vaughan secured a horse, galloped to the nearest telegraph line and sent the thrilling news to his paper. Already the wires were flashing it to the farthest cities of the North and West.

Victory! The first and last battle of the war had been settled. He spurred his horse through the blistering heat back to his regiment to join in the pursuit of the flying enemy.

They were just dashing across Bull Run going into action, their battle flag flying and their band playing. They were not long in finding the foe. The obstruction still remained in the path of the advancing hosts. The grim figure on the little sorrel horse had just ordered his brigade to fix bayonets.

In sharp tones his command was snapped:

"Charge and take that battery!"

A low grey cloud rose from the hill, swept over the crack Federal battery of Ricketts and Griffin and captured their guns.

John's regiment reached the field just in time to see the cannoneers fall in their tracks at the first deadly volley from the charging men.

Every horse was down dead or wounded. The pitiful cries of the stricken horses rang over the field above the roar of the battle, pathetic, heartrending, sickening.

The two armies had clinched now in the grim struggle which meant defeat or victory. It was incredible that the army which swept the field for four terrible hours should fail. The new regiments formed in line and with a shout of desperation charged Jackson's men and retook the captured battery.

Again the men in grey rallied and tore the guns a second time from the hands of their owners.

John saw a shell explode directly beneath a magnificent horse on which a general sat directing his men. The horse was blown to atoms, the general was hurled twenty feet into the air and struck the ground on his feet. He was unhurt, called for another horse, mounted and led the third charge to recover the guns. For a moment the two battle lines mingled in deadly hand to hand combat and once more the guns were retaken.

It had scarcely been done before Jackson's men rallied, turned and swift as a bolt of lightning from the smoke-covered hill captured the guns the third time and held them.

And then the unexpected, unimaginable thing happened. A new dust cloud rose over the hill toward Manassas Junction. The Southerners were hoping against hope that it might be Kirby Smith with his lost regiment from the Shenandoah Valley. The regiment had been expected since noon. It was now half past three o'clock. General McDowell, the Union Commander, was hoping against hope that Patterson's army from the Shenandoah would join his.

They were not long in doubt. The fresh troops suddenly swung into position on McDowell's right flank. If they were allies all was well. If they were foes! Suddenly from this line of battle rose a new cry on the face of the earth. From two thousand dusty throats came a heaven-piercing, soul-shivering shout, the cry of the Southern hunter in sight of his game, a cry that was destined to ring over many a field of death--the fierce, wild "Rebel Yell."

They charged McDowell's right flank with resistless onslaught. Kirby Smith fell desperately wounded and Elzey took command. Beckham's battery unlimbered and poured into the ranks from the rear a storm of shell. McDowell swung his battle line into a fiery crescent and made his last desperate stand.

Jubal Early, Elzey's brigade, and Stonewall Jackson charged at the same signal--and then--pandemonium!

Blind, unreasoning panic seized the army of the North. They broke and fled. Brave officers cursed and swore in vain. The panic grew. Men rushed pell mell over one another, white with terror. They threw down their muskets, their knapsacks, their haversacks and ran for their lives, every man for himself, and the devil take the hindmost. In vain the regular army, with splendid discipline, formed a rear guard to effect an orderly retreat. The crack of their guns only made the men run faster.

The wildest rumors flew from parched tongue to throbbing ear.

An army of a hundred thousand fresh troops had fallen on their tired, bloody ranks. They were led by Jeb Stuart at the head of four thousand Black Horse Cavalry. If a single man escaped alive it would be for one reason, only they could outrun them. It was a crime for officers to try to round them up for a massacre. That's all it was--a massacre! With each mad thought of the rushing mob the panic grew. They cut the traces of horses from guns and left them on the field. The frantic mob engulfed the buggies and carriages of the Congressmen and picnickers from Washington who had come out to see the Rebellion put down at a single blow. The road became a mass of neighing, plunging horses, broken and tangled wagons, ambulances and riderless artillery teams. Horses neighed in terror more abject than that which filled the hearts of men. Men once had reason--the poor horse had never claimed it. The blockades on the road formed no barrier to the flying men on foot. They streamed around and overflowed into the woods and fields and pressed on with new terror. God in Heaven! They pitied the poor fools engulfed in those masses of maddened plunging brutes and smashing wagons. It was only a question of a few minutes when Stuart's sabres would split every skull.

John Vaughan was swept to the rear on the crest of this wave of terror. Up to the moment it began he had scarcely thought of danger. After the first few minutes of nerve tension under fire his spirit had risen as the combat raged and deepened. It didn't seem real, the falling of men around him. He had no time to realize that they were being torn to pieces by shot and shell and the hail of lead that whistled from those long sheets of flaming smoke-banks before him.

And then the panic had seized him. He had caught its mad unreasoning terror from the men who surged about him. And it was every man for himself. The change was swift, abject, complete from utter unconsciousness of fear to the blindest terror. Some ran mechanically, with their eyes set in front as if stiff with fear, expecting each moment to be struck dead, knowing it was useless to try but going on and on because involuntary muscles were carrying them.

A fat man caught hold of John's coat and held on for half a mile before he could shake him off. He begged piteously for help.

"Don't leave me, partner!" he panted. "I'm a sinful man. I ain't fit to die. You're young and strong--save me!"

The dead weight was pulling him down and John shook the fellow off with an angry jerk.

"To hell with you!"

They suddenly came to a lot of horses hid in the woods, rearing and plunging and neighing madly.

John swerved out of their way and an officer rushed up to him crying:

"Why don't you take a horse?"

He looked at him in a dazed way before he could realize his meaning.

"Take a horse!" he yelled. "The rebels will get 'em if you don't----"

The men were too intent on running to try to save horses. Horses would have to look out for themselves.

It suddenly occurred to John that a horse might go faster. Funny he hadn't thought of it at once. He turned, seized one, mounted, and galloped on. There was a quick halt. A panting mob came surging back over the way they had just fled. A ford in front had been blocked, and in the scramble the cry was raised that Stuart's cavalry were on them and cutting every soul down in his tracks at the crossing.

John leaped from his horse, turned, and ran straight for the woods. He didn't propose to be captured by Stuart's cavalry, that was sure. He turned to look back and ran into a tree. He climbed it. If he could only get to the top before they saw him. He had been an expert climber when a boy in Missouri and he thanked God now for this. He never paused for breath until he had reached the very top, where he drew the swaying branches close about his body to hide from the coming foe. The sun was yet hanging over the trees in the woods--a ball of sullen red fire lighting up the hiding place of the last poor devil for the eyes of the avenging hosts who were sweeping on. If it were night it would be all right. But this was no place for a man with an ounce of sense in broad daylight. The sharpshooters would see him in that tall tree sure. They couldn't take him prisoner up there--they would shoot him like a squirrel just to see him tumble and, by the Lord Harry, they would do it, too!

He got down from the tree faster than he climbed up and from the edge of the woods spied a dense swamp. He never stopped until he reached the centre of it, and dropped flat on his stomach.

"Thank God, at last!" he sighed.

The Northern army fleeing for Washington had left on the field twenty-eight guns, four thousand muskets, nine regimental flags, four hundred and eighty-one dead, a thousand and eleven wounded and fourteen hundred captured. The road to the rear was literally sown with pistols, knapsacks, blankets, haversacks, wagons, tools and hospital stores.

And saddest of all the wreck, lay the bright new handcuffs with coils of hangman's rope scattered everywhere.

The Southern army had lost three hundred and eighty-seven killed, including two brigadier generals, Bee and Barton, and fifteen hundred wounded. They were so completely scattered and demoralized by their marvellous and overwhelming victory that any systematic pursuit of their foe was impossible.

The strange silent figure on the little sorrel horse turned his blue eyes toward Washington from the last hilltop as darkness fell, lifted his head suddenly toward the sky, and cried:

"Ten thousand fresh troops and I'd be in Washington to-morrow night!"

The troops were not to be had, and Stonewall Jackson ordered his men to bivouac for the night and sent out his details to bury the dead and care for the wounded of both armies.

Monday morning dawned black and lowering and before the sun rose the rain poured in steady torrents. Through every hour of this desolate sickening day the weary, terror-stricken stragglers trailed through the streets of Washington--their gorgeous plumes soaked and drooping, the Scotch bonnets dripping the rain straight down their necks and across their dirty foreheads, the Garibaldi shirts, the blue and grey, the black and yellow and gold and blazing Zouave uniforms rain-soaked and mud-smeared.

Betty Winter bought out a peddler's cake and lemonade stand on the main line of this ghastly procession and through every bitter hour from sunrise until dark stood there cheering and serving the men without money and without price, while the tears slowly rolled down her flushed cheeks.

CHAPTER IX
VICTORY IN DEFEAT

The President had risen at daylight on the fateful Sunday morning. He was sorry this first action must be fought on Sunday. It seemed a bad omen. The preachers from his home town of Springfield, Illinois, had issued a manifesto against his election without regard to their party affiliations on account of his supposed hostility to religion. It had hurt and stung his pride more than any single incident in the campaign. His nature was profoundly religious. He was not a church member because his religion had the unique quality of a personal faith which refused from sheer honesty to square itself with the dogmas of any sect. The preachers had not treated him fairly, but he cherished no ill will. He knew their sterling worth to the Republic and he meant to use them in the tremendous task before him. He had hoped the battle would not be joined until Monday. But he knew at dawn that a clash was inevitable.

At half past ten o'clock, though keenly anxious for the first news from the front, he was ready to accompany Mrs. Lincoln to church. The breeze was from the South--a hot, lazy, midsummer heavy air.

The Commander-in-Chief bent his giant figure over a war map, spread on his desk, fixed the position of each army by colored pins, studied them a moment and quietly walked with his wife to the Presbyterian Church to hear Dr. Gurley preach. He sat in reverent silence through the service, his soul hovering over the distant hills.

Before midnight the panic stricken Congressmen began to drop into the White House, each with his story of unparalleled disaster. At one o'clock the President

The Southerner

stood in the midst of a group of excited, perspiring statesmen who had crowded into the executive office, the one cool, shrewd, patient, self-possessed courageous man among them. He reviewed their stories quietly and with no sign of excitement, to say nothing of panic.

They marvelled at his dull intellect.

He was listening in silence, shaping the big new policy of his administration.

He spent the entire night calmly listening to all these stories, speaking a word of good cheer where it would be of service.

Mr. Seward entered as he had just finished a light breakfast.

The Secretary's hair was disheveled, his black string tie under his ear, and he was taking two pinches of snuff within the time he usually took one.

In thirty minutes the outlines of his message to Congress and his new proclamation were determined. Mr. Seward left with new courage and a growing sense of reliance on the wisdom, courage and intellectual power of the Chief he had thought to supplant without a struggle.

At eight o'clock the man with a grievance made his first appearance. His wrath was past the boiling point, in spite of the fact that his handsome uniform was still wet from the night's wild ride.

He went straight to the point. He was a volunteer patriot of high standing in his community. As a citizen of the Republic, wearing its uniform, he represented its dignity and power. He had been grossly insulted by a military martinet from West Point and he proposed to test the question whether an American citizen had any rights such men must respect.

The President lifted his calm, deep eyes to the flushed angry face, glanced at the gold marks of his rank, and said:

"What can I do for you, Captain?"

"I've come to ask you, Mr. President," he began with subdued intensity, "whether a volunteer officer of this country, a man of culture and position, is to be treated as a dog or a human being?"

The quiet man at the desk slipped his glasses from his ears, polished them with his handkerchief, readjusted them, and looked up again with kindly interest:

"What's the trouble?"

"A discussion arose in our regiment on the day we were ordered into battle over the expiration of our enlistment. I held, as a lawyer, sir, that every day of rotten manual labor we had faithfully performed for our country should be counted in our three months military service. Our time had expired and I demanded that we be discharged then and there----"

"On the eve of a battle?"

"Certainly, sir--what had that to do with our rights? We could have reenlisted on the spot. I refused to take orders from the upstart who commanded our brigade."

"And what happened?" the calm voice asked.

"He dared to threaten my life, sir!"

"Who was he?"

"A Colonel in command of our brigade--named Sherman!"

"William Tecumseh Sherman?"

"Yes, sir."

"What did he say to you?"

"Swore that if I moved an inch to leave his command he'd shoot me----"

"He said that to you?"

"Swore he'd shoot me down in my tracks like a dog!"

The President gravely rose, placed a big hand on the young officer's shoulder and in serious, friendly tones said:

"If I were in your place, Captain, I wouldn't trust that man Sherman--I believe he'll do it!"

The astonished volunteer looked up with a puzzled sheepish expression, turned and shot out of the room.

The long figure dropped into a chair and doubled with laughter. He rose and walked to his window, looking out on the trees swaying beneath the storm, still laughing.

"They say that every cloud has its silver lining!" he laughed again. "I'll remember that fellow Sherman."

Late in the day a report reached him of a beautiful young woman serving refreshments without pay to the straggling, broken men.

He turned to Nicolay, his secretary:

"Get my carriage, find her, and bring her to me. I want to see her."

Betty's eyes were still red when she walked into his office.

He sprang to his feet, and with long strides met her. He grasped her hand in both his and pressed it tenderly.

"So it's *you*!" he whispered.

Betty nodded.

"My little Cabinet comforter----"

"I'm afraid I'll be no good to-day," she faltered.

"Then I'll cheer *you*," he cried. "I just wanted to thank the woman who's been standing behind a lemonade counter through this desolate day giving her time, her money, and her soul to our discouraged boys----"

"And you are not discouraged?" Betty asked pathetically.

"Not by a long shot, my child! Brush those tears away. Jeffy D.'s the man to be discouraged to-day. This will be a dearly bought victory. Mark my word. For the South it's the glorious end of the war. While they shout, I'll be sawing wood. It needed just this shock and humiliation to bring the North to their senses. Watch them buckle on their armor now in deadly earnest. The demagogues howled for a battle. They pushed us in and they got it. Some of the Congressmen who yelled the loudest for a march straight into Richmond without a pause even to water the horses got tangled up in that stampede from Bull Run. They thought Jeb Stuart's cavalry were on them and lost their lunch baskets in the scramble. They've seen a great light. I'll get all the money I ask Congress for and all the soldiers we need for any length of time. I've asked for four hundred million dollars and five hundred thousand men for three years. I shouldn't be surprised if they voted more. The people will have sense enough to see that this defeat was exactly what they should have expected under such conditions."

His spirit was contagious. Betty forgot her shame and fear.

"You're wonderful, Mr. President," the girl cried in rapt tones. "Now I know that you have come into the kingdom for such a time as this."

"And so have you, my child," he answered reverently. "And so has every brave woman who loves this Union. That's what I wanted to say to you and thank you for your example."

Betty left the White House with a new sense of loyal inspiration. She walked on air unconscious of the pouring rain. She paused before a throng that blocked the sidewalk.

Some of them were bareheaded, the rain drops splashing in their faces, apparently unconscious of anything that was happening.

She pushed her way into the crowd. They were looking at the bulletin board of the **Daily Republican**, reading the first list of the dead and wounded. Her heart suddenly began to pound. John Vaughan had not reported his return. He might be lying stark and cold with the rain beating down on his mangled body. She read each name in the list of the dead, and drew a sigh of relief. But the last bulletin was not cheering. It promised additional names for a later edition. Besides, the War Department might not be relied on for reports of non-combatants. A newspaper correspondent was not enrolled as a soldier. His death might remain unrecorded for days.

On a sudden impulse she started to enter the office and ask if he had returned, stopped, blushed, turned and hurried home with a new fear mingled with a strange joy beating in her heart.

CHAPTER X
THE AWAKENING

John Vaughan had secured a loose horse on emerging from his friendly swamp. The shadows of night had given him the chance to escape. His horse was fresh, the rain had begun to fall, the heat had abated and he made good time.

He reached the office before midnight, took his seat at his desk, pale and determined to tell the truth. He wrote an account of the battle and the panic in which it had ended so vivid, so accurate, so terrible in its confession of riot and dismay, the editor refused to print it.

"Why not?" John sternly demanded.

"It won't do."

"It's true!"

"Then the less said about it the better. Let's hush it up."

John smiled:

"I'm sorry. I would like to see that thing in type just as I saw and felt and lived it. It's a good story and it's my last--it's a pity to kill it----"

"Your last? What do you mean?" the chief broke in.

"That I'm going into the ranks, and see if I am a coward--" he paused and scowled--"it looked like it yesterday for a while, and my curiosity's aroused. Besides, the country happens to need me."

"Rubbish," the editor cried, "the country will get all the men it needs without you. You're a trained newspaper man. We need you here."

"Thanks. My mind's made up. I'm going to Missouri and raise a company."

The chief laid a hand on John's shoulder. "Don't be a fool. Stand by the ship. I'll put your damned story in just as you wrote it if that's what hurts."

John flushed and shook his head:

"But it isn't. You may be right about the stuff. If I were editor I'd kill it myself. No. My dander's up. I want a little taste of the real thing. I saw enough yesterday to interest me. The country's calling and I've got to go."

The boys crowded around him and shook hands. From the door he waved his good-bye and they shouted in chorus:

"Good luck!"

Arrived at his room, he wrote a note to Betty Winter. He read it over and it seemed foolishly cold and formal. He tore it up and wrote a simpler one. It was flippant and a little presumptuous. He destroyed that and decided on a single line:

"MY DEAR MISS BETTY:

"Can I see you a few minutes before leaving to-night?

"JOHN VAUGHAN."

He sent it and began hurriedly to dress, his mind in a whirl of nervous excitement. His vanity had not even paused to ask whether her answer would be yes. He was sure of it. The big exciting thing was that he had made a thrilling discovery in the midst of that insane panic. He was in love--for the first time in life foolishly and madly in love. Fighting and elbowing his way through that throng of desperate terror-stricken men and horses it had come to him in a flash that life was sweet and precious because Betty Winter was in it. The more he thought of it the more desperate became his determination not to be killed until he could see and tell her. Through every moment of his wild scramble through woods and fields and crowded road, up that tree and down again, his heart was beating her name:

"Betty--Betty--Betty!"

What a blind fool he had been not to see it before! She, too, had been blind. It was all clear now--this mysterious power that had called them from the first, neither of them knowing or understanding.

When Betty took his note from the maid's hand her eyes could see nothing for a moment. She turned away that Peggy should not catch her white face. She knew instinctively the message was from John Vaughan. It may have been written with his last breath and sent by a friend. She broke the seal with slow, nervous dread, looked quickly, and laughed aloud when she had read, a joyous, half hysterical little laugh.

"The man's waiting for an answer, Miss," the maid said.

Betty looked at her stupidly, and blushed:

"Why, of course, Peggy, in a moment tell him."

She wrote half a page in feverish haste, telling him how happy she was to know that he had safely returned, read it over twice, flushed with anger at her silly confusion and tore it into tiny bits. She tried again, but afraid to trust herself, spread John's note out and used it for a model,

"MY DEAR MR. VAUGHAN:

"Certainly, as soon as you can call.

"BETTY WINTER."

And then she sat down by her window and listened to the splash of the rain against the glass, counting the minutes until he should ring her door bell.

And when at last he came, she had to stand before her clock and count the seconds off for five minutes lest she should disgrace herself by rushing down stairs.

Their hands met in a moment of awkward silence. The play of mind on mind had set each heart pounding. The man of easy speech found for the first time that words were difficult.

"You've heard the black news, of course," he stammered.

"Yes----"

Her eyes caught the haggard drawn look of his face with a start.

"You saw it all?" she asked.

"I saw so much that I can never hope to forget it," he answered bitterly.

He led her to a seat and she flushed with the sudden realization that he had been holding her hand since the moment they met. She drew it away with a quick, nervous movement, and sat down abruptly.

"Was it really as bad as it looks to-day?" she asked with an attempt at conventional tones.

"Worse, Miss Betty. You can't imagine the sickening shame of it all. I was never in a battle before. I wouldn't mind repeating that experience at close quarters--but the panic----"

"The President is the coolest and most courageous man in the country to-day," she put in eagerly. "It's inspiring to talk to him."

A bitter speech against a Commander-in-Chief who could allow himself to be driven into a battle by the chatter of fools rose to his lips, but he remembered her admiration and was silent. He fumbled at his watch chain and pulled the corner of his black moustache with growing embarrassment. The thing was more difficult than he had dreamed.

"I have resigned from the paper," he said at last.

"Resigned?" she repeated mechanically.

"Yes. I'm going back home to-night and help raise a company in answer to the President's proclamation."

The room was very still. Betty turned her eyes toward the window and listened to the splash of the wind driven rain.

"To your home town?" she faltered.

"Yes. To Palmyra."

"Where your brother went to raise a company to fight us--strange, isn't it?" Her voice had a far-away sound as if she were talking to herself.

"Yes--to fight us," he repeated in low tones.

Again a silence fell between them. He looked steadily into her brown eyes that were burning now with a strange intensity, tried to speak, and failed. He caught the gasp of terror in the deep breath with which she turned from his gaze.

"My chief was bitter against my going--I--I hope you approve--Miss Betty?" He spoke with pauses which betrayed his excitement.

"Yes, I'm glad----"

She stopped short, turned pale and fumbled at the lace handkerchief she carried.

"Every brave man who loves the Union must feel as you do to-day--and go--no matter how hard it may be for those who--for those he leaves at home----"

She paused in embarrassment at the break she had almost made, and flushed scarlet.

He leaned close:

"I'm afraid I'm not brave, Miss Betty. I ran with the rest of them yesterday, ran like a dog for my life"--he paused and caught his breath--"but I'm not sorry for it now. In the madness of that scramble to save my skin I had a sudden revelation of why life was sweet----"

He stopped and she scarcely breathed. Her heart seemed to cease beating. Her dry lips refused to speak the question she would ask. The sweet moment of pain and of glory had come. She felt his trembling hand seize her ice-cold fingers as he went on impetuously:

"Life was sweet because--because--I love you, Betty."

She sprang to her feet trembling from head to foot. He followed, whispering:

"My own, I love you--I love you----"

With sudden fierce strength he clasped her in his arms and covered her lips with kisses.

She lifted her trembling hands:

"Please--please----"

Again he smothered her words and held her in mad close embrace.

"Let me go--let me go!" she cried with sudden fury, thrusting him from her, breathless, her eyes blinded with tears.

"Tell me that you love me!" he cried with desperate pleading.

The splendid young figure faced him tense, quivering with rage.

"How dare you take me in your arms like that without a word?" Her eyes were flashing, her breast rising and falling with quick furious breathing.

He seized her hand and held it with cruel force. Her eyes blazed and he dropped it. She was thinking of the scene with his slender chivalrous brother. She could feel the soft kiss on the tips of her fingers and the blood surged to her face at the thought of this man's lips pressed on hers in mad, strangling passion without so much as by your leave! She could tear his eyes out.

He looked at her now in a hopeless stupor of regret.

"Forgive me, Betty," he faltered. "I--I couldn't help it."

Her eyes held his in a cold stare:

"I suppose that's all any woman has ever meant to you, and you took me for granted----"

He lifted his hand in protest.

"Please, please, Miss Betty," he groaned.

"You may go now," she said with slow emphasis.

He looked at her a moment dazed, and a wave of sullen anger slowly mounted his face to the roots of his black tangled hair, which he suddenly brushed from his forehead.

Without a word he walked out into the storm, his jaws set. The door had scarcely closed, when the trembling figure crumpled on the lounge in a flood of bitter tears.

CHAPTER XI
THE MAN ON HORSEBACK

Before the sun had set on the day of storm which followed the panic at Bull Run, the President had selected and summoned to Washington the man who was to create the first Grand Army of the Republic--a man destined to measure the full power of his personality against the Chief Magistrate in a desperate struggle for the supremacy of the life of the Nation itself.

General George Brinton McClellan, in answer to the summons, reached Washington on July the 20th, and immediately took command of the Army of the Potomac--or of what was left of it.

The President did not make this selection without bitter opposition and grave warning. He was told that McClellan was an aggressive pro-slavery Democrat, a political meddler and unalterably opposed to him and his party on every essential issue before the people. These arguments found no weight with the man in the White House. He would ask but one question, discuss but one issue:

"Is McClellan the man to whip this new army of 500,000 citizens into a mighty fighting machine and level it against the Confederacy?"

The all but unanimous answer was:

"Yes."

"Then I'll appoint him," was the firm reply. "I don't care what his religion or his politics. The question is not *whether I shall save the Union--but that the Union shall be saved*. My future and the future of my party can take care of themselves--if they can't, let them die!"

The new Commander was a man of striking and charming personality, but thirty-four years old, and graduated from West Point in 1846. He had served with distinction in the war against Mexico, studied military science in Europe under the great generals in command at the Siege of Sebastopol, and had achieved in West Virginia the first success won in the struggle with the South. He had been opposed in West Virginia by General Robert E. Lee, the man of destiny to whom the President, through General Scott, had offered the command of the Union army before Lee had drawn his sword for Virginia. He was a past master of the technical science of engineering, defense and military drill.

In spite of his short physical stature, he was of commanding appearance. On horseback his figure was impressively heroic. It took no second glance to see that he was a born leader of men.

On the first day of his active command he had already conceived the idea that he was a man of destiny. He wrote that night to his wife:

"I find myself in a new and strange position here--President, Cabinet, General Scott and all deferring to me. By some strange operation of magic, I seem to have become the power of the land----"

Three days later he wrote again of his sensational reception in the Senate Chamber:

"I suppose half a dozen of the oldest members made the remark I am becoming so much used to:

"'Why how young you look and yet an old soldier!'

"They give me my way in everything, full swing and unbounded confidence. All tell me that I am held responsible for the fate of the Nation, and that all its resources shall be placed at my disposal. It is an immense task that I have on my hands, but I believe I can accomplish it. When I was in the Senate Chamber to-day and found those old men flocking around me; when I afterward stood in the library looking over the Capital of a great Nation, and saw the crowd gathering to stare at me, I began to feel how great the task committed to me. How sincerely I pray God that I may be endowed with the wisdom and courage necessary to accomplish the work. Who would have thought when we were married, that I should so soon be called upon to save my country?"

Nor was McClellan the only man who saw this startling vision. He made friends with astounding rapidity, and held men to him with hooks of steel.

With utter indifference to his own fame or future, the President joined the public in praise of the coming star. The big heart at the White House rejoiced in the strength of his Commanding General. But the man who measured the world by the fixed standards of an exact science had no powers of adjustment to the homely manners, simple unconventional ways, and whimsical moods of Abraham Lincoln.

McClellan's one answer to all inquiries about his relation to the Chief Executive was:

"The President is honest and means well!"

The smile that played about the corners of his fine, keen, blue eyes when he said this left no doubt in the mind of his hearer as to his real opinion of the poor country lawyer who had by accident been placed in the White House.

And so the inevitable happened. The suggestions of the President and his War Department were early resented as meddling with affairs which did not concern them.

The President saw with keen sorrow that there were brewing schemes behind the compelling blue eyes of the "Napoleon" he had created. The talk of McClellan's aspirations to a military dictatorship, which would include the authority of the Executive and the Legislative branches of the Government, had been current for more than two months. His recent manner and bearing had given color to these reports.

The splendor and ceremony of his headquarters could not have been surpassed by Alexander or Napoleon. His growing staff already included a Prince of the Royal Blood, the distinguished son of the Emperor of France, and the Comte de Paris his attendant. His baggage train was drawn by one hundred magnificent horses perfectly matched, hitched in teams of four to twenty-five glittering new vans. His Grand Army spread over mile after mile of territory far back into the hills of Virginia. The autumnal days were brilliant with fresh uniforms, stars, sabres, swords, spurs, plate, dinners, wines, cigars, the pomp and pride and glory of war.

Men stood in little groups and discussed in whispers the significance of his continued stay in the Capital.

"If the President has any friends, the hour has come when they've got to stand by him!" The speaker was a man of fifty, a foreigner who had made Washington his home and liked Lincoln.

"Nonsense, my dear fellow," a tall Westerner replied, "we may have to get a few rifles and guard the White House from somebody's attempt to occupy it, but we'll not need any big guns."

"If you'd heard the talk last night," the foreigner replied, with a shrug of his shoulder, "you'd change your mind----"

The Westerner shook his head:

"No! The General's not that big a fool and the men around him have better sense. And if they haven't--if they all should go crazy--it couldn't be done. They couldn't control the army."

"Did you ever hear the army cheer as 'Little Mac' rides along the line?"

"Yes, but it don't mean an Emperor for all that----"

"I'm not so sure!"

And there were men of National reputation who considered the chances of the man on horseback good at this moment. Such a man had openly attached himself to the General as his attorney--no less a personage than the distinguished Attorney General of the late Cabinet, Edwin M. Stanton. During the closing days of Buchanan's crumbling administration Stanton had become the dominating force of the Capital. His daring and his skill had defeated the best laid schemes of the Southern party and broken its grip on the administration. He had remained in Washington as a lawyer practicing before the Supreme Court and had become the most aggressive observer and critic of Lincoln and his Cabinet. His scorn for the President knew no bounds.

"No one," he wrote to General John A. Dix, "can imagine the deplorable condition of this city and the hazard of the Government, who did not witness the weakness and the panic of the administration and the painful imbecility of Lincoln."

To Buchanan, his ex-Chief, he wrote:

"A strong feeling of distrust in the candor and sincerity of Lincoln's personality and of his Cabinet has sprung up. It was the imbecility of this administration which culminated in the catastrophe of Bull Run. Irretrievable misfortune and National disgrace never to be forgotten are to be added to the ruin of all peaceful pursuits and National bankruptcy as the result of Lincoln's running the machine for five months. Jefferson Davis will soon be in possession of Washington."

Not only in letters to the leaders of public opinion in the Nation did the aggressive and powerful lawyer seek to destroy the Government, but in his conversation in Washington he was equally daring, venomous and personal in his abuse of the President. "A low, cunning clown" and "the original gorilla" were his choice epithets.

Stanton's influence over McClellan was decided and vital from the moment of their introduction. It was known among the General's intimate friends that he had advised again and again that he use his power as Commander of the Army to declare a Dictatorship, depose the President and dissolve the sittings of Congress until the war should be ended.

How far McClellan had dallied with this dangerous and alluring scheme was a matter of conjecture. It is little wonder that the wildest rumors of intrigues, of uprisings, of mutiny, filled the air.

McClellan had doggedly refused either to move his army or to formally go into winter quarters until the middle of December, when he took to his bed and announced that he was suffering from an attack of typhoid fever.

The President was further embarrassed by the course of his Secretary of War, Cameron, who, while laboring under the censure of Congress for the conduct of his office, had allowed Senator Winter to stab his chief in the back by recommending in his report that the slaves be armed by the Government and put into the ranks of the armies. Senator Winter, as the Radical leader, knew that to meet such an issue once raised the President must rebuke his Secretary and apologize to the Border Slave States. He would thus alienate from his support all Cameron's friends, and all friends of the negro. The Senator did not believe the President would dare to fight on such an issue.

He had misjudged his man. The President not only rebuked his Secretary by suppressing his report and revising its language, he demanded and received his resignation, notwithstanding the fact that Cameron was the most powerful politician in the most powerful State of the North.

He at once sought a new Secretary of War, free from all party entanglements, who could not be influenced by contractors or jobbers or scheming politicians, who was absolutely honest and who had a boundless capacity for work.

Strangely enough, his eye rested on Edward M. Stanton, his arch enemy, the man who had become McClellan's confidential attorney.

As an aggressive patriotic Democrat, Stanton had won the confidence of the public in the last administration. His capacity for work had proved limitless. He was under no obligations to a living soul who could ask aught of Lincoln's administration. He was savagely honest. At the moment the discovery of gigantic frauds practiced on the War Department by thieving contractors, coupled with fabulous expenditures in daily expenses, had destroyed the confidence of the money lenders in the integrity of the Government. The Treasury was facing a serious crisis.

And then the astounding thing happened. Without consulting a soul inside his Cabinet or out, Abraham Lincoln appointed his bitterest foe from the party of his enemies his Secretary of War. He offered the place to Edwin M. Stanton.

Perhaps the most astonished man in America was Stanton himself. To the amazement of his friends, as well as his critics, he promptly accepted the position.

Senator Winter, whose radical temperament had found in Stanton a congenial spirit, though as wide as the poles apart in politics, met him in the lobby of the Senate Chamber on the day his appointment was confirmed.

He broke into a cynical laugh and asked:

"And what will you do?"

Stanton's keen spectacled eyes bored him through in silence as he snapped:

"I may make Abe Lincoln President of the United States."

Evidently another man was entering the Cabinet under the impression that the hands of an impotent Chief Magistrate needed strengthening. The merest glance at this man's burly thick set body, his big leonine head with its shock of heavy black hair, long and curling, his huge grizzly beard and full resolute lips, was enough to convince the most casual observer that he could be a dangerous enemy or a powerful ally.

The President was warned of this appointment, but his confidence was unshaken. His reply was a revelation of personality:

"I have faith in affirmative men like Stanton. They stand between a nation and perdition. He has shown a loyalty to the Union that rose above his own partisan creed of a lifetime. I like that kind of a man."

"He'll run away with the whole concern," was his friend's laconic reply.

The President's big generous mouth moved with a smile:

"Well, we may have to treat him as they sometimes did a Methodist minister I knew out West. He was a mighty man in prayer and exhortation. At times his excitement rose to such threatening heights the elders put brick bats in his pockets to hold him down. We may be obliged to serve Stanton the same way----"

He paused and laughed.

"But I guess we'll let him jump awhile first!"

The men who knew the inner secrets of Stanton's relations to McClellan watched this drama with keen interest. Had he gone into the Cabinet to place the General in supreme power in a moment of crisis? Or had he at heart deserted the Commander with the intention of using the enormous power of the War Department to further a scheme of equal daring for himself? They could only watch the swiftly moving scenes of the war pageant for their answer.

One fact was standing out each day with sharp and clean cut distinctness, a struggle of giants was on beneath the surface. Startling surprise had followed startling surprise during the past months. Men everywhere were asking one another, what next? The air of Washington was foul with the breath of passion and intrigue. Purposes and methods were everywhere assailed. Men high in civil life were believed to be plotting with military conspirators to advance their personal fortunes on the ruins of the Republic.

Around two men were gathering the forces whose clash would decide the destiny of the Nation--the struggle between the supremacy of civil authority in the President, and the war-created strength of the Military Commander represented by McClellan. Could the Republic survive this war within a war?

CHAPTER XII
LOVE AND PRIDE

Betty Winter had found her fierce resolution to blot John Vaughan from her life a difficult one to keep. The first two weeks were not so hard. Every instinct of her pure young girlhood had cried out against the conceit which had imagined her conquest so easy. The memory of his arms about her crushing with cruel force, his hot lips on hers in mad, unasked kisses brought the angry blood mounting to her cheeks. She walked the floor in rage and dropped at last exhausted:

"I could kill him!"

The memory which stung deepest was the terror she had felt in his arms--the sudden fear of the brute quivering in tense muscles and throbbing in passionate kisses. She had thought this man a gentleman. In that flash of self-revealing he was simply a beast. It had unsettled her whole attitude toward life. For the first time she began to suspect the darker side of passion. If this were love, she would have none of it.

Again she resolved for the hundredth time, to banish the last thought of him. If there were no cleaner, more chivalrous men in the world she could live without them. But there were men with holier ideals. Ned Vaughan was one. She drew from the drawer the only letter she had received from him and the last she would probably get in many a day, as he had crossed the dead line of war and was now somewhere in the great silent South. She read it over and over with tender smiles:

"DEAR MISS BETTY;

"I can't disappear behind the battle lines without a last word to you. I just want to tell you that every hour, waking or dreaming, the memory of you is my inspiration. The hardest task is easy because my heart is beating with your name with every stroke. For me the drums throb it, the bugle calls it. I hear it in the tramp of soldiers, the rumble of gun, the beat of horses' hoofs and the rattle of sabre,--for I am fighting my way back, inch by inch, hour by hour, to you, my love!

"You cannot answer this. There will be no more mails from the South--no more mails from the North until I see you again on the Capitol Hill in Washington. There has never been a doubt in my heart that the South shall win--that I shall win. And when I stand before you then it will not be as conqueror, though victorious. I shall bow at your feet your willing slave. And I shall kiss my chains because your dear hands made them. I can expect no answer to this. I ask none. I need none. My love is enough. It's so big and wonderful it makes the world glorious.

"NED."

How sharp and bitter the contrast between the soul of this chivalrous boy and his vain conceited brother! She loathed herself for her blind stupidity. Why had she preferred him? Why--why--why! The very question cut her. It was not because John Vaughan had chosen to cast his lot with her people of the North. Rubbish! She had a sneaking admiration for Ned because he had dared her displeasure in making his choice. There must be something perverse in her somewhere. She could see it now. It must be so or the evil in John Vaughan's character would not have drawn her as a magnet from the first. She hadn't a doubt now that all the stories about his fast life and his contempt for women were true and much more than gossip had dreamed.

He would write a letter of apology, of course, in due season. He was too shrewd a man of the world, too skillful an interpreter of the whims of women to write at once. He was waiting for her to cool--waiting until she should begin to be anxious. It was too transparent. She would give him a surprise when his letter came. The shock would take a little of the conceit out of him. She would return his letter unopened by the next mail.

When four weeks passed without a word the first skirmish between love and pride began. Perhaps she had been unreasonable after all. Was it right to blame a man too harshly for being mad about the woman he loved? In her heart of hearts did she desire any other sort of lover? Tears of vexation came in spite of every effort to maintain her high position. She had to face the plain truth. She didn't desire a cold lover. She wished him to be strong, manly, masterful--yes, masterful, that was it--yet infinitely tender. This man was simply a brute. And yet the memory of his mad embrace and the blind violence of his kisses had become each day more vivid and terrible--terrible because of their fascination. She accepted the fact at last in a burst of bitter tears.

And then came the announcement in the ***Daily Republican*** of his return to the city and his attachment to the company of cavalry at McClellan's headquarters. The thought of his presence sent the blood surging in scarlet waves to her face. There was no longer any question in her mind that she had wounded him too deeply for forgiveness. Her dismissal had been so cold, so curt, it had been an accusation of dishonor. She could see it clearly now. He had poured out his confession of utter love in a torrent of mad words and clasped her in his arms without thought or calculation, an act of instinctive resistless impulse. He had justly resented the manner in which she had repulsed him. Yet she had simply followed the impulse of her girlish heart, and she would die sooner than apologize.

She accepted the situation at last with a dull sense of pain and despair, and tried to find consolation in devotion to work in the hospitals which had begun to grow around the army of drilling volunteers.

Events were moving now with swift march, and her championship of the President gave her days of excitement which brought unexpected relief from her gloomy thoughts. She was witnessing the first movements of the National drama from the inside and its passion had stirred her imagination. Her father's growing hatred of Abraham Lincoln left her in no doubt as to whose master hand had guided the assaults on the rear of his distracted administration.

The fall of Cameron, the Secretary of War, had been the work of her father, with scarcely a suggestion from without. The Abolitionist had determined to force Lincoln to free the slaves at once or destroy him and his administration. They also were whispering the name of their chosen dictator who would assume the reins of power on his downfall.

The President was equally clear in his determination not to allow his hand to be forced and lose control of the Border Slave States, whose influence and power were becoming each day more and more essential to the preservation of the Union. He had succeeded in separating the counties of Western Virginia and had created a new State out of them. His policy of conciliation and forbearance was slowly, but surely, welding Kentucky, Missouri and Maryland to the Nation.

Any tinkering at this moment with the question of Slavery would imperil the loyalty of these four States. He held them now and he refused to listen to any man or faction who asked him to loosen that grip.

The true policy of the Radicals, Senator Winter realized, was to fire into the President's back through his generals in the field in an emancipation crusade which would work the North into a frenzy of passion. He had shrewdly calculated the chances, and he did not believe that Lincoln would dare risk his career on a direct order revoking such a proclamation.

General Hunger was the first to accept the mutinous scheme. He issued a proclamation declaring all slaves within the lines of the Union army forever free, and a wave of passionate excitement swept the North. The quiet self-contained man in the White House did not wait to calculate the force of this storm. He revoked Hunter's order before the ink was dry on it.

Again Senator Winter invaded the Executive office:

"You dare, sir," he thundered, "to thus spit in the face of the millions of the loyal North who are pouring their blood and treasure into this war?"

"I do," was the even answer. "I am the President of the United States and as Commander-in-Chief of its Army and Navy I will not be disobeyed by my subordinates on an issue I deem vital to the Nation's existence. If in the fulness of God's time an emancipation proclamation must be issued in order to save the Union, I know my duty and I'll do it without the interference of any of my generals in the field----"

He paused and glanced over the rims of his spectacles with a sudden flash from his deep set eyes:

"Do I make myself clear?"

Winter's face went white with anger as he slowly answered:

"Perfectly. It seems you have learned nothing from the wrath with which your sacrifice of John C. Fremont to appease the slave power was received?"

"So it seems," was the laconic response. "Fremont issued, without consulting me, his famous proclamation last August. I saw your hand, Senator, in that clause 'freeing' the slaves in the State of Missouri."

"And I warn you now," the Senator growled, "that the storm of indignation which met that act was nothing to one that will break about your head to-morrow! The curses of Fremont's soldiers still ring in your ears. The press, the pulpit, the platform and both Houses of Congress gave you a taste of their scorn you will not soon forget. Thousands of sober citizens who had given you their support, whose votes put you in this office, tore your picture down from their walls and trampled it under their feet. For the first time in the history of the Republic the effigy of a living President was burned publicly in the streets of an American city amid the jeers and curses of the men who elected him. Your sacrifice of Fremont has made him the idol of the West. He is to them to-day what Napoleon in exile was to France. This is a Government of the people. Even a President may go too far in daring to override public opinion!"

The giant figure slowly rose and faced his opponent, erect, controlled, dignified:

"But the question is, Senator, who is a better judge of true public opinion, you or I? It remains to be seen. In the meantime I must tell you once more that I am not the representative of a clique, or faction. I am the Chief Magistrate of all the people--I am going to save this Union for them and their children. I hope to live to see the death of Slavery. That is in God's hands. My duty to-day is as clear as the noonday sun. I can't lose the Border Slave States at this stage of the game and save the Union--therefore I must hold them at all hazards. Let the heathen rage and the people imagine vain things if they will----"

"Then it's a waste of breath to talk!" the Senator suddenly shouted.

The rugged head bowed gracefully:

"I thought so from the first--but I've tried to be polite----"

"Good day, sir!"

"Good day, Senator," the President laughed, "come in any time you want to let off steam. It'll make you feel easier and it won't hurt me."

Abraham Lincoln knew the real cause of public irritation and loss of confi-

The Southerner

dence. The outburst of wrath over Fremont was but a symptom. The disease lay deeper. The people had lost confidence in his War Department through the failure of his first Secretary and the inactivity of the army under McClellan. He had applied the remedy to the first cause in the dismissal of Cameron and the appointment of Stanton. It remained to be seen whether he could control his Commanding General, or whether McClellan would control the Government.

The situation was an intolerable one--not only to the people who were sacrificing their blood and money, but to his own inherent sense of honor and justice. He had no right to organize and drill a mighty army to go into winter quarters, drink and play cards, and dance while a victorious foe flaunted their flag within sight of the Capitol.

Besides, the Western division under two obscure Generals, Grant and Sherman, had moved in force in mid-winter and with a mere handful of men compared to the hosts encamped in Washington had captured Fort Henry and Fort Donelson and taken fourteen thousand prisoners. The navy had brilliantly cooeperated on the river, and this fact only made more painful the disgrace of the Confederate blockade of the Capital by its half dozen batteries on the banks of the Potomac.

The President was compelled to test the ugly question of the extent and power of General McClellan's personal support.

He returned from a tour of inspection and stood on the hilltop overlooking McClellan's miles of tents and curling camp fires. He turned to Mrs. Lincoln, who had accompanied him:

"You know what that is?"

"The Army of the Potomac, of course, Father."

"No!" he replied bitterly, "that's only McClellan's body guard--a hundred and eighty thousand."

The General had persistently refused to take any suggestion from his superior as to the movement of his army. Would Lincoln dare to force the issue between them and risk the mutiny of this Grand Army undoubtedly devoted to their brilliant young leader? There were many who believed that if he dared, the result would be a ***coup d'etat*** which would place the man on horseback in supreme power.

The moment the President reached the point where he saw that further delay would mean grave peril to the Nation, he acted with a promptness which stunned the glittering military court over which the young Napoleon presided. From the White House, as Commander-in-Chief of the Army and Navy, he issued a military order for the advance of McClellan's forces on Richmond!

The idea of such an order coming from a backwoods lawyer without military training was preposterous. Its audacity for a moment stunned the Commander of all the divisions of the army, but when the excitement had subsided on the day it was done, General McClellan, for the first time, squarely faced the fact that there was a real man in the White House.

The issue was a square one. He must obey that order or march on the Capital with his army, depose the President, and declare a dictatorship.

He decided to move on Richmond. He wrangled over the route he would take, but he moved, when once in motion, with remarkable swiftness.

Within two weeks a magnificent army of one hundred and twenty thousand men, fourteen thousand horses, forty-four batteries with endless trains of wagons, supplies, and pontoon bridges were transported by water two hundred miles to the Virginia Peninsula without the loss of a life.

The day was a glorious one toward the end of March, when Betty stood on the hill above Alexandria and watched, with heavy heart, the magnificent pageant of the embarking army. The spring was unusually early. The grass was already a rich green carpet in the shaded lanes. Jonquils were flaming from every walkway, the violets beginning to lift their blue heads from their dark green leaves and the trees overhead were hanging with tassels behind which showed the clusters of fresh buds bursting into leaf.

The armed host covered hill and plain and stretched out in every direction as far as the eye could reach. Four hundred ships had moved up the river to receive them. Companies and regiments of magnificently equipped soldiers were marching to the throb of drum and the scream of fife. Thousands of cavalrymen, in gay uniforms, their golden yellow shining in the sun, were dashing across a meadow at the foot of the hill. The long lines of infantry stretched from the hills through the streets of Alexandria down to the water's edge. Everywhere the regimental bands were playing martial music.

Somewhere among those marching, cheering, laughing, shouting thousands was the man she loved, leaving without a word.

An awkward private soldier passed with his arm around his sweetheart. Her eyes were red and she leaned close. They were not talking any more. But a few minutes were left and he must go--perhaps to die. Words had ceased to mean anything.

Her heart rose in fierce rebellion against the wall of silence her pride had reared. A group of magnificently equipped young officers passed on horseback. Perhaps of General McClellan's staff! She looked in vain among them for his familiar face. If he passed she would disgrace herself--she felt it with increasing certainty. Why had she come here, anyway? As well tell the truth--in the vague hope of a meeting.

The quick beat of a horse's hoof echoed along the road. She looked and recognized John Vaughan! He was coming straight toward her. Instinctively and resistlessly she moved to meet him.

She waved her hand in an awkward little gesture as if she had tried to stop after beginning the movement. His eye had been quick to see and with a graceful pull on his horse's bridle he had touched the pommel of the saddle, leaped to his feet, cap in hand, and stood trembling before her.

"It's too good to be true!" he exclaimed breathlessly.

She extended her bare hand and he held it without protest. It was trembling violently.

"You were going to leave without an effort to see me?" she asked in low tones.

"I was just debating that problem when I saw you standing by the road," he answered soberly. "I don't think I could have done it. It's several hours before we embark. I was just figuring on how I could reach you in time."

"Really?" she murmured.

"Honestly."

"Well, if you had gone without a word, I couldn't have blamed you"--she paused and bit her lips--"I was very foolish that day."

"It was my fault," he broke in, "all my fault. I was a brute. I realized it too late. I'd have eaten my pride and gone back to see you the day I reached Washington if I had thought it any use. I have never seen such a look in the eyes of a woman as you gave me that day, Miss Betty. If there had been any love in your heart I knew that I had killed it----"

She looked into his eyes with a tender smile:

"I thought you had----"

He pressed her hand tenderly.

"But now?"

"I know that love can't be killed by a kiss."

She stopped suddenly, threw her arms around his neck, and kissed him. He held her close for a moment, murmuring:

"My sweetheart--my darling!"

Through four swift beautiful hours they sat on a log, held each other's hands, and told over and over the old sweet story. Another long, tender embrace and he was gone. She stood on the little wharf, among hundreds of weeping sisters and mothers and sweethearts, and watched his boat drift down the river. He waved his handkerchief to her until the big unfinished dome of the Capitol began to fade on the distant horizon.

CHAPTER XIII
THE SPIRES OF RICHMOND

To meet three great armies converging on Richmond along the James under McClellan, from the North under McDowell, and the West by the Shenandoah Valley, the South had barely fifty-eight thousand men commanded by Joseph E. Johnston and eighteen thousand under Stonewall Jackson.

The Southern people were still suffering from the delusion of Bull Run and had not had time to adjust themselves to the amazing defeats suffered at Fort Henry and Fort Donaldson, to say nothing of the stunning victory of the **Monitor** in Hampton Roads, which had opened the James to the gates of the Confederate Capital.

Jackson was ordered into the Shenandoah Valley to execute the apparently impossible task of holding in check the armies of Fremont, Milroy, Banks and Shields, and at the same time prevent the force of forty thousand men under McDowell from reaching McClellan. The combined forces of the Federal armies opposed thus to Jackson were eight times greater than his command. And yet, by a series of rapid and terrifying movements which gained for his little army the title of "foot cavalry," he succeeded in defeating, in quick succession, each army in detail.

McDowell was despatched in haste to join Fremont and crush Jackson. And while his army was rushing into the Shenandoah Valley, Jackson withdrew and quietly joined the army before Richmond which moved to meet McClellan.

Little Mac, with his hundred and twenty thousand men, had moved up the Peninsula with deliberate but resistless force, Johnston's army retiring before him without serious battle until the Army of the Potomac lay within sight of the spires of Richmond. Faint, but clear, the breezes brought the far-off sound of her church bells on Sunday morning.

The two great armies at last faced each other for the first clash of giants, McClellan with one hundred and ten thousand men in line, Johnston with seventy thousand Southerners.

John Vaughan rode along the lines of the Federal host on the afternoon of May 30th, to inspect and report to his Commander. Through the opening in the trees the Confederate army could be plainly seen on the other side of the clearing. The Federal scouts had already reported the certainty of an attack.

The Confederates that night lay down on their arms with orders to attack at daylight. Dark clouds had swirled their storm banks over the sky before sunset and the heavens were opened. The rain fell in blinding torrents, until the sluggish little stream of the Chickahominy had become a rushing, widening, treacherous river which threatened to sweep away the last bridge McClellan had constructed.

The Confederate Commander was elated. The army of his enemy was divided by a swollen river. The storm increased until it reached the violence of a hurricane. Through the entire night the lightning flashed and the thunder pealed without ceasing. At times the heavens were livid with blinding, dazzling light. Tents were a mockery. The earth was transformed into a vast morass.

The storm had its compensations for the Northern army though divided. Its frightful severity had so demoralized the Confederates that it was nearly noon before General A. P. Hill moved to the attack.

The entrenched army was ready. The Union pickets lay in the edge of the woods and every soldier in the pits had been under cover for hours awaiting the onset.

With a shout the men in grey leaped from their shelter, pouring their volleys from close charging columns. The rifle balls whistled through the woods, clipping boughs, barking the trees, and hurling the Federal pickets back on their support. In front of the abatis had been planted a battery of four guns. The grey men had fixed their eyes on them. General Naglee saw their purpose and threw his four thousand men into the open field to meet them. Straight into each other's faces their muskets flamed, paused, and flamed again. The Northern men fixed their bayonets, charged, and drove the grey line slowly back into the woods. Here they met a storm of hissing lead that mowed their ranks. They broke quickly and rushed for the cover of their rifle pits.

The grey lines charged, and for three hours the earth trembled beneath the shock of their continued assaults.

Suddenly on the left flank of the Federal army a galling fire was poured from a grey brigade. The movement had been quietly and skillfully executed. At the same moment General Rodes' brigade rushed on their front with resistless force. The officers tried to spike their guns and save them, but were shot down in their tracks to a man. Their guns were lost, and in a moment the men in grey had wheeled them and were pouring a terrible fire on the retreating lines.

The Confederates now charged the Federal centre, and for an hour and a half the fierce conflict raged--charge and countercharge by men of equal courage led by dauntless officers. The Union right wing had already been crumpled in hopeless confusion, the centre had yielded, the left wing alone was holding its own. It looked as if the whole Union army on the South side of the Chickahominy would be wiped out.

At Seven Pines Heintzelman had made a stubborn stand. General Keyes saw a hill between the lines of battle which might save the day if he could reach it in time. He must take men between two battle lines to do so. The Confederate Commander, divining his intention, poured a galling fire into his ranks and began a race with him for the heights. Keyes won the race and formed his line in the nick of time. The tremendous fire poured down from this new position was too much for the assaulting Southern column and it halted.

The Confederate forces had forced the Federal lines back two miles as the river fog and the darkness slowly rose and enveloped the field. General Johnston ordered his men to sleep on the fields and camps they had captured. A minute later he was hurled from his horse by an exploding shell and was borne from the field dangerously wounded. The first day's struggle had ended in reverses for the invading enemy. The Confederates had captured ten guns, six thousand muskets, and five hundred prisoners, besides driving McClellan's forces two miles from the opening battle lines.

Between the two smoke-grimed, desperate armies locked thus in close embrace there could be no truce for burying the fallen or rescuing the wounded. Over the rain-soaked fields and woods for two miles behind the Confederate front lay the dead, the dying, and the wounded, the blue side by side with their foes in grey. Dim fog-ringed lanterns flickered feebly here and there like wounded fireflies over the dark piles on the ground.

The Southern ambulance corps did its best at its new trade. Their long lines of wagons began to creep into Richmond and fill the hospitals. Shivering white-faced women, wives, sweethearts, mothers, sisters were there looking for their own, praying and hoping. All day they had shivered in their rooms at the deep boom of cannon, whose thunder rattled the glass in the windows through which they gazed on the deserted streets. It was the first lesson in real war, this hand to hand grip of the two giants whose struggle must decide the fate of Richmond.

The wagons left their loads and rattled back over the rough cobble stones and out on the muddy roads to the front again. The night would be all too short for their work.

In their field hospital, the surgeons, with bare, bloody arms, were busy with knife and saw. Boys who had faced death in battle without a tremor, now pale and trembling, watched the growing pile of legs and arms. Alone in the darkness beyond the voice or touch of a loved hand they must face this awful thing and hobble through life maimed wrecks. They looked over their shoulders into the murky darkness and envied the silent forms that lay there beyond the reach of pain and despair. All night the grim tragedy of the knife and saw, and the low moans that still came from the darkness of the woods!

Sunday morning, the second day of June, dawned over the battle-scarred earth--an ominous day for the armies of the Republic--for the sun rose on a new figure in command of the men in grey. Robert E. Lee had taken the place of Joseph E. Johnston.

General G. W. Smith, second in command when Johnston fell, had formed his plan of battle, and the new head of the Confederacy, with his high sense of courtesy and justice, permitted his subordinate to direct the conflict for the day.

As the sun rose, red and ominous through the dark pine forest, General Smith quickly advanced his men at Fair Oaks Station, down the railroad, and fell with fury on the men in blue, who crouched behind the embankment. The men were less than fifty yards apart, and muskets blazed in long level sheets of yellow flame. No longer could the ear catch the effect of ripping canvas in the fire of small arms. The roar was endless. For an hour and a half the two blazing lines mowed each other down in their tracks without pause. The grey at last gave way and fell back to the shelter of their woods and gathered reinforcements. The Union lines had been cut to pieces and suddenly ceased firing while their support advanced.

The roaring hell had died into a strange ominous stillness. John Vaughan had just dashed up to the embankment with orders from McClellan to hold this position until Haskin's division arrived. He sprang on the embankment and looked curiously at the long piles of grey bodies lying in an endless row as far as the eye could reach. Over the tree tops, faintly mingling with the low cry of a dying boy of sixteen, came the sweet distant notes of a church bell in Richmond.

"God in heaven--the mockery of it!" he cried.

A great shout swept the blue lines. Hooker's magnificent division of fresh troops swept into view, eager for the fray. They rapidly deployed to the right and left. In front of them lay the open blood-soaked field, and beyond the deep woods bristling with Southern bayonets. The new division leaped into this open field, with a wild shout, their eyes set on the woods. They paused, only to fire, and their double quick became a race.

The Southern batteries followed and tore great holes in their ranks. They closed them with low quick sullen orders sweeping on. They reached the edge of the woods and poured into its friendly shelter. And then above the tops of oak and pine and beech and ash and tangled undergrowth came the soul-piercing roar of two great armies, fearless, daring, scorning death, fighting hand to hand, man to man, for what they believed to be right.

The people in church turned anxious faces toward the sound. Its roar rang above the sob of organ and the chant of choir.

Bayonet clashed on bayonet, as regiment after regiment were locked in close mortal combat. Hour after hour the stubborn unyielding hosts held fast on both sides. The storm weakened and slowly died away. Only the intermittent crack of a rifle here and there broke the stillness.

There was no shout of victory, no sweep of cheering hosts--only silence. The Confederate General in command for the day had lost faith in his battle plan and withdrew his army from the field. The men in blue could move in and camp on the ground they had held the day before if they wished.

But there was something more important to do now than maneuver for position in history. The dead and the dying and wounded crying for water were everywhere--down every sunlit aisle of the forest they lay in heaps. In the open fields they lay faces up, the scorching Southern sun of June beating piteously down in their eyes--the blue and the grey side by side in death as they fought hand to hand in life.

The trenches were opened and they piled the bodies in one on top of the other, where they had fallen. They turned their faces downward, these stalwart, brave American boys that the grave-diggers might not throw the wet dirt into their eyes and mouths. O, aching hearts in far-away homes, at least you were not there to see!

Both armies paused now to gird their loins for the crucial test. General Lee was in the saddle gathering every available man into his ranks for his opening assault on McClellan's host. Jackson was in the Shenandoah Valley holding three armies at bay, defeating them in detail and paralyzing the efficiency of McDowell's forty thousand men at Fredericksburg, by the daring uncertainty of his movements.

The first act of Lee was characteristic of his genius. Wishing to know the exact position of McClellan's forces, and with the further purpose of striking terror into his antagonist's mind for the safety of his lines of communication, he conceived the daring feat of sending a picked body of cavalry under the gallant J. E. B. Stuart completely around the Northern army of one hundred and five thousand men.

On June the 12th, Stuart with twelve hundred troopers, fighting, singing, daredevil riders to a man, slipped from Lee's lines and started toward Fredericksburg. The first night he bivouacked in the solemn pines of Hanover. At the first streak of dawn the men swung into their saddles in silence.

Turning suddenly to the east he surprised and captured the Federal pickets without a shot. In five minutes he confronted a squadron of Union cavalry. With piercing rebel yell his troopers charged and scattered their foes.

Sweeping on with swift, untiring dash they struck the York River Railroad, which supplied McClellan's army, surprised and captured the company of infantry which guarded Tunstall's Station, cut the wires and attacked a train passing with troops.

Riding without pause through the moonlit night they reached the Chickahominy at daybreak. The stream was out of its banks and could not be forded. They built a bridge, crossed over at dawn, and the following day leaped from their saddles before Lee's headquarters and reported.

A thrill of admiration and dismay swept the ranks of the Northern army and started in Washington a wave of bitter criticism against McClellan. No word of reply reached the world from the little Napoleon. He was busy digging trenches, felling trees and pushing his big guns steadily forward and always behind impregnable works. He was a born engineer and his soul was set on training his great siege guns on the Confederate Capital.

On the 25th of June his advance guard had pressed within five miles of the apparently doomed city. His breastworks bristled from every point of advantage. His army was still divided by the Chickahominy River, but he had so thoroughly bridged its treacherous waters he apparently had no fear of coming results.

On June the 27th Stonewall Jackson had slipped from the Shenandoah Valley, baffling two armies converging on him from different directions, and with a single tiger leap had landed his indomitable little army by Lee's side.

Anticipating his arrival, the Confederate general had hurled Hill's corps against the Union right wing under Porter. Throughout the day of the 26th and until nine o'clock at night the battle raged with unabated fury. The losses on both sides were frightful and neither had gained a victory. But at nine o'clock the Federal Commander ordered his right wing to retreat five miles to Gaines Mill and cover his withdrawal of heavy guns and supplies. They were ordered at all hazards to hold Jackson's fresh troops at bay until this undertaking was well under way. It was a job that called for all his skill in case of defeat. It involved the retreat of an army of one hundred thousand men with their artillery and enormous trains of supplies across the mud-scarred marshy Peninsula. Five thousand wagons loaded to their utmost capacity, their wheels sinking in the springy earth, had to be guarded and transported. His siege guns, so heavy it was impossible to hitch enough horses to move them over roads in which they sank to the hubs, had to be saved. Three thousand cattle were there, to be guarded and driven, and it was more than seventeen miles to the shelter of his gunboats on the James.

During the night his wagon trains and heavy guns were moved across the Chickahominy toward his new base on the James.

The morning of the 27th dawned cool and serene. Under the cover of the night the silent grey army had followed the retiring one in blue. The Southerners lay in the dense wood above Gaines Mill dozing and waiting orders.

A balloon slowly rose from the Federal lines and hung in the scarlet clouds that circled the sun. The signal was given to the artillery that the enemy lay in the deep woods within range and a storm of shot and shell suddenly burst over the heads of the men in grey and the second day's carnage had begun.

For once Jackson, the swift and mysterious, was late in reaching the scene. It was two o'clock when Hill again unsupported hurled his men on the Federal lines in a fierce determined charge. Twenty-six guns of the matchless artillery of McClellan's army threw a stream of shot and shell into his face. Never were guns handled with deadlier power. And back of them the infantry, thrilled at the magnificent spectacle, poured their hail of hissing lead into the approaching staggering lines.

The waves of grey broke and recoiled. A blue pall of impenetrable smoke rolled through the trees and clung to the earth. Under the protection of their great guns the dense lines of blue pushed out into the smoke fog and charged their foe. For two hours the combat raged at close quarters. A division of fresh troops rushed to the Northern line, and Lee observing the movement from his horse on an eminence, ordered a general attack on the entire Union front.

It was a life and death grapple for the mastery. Jackson's corps was now in action. A desperate charge of Hood's division at last broke the Union lines and the grey men swarmed over the Federal breastworks. The lines broke and began to roll back toward the bridges of the Chickahominy. The retreat threatened to become a rout. The twilight was deepening over the field when a shout rose from the tangled masses of blue stragglers by the bridge. Dashing through them came the swift fresh brigades of French and Meager. General Meager, rising from his stirrups in his shirt sleeves, swung his bare sword above his head, hurled his troops against the advancing Confederate line and held it until darkness saved Porter's division from ruin.

McClellan's one hope now was to pull his army out of the deadly swamps in which he had been caught and save it from destruction. He must reach the banks of the James and the shelter of his gunboats before he could stop to breathe. At every step the charging grey lines crashed on his rear guard. Retreating day and night, turning and fighting as a hunted stag, he was struggling only to escape.

That there was no panic, no rout, was a splendid tribute to his organizing and commanding powers. His army was an army at last in fact as well as in name--a compact and terrible fighting machine. The oncoming Confederate hosts learned this to their sorrow again and again in the five terrible days which followed.

On July 1st, McClellan reached the shelter of his gunboats and intrenched himself on the heights of Malvern Hill. On its summit he placed tier after tier of batteries swung in crescent line, commanding every approach. Surmounting those on the highest point he planted seven of his great siege guns. His army surrounded this hill, its left flank resting on the James and covered by his gunboats.

It was late in the afternoon before Lee ordered a general attack. The grey army was floundering in the mud in a vain effort to reach its fleeing enemy in force. At noon they were still burying the dead on the blood-soaked field of Glendale where McClellan's gallant rear guard had stood until the last wagon train had safely arrived at Malvern Hill.

Ned Vaughan's company had been hurried from the West to the defense of Richmond, and reached the field on the night of the 30th, too late for the battle of Glendale, but in time to walk over its scarred soil in the soft moonlight and get his first glimpse of war. He was yet to see a battle.

A group of grey schoolboy comrades were burying one of their number beneath a tall pine in the edge of an old field. He joined the circle and watched them. They dug the grave with their bayonets, tenderly wrapped the body in the battle flag of the South and covered it with their hands. One of them recited a beautiful Psalm from memory, and not a word was spoken as they drew the damp earth up into a mound. A whip-poor-will began his song in the edge of the woods as he passed on.

A few yards further a man in grey was cutting a forked limb into a crutch.

Something dark lay huddled on the brown straw. It was a wounded man in blue. The Southerner lifted his enemy, and placed the crutch under him.

"Now, partner," he said cheerfully, "you're all right. You'll find the hospital down there by them lights. They'll look out for ye."

Ned wondered vaguely how he would really feel under his first baptism of fire. He was only a private soldier in this company which had been ordered East. He had resigned from the first he had helped to raise--the ambitions and intrigues of its officers had aroused his disgust and he had taken a place in the ranks of the first company sent to Virginia. He had made up his mind he would wear no signs of rank that were not fairly won on the field of battle.

To-morrow he was going to face it at short range. Everywhere were strewn canteens, knapsacks, broken guns and blankets. He came suddenly on a trench behind which the men in blue had fought from dark to dark. It was full of dead soldiers.

His regiment was up before day to move at dawn. His company had been assigned to a regiment of veterans who had fought at Bull Run and had been in three of the battles before Richmond. Their ranks were thin and the Western boys were given a royal welcome.

The seasoned men were in good humor, the new company serious. Ned was carefully shaving by the flickering light of the camp fire.

"What the divil are you doin' that for?" his Irish messmate asked in amazement.

"You want to know the truth, Haggerty?" Ned drawled.

"That's what I want----"

"We're going into our first battle, aren't we?"

"Praise God, we are!"

"And we may come out a corpse?"

"Yis----"

"I'm going to be a decent one."

"Ah, go'long wid ye--ye bloody young spalpeen--ye're no more afraid than I am!"

"Maybe not, Haggerty, but it's a solemn occasion, and I'm going to look my best."

"Ye'll live ter see many a scrap, me bye!"

"Same to you, old man! But I'm going to be clean for this one, anyhow."

The regiment marched toward Malvern Hill at the first streak of dawn. It was slow work. Always the artillery ahead were sticking in the mud and the halts were interminable.

The new company grew more and more nervous:

"What's up ahead?"

They asked it at every halt the first three hours. And then their disgust became more pronounced.

"What in 'ell's the matter?" Ned groaned.

"Don't worry, Sonny," an old corporal called, "you'll get there in time to see more than you want."

The regiment reached the battle lines at one o'clock. The morning hours had been spent in driving in the skirmishers and feeling the enemy's positions. Lee had given orders for a general charge on a signal yell from Armistead's brigade. He was now waiting the arrival of all his available forces before attacking.

Late in the afternoon General D. H. Hill heard a shout followed by a roar of musketry and immediately ordered his division to charge. No other General seemed to have heard it and the charge was made without support. It was magnificent, but it was not war, it was sheer butchery. No army could have stood before the galling fire of those massed batteries.

Ned's regiment had deployed in a wood on the edge of a wide field at the foot of the hill. Their movement caught the eye of a battery on the heights which opened with six guns squarely on their heads.

The struggling, shattered remnants of a regiment which had been all but annihilated fell back through these woods, stumbling against the waiting men.

Ned saw a soldier with a Minie ball sticking in the centre of his forehead, the blood oozing from the round, clean-cut hole beside the lead. He was walking steadily backward, loading and firing with incredible rapidity. The company halted behind the troops held in reserve, but the man with the ball in his forehead refused to go to the rear. He wouldn't believe that he was seriously hurt. He jokingly asked a comrade to dig the ball out. He did so, and the fellow dropped in his tracks, the blood gushing from the wound in a stream.

The uncanny sight had sickened Ned. He looked at his hand and it was trembling like a leaf.

And this division was charging up that awful hill again. Ned saw a private soldier who belonged to one of its regiments deliberately walk across the field alone and join his comrades as if nothing of importance were going on. And yet the bullets were whistling so thickly that their "Zip! Zip!" on the ground kept the air filled with flying dirt and tufts of grass--a veritable hail of lead through which a sparrow apparently couldn't fly.

The fellow was certainly a fool! No man with a grain of sense would do such a thing *alone*--maybe with a crowd of cheering men, but only a maniac *could* do it alone--Ned was sure of that.

A shell smashed through the top of a tree, clipped its trunk in two and down it came with a crash that sent the men scampering.

A solid shot came bounding leisurely down the hill and rolled into the woods. A man just in front put out his foot playfully to stop it and it broke his leg.

The shriek of shell and the whistle of lead increased in terrifying roar each moment and Ned felt a queer sensation in his chest--a sort of shortness of breath. In a moment he was going to bolt for the rear! He felt it in his bones and saw no way to stop it. He lifted his eyes piteously toward the Colonel who sat erect in his saddle stroking the neck of a restless horse with his left hand.

The veteran saw the boy's terror under his trial of fire and his heart went out to him in a wave of fatherly sympathy.

He rode quickly up to Ned:

"Won't you hold my horse's bridle a minute, young man, while I use my glasses?" he asked coolly.

Ned's trembling hand caught the reins as a drowning man a straw. The act steadied his shaking nerves. As the Colonel slowly lowered his glasses Ned cried through chattering teeth:

"D-d-d-on't y-you think--I-I-I--am d-d-doing p-pretty well, C-colonel, f-f-f-for my f-f-ffirst battle?"

The Colonel nodded encouragingly:

"Very well, my boy. It's a nasty situation. You'll make a good soldier."

And then the order to charge!

Across the level field torn by shot and shell, the regiment swept in grey waves. The gaps filled up silently. They started up the hill and met the sleet of hissing death. The hill top blazed streams of yellow flame through the pall of smoke. Men were falling--not one by one, but in platoons and squads, rolling into heaps of grey blood-soaked flesh and rags. The regiment paused, staggered, reeled and rallied.

Haggerty fell just in front of Ned, who was loading and firing with the precision of a machine. If he had a soul--he didn't know it now. The men were ordered to lie down and fire from the ground.

Haggerty caught Ned's eye as it glanced along his musket searching for his foe through the cloud of blue black smoke that veiled the world.

"Roll me around, Bye," the Irishman cried, "and make a fince out of me--I'm done for."

Ned paid no attention to his call, and Haggerty pulled his mangled body down the hill and doubled himself up in front of his friend.

"Keep down behind me, Bye," he moaned. "I'll make a good fort for ye!"

It was useless to protest, he had erected the fort to suit himself and Ned was fighting now behind it. The sight of his dying friend steadied his nerves and sent a thrill of fierce anger like living fire through his veins. His eye searched the hilltop for his foe. The smoke rolled in dark grey sulphurous clouds down the slope and shut out the sky line. He waited and strained his bloodshot eyes to find an opening. It was no use to waste powder shooting at space. He was too deadly angry now for that.

A puff of wind lifted the clouds and the blue men could be seen leaping about their guns. They looked like giants in the smoke fog. Again he fired and loaded, fired and loaded with clock-like, even steady, hand. It was tiresome this ramming an old-fashioned muzzle-loading musket lying flat on the ground. But with each round he was becoming more and more expert in handling the gun. His mouth was black with powder from tearing the paper ends of the cartridges. The sulphurous taste of the powder was in his mouth.

From the centre of the field rose the awful Confederate yell again. A regiment of Georgians, led by Gordon were charging. Waiting again for the smoke to clear in front Ned could see the grey waves spread out and caught the sharp word of command as the daring young officers threw their naked swords toward the sky crying:

"Forward!"

And then they met the storm. From grim, black lips on the hill crest came the answer to their yell--three hundred and forty mighty guns were singing an oratorio of Death and Hell in chorus now from those heights. Half the men seemed to fall at a single crash and still the line closed up and rushed steadily on, firing and loading, firing and loading,--running and staggering, then rallying and pressing on again.

On the right ten thousand men under Hill slipped out into line as if on dress parade--long lines of handsome boyish Southerners. The big guns above saw and found them with terrible accuracy. A wide lane of death was suddenly torn through them before they moved. They closed like clock work and with a cheer swept forward to the support of the men who were dying on the blood-soaked slope.

Ned's heart was thumping now. He felt it coming, that sharp low order from the Colonel before the words rang from his lips. His hour had come for the test--coward or hero it had to be now. It was funny he had ceased to worry. He had entered a new world and this choking, blinding smoke, the steady thunder of guns, the long sheets of orange fire that flashed and flashed and blazed in three rings from the hill, the ripping canvas of musketry fire in volleys, the dull boom of the great guns on the boats below, were simply a part of the routine of the new life. He had lived a generation since dawn. The years that had gone before seemed a dream. The one real thing was Betty's laughing eyes. They were looking at him now from behind that flaming hill. He must pass those guns to reach her. Not a doubt had yet entered his soul that he would do it. Men were falling around him like leaves in autumn, but this had to be. He saw the end. No matter how fierce this battle, McClellan was only fighting to save his army from annihilation. Lee was destroying him.

The order came at last. The Colonel walked along in front of his men with bared head.

"Now, boys,--that battery on the first crest--we've half their men--charge and take those guns!"

The regiment leaped to their feet and started up the hill. They had lost two hundred men in their first sweep. There were six hundred left.

"Hold your fire until I give the word!" the Colonel shouted.

The smoke was hanging low, and they had made two hundred yards before the blue line saw them through the haze. The hill blazed and hissed in their faces. The massed infantry behind the guns found their marks. Men dropped right and left, sank in grey heaps or fell forward on their faces--some were knocked backwards down the slope. Yet without a pause they climbed.

Three hundred yards more and they would be on the guns. And then a sheet of blinding flame from every black-mouthed gun in line double shotted with grape and canister! The regiment was literally knocked to its knees. The men paused as if dazed by the shock. The sharp words of cheer and command from their officers and they rallied. From both flanks poured a murderous hail of bullets--guns to the right, left and front, all screaming, roaring, hissing their call of blood.

The Colonel saw the charge was hopeless and ordered his men to fire and fall back fighting. The grey line began to melt into the smoke mists down the hill and disappeared--all save Ned Vaughan. His eyes were fixed on that battery when the order to fire was given. He fired and charged with fixed bayonet alone. He never paused to see how many men were with him. His mind was set on capturing one of those guns. He reached the breastworks and looked behind him. There was not a man in sight. A blue gunner was ramming a cannon. With a savage leap Ned was on the boy, grabbed him by the neck and rushed down the hill in front of his own gun before the astounded Commander realized what had happened. When he did it was too late to fire. They would tear both men to pieces.

The regiment had rallied in the woods at the edge of the field from which they had first charged.

Ned Vaughan led his prisoner, in bright new uniform of blue, up to the Colonel and reported.

"A prisoner of war, sir!"

The Colonel took off his hat and gazed at the pair:

"Aren't you the boy who held my horse?"

Ned saluted:

"Yes, sir."

"Then in the name of Almighty God, where did you get that man?"

Ned pointed excitedly to the hilltop:

"Right yonder, sir,--there's plenty more of 'em up there!"

The Colonel scratched his head, looked Ned over from head to heel and broke into a laugh.

"Well, I'll be damned," he said at last. "Take him to the rear and report to me to-night. I want to see you."

Ned saluted and hurried to the rear with his prisoner.

The sun was slowly sinking in a sea of blood. The red faded to purple, the purple to grey, the grey into the shadows of night and still the guns were thundering from their heights. It was nine o'clock before they were silent and Lee's torn and mangled army lay down among their dead and wounded to wait the dawn and renew the fight. They had been compelled to breast the most devastating fire to which an assaulting army had been subjected in the history of war. The trees of the woods had been literally torn and mangled as if two cyclones had met and ripped them to pieces.

The men dropped in their tracks to snatch a few hours' sleep.

The low ominous sounds that drifted from the darkness could not be heeded till to-morrow. Here and there a lantern flickered as they picked up a wounded man and carried him to the rear. Only the desperately wounded could be helped. The dead must sleep beneath the stars. The low, pitiful cries for water guided the ambulance corps as they stumbled over the heaps of those past help.

The clouds drew a veil over the stars at midnight and it began to pour down rain before day. The sleeping, worn men woke with muttered oaths and stood against the trees or squatted against their trunks seeking shelter from the flood. As the mists lifted, they looked with grim foreboding but still desperate courage to the heights. Every rampart was deserted. Not one of those three hundred and forty guns remained. McClellan had withdrawn his army under the cover of the night to Harrison's Landing.

It would be difficult to tell whose men were better satisfied.

"Thank God, he's gone from there anyhow!" the men in grey cried with fervor.

Now they could get something to eat, bury their dead and care for all the wounded. McClellan's Peninsula Campaign had ended. His Grand Army had melted from a hundred and ten thousand fighting men in line to eighty-six thousand. The South had lost almost as many.

From the wildest panic into which the advance of his army had thrown Richmond, the Confederate Capital now swung to the opposite extreme of rejoicing for the deliverance, mingled with criticism of their leaders for allowing the Federal army to escape at all.

The gloom in Washington was profound.

An excited General rushed to the White House at two o'clock in the morning, roused the President from his bed and pleaded for the immediate dispatch of a fleet of transports to Harrison's Landing as the only possible way to save the army from annihilation.

The President soothed his fears and sent him home. He was not the man to be thrown into a panic. Yet the incredible thing had happened. His army of more than two hundred thousand men, under able generals, had been hurled back from the gates of Richmond in hopeless, bewildering defeat, and he must begin all over again.

One big ominous fact loomed in tragic menace from the smoke and flame of this campaign--the South had developed two leaders of matchless military genius--Robert E. Lee and Stonewall Jackson. It was a fact the President must face and that without fear or favor to any living man in his own army.

He left Washington for the front at once. He must see with his own eyes the condition of the army. He must see McClellan. The demand for his removal was loud and bitter. And fiercest of all those who asked for his head was the iron-willed Secretary of War, Edwin M. Stanton, his former champion.

CHAPTER XIV
THE RETREAT

John Vaughan had become one of his General's trusted aides. His services during the month's terrific struggle had proven invaluable. The Commander was quick to discern that he was a man of culture and possessed a mind of unusual power. More than once the General had called him to his headquarters to pour into his ears his own grievances against the authorities in Washington. Naturally his mind had been embittered against the man in the White House. The magnetic personality of McClellan had appealed to his imagination from their first meeting.

The General was particularly bitter on the morning the President was expected. His indignation at last broke forth in impassioned words to his sympathetic listener.

The tragic consequence of the impression made in that talk neither man could dream at the moment.

Pacing the floor with the tread of a caged lion McClellan suddenly paused and his fine blue eyes flashed.

"I tell you, Vaughan, the wretches have done their worst. They can't do much more----"

He stopped suddenly and drew from his pocket the copy of a dispatch he had sent to the war office. He read it carefully and looked up with flashing eyes:

"I'll face the President with this dispatch to Stanton in my hands, too. They would have removed me from my command for sending it--if they had dared!"

He slowly repeated its closing words:

"I know that a few thousand more men would have changed this battle from a defeat to a victory. As it is, the Government must not and cannot hold me responsible for the result. I feel too earnestly to-night. I have seen too many dead and wounded comrades to feel otherwise than that the Government has not sustained this army. If you do not do so now, the game is lost. If I save this army now, I tell you plainly that I owe no thanks to you, or to any other person in Washington. You have done your best to sacrifice this army----"

He paused and his square jaws came together firmly.

"And if that be treason, they can make the most of it!"

"I am curious to know how he meets you to-day," John said with a smile.

An orderly announced the arrival of the President and the Commanding General promptly boarded his steamer. In ten minutes the two men were facing each other in the stateroom assigned the Chief Magistrate.

Lincoln's tall, rugged figure met the compact General with the easy generous attitude of a father ready to have it out with a wayward boy. His smile was friendly and the grip of his big hand cordial.

"I am satisfied, sir, that you, your officers and men have done the best you could. All accounts say that better fighting was never done. Ten thousand thanks, in the name of the people for it."

The words were generous, but the commander put in a suggestion for more.

"Never, Mr. President," he said emphatically, "did such a change of base, involving a retrogressive movement under incessant attacks from a vastly more numerous foe partake of so little disaster. When all is known you will see that the movement just completed by this army is unparalleled in the annals of war. We have preserved our trains, our guns, our material, and, above all, our honor."

"Rest assured, General," the quiet voice responded, "the heroism and skill of yourself, officers and men, is and forever will be appreciated."

The President returned to Washington profoundly puzzled as to his duty. He was alarmed at the display of self esteem which his defeated General had naively made, and his loyalty was boldly and opened questioned by his advisers, and yet he was loath to remove him from command. Down in his square, honest heart he felt that with all his faults, McClellan was a man of worth, that he had never been thoroughly whipped in a single battle and that he hadn't had a fair trial.

Any other man in power than Abraham Lincoln would have removed him instantly on the receipt of his insolent and insulting dispatch. Instead, the President had gone to see him with an open mind. He returned determined to strengthen his military council by the addition of an expert in Washington as his Commander-in-Chief.

He called to this post Henry W. Halleck. Although McClellan had waived the crown of such power aside with lofty words of unselfish patriotism, he received the announcement of Halleck's promotion and his subordination with sullen rage.

"In this thing," he wrote his wife, "the President and those around him have acted so as to make the matter as offensive as possible to me."

And yet against every demand that McClellan should be removed from command the President was obdurate. Again and again his friends urged:

"McClellan is playing for the Presidency."

The tall man merely nodded:

"All right. Let him. I am perfectly willing that he shall have it if he will only put an end to this war."

But if the President refused to remove him from command, Halleck and Stanton managed quickly to strip him of half his army by detaching and sending it to join the new army of General Pope. McClellan, with the remainder of his men, had been sent by transport back to Alexandria. General John Pope was summoned from the West to take command of the new "Army of Virginia," composed of the divisions of Fremont, Banks and McDowell, and the detached portion of McClellan's men.

All eyes were now centred on the new Commander. The West had only seen success--Fort Henry, Fort Donelson, Pea Ridge, Shiloh, and Island No. 10.

The new General on the day he began his advance against Lee and Jackson issued an address to his army which sent a chill to the heart of the President.

"I have come to you from the West," he proclaimed, "where we have always seen the backs of our enemies--from an army whose business has been to seek the adversary and beat him when found. I desire you to dismiss from your minds certain phrases which I am sorry to find much in vogue among you. I hear constantly of 'lines of retreat' and 'bases of supplies.' Let us discard such ideas. Let us look before us, not behind. From to-day my headquarters will be in the saddle."

Every man in the Army of the Potomac which McClellan had created and fought with such fierce and terrible, if unsuccessful power, resented this address as an insult. McClellan himself was furious. For some reason only part of the forces from his army which were detached ever reached Pope, and those who did were not enthusiastic. It was expecting too much of human nature to believe that they could be.

The outlook for the coming battle was ominous.

CHAPTER XV
TANGLED THREADS

Betty Winter received a telegram from John Vaughan announcing his arrival at Alexandria with McClellan on the last day of August. Her heart gave a bound of joy. She could see him to-morrow. It had been five years instead of five months since she had stood on that little pier and watched him float away into the mists of the river! All life before the revelation which love had brought was now a shadowy memory. Only love was real. His letters had been her life. They hadn't come as often as she had wished. She demanded his whole heart. There could be no compromise. It must be all, **all** or nothing.

She tried to sleep and couldn't. Her brain was on fire.

"I must sleep and look my best!" she laughed softly, buried her face in the pillow and laughed again for joy. How could she sleep with her lover standing there alive and strong with his arms clasping her to his heart!

She rose at daylight and threw open her window. The air was crisp with the breath of fall. She watched the sun rise in solemn glory. A division of cavalry dashed by, the horses' hoofs ringing sharply on the cobble stones, sabres clashing. Behind them came another and another, and in a distant street she heard the rumble of big guns, the crack of their drivers' whips and the sharp cries of the men urging the horses to a run.

Something unusual was on foot. The sun was barely up and the whole city seemed quivering with excitement.

She dressed hurriedly, snatched a bite of toast and drank a cup of coffee. In twenty minutes she entered the White House to get her pass to the front. She wouldn't go to the War Department. Stanton was rude and might refuse. The hour was absurd, but she knew that the President rose at daylight and that he would see her at any hour.

She found him seated at his desk alone pretending to eat an egg and drink his coffee from the tray that had been placed before him. His dishevelled hair, haggard look and the pallor of his sorrowful face showed only too plainly that he had not slept.

"You have bad news, Mr. President?" Betty gasped.

He rose, took her hand and led her to a seat.

"Not yet, dear, but I'm expecting it."

"We lost the battle yesterday?" she eagerly asked.

"Apparently not. You may read that. I trust you implicitly."

He handed her the dispatch he had received from General Pope after the first day's fight at Manassas. Betty read it quickly:

"We fought a terrific battle here yesterday with the combined forces of the enemy, which lasted with continuous fury from daylight until dark, by which time the enemy was driven from the field which we now occupy. The enemy is still in our front, but badly used up. We lost not less than eight thousand men killed and wounded, but from the appearance of the field the enemy lost two to one. The news has just reached me from the front that the enemy is retreating toward the mountains."

Betty looked up surprised:

"Isn't that good news?"

"Nothing to brag about. It's the last sentence that worries me----"

"But that seems the best!"

"It might be but for the fact that Jackson is leading that retreat toward the mountains! I've an idea that he will turn up to-day on Pope's rear with Lee's whole army on his heels. Jackson is in the habit of appearing where he's least expected----"

He paused, paced the floor a moment in silence and threw his long arms suddenly upward in a hopeless gesture:

"If God would only give me such a man to lead our armies!"

"Is General McClellan at Alexandria to-day?" Betty suddenly asked.

"I'm wondering myself. He should be on that field with every soldier under his command."

"I've come to ask you for a pass to Alexandria----"

"Then my worst fears are confirmed!" he broke in excitedly. "Your sweetheart's on McClellan's staff--his men will never reach the field in time!"

He dropped into a chair, hurriedly wrote the pass and handed it to Betty.

"God bless you, child. See me when you get back and tell me all you learn of McClellan and his men to-day. The very worst is suspected----"

"You mean?"

"That this delay and deliberate trifling with the most urgent and positive orders is little short of treason. Unless his men reach Pope to-day and fight, the Capital may be threatened to-morrow."

"Surely!" Betty protested.

"It's just as I tell you, child, but I'll hope for the best. Be eyes and ears for me to-day and you may help me."

The agony of his face and the deep note of tragedy in his voice had taken the joy out of her heart. She threw the feeling off with an effort.

"What has it all to do with my love!" she cried with a toss of her pretty head as she sprang into the saddle for the gallop to Alexandria.

The cool, bracing air of this first day of September, 1862, was like wine. The dew was yet heavy on the tall grass by the roadside and a song was singing in her heart that made all other music dumb.

John had dismounted and was standing beside the road, the horse's bridle hanging on his arm in the very position he had stood and looked into her soul that day.

She leaped to the ground without waiting for his help and sprang into his arms.

"I like you better with that bronzed look--you're handsomer than ever," she sighed at last.

His answer was another kiss, to which he added:

"No amount of sunburn could make you any prettier, dear--you've been perfect from the first."

"Your General is here?" Betty asked.

"Yes."

"And you can give me the whole day?"

"Every hour--the General is my friend."

The moment was too sweet to allow any shadow to cloud it. The girl yielded to its spell without reserve. They mounted and rode side by side over the hills. And the man poured into her ears the unspoken things he had felt and longed to say in the lonely nights of camp and field. The girl confessed the pain and the longing of her waiting.

They mounted the crest of a hill and the breeze from the southwest brought the sullen boom of a cannon.

Instinctively they drew rein.

"The battle has begun again," John said casually.

"It stirs your blood, doesn't it?" she whispered.

A frown darkened his brow:

"Not to-day."

The girl looked with quick surprise.

"You don't mean it?"

"Certainly. Why get excited when you know the end before it begins."

"You know it?"

"Yes."

"Victory?"

He laughed cynically:

"Victory for a pompous braggart who could write that address to an army reflecting on the men who fought Lee and Jackson before Richmond with such desperate courage?"

"You are sure of defeat then?"

"Absolutely."

Betty looked at him with a flush of angry excitement:

"General McClellan is counting on Pope's defeat to-day?"

"Yes."

"Then it's true that he is not really trying to help him?"

"Why should he wish to sacrifice his brave men under the leadership of a fool?"

"He is, in fact, defying the orders of the President, isn't he?"

"You might say that if you strain a point," John admitted.

Again the long roar of guns boomed on the Western horizon, louder, clearer. The dull echoes became continuous now, and the quickening breeze brought the faint din from the vast field of death whose blazing smoke covered lines stretched over seven miles.

"*Boom-boom-boom, boom!--boom! boom!*"

Again they drew rein and listened.

John's brow wrinkled and his right ear was thrown slightly forward.

"Those are our big guns," he said with a smile. "The Confederate artillery can't compare with ours--their infantry is a terror--stark, dead game fighters----"

"*Boom--Boom!----Boom! Boom! Boom!*"

"How do you know those are our guns?" Betty asked with a shiver.

"The rebels have none so large. They'll have some to-night."

Again an angry flush mounted her cheeks:

"You wish them to be captured?"

"It will be a wholesome lesson."

Betty leaned closer and grasped his hand with trembling eagerness.

"O John--John, dear, this is madness! General McClellan has been accused of treason already--this surely is the basest betrayal of his country----"

The man shook his head stubbornly:

"No--it's the highest patriotism. My Commander is brave enough to dare the authorities at Washington for the good of his country. The sooner this farce under Pope ends the better--no man of second rate ability can win against the great Generals of the South."

The girl's keen brown eyes looked steadily into his and her lips trembled.

"I call it treachery--the betrayal of his country for his selfish ambitions! I'm surprised that you sympathize with him."

John frowned, was silent and then turned to her with a smile:

"Let's not talk about it, dear. The day's too beautiful. We're alone together. This is not your battle--nor mine--it's Pope's--let him fight it out. I love you--that's all I want to think about to-day."

The golden brown curls were slowly shaken:

"It *is* your battle and it's mine--O John dear, I'm heartsick over it! The President's anguish clouded the morning for me, but the thought of you made me forget. Now I'm scared. You've surprised and shocked me."

"Nonsense, dear!" he pleaded.

She looked at him with quick, eager yearning.

"You love me?" she asked.

"Can you doubt it?"

"With every beat of your heart?"

"Yes."

"Will you do something for me?" she begged.

"What is it?"

"Just for me, because I ask it, John, and you love me?"

"If I can."

"I want you to resign immediately from McClellan's staff, report at the War Department and let the President give you new duties----"

The man shot her a look of angry amazement:

"You can't mean this?"

Again the soft, warm hand that had slipped its glove grasped his. He could feel her slim, little fingers tremble. She had turned very pale:

The Southerner

"I'm in dead earnest. I love you, dear, with my whole heart, and it's my love that asks this. I can't think of you betraying a solemn trust. The very thought of it cuts me to the quick. If this is true, General McClellan should be court-martialed."

The man's square jaws closed with a snap:

"Let them try it if they dare----"

"The President will dare if he believes it his duty."

"Then he'll hear something from the hundred and fifty thousand soldiers who have served under McClellan."

The little hand pressed harder.

"Won't you, for my sake, dear,--just because I'm your sweetheart and you love me?"

The stalwart figure suddenly stiffened:

"And you could respect a man who would do a thing like that?"

"For my sake?--Yes."

"No, you think you could. But you couldn't. No woman can really love a poltroon or a coward."

"I'm not asking you to do a cowardly thing----"

"To desert my leader in a crisis?"

"To wash your hands of treachery and selfish ambitions."

"But it's not true," he retorted. "You mustn't say that. McClellan's a leader of genius--brave, true, manly, patriotic."

"I've a nobler ideal of patriotism----"

"Your blundering backwoodsman in the White House?"

"Yes. He has but one thought--that the Union shall be saved. He has no other ambition. If McClellan succeeds, he rejoices. If he fails, he is heartbroken. I know that he has defended him against the assaults of his enemies. He has refused to listen to men who assailed his loyalty and patriotism. This generous faith your Chief is betraying to-day. That you defend him is horrible--O John, dear, I can't--I won't let you stay! You must break your connection with this conspiracy of vain ambition. The country is calling now for every true, unselfish man--please!"

He lifted his hand in firm protest:

"And for that very reason I stand firmly by the man I believe destined to save my country."

"You won't change Commanders because I ask it?"

He was silent a moment and a smile played about the corners of his lips:

"Would you change because I asked it?"

"Yes."

"Then come over from Lincoln to McClellan," he laughed.

"And join your group of conspirators--never!"

"Not if I ask it, because I love you?"

Her brown eyes sparkled with anger:

"You'll not find this a joke!"

"That's why I treat it seriously, my dear," was the firm reply. "If I could throw up my position in this war on the sudden impulse of my sweetheart, I'd be ashamed to look a man in the face--and you would despise me!"

"If your Commander succeeds to-day in bringing disaster to our army I'll despise you for aiding him----"

"Let's not discuss it--please, dear!" he begged with a frown.

"As you please," was the cold reply.

They rode on in silence, broken only by the increasing roar of the great guns at Manassas. Betty glanced at the stolid, set face and firm lips. Her anger steadily rose with every throb of Pope's cannon. Each low thunder peal on the horizon now was a cry for help from dying mangled thousands and the man she loved refusing to hear.

Suddenly the picture of his brother flashed before her vision, the high-strung, clean young spirit, chivalrous, daring, fighting for what he knew to be right--right because right is right, and wrong is wrong.

She looked at John Vaughan with a feeling of fierce anger. Between the two men she preferred the enemy who was fighting in the open to win or die. Her soul went out to Ned in a wave of tender admiration. Her wrath against his brother steadily rose.

Suddenly she drew her rein:

"You need come no further. I'll ride back home alone."

He bit his lips without turning and was silent. She touched her horse with her whip and galloped swiftly toward Washington.

* * * * *

The last day of Pope's brief campaign ended in the overwhelming disaster of the second battle of Bull Run. The sound of his cannon reached McClellan's ears, but the organizer of the Army of the Potomac, though ordered to do so, never joined his rival.

Once more the army of the Union was hurled back on Washington in panic, confusion and appalling disaster. Lee and Jackson had crushed Pope's hosts with a rapidity and case that struck terror to the heart of the Nation. General Pope lost fifteen thousand men in a single battle. Lee and Jackson lost less than half as many.

The storm broke over McClellan's head at Washington on his arrival. Stanton and Halleck and Pope accused him of treachery. The hot heads demanded his arrest and trial by court-martial.

The President shook his head, but sadly added:

"He has acted badly toward Pope. He really wanted him to fail."

And then began the search to find the man once more to weld the shattered army into an efficient fighting force.

Abraham Lincoln asked himself this question with a sense of the deepest and most solemn responsibility. He must answer at the bar of his conscience before God and his country. Again he brushed aside every adviser inside and outside his Cabinet and determined on his choice absolutely alone.

Early on the morning of September 2nd John Vaughan looked from the window of General McClellan's house and saw the giant figure of the President approaching, accompanied by Halleck.

When his aide announced this startling fact, the General coolly said:

"It means my arrest, no doubt. I'm ready. Let them come."

The President was not kept waiting this time. His General was there to receive him.

The rugged face was pale and drawn.

"General McClellan," he began without ceremony, "I have come to ask you to take command of all the returning troops for the defense of Washington."

The short, stalwart figure of the General suddenly straightened, his blue eyes flashed with amazement and then softened into a misty expression. He bowed with dignity and quietly said:

"I accept the position, sir."

"I need not repeat," the President went on, "that I disapprove some things you have done. I have made this plain to you. I do this because I believe it's best for our country. I assume its full responsibility and I expect great things of you."

The President bowed and left the astonished General and his still more astonished aide gazing after his long swinging legs returning to the White House.

He had done the most unpopular act of his entire administration. His decision had defied the fiercest popular hostility. He faced a storm of denunciation which would have appalled a less simple and masterful man. The Cabinet meeting which followed the startling news was practically a riot. He listened to all his excited Ministers had to say with patience. When they had spoken their last word of bitter disapproval he quietly rose and ended the tumultuous session with two or three sentences which none could answer:

"There is no one in the army who can man these fortifications and lick these troops of ours into shape half as well as he can. McClellan is a great engineer--of the stationary type, perhaps. But we must use the tools we have! If he cannot fight himself, at least he excels in making others ready to fight."

He waited for an answer and none came. He had not only averted a Cabinet crisis but his remorseless common sense and his unswerving adherence to what he saw was best had strengthened his authority over all his councillors.

When the rest had gone he turned to the young man who knew him best, his Secretary, John Nicolay, and gripped his arm with a big hand which was trembling:

"The most painful duty of my official life, Boy! There has been a design, a purpose in breaking down Pope without regard to the consequences to the country that is atrocious. It's shocking to see and know this, but there is no remedy at present. McClellan has the army with him and I must use him."

CHAPTER XVI
THE CHALLENGE

"One war at a time," the President said to his Secretary of State when he proposed a foreign fight. He must now strangle Northern public opinion to enforce this principle.

Captain Wilkes had overhauled the British Steamer *Trent* on the high seas, searched her and taken the Confederate Commissioners Mason and Slidell by force from her decks.

The people of the North were mad with joy over the daring act. Congress, swept off its feet by the wave of popular hysteria, proclaimed Wilkes a hero and voted their thanks. The President did not move with current opinion. He had formed the habit in boyhood of thinking for himself, and had never allowed himself to take his cues for action from second-hand suggestions. From the first he raised the question of Wilkes' right to stop the vessel of a friendly nation on the high seas, search her and take her passengers prisoners by force of arms.

The backwoods lawyer questioned, too, the right of a naval officer to turn his quarter-deck into a court and decide questions of international law offhand. He raised the point at once whether these men thus captured might not be white elephants on the hands of the Government. Moreover he reminded his Cabinet that we had fought England once for daring to do precisely this thing.

Great Britain promptly drew her sword and made ready for war.

Queen Victoria's Government not only demanded that the return of these passengers be made at once with an apology, but did it in a way so offensive that a less balanced man in power would have lost his head and committed the fatal blunder.

The tall, quiet Chief Magistrate was equal to the occasion. Great Britain had ordered her navy on a war footing, dispatched eight thousand troops to Canada to strike by land as well as sea, allowing us but seven days in which to comply with all her demands or hand Lord Lyons his passports.

The President immediately dictated a reply which forced her Prime Minister to accept it and achieved for the Nation the establishment of a principle for which we had fought in vain in 1812.

He ordered the prisoners returned and an apology expressed. His apology was a two-edged sword thrust which Great Britain was compelled to take with a groan.

"In 1812," the President said, "the United States fought because you claimed the right to stop our vessels on the high seas, search them and take by force British subjects found thereon. Our country in making this surrender, adheres to the ancient principle for which we contended and we are glad to find that Her Majesty's

Government in demanding this surrender thereby renounces an error and accepts our position."

Lord Palmerston made a wry face, but was compelled to accept the surrender, and with it seal his own humiliation as a beaten diplomat. War with England at this moment would have meant unparalleled disaster. France had ambitions in Mexico and she was bound in friendship to England. The two great Nations of Europe would have been hurled against our divided country with the immediate recognition of the Confederacy.

The President forced this return of the prisoners and apparent surrender to Great Britain in the face of the blindest and most furious outbursts of popular rage.

Gilbert Winter rose in the Senate and in thunderous oratory voiced the well-nigh unanimous feeling of the millions of the North of all parties and factions:

"I warn the administration against this dastardly and cowardly surrender to a foreign foe! The voice of the people demand that we stand firm on our dignity as a Sovereign Nation. If the President and his Cabinet refuse to listen they will find themselves engulfed in a fire that will consume them like stubble. They will find themselves helpless before a power that will hurl them from their places!"

The President was still under the cloud of public wrath over this affair when the crisis of the problem of emancipation became acute. The gradual growth of the number of his bitter foes in Washington he had seen with deep distress. And yet it was inevitable. No man in his position could administer the great office whose power he was wielding without fear or favor and not make enemies. And now both friend and foe were closing in on him with a well-nigh resistless demand for emancipation.

Hour after hour he sat patiently in his office receiving these impassioned delegations.

Old Edward was standing at the door again smiling and washing his hands:

"A delegation of editors, presenting Mr. Horace Greeley's 'Prayer of Twenty Millions.'"

The patient eyes were lifted front his desk, and the strong mouth firmly pressed:

"Let them in."

The President rose in his easy, careless manner:

"I'm glad to see you, gentlemen. You are the leaders of public opinion. The people rule this country and I am their servant. What is it?"

The Chairman of the Committee stepped forward and gravely handed him an engrossed copy of Greeley's famous editorial, "The Prayer of Twenty Millions," demanding the immediate issue of a proclamation of emancipation.

The Chairman bowed and spoke in earnest tones:

"As the representatives of millions of readers we present this 'Prayer' with our endorsement and the request that you act. In particular we call your attention to these paragraphs:

"'A great portion of those who brought about your election and all those who desire the unqualified suppression of the rebellion, are sorely disappointed, pained and surprised by the policy you seem to be pursuing with regard to the slaves of rebels. I write to set before you succinctly and unmistakably what we require, what we have a right to expect and of what we complain.

"'We think you are unduly influenced by the counsels, the representations and the menaces of certain fossil politicians from the Border Slave States, knowing as you do, that the loyal citizens of these States do not expect that Slavery shall be upheld, to the prejudice of the Union.

"'We complain that the Union cause has suffered and is now suffering immensely from the mistaken course which you are pursuing and persistently cling to, in defense of slavery. We complain that the confiscation act which you approved is being wantonly and wholly disregarded by your Generals, apparently with your knowledge and consent.

"'The seeming subserviency of your policy to the slave holding, slave upholding interest is the perplexity and the despair of statesmen of all parties. Whether you will choose to listen to their admonishment or wait for your verdict through future history, or at the bar of God, I do not know. I can only hope.'"

The President's sombre eyes met his with a penetrating flash and rested on Senator Winter who remained in the background. He took the paper, laid it carefully on his desk, threw his right leg across the corner of the long table in easy, friendly attitude and began his reply persuasively:

"The editor of the *Tribune*, gentleman, if on my side, is equal to an army of a hundred thousand men in the field. I've known this from the first. Against me he throws this army in the rear and fires into my back. My grievance is that his Prayer which you have made yours is being used for ammunition in this rear attack. It should have been presented to me first, if it were a genuine prayer. I have read it carefully. It is full of blunders of fact and reasoning, but it fairly expresses the discontent in the minds of many. Its unfair assumptions will poison millions of readers against me----"

He paused, opened a drawer in his desk, took from it a sheet of paper on which he had written in firm, clear hand a brief message in reply, and turned to his petitioners:

"And therefore, gentlemen, I have written a few words in answer to this attack. I ask you to give it the same wide hearing you have accorded the assault. I'll read it to you:

"'Dear Sir:--I have just read yours of the 19th instant addressed to myself through the **New York Tribune**.

"'If there be in it any statements or assumptions of fact, which I know to be erroneous, I do not now and here controvert them.

"'If there be any influences which I believe to be falsely drawn, I do not now and here argue against them.

"'If there be perceptible in it an impatient and dictatorial tone, I waive it in deference to an old friend, whose heart I have always supposed to be right.

"'As to the policy I seem to be pursuing, as you say, I have not meant to leave anyone in doubt. I would save the Union. I would save it in the shortest way under the Constitution.

"'The sooner the National authority can be restored, the nearer the Union will be,--the Union as it was.

"'If there be those who would not save the Union, unless they could at the same time save Slavery, I do not agree with them.

"'If there be those who would not save the Union, unless they could at the same time destroy Slavery, I do not agree with them.

"'***My paramount object is to save the Union, and not either to save or destroy Slavery***.

"'If I could save the Union without freeing any slave I would do it. And if I could save it by freeing all the slaves I would do it. And if I could save it by freeing

The Southerner

some, and leaving others alone, I would also do that.

"'What I do about Slavery and the colored race I do because I believe it helps to save the Union, and what I forbear, I forbear because I do not believe it would help to save the Union.

"'I shall do less whenever I believe what I am doing hurts the cause, and I shall do more, whenever I believe doing more will help the cause.

"'I shall try to correct errors, when shown to be errors, and I shall adopt new views so fast as they shall appear to be true views.

"'I have stated my purpose, according to my view of official duty, and I intend no modification of my oft expressed personal wish, that all men everywhere could be free.'"

A moment of death-like stillness followed the reading. The members of the committee had unconsciously pressed nearer. Some of them stood with shining eyes gazing at the rugged, towering figure as if drawn by a magnet. The stark earnestness and simplicity of his defense had found their hearts. The daring of it fairly took their breath.

Senator Winter turned to his nearest neighbor and growled:

"Bah! The trouble is Lincoln's a Southerner--born in the poisoned slave atmosphere of the South. He grew up in Southern Indiana and Illinois. His neighbors there were settlers from the South. He has never breathed anything but Southern air and ideals. It's in his blood. Only a man born in the South could have written that document----"

The listener looked up suddenly:

"I believe you are right. Excuse me--I want to speak to the long-legged Southerner. I've never seen him before."

To the astonishment of the Senator, the editor pushed his way into the group who were shaking hands with the President.

He paused an instant, extended his hand and felt the rugged fingers close on it with a hearty grip. Before he realized it he was saying something astounding-- something the farthest possible removed from his thoughts on entering the room.

"I want to thank you, sir, for that document. The heart of an unselfish patriot speaks through every word. I came here to criticise and find fault. I'm going home to stand by you through thick and thin. You've given us a glimpse inside."

Both big hands were now clasping his and a mist was clouding the hazel-grey eyes.

"The Senator accuses you," he went on, "of being a Southerner. He must be right. No Northern man could have seen through the clouds of passion to-day clearly enough to have written that letter. You can see things for all the people, North, South, East and West. God bless you--I'm going home to fight for you and with you----"

In angry amazement Senator Winter saw most of the men he had led to this carefully planned attack walk up and pledge their loyalty to his smiling foe. He turned on his heel and left, his jaw set, his blue eyes dancing with fury.

Old Edward was again rubbing his hands apologetically at the door:

"A body of clergymen from Chicago, sir----"

"Clergymen from Chicago?"

"Yes, sir."

"I didn't know they ever used such things in Chicago!"

He caught his knee in his big hands, leaned back and laughed heartily. The doorman looked straight ahead and managed to keep his solemn countenance under control.

"All right, let them in, Edward."

The reverend gentlemen solemnly filed into the executive office. They looked around in evident amazement at its bare poverty-stricken appearance. They had been shocked at the threadbare appearance of the White House grounds as they entered. This room was a greater shock--this throbbing nerve centre of the Nation. In the middle stood the long, plain table around which the storm-racked Cabinet were wont to gather. There was not a single piece of ornamental or superfluous furniture visible. It appeared almost bare. A second-hand upright desk stood by the middle window. In the northwest corner of the room there were racks with map rollers, and folios of maps on the floor and leaning against the wall.

The well-dressed, prosperous-looking gentlemen gazed about in a critical way.

Their spokesman was a distinguished Bishop who knew that he was distinguished and conveyed the information in every movement of his august body.

"We have come, Mr. President," he solemnly began, "as God's messengers to urge on you the immediate and universal emancipation of every slave in America."

The faintest suggestion of a smile played about the corners of the big, firm mouth as he rose and began a reply which greatly astonished his visitors. They had come to lecture him and before they knew it the lamb had risen to slay the butchers.

"I am approached, gentlemen," he said softly, "with the most opposite opinions and advice, and that by religious men, who are equally certain that they represent the Divine Will. I am sure that either one or the other class is mistaken in that belief, and perhaps in some respects, both. I hope it will not be irreverent for me to say that if it is probable that God would reveal His will to others on a point so connected with my duty, it might be supposed He would reveal it directly to me----"

He paused just an instant and his bushy eyebrows were raised a trifle as if in search of one friendly face in which the sense of humor was not dead. He met with frozen silence and calmly continued:

"Unless I am more deceived in myself than I often am, it is my earnest desire to know the will of Providence in this matter. And if I can learn what it is I will do it! These are not, however, the days of miracles, and I suppose it will be granted that I am not to expect a direct revelation. I must study the plain physical facts of the case, ascertain what is possible, and learn what appears to be wise and right. The subject is difficult and good men do not agree----"

"We are all agreed to-day!" the leader interrupted.

"Even so, Bishop, but we are not all here to-day."

The gentle irony was lost on the great man, and the President went on good-naturedly:

"What good would a proclamation of emancipation do as we are now situated? Shall I issue a document that the whole world will see must be of no more effect that the Pope's bull against the comet? Will my words free the slaves when I cannot even enforce the Constitution in the rebel States? Is there a single court or magistrate, or individual that will be influenced by it there? I approved the law of Congress which offers protection and freedom to the slaves of rebel masters who come within our lines. Yet I can not learn that the law has caused a single slave to come over to us.

"Now then, tell me, if you please, what possible result of good would follow the issuing of such a proclamation as you desire? The greatest evils might follow it--among them the revolt of the Border Slave States which we have held loyal with so much care, and the desertion from the ranks of our armies of thousands of Democratic soldiers who tell us plainly that they are not fighting and they're not going to fight to free negroes!

"Understand me, I raise no objection against it on legal grounds. As Commander-in-Chief of the Army and Navy in time of war, I suppose I have a right to take any measure which may best subdue the enemy. Nor do I urge objections of a moral nature in view of possible consequences of servile insurrection and massacre in the South. I view this matter now as a practical war measure. Has the moment arrived when I can best strike with this weapon?

"Do not misunderstand me because I have mentioned objections. They indicate some of the difficulties that have thus far prevented my action in some such way as you desire. I have not decided against a proclamation of liberty to the slaves. I hold the matter under advisement. And I can assure you that the subject is on my mind, by day and night more than any other. What shall appear to be God's will I will do----"

He stopped suddenly and a smile illumined his dark face:

"But I cannot see, gentlemen, why God should be sending his message to me by so roundabout route as the sinful city of Chicago. I trust that in the freedom with which I have canvassed your views and expressed my own, I have not in any respect injured your feelings."

The ice was broken at last and the men of God began to smile, press forward and shake his hand. They came his critics, and left his friends.

And yet no hint was given to a single man present that his Emancipation Proclamation had been written two months before and at this moment was lying in the drawer of the old desk before which he sat. Long before the revelation of God's will through these clergymen he had discussed its provisions before his Cabinet and enjoined absolute secrecy. Men from all walks of life came to advise the backwoods lawyer on how to save the country. He listened to all and then did exactly what he believed to be best.

His plan had long been formed on the subject of the destruction of Slavery. His purpose was to accomplish this great task in a way which would give his people a just and lasting peace. He held the firm conviction that the North was equally responsible with the South for the existence of Slavery, and that the Constitution which he had sworn to defend and uphold guaranteed to the slave owner his rights. He was determined to free the slaves if possible, but to do it fairly and honestly and then settle the question for all time by colonizing the negro race and removing them forever from physical contact with the white.

At his request Congress had already passed a bill providing for the colonization of emancipated slaves. He now sent for a number of representative negroes to hear his message and deliver it to their people.

Old Edward ushered them into his office with a look of unmistakable superiority.

It was a strange meeting--this facing for the first time between the supreme representative of the dominant race of the new era and the freed black men whose very existence the President held to be an eternal menace against the Nation's future. It is remarkable that the first words Abraham Lincoln ever addressed as President to an assemblage of negroes should have been the words which fell from his lips.

The ebony faces, their cream-colored teeth showing with smiles and their wide rolling eyes roaming the room made a striking and dramatic contrast to the rugged face and frame of the man who addressed them.

"Your race is suffering," he began with distinct, clean cut emphasis, "in my judgment the greatest wrong inflicted on any people. But even when you cease to be slaves, you are yet far removed from being placed on an equality with the white race. On this broad continent not a single man of your race is made the equal of a single man of ours. Go where you are treated best and the ban is still upon you. I cannot alter it if I would.

"It is better for us both, therefore, to be separated. One of the principal difficulties in the way of colonization is that the free colored man cannot see that his comfort would be advanced by it. For the sake of your race you should sacrifice something of your present comfort. In the American Revolution sacrifices were made by the men engaged in it. They were cheered by the future.

"The Colony of Liberia is an old one, is in a sense a success and it is open to you. I am arranging to open another in Central America. It is nearer than Liberia--within seven days by steamer. You are intelligent and know that success does not so much depend on external help as on self-reliance. Much depends on yourself. If you will engage in the enterprise, I will spend some of the money intrusted to me. This is the practical part of my wish to see you. I ask you then to consider it seriously, not for yourselves merely, ***nor for your race and ours for the present time, but for the good of mankind***."

He dismissed his negro hearers and sent again for the representatives of the Border Slave States. Here his plan must be set in motion. He proposed to pay for the slaves set free and arrange for their colonization.

He spoke with deep emotion. His soul throbbed with passionate tenderness in every word.

"You are patriots and statesmen," he solemnly declared, "and as such I pray you to consider this proposition, and at the least commend it to the consideration of your States and people. Our common country is in grave peril demanding the loftiest views and boldest action to bring it speedy relief. You can make it possible to accomplish the just destruction of this curse of our life. It will bring emancipation as a voluntary process, leaving the least resentment in the minds of our slave-holders. It will not be a violent war measure, to be remembered with fierce rebellious anger. It will pave the way for good feeling at last between all sections when reunited. It is reasonable. It is just. It will leave no cause for sectional enmity. This plan of gradual emancipation with pay for each slave to his owner will secure peace more speedily and maintain it more permanently than can be done by force alone. Its cost could be easier paid than the additional cost of war and would sacrifice no blood at all.

"In giving freedom to the *slave*, we *assure* freedom to the *free*--honorable alike in what we give and what we preserve. We shall nobly save or meanly lose the last best hope of earth. Other means may succeed. This could not fail. The way is plain, peaceful, generous, just--a way which if followed, the world will forever applaud, and God must forever bless."

His tender, eloquent appeal fell on deaf ears. The men who represented the Border Slave States refused to permit the question of tampering with Slavery to be submitted to their people--no matter by what process, with or without pay.

They demanded with sullen persistence that the President defy all shades of

Northern opinion and stand squarely by his Inaugural address. In vain he pointed out to them that the fact of a desperate and terrible war, costing two million dollars a day and threatening the existence of the Government itself, had changed the conditions under which he made that pledge.

When the President at last introduced into Congress through his spokesman the bill appropriating fifteen million dollars with which to pay for their slaves, the men from the Border States united with the Democrats and defeated it!

With a sorrowful heart and deep forebodings of the future he turned to his desk and drew forth the document he had written declaring as an act of war against the States in rebellion that their slaves should be free.

He read its provisions again with the utmost care. He made no attack on Slavery, or the slave-holder. He was striking the blow against the wealth and power of the South for the sole purpose of crippling her resources and weakening her power to continue the struggle to divide the Union. There was in it not one word concerning the rights of man or the equal rights of black and white men. His mind was absolutely clear on that point. The negro when freed would be an alien race so low in the scale of being, so utterly different in temperament and character from the white man that their remaining in physical contact with each other in our Republic was unthinkable. In the Emancipation Proclamation itself, therefore, he had written the principles of the colonization of the negro race. The two things were inseparable. He could conceive of no greater calamity befalling the Nation than to leave the freed black man within its borders as an eternal menace to its future happiness and progress.

He called his Secretary and ordered a Cabinet meeting to fix the date on which to issue this momentous document to the world--a challenge to mortal combat to his foes in all sections.

CHAPTER XVII
THE DAY'S WORK

Betty Winter held John Vaughan's note in her hand staring at its message with increasing amazement:

"DEAR LITTLE SWEETHEART:

"The President has just called General McClellan again to the chief command. His act vindicates my loyalty. Our quarrel is too absurd. Life is too short, dear, for this--it's only long enough for love.
May I see you at once?

"JOHN."

Could it be true? For a moment she refused to believe it. The President had expressed to her his deep conviction of McClellan's guilt. How could he reverse his position on so vital and tremendous a matter over night? And yet John Vaughan was incapable of the cheap trick of lying to make an engagement.

A newsboy passed yelling an extra.

"Extra--Extra! General McClellan again in the saddle! Extra!"

It was true--he had made the appointment. What was its meaning? Had they forced the President into this humiliating act? If the General were really guilty of destroying Pope and overwhelming the army in defeat, his treachery had created the crisis which forced his return to power. The return under such conditions would not be a vindication. It would be a conviction of crime.

She would see the President at once and know the truth. The question cut the centre of John Vaughan's character. The orderly who brought the note was waiting for an answer.

She called from the head of the stairs:

"Tell Mr. Vaughan there is no answer to-day."

"Yes, Miss."

With quick salute he passed out and Betty stood irresolute as she listened to the echo of his horse's hoof-beat growing fainter. It was only six o'clock, but the days were getting shorter and it was already dark. She could walk quickly down Pennsylvania Avenue and reach the White House before dinner. He would see her at any hour.

In five minutes she was on the way her mind in a whirl of speculation on the intrigue which might lie behind that sensational announcement. She was beginning to suspect her lover's patriotism. A man could love the South, fight and die for it and be a patriot--he was dying for what he believed to be right--God and his country. But no man could serve two masters. Her blood boiled at the thought of a conspiracy within the lines of the Union whose purpose was to betray its Chief. If John Vaughan were in it, she loved him with every beat of her heart, but she would cut her heart out sooner than sink to his level!

She became conscious at last of the brazen stares of scores of brutal-looking men who thronged the sidewalks of the Avenue.

Gambling dens had grown here like mushrooms during the past year of war's fevered life. The vice and crime of the whole North and West had poured into Washington, now swarming with a quarter of a million strange people.

The Capital was no longer a city of sixty thousand inhabitants, but a vast frontier post and pay station of the army. And such a pay station! Each day the expenditures of the Government were more than two millions. The air was electric with the mad lust for gain which the scent of millions excites in the nostrils of the wolves who prey on their fellow men. The streets swarmed with these hungry beasts, male and female. They pushed and crowded and jostled each other from the sidewalks. The roar of their whiskey-laden voices poured forth from every bar-room and gambling den on the Avenue.

A fat contractor who had made his pile in pasteboard soles for army shoes and sent more boys to the grave from disease than had been killed in battle, touched elbows with the hook-nosed vulture who was sporting a diamond pin bought with the profits of shoddy clothes that had proven a shroud for many a brave soldier sleeping in a premature grave.

They were laughing, drinking, smoking, swearing, gambling and all shouting for the flag--the flag that was waving over millions they hoped yet to share.

A feeling of sickening fear swept the girl's heart. For the first time in her life she was afraid to be alone on the brightly lighted streets of Washington at dusk. The poison of death was in the air. Every desperate passion that stirs the brute in man was written in the bloodshot eyes that sought hers. The Nation was at war. To cheat, deceive, entrap, maim, kill the enemy and lay his home in desolation was the daily business now of the millions who backed the Government. Whatever the lofty aims of either of the contending hosts, they sought to win by war and this was war. It was not to be wondered at that this spirit should begin to poison the springs of life in the minds of the weak and send them forth to prey on their fellows. It was not to be wondered at that men planned in secret to advance their own interests at the expense of their fellows, to climb the ladder of wealth and fame in this black hour no matter on whose dead bodies they had to walk.

With a pang of positive terror Betty asked herself the question whether the man she loved had been touched by this deadly pestilence? A wave of horror swept her. A drunken brute brushed by and thrust his bloated face into hers.

With a cry of rage and fear she turned and ran for two blocks, left the Avenue at the corner and hurried back to her home.

She would wait until morning and see the President before the crowd arrived.

He greeted her with a joyous shout:

"Come right in, Miss Betty!"

With long, quick stride he met her and grasped her hand, a kindly twinkle in his eye:

"And how's our old grizzly bear, your father, this morning?"

"He's still alive and growling," she laughed.

The President joined heartily:

"I'll bet he is," he said, "and hates me just as cordially as ever?"

Betty nodded.

"But his beautiful daughter?"

"Was never more loyal to her Chief!"

"Good. Then my administration is on a sound basis. You want no office. You ask no favors. Such clear, pure, young eyes in the morning of life don't make mistakes. They know."

"But I've come to ask you something this morning----"

The smile faded into a look of seriousness.

"What's the matter?" he asked quickly.

Betty hesitated and the red blood slowly mounted to her cheeks. He led her to a seat, beside his chair, touched her hand gently and whispered:

"Tell me."

"I hope you won't think me presumptuous, Mr. President, if I ask you to tell me why you recalled General McClellan?"

The rugged face suddenly flashed with a smile.

"Presumptuous?" he laughed. "My dear child, if you could have heard a few things my Cabinet had to say to me in this room on that subject! The tender deference with which you put the question is the nearest thing to an endorsement I have so far received! Go as far as you like after that opening. It will be a joy to discuss it with you. Presumptuous--Oh, my soul!"

He caught his knee between his hands and rocked with laughter at the memory of his Cabinet scene.

Reassured by his manner Betty leaned closer:

"You remember the morning you gave me the pass to Alexandria?"

"To see a certain young man?"

"Yes."

"Perfectly."

"You distinctly gave me the impression that morning that you were sure General McClellan was betraying his trust in his failure to support General Pope and that your confidence in him was gone forever."

"Did I?"

"Yes."

"Then it wasn't far from the truth," he gravely admitted.

"And yet you recalled him to the command of the army?"

"I had to."

"Had to?"

"It was the only thing to do."

Betty spoke in a whisper:

"You mean that their conspiracy had become so dangerous there was no other way?"

He threw her a searching look, was silent a moment and slowly said:

"That's a pointed question, isn't it?"

"I'm a member of your Cabinet, you know----"

"Yes, I know--but why do *you* happen to ask me such a dangerous question at this particularly trying moment? Come, my little bright eyes, out with it?"

"The certain young man and I are not very happy----"

"You've quarrelled?"

"Yes."

"About what?"

"You."

"You don't mean it, Miss Betty?" he said incredulously.

Her eyes were dim and she nodded.

"But why about me?"

"I saw things which confirmed your suspicions. He admitted his desire that General Pope should fail and defended McClellan's indifference. We quarrelled. I asked him to resign from the staff of his Chief----"

"You didn't!" he exclaimed softly, his deep eyes shining.

"I did--and he refused."

Again the big hands both closed on hers:

"God bless you, child! So long as I hold such faith from hearts like yours, I know that I'm right. They can say what they please about me----"

"You see," she broke in, "if he is in this conspiracy and they have forced you to this surrender, he is equally guilty of treachery----"

"And you hold him responsible for his Commander's ambitions?"

"Yes."

The President sprang to his feet and paced the floor a moment, stopped and gazed at her with a look of curious tenderness:

"By jinks, Miss Betty, if I had a few more like you in my Cabinet I wouldn't be so lonesome!"

"They did force you?" she demanded.

"Not as you mean it, my child. I'm not going to pretend to you that I don't understand the seriousness of the situation. The Army of the Potomac is behind McClellan to a man. It amounts to infatuation. I sounded his officers. I sounded his men. To-day they are against me and with him. If the issue could be sprung--if the leaders dared to risk their necks on such a revolution, they might win. They don't know this as clearly as I do. Because they are not so well informed they are afraid to move. I have chosen to beat them at their own game----"

He paused and laughed:

The Southerner

"I hate to shatter your ideal, Miss Betty, but I'm afraid there's something of the fox in my make-up after all. Will it shock you to learn this?"

"I shall be greatly relieved to know it," she responded firmly.

"Think, then, for a moment. I suspend McClellan for his failure and replace him with a man I believe to be his superior. The army sullenly resent this change. They do not agree with me. They believe McClellan the greatest General in sight. It's a marvellous thing this power over men which he possesses. It can be used to create a Nation or destroy one. It's a dangerous force. I must handle it with the utmost care. So long as their idol is a martyr the army is unfit for good service. The moment I restore the old commander, in whom both officers and men have unbounded faith, I show them that I am beyond the influence of the political forces which demand his destruction--don't I?"

"Yes."

"And the moment I dare to brave popular disapproval and restore their commander don't you see that I win the confidence of the army in my fairness and my disinterested patriotism?"

"Of course."

"See then what must happen. Now mind you, I would never have restored McClellan to command if I did not know that at this moment he can do the work of putting this disorganized and defeated army into fighting shape better than any other. McClellan thus returned to power must fight. He must win or lose. If he wins I am vindicated and his success is mine. If he loses, he loses his power over the imagination of his men and at last I am master of the situation. I shall back him with every dollar and every man the Nation can send into his next campaign. No matter whether he wins or loses, I *must* win because the supremacy of the civil power will be restored."

"I see," Betty breathed softly.

She rose with a new look of reverence for a great mind.

"And the civil power was not supreme when you restored McClellan to his command?"

"Miss Betty, you'd make a good lawyer!" he laughed.

"Was it?" she persisted.

"No."

"Thank you," she said, rising and extending her hand. "I learned exactly what I wished to know."

"And you'll stop quarreling?"

"If he's reasonable----"

He lifted his long finger in solemn warning.

"Remember now! This administration is honestly and sincerely backing General McClellan for all it's worth. It has always done this. We are going to try to make even a better record in the next campaign----"

"When will it open?"

"Sooner than any of us wish it, if our scouts report the truth. Flushed with his great victory over Pope, General Lee is sure to invade Maryland. The campaign will be a dangerous and crucial one. The moment Lee crosses the Potomac, his communications with Richmond will be imperiled. If he dares to do it we can crush his army in a great battle, cut his communications with Richmond, drive his men into the Potomac and end the war. I have given McClellan the opportunity of his life. I pray God to give success----"

Edward appeared at the door.

"Well, what is it?"

"The crowd, sir--they are clamoring to get in."

Betty hurried into the family apartments to speak to Mrs. Lincoln, her mind in a whirl of resentment against John Vaughan.

The President turned to the crowd which had already poured into the room.

As usual, the cranks and inventors led the way. The inventors found the President an easy man to talk to. His mind was quick to see a good point and always open to conviction. He had once patented a device for getting flat boats over shoals himself. His immediate approval of the first model of Ericsson's famous **Monitor** had led to its adoption in time to meet and destroy the **Merrimac** in Hampton Roads on the very day the iron terror had sent his big ships to the bottom. He allowed no inventor to be turned from the door of the White House no matter how ridiculous his hobby might appear. The inventions relating to the science of war he would test himself on the big open field between the White House grounds and the river.

The first inventor in line carried the model of a new rifle which would shoot sixteen times. The army officers believed in the idea of a single shell breech loader on account of the simplicity of its mechanism. Our muskets were still muzzle loaders and the men were compelled to use ramrods to load.

The President examined the new gun with keen interest, pulled his black, shaggy beard thoughtfully, looked at the breathless inventor, and slowly mused:

"Well, now as the fat girl said when she pulled on her stocking, it strikes me there's something in it!"

The inventor laughed with nervous joy, and watched him write a card of endorsement:

"Take that to the War Department, and tell them I like your idea--I want them to look into it."

His face wreathed in smiles, the man pushed his way through the crowd, and hurried to the War Department.

The next one was a little fellow who had a gun of marvellous model, double-barrelled, with the barrels crossed. The President adjusted his spectacles and took a second look before he made any comment. He lifted his bristling eyebrows:

"What's it for?"

"For cross-eyed men, sir!" he whispered.

"You don't say?" he roared.

"Yes, sir," the little man continued eagerly. "The cross-eyed men ain't never had no chance in this war. They turn 'em all down. They won't take 'em as soldiers. That gun'll fix 'em. Push a regiment o' good cross-eyed men to the front with that gun a-pourin' hot lead from two barrels at the same time an' every man er cross firin' at the enemy an' we'll jist natchally make hash outen 'em, sir----"

"And we may need the cross-eyed men, too, before the war ends." The sombre eyes twinkled thoughtfully. "Thank you, my friend, when I draft the cross-eyed men come in again and we'll talk it over. Your heart's in the right place, anyhow."

He glanced doubtfully at the little skillet-shaped head and reached over his shoulder for the next one. It was a bullet proof shirt for soldiers--a coat of mail which weighed fifty pounds.

"How long do you think a man could march with that thing on and the thermometer at ninety-eight in the shade?"

He handed it back with a shake of his head and grasped the next one--a model water-tight canoe to fit the foot like a snow shoe.

"What's the idea?" he asked.

"Shoe the army with *my* canoes, sir, and they can all walk on water----"

"And yet they say the age of miracles has passed! Take it over to old Neptune's office. He's a sad man at times and I like him. This ought to cheer him."

The next one was a man of unusually interesting face. A typical Yankee farmer with whiskers spilling over his collar from his neck and bristling up against his clean shaven chin. He handed the President a model of a new musket. He examined it with care and fixed the man with his gaze:

"Well, sir?"

"Hit's the rekyle, sir," he explained softly. "Hit's the way she's hung on the stock."

"Oh----"

"Ye see, sir," he went on earnestly, "a gun ought not to rekyle, and ef hit rekyles at all, hit ought to rekyle a leetle forred----"

"Right you are!" the President roared with laughter. "Your logic's sound whether your gun kicks or not. I say so, too. A gun ought *not* to rekyle at all, and if it does rekyle, by jinks, it ought to rekyle and hit the other fellow, not us!"

The tall figure dropped into the chair by his desk and laughed again.

"Come in again, Brother 'Rekyle' and we'll talk it over when I've got more time."

The stocky, heavy set figure of the Secretary of War suddenly pushed through the crowd and up to the desk. Stanton's manner had always been rude to the point of brusqueness and insult. The tremendous power he was now wielding in the most important Department of the Government had not softened his temper or improved his manners. The President had learned to appreciate his matchless industry and sterling honesty and overlooked his faults as an indulgent father those of a passionate and willful child.

Stanton's eyes were flashing through his gold rimmed glasses the wrath he found difficult to express.

The President looked up with a friendly smile:

"Well, Mars, what's the trouble now?"

Stanton shook his leonine locks and beard in fury at the use of the facetious word. He loathed levity of any kind and the one kind he could not endure was the

The Southerner

quip that came his way.

He regarded himself seriously every day, every hour, every minute in every hour. He was the incarnate soul of Mars on earth. He knew and felt it. He raged at the President's use of the term because he had a sneaking idea that he was being laughed at--and that by a man who was his inferior and yet to whom he was rendering indispensable service.

An angry retort rose to his lips, but he suppressed the impulse. It was a waste of breath. The President was a fool--he would only laugh again as he had done before. And so he plunged straight to the purpose of his call:

"Before you get to your usual batch of passes and pardons this morning I want to protest again, Mr. President, against your persistent interference with the discipline of the army and the affairs of my Department. Your pardons are hamstringing the whole service, sir. It must stop if you expect your generals to control their men!"

"Is that all, Mars?" the even voice asked.

"It is, sir!"

"Thanks for the spirit that prompts your rage. I know you're right about most of these things. I'll do my best to help and not hinder you----"

"There's a woman coming here this morning to present a petition over my head."

"Oh, I see----"

"I have refused it and I demand that you support, not make a fool of me."

He turned without waiting for an answer and strode from the room.

The President whispered to Nicolay:

"We may have to put a few bricks in Stanton's pocket yet, John!"

He glanced toward the waiting crowd and whispered again:

"Any news to-day from the front before I go on?"

Nicolay drew a telegram from his file:

"Only this dispatch, sir, announcing the capture of fifty mules and two brigadier generals by Stuart's cavalry----"

"Fifty mules?"

"And two brigadier generals."

"Fifty mules--and they're worth two hundred dollars a piece. Tell 'em to send a regiment after those mules. Jeffy D. can have the generals."

A slender little dark-haired girl about fifteen years old, with big wistful blue eyes, had taken advantage of the pause to slip close. When the President lifted his head she caught his eyes. He rose immediately and drew her to his side.

"You're all alone, little girl?"

"Yes, sir," she faltered.

"And what can I do for you?"

"If you please, I want to pass through the lines to Virginia--my brother's there--he was shot in the last battle. I want to see him."

"Of course you do," the kindly voice agreed, "and you shall."

He wrote the pass and handed it to her.

She murmured her thanks and he placed his big hand on her dark head and asked casually:

"Of course you're loyal?"

The young lips quivered, she hesitated, looked up into his face through dimmed eyes, and the slender body suddenly stiffened, as she slowly said:

"Yes--to the heart's core--to Virginia!"

The trembling fingers handed the pass back and the tears rolled down her cheeks.

The tall man dared not look down again. Something about this slim wistful girl brought back over the years the memory of the young mother who had come from the hills of old Virginia.

He was still for a moment, stooped, and took her hand in his. His voice was low and tender and full of feeling:

"I know what it cost you to say that, child. You're a brave, glorious little girl, if you are a rebel. I love you for this glimpse you've given me of a great spirit. I'm sure I can trust you. If I let you go, will you promise me faithfully that no word shall pass your lips of what you've seen inside our lines?"

"I promise!" she cried, smiling through her tears.

He handed her back the pass and slowly said:

"May God bless you--and speed the day when your people and mine shall be no longer enemies."

He turned again to his desk, and beside it stood a quiet woman dressed in black.

He bowed to her with easy grace:

"And how can I serve you, Madam?"

She smiled hopefully:

"You have children, Mr. President?"

A look of sorrow overspread the dark face.

"Yes," he said reverently, "I have two boys now. I had three, but God has just taken one of them."

"I had two," the mother responded. "Both of them went into the army to fight for their country and left me alone. One has been killed in battle. I tried to be brave about it. I said over and over again, 'the Lord gave and the Lord has taken away, blessed is the name of the Lord!' But I had to give up. I'm all alone in my little place in the mountains of Pennsylvania and I can't endure it. I know they say I have no right to ask, but I want my last boy to come home. All night I lie there alone and cry. Can't you let me have my boy back? He's all I've got on earth--others have more. I have only this one. I'm just a woman--lonely, heartsick and afraid. They say I can't have him. But I've come to ask you. I've heard that you have a loving heart----"

She stopped suddenly.

"You have seen Stanton?" the President asked.

"Yes. He wouldn't listen. He swore I shouldn't have him."

The hazel-grey eyes gazed thoughtfully out the window across the shining river for a moment.

"I have two," he murmured, "and you have only one. It isn't fair. You shall have your boy."

He turned to his desk and wrote the order for his discharge. The mother pressed close, gently touched with the tips of her fingers his thick black hair and softly cried while he was writing.

She took the precious paper, tried to speak and choked.

"Go away now," the President whispered, "or you'll have me crying in a minute."

When the last man had gone he stood alone before his window in brooding silence. A tender smile overspread his face and he drew a deep breath. In the hills of Pennsylvania he saw a picture--a mother in the door of a humble home waiting for her boy. He is coming down the road with swift, strong step. She sees and rushes to meet him with a cry of joy, holds him in her arms without words a long, long while and will not let him go. And then she leads him into the house, falls on her knees and thanks God.

He smiles again and forgets the burden of the day.

CHAPTER XVIII
DIPLOMACY

In the whirlwind of passion, intrigue, slander and hate which had circled the head of the new President since the day of his Inauguration, the mother of his children had not been spared.

The First Lady of the Land had found her position as difficult in its way as her husband had found his. She had met the cynical criticism at first with dignity, reserve, and contempt. But as it increased in violence and virulence she had more than once lost her temper. She had never been blessed with the serenity of spirit that with Lincoln in his trying hours touched the heights of genius.

She was just a human little woman who loved her husband devotedly and hated every man and woman who hated him. And when her patience was exhausted she said things as she thought them, with a contempt for consequences as sublime as it was dangerous.

From the moment of the opening of the war she hated the South, not only because the Southern people had flung the shadow of death over her splendid social career and blighted the brightest dream of her life by war, but she had a more intimate and personal reason for this hatred. Her own flesh and blood had gone into the struggle against her and the husband she loved. Both her brothers born in the South, were in the Confederate army fighting to tear the house down over her head. One of these brothers had been made the Commandant of Libby Prison in Richmond. The woman in her could never forgive them.

And yet men in the North who sought the destruction of her husband saw how they might use the fact of her Southern kin to their own gain, and did it with the most cruel and bitter malignity.

One thing she was determined to do--maintain her position in a way to put it beyond the reach of petty spite and gossip. She had always resented the imputation of boorishness and lack of culture his enemies had made against the man she loved. She held it her first duty, therefore, to maintain her place as the First Lady of the Land in a way that would still those slanderous tongues. For this reason her dresses had been the most elaborate and expensive the wife of any Chief Magistrate of the Republic had ever worn. Her big-hearted, careless husband had no more idea of the cost of such things than a new-born babe.

Lizzie Garland, the negro dressmaker, to whom she had given her patronage, practically spent her entire time with the President's wife, who finally became so contemptuous of unreasonable public criticism in Washington that she was often seen going to Lizzie Garland's house to be fitted.

As Lizzie bent over her work basting the new seams in fitting her last dress, the Mistress of the White House suddenly stopped the nervous movement of her rocking-chair.

"He demands a thousand dollars to-night, Lizzie?"

"Swears he'll take the whole account to the President to-morrow unless he gets it, Madam."

"You tried to make him reasonable?"

"Begged him for an hour."

"That's what I get for trading with a little rat in Philadelphia. I'll stick to Stewart hereafter."

She rose with a gesture of nervous rage:

"Well, there's no help for it then. I must ask him. I dread it. Mr. Lincoln calls me a child--a spoiled child. He's the child. He has no idea of what these things cost. Why can't a Nation that spends two millions a day on contractors and soldiers give its President a salary he can live on?"

She threw herself on the lounge and gave way for a moment to despair.

"He'll give it to you, of course, when you ask it," Lizzie ventured cheerfully.

"If I'm diplomatic, yes. But I hate to do it. He's harassed enough. I wonder sometimes if he's human to stand all he does. If he knew the truth--O my God----"

"Don't worry, Madam," Lizzie pleaded. "It will come out all right. The President is sure to be re-elected."

"That's it, is he? I'm beginning to lose faith. He'll never win if the scoundrels in Washington can prevent it. There's just one man in Congress his real friend. I can't make him see that the hypocrites he keeps in his Cabinet are waiting and watching to stab him in the back. But what's the use to talk, I've got to face it to-day--ask Phoebe to come here."

"Let me go, Madam," Lizzie begged. "I hate the sight of that woman. I suspect her of nosing into our affairs."

"Nonsense!" was the contemptuous answer. "Phoebe's just a big, fat, black, good-natured fool. It rests me to look at her--she's so much fatter than I am."

With a shrug of her shoulders the dressmaker rose and rang for the colored maid, who had just entered Mrs. Lincoln's service.

Phoebe walked in with a glorious smile lighting her dusky face. Seeing her mistress lying down at the unusual hour of eleven o'clock in the morning, she rushed to her side:

"Laws of mussy, Ma'am, ain't you well!"

"Just a little spell of nerves, Phoebe, something that never worries your happy soul----"

"No, Ma'am, dat dey don't!" the black woman laughed.

"Hand me a pencil and pad of paper."

Phoebe executed her order with quick heavy tread, and stood looking while her mistress scribbled a note to her husband.

"Take that to the President, and see that he comes."

Phoebe courtesied heavily:

"Yassam, I fetch him!"

The Hon. Salmon P. Chase, Secretary of the Treasury, was engaged with the President when Phoebe presented herself at the door of the executive office.

John Hay tried in vain to persuade her to wait *a* few minutes. Phoebe brushed the young diplomat aside with scant ceremony.

"G'way fum here, Boy!" she laughed. "Miss Ma'y sent me ter fetch 'im right away. An' I gwine ter fetch 'im!"

She threw her ponderous form straight through the door and made for the Chief Magistrate.

Mr. Chase was delivering an important argument, but it had no weight with her.

She bowed and courtesied to the President.

"Excuse me, Governor," he said with a smile. "Good morning, Phoebe."

"Good mornin', sah."

She extended the note with a second dip of her ponderous form:

"Yassah, Miss Ma'y send dis here excommunication ter you, sah!"

"You don't say so?" the President cried, breaking into a laugh.

"Yassah."

"Then I'm excommunicated, Governor!" he nodded to Chase. "I must read the edict." He adjusted his glasses and glanced at the note:

"Your mistress is lying down?"

"Yassah, she's sufferin' fum a little spell er nervous prosperity, sah--dat's all--sah----"

"Oh, that's all?"

"Yassah."

The President roared with laughter, in which Phoebe joined.

"Thank you, Phoebe, tell her I'll be there in a minute----"

"Yassah."

"And Phoebe----"

The maid turned as she neared the door:

"Yassah?"

"I hope you'll always bring my messages from your mistress----"

"Yassah."

"I like you, Phoebe. You're cheerful!"

"I tries ter be, sah!" she laughed, swinging herself through the door.

The President threw his big hands behind his head, leaned back, and laughed until his giant frame shook.

The dignified and solemn Secretary of the Treasury scowled, rose, and stalked from the room.

"Sorry I couldn't talk longer, Chase."

"It's all right," the Secretary replied, with a wave of his hand.

The President found his wife alone.

"I hope nothing serious, Mother?" he said tenderly.

"I've a miserable headache again. Why were you so long?"

"I was with Governor Chase."

"And what did the old snake in the grass want this time?"

The President glanced toward the door uneasily, sat down by her side and touched her hand:

"You should be more careful, Mother. Servants shouldn't hear you say things like that----"

The full lips came together with bitter firmness:

"I'll say just what I think when I'm talking to you, Father--what did he want?"

"He offered his resignation as my Secretary of the Treasury."

His wife sprang up with flashing eyes:

"And you?"

"Refused to accept it."

"O my Lord, you're too good and simple for this world! You're a babe--a babe in the woods with wolves prowling after you from every tree and you won't see them! You know that he's a candidate against you for the Presidency, don't you?"

"Yes."

"You know that he never loses an opportunity to sneer at you behind your back?"

"I've heard so."

"You know that he's hand in glove with the conspirators in Congress who are trying to pull you down?"

"Perhaps."

"You know that he's the greatest letter writer of the age? That he writes as many letters to your generals in the field as old Winter--that he writes to every editor he knows and every politician he can influence, and that the purpose of these letters is always the same--to pull you down?"

"Possibly."

"You have this chance to put your foot on this frozen snake's head and yet you bring him into your house again to warm him into life?"

"Chase is a great Secretary of the Treasury, my dear. The country needs him. I can't afford to take any chances just now of a change for the worse."

"He has no idea of leaving. He's only playing a game with you to strengthen himself--can't you see this?"

"Maybe."

"And yet you submit to such infamy in your own Cabinet?"

"It's not a crime, Mother, to aspire to high office. The bee is in poor Chase's bonnet. He can't help it. I've felt the thing tickle myself. If he can beat me let the best man win----"

"Don't--don't--don't say such fool things," his wife cried. "I'll scream! You need a guardian. You have three men in your Cabinet who are using their positions to climb into the Presidency over you--old Seward, Chase and now Stanton, and you smile and smile and let them think you don't know. You'll never have a united and powerful administration until you kick those scoundrels out----"

"Mother--Mother--you mustn't----"

"I will--I'll tell you the truth--nobody else does. I tell you to kick these scoundrels out and put men in their places who will loyally support you and your policies!"

"I've no right in such an hour to think of my own ambitions, my dear," was the even, quiet answer. "Seward is the best man for his place I know in the country. Stanton is making the most efficient War Secretary we have ever had. Chase is a great manager of our Treasury. I'm afraid to risk a new man. If these men can win over me by rendering their country a greater service than I can, they ought to win----"

"But can't you see, you big baby, that it isn't the man who really gives the greatest service that may win? It's the liar and hypocrite undermining his Chief who may win. Won't you have common sense and send those men about their business? Surely you won't lose this chance to get rid of Chase. Won't you accept his resignation?"

"No."

There was a moment's tense silence. The wife looked up appealingly and the rugged hand touched hers gently.

"I think, Father, you're the most headstrong man that God ever made!"

The dark, wistful face brightened:

"And yet they say I'm a good-natured, easy-going fellow with no convictions?"

"They don't know you----"

"I'm sorry, Mother, we don't see it the same way, but one of us has to decide these things, and I suppose I'm the one."

"I suppose so," she admitted wearily.

"But tell me," he cried cheerfully, "what can I do right now to make you happy? You sent for me for something. You didn't know that Chase was there, did you?"

She hesitated and answered cautiously:

"It doesn't matter whether I did or not. You refuse to listen to my advice."

He bent nearer in evident distress:

"What can I do, Mother?"

"I need some money. Since Willie's death last winter I've thought nothing of my dresses for the next season. I must begin to attend to them. I need a thousand dollars."

"To-day?"

"Yes."

He looked at her with a twinkle playing around the corner of his eyes as he slowly rose:

"Send Phoebe in for the check."

"Ring for her, please."

He pulled the old-fashioned red cord vigorously, walked back to the lounge, put his hands in his pockets and looked at his wife in a comical way.

"Mother," he said at last, "you're a very subtle woman. You'd make a great diplomat if you didn't talk quite so much."

CHAPTER XIX
THE REBEL

While Betty Winter was still brooding in angry resentment over the problem of John Vaughan's guilt in sharing the treason of his Chief, the army was suddenly swung into the field to contest Lee's invasion of Maryland.

The daring venture of the Confederate leader had developed with startling rapidity. The President was elated over the probable annihilation of his army. He knew that half of them were practically barefooted and in rags. He also knew that McClellan outnumbered Lee and Jackson two to one and that the Southerners, no longer on the defensive, but aggressors, would be at an enormous disadvantage in Maryland territory.

That Lee was walking into a death trap he was morally sure.

The Confederate leader was not blind to the dangers of his undertaking. Conditions in the South practically forced the step. It was of the utmost importance that he should have full and accurate information before his move, and a group of the coolest and bravest young men in his army were called on to go into Washington as scouts and spies and bring this report. Men who knew the city were needed.

Among the ten selected for the important mission was Ned Vaughan. He had been promoted for gallantry on the field at Malvern Hill, and wore the stripes of a lieutenant. He begged for the privilege of risking his life in this work and his Colonel could not deny him. He had proven on two occasions his skill on secret work as a scout before the second battle of Bull Run. His wide circle of friends in Washington and the utter change in his personal appearance by the growth of a beard made his chances of success the best of any man in the group.

He was anxious to render his country the greatest possible service in such a crisis, but there was another motive of resistless power. He was mad to see Betty Winter. He knew her too well to believe that if he took his life in his hand to look into her eyes she could betray him.

His disguise in the uniform of a Federal Captain was perfect, his forged pass beyond suspicion. He passed the lines of the Union army unchallenged and spent his first night in Washington in Joe Hall's famous gambling saloon on Pennsylvania Avenue. He arrived too late to make any attempt to see Betty. He stood for half an hour on the corner of the street, gazing with wistful eyes at the light in her window. He dared not call and involve her in the possibility of suspicion. He must wait with caution until she left the house and he could speak to her without being recognized. If he failed to get this chance he would write her as a last resort.

In Hall's place he found scores of Congressmen and men from every department of the Government service. Old Thaddeus Stevens, the leader of the war party in the House, was playing for heavy stakes, his sullen hard face set with grim determination.

He watched a young clerk from the War Department stake his last dollar, lose, and stagger from the table with a haunted, desperate look. Ned followed him into two saloons and saw the bartenders refuse him credit. He walked through the door of the last saloon, his legs trembling and his white lips twitching, stopped and leaned against the wall of the little bookstore on the corner, the flickering street lamp showing dimly his ghastly face and eyes.

Ned glanced uneasily behind him to see that he had not been followed. He had left under the impression that a secret service man had seen them both leave. He knew that Baker, the head of the Department, might know the name of every clerk who frequented a gambling den. No one was in sight and he debated for a moment the problem of offering this boy the bribe to get from Stanton's office the information he wanted.

It was a question of character and his judgment of it. Could he speak the word to this boy that might send one or both to the gallows? He was well born. His father was a man of sterling integrity and a firm supporter of the Union. The boy was twenty-two years old and had been a pet in the fast circle of society in which he had moved for the last three years. If his love for his country were the real thing, he would hand Ned over as a spy without a moment's hesitation. If the mania for gambling had done its work he would do anything for money.

Ned's own life was in the decision. He took another look into the haggard face and made up his mind.

He started on as if to pass him, stopped suddenly and extended his hand:

"Hello, Dick, what's up?"

The boy glowered at him and answered with a snarl:

"I don't know you----"

Ned drew a sigh of relief. One danger was passed. He couldn't recognize him. The rest should be easy.

"You don't need to, my boy," he whispered. "You're looking for a friend--money?"

"Yes. I'll sell my soul into hell for it right now," he gasped.

"You don't need to do that." Ned drew two hundred dollars in gold from his pocket and clinked the coin.

"You see that gold?"

"Yes, yes--what do you want for it?"

"I want you to get for me to-morrow morning the exact number of men in McClellan's army. I want the figures from Stanton's office--you understand. I want the name of each command, its numbers and its officers. I know already half of them. So you can't lie to me. Give me this information here to-morrow night and the gold is yours. Will you do it?"

The boy glanced at Ned for a moment:

"I'll see you in hell first. I've a notion to arrest you--damned if I don't----"

He wheeled and started toward the corner.

Ned's left hand gripped his with the snap of a steel trap, his right holding his revolver.

"Don't you be a fool. I know that you're ruined. I saw you in Joe Hall's----"

The boy's jaw dropped.

"You saw me?" he stammered.

"Yes. You're done for, and you know it. Bring me those figures and I'll double the pile--four hundred dollars."

The weak eyes shifted uneasily. He hesitated and faltered:

"All right. Meet me here at seven o'clock. For God's sake, don't speak to me if there's anyone in sight."

All next day Ned watched Betty's house in vain. At dark, in despair and desperation, he wrote a note.

"DEAR MISS BETTY:

"For one look into your dear eyes I am here. I've tried in vain to meet you. I can't leave without seeing you. I'll wait in the park at the foot of the avenue to-morrow night at dusk. Just one touch of your hand and five minutes near you is all I ask----"

There was no signature needed. She would know. He mailed it and hurried to his appointment.

The boy was prompt. There was no one in sight. Ned hurriedly examined the sheet of paper, verified the known commands and their numbers and, convinced of its genuineness, handed the money to the traitor.

"For God's sake, never speak to me again or recognize me in any way," he begged through chattering teeth. "I got those things from Stanton's desk and copied them."

Ned nodded, placed the precious document in his pocket, and watched the fool hurry with swift feet straight to Joe Hall's place and disappear within.

Betty failed to come at the appointed time and he was heartsick. He would finish his work in six hours to-morrow and he should not lose a moment in passing the Federal lines. The precious figures he had bought were memorized and the paper destroyed. In six hours next day he completed the drawings of the fort on which information had been asked and was ready to leave.

But he had not seen Betty. He tried to go and each effort only led him to the corner from which he watched her house. He lingered until night and waited an hour again in the dark. And still she had not come. And then it slowly dawned on him that she must have realized from the moment she read his message the peril of his position and the danger of his betrayal in their meeting.

He turned with quick, firm tread to pass the Federal lines without delay, and walked into the arms of two secret service men.

Without a word he was manacled and led to prison. The boy he had bribed had been under suspicion since his first visits to Joe Hall's. Stanton had discovered that his desk had been rummaged. Five of his nine Southern comrades had been arrested and he was the sixth. The rage of the Secretary of War had been boundless. He had thrown out a dragnet of detectives and every suspicious character in the city was passing through it or landing in prison.

The men stripped him and searched with the touch of experts every stitch of his clothing, ripped the lining of his coat, opened the soles of his shoes, split the heels and found nothing. He had been ordered to dress and given permission to go, when suddenly the officer conducting the search said:

"Wait!"

Ned stopped in the doorway. It was useless to protest.

"Excuse my persistence, my friend," he said apologetically. "You seem all right and my men have apparently made a mistake, all the same I'm going to examine your mouth----"

Ned's eyes suddenly flashed and his figure unconsciously stiffened.

"I thought so!" the officer laughed.

The door was closed and the guard stepped before it.

And then, with quick sure touch as if he saw the object of his search through the flesh, the detective lifted Ned Vaughan's upper lip and drew from between his lips and teeth the long, thin, delicately folded tinfoil within which lay the tissue drawing of the fort.

The drumhead court-martial which followed was brief and formal. The prisoner refused to give his name or any clue to his identity. He was condemned to be hanged as a spy at noon the next day and locked in a cell in the Old Capitol Prison.

On his way they passed Senator Winter's house. Six hours' delay just to look into her face had cost him his life, but his one hopeless regret now was that he had failed to see her.

Betty Winter read the account of the sensational arrest and death sentence. He had been arrested at the trysting place he had appointed. She dropped the paper with a cry and hurried to the White House. She thanked God for the loving heart that dwelt there.

Without a moment's hesitation the President ordered a suspension of sentence and directed that the papers be sent to him for review.

In vain Stanton raged. He shook his fist in the calm, rugged face at last:

"Dare to interfere with the final execution of this sentence and I shall resign in five minutes after you issue that pardon! I'll stand for some things--but not for this--I warn you!"

"I understand your position, Stanton," was the quiet answer. "And I'll let you know my decision when I've reached it."

With a muttered oath, the Secretary of War left the room.

Betty bent close to his desk and whispered:

"You'll give me three days to get his mother here?"

"Of course I will, child, six days if it's necessary. Get word to her. If I can't save him, she can say good-bye to her boy. That can't hurt anybody, can it?"

With a warm grasp of his hand Betty flew to the telegraph office and three days later she saw for the first time the broken-hearted mother. The resemblance was so startling between the mother and both sons she couldn't resist the impulse to throw her arms around her neck.

"I came alone, dear," the mother said brokenly, "because his father is so bitter. You see we're divided at home, too. I'm with John in his love for the Union--but his father is bitter against the war. It would do no good for him to come. He hates the President and says he's responsible for all the blood and suffering--and so I'm alone--but you'll help me?"

"Yes, I'll help and we'll fight to win."

The mother held her at arms' length a moment:

"How sweet and beautiful you are! How happy I am that you love my John! I'm proud of you. Is John here?"

Betty's face clouded:

"No. I telegraphed him to come. He answered that a great battle was about to be fought and that it was absolutely useless to ask for pardon----"

"But it isn't--is it, dear?"

"No, we'll fight. John doesn't know the President as I do. We'll never give up--you and I--Mother!"

Again they were in each other's arms in silence. The older woman held her close.

And then came the long, hard fight.

The President heard the mother's plea with tender patience and shook his head sorrowfully.

"I'm sorry, dear Madam," he said at last, "to find this case so dangerous and difficult. Our army is approaching a battle. Tremendous issues hang on the results. It looks now as if this battle may end the war. The enemy have as good right to send their brave scouts and spies among us to learn our secrets as we have to send ours to learn theirs. They kill our boys without mercy when captured. I have just asked Jefferson Davis to spare the life of one of the noblest and bravest men I have ever known. He was caught in Richmond on a daring errand for his country. They refused and executed him. How can I face my Secretary of War with such a pardon in my hands?"

The mother's head drooped lower with each sorrowful word and when the voice ceased she fell on her knees, with clasped hands and streaming eyes in a voiceless prayer whose dumb agony found the President's heart more swiftly and terribly than words.

"O my dear little mother, you mustn't do that!" he protested, seizing her hands and lifting her to her feet. "You mustn't kneel to me, I'm not God--I'm just a distracted man praying from hour to hour and day to day for wisdom to do what's right! I can't stand this--you mustn't do such things--they kill me!"

He threw his big hands into the air with a gesture of despair, his face corpse-like in its ashen agony. He took a step from her and leaned against the long table in the centre of the room for support.

Betty whispered something in the mother's ear and led her near again.

"If you'll just give my boy to me alive," she went on in low anguish, "I'll take him home and keep him there and I'll pledge my life that he will never again take up arms against the Union----"

"You can guarantee me that?" he interrupted, holding her gaze.

"I'm sure of it. He's noble, high-spirited, the soul of honor. He was always good and never gave me an hour's sorrow in his life until this war came----"

The long arm suddenly swung toward his Secretary:

"Have the prisoner, Ned Vaughan, brought here immediately. When he comes, Madam, I'll see what can be done."

With a sob of joy the mother leaned against Betty, who took her out into the air until the wagon from the jail should come.

They had led Ned quickly into the President's office before his mother and Betty knew of his arrival. His wrists were circled with handcuffs. The President looked over his spectacles at the irons and spoke sharply:

"Take those things off him----"

The guard hesitated, and the high pitched voice rang with angry authority:

"Take off those handcuffs, I tell you. His mother'll be here in a minute--take 'em off!"

The guard quickly removed the manacles and the President turned to him and his attendants:

"Clear out now. I'll call you when I want you."

Ned bowed:

"Thank you, sir."

"I hope I can do more than that for you, my boy. It all depends on you----"

The mother's cry of joy stopped him short as she walked into the door. With a bound she reached Ned's side, clasped him in her arms and kissed him again and again with the low caressing words that only a mother's lips can breathe. He loosened her hands tenderly:

"I'm glad you came, dear. It's all right. You mustn't worry. This is war, you know."

"But we're going to save you, my darling. The President's going to pardon you. I feel it--I know it. That's why he sent for you. God has heard my prayer."

"I'm afraid you don't understand these things, dear," Ned replied tenderly. "The President can't pardon me--no one understands that better than I do----"

"But he will, darling! He will----"

Ned soothed her and turned to Betty.

"Just a moment, Mother, I wish to speak to Miss Betty."

He took her hand and looked into her face with wistful intensity.

"One long look at the girl of my dreams and I'll wait for you on the other side! This is not the way I told you I would return, is it? But it's war. We must take it as it comes--good-bye--dearest----"

"O Ned, Boy, the President will pardon you if you'll be reasonable. You must, for her sake, if not because I ask it."

"It's sweet of you to try this, dearest, but of course, it's useless. The President must be just."

The tall figure rose and Ned turned to face his desk.

"Young man," he began gently, "you're a soldier of exceptional training and intelligence. You knew the danger and the importance of your mission. You have failed and your life is forfeited to the Nation, but for your mother's sake, because of her love and her anguish and her loyalty, I have decided to trust you and send you home on parole in her custody if you take the oath of allegiance----"

The mother gave a sob of joy.

"I thank you, Mr. President," was the firm reply, "for your generous offer for my mother's sake, but I cannot take your oath. I have sworn allegiance to another

Government in the righteousness and justice of whose cause I live and am ready to die----"

"Ned--Ned!" the mother moaned.

"I must, Mother, dear," he firmly went on. "Life is sweet when it's worth living. But man can not live by bread alone. They have only the power to kill my body. You ask me to murder my soul."

He paused and turned to the President, whose eyes were shining with admiration.

"I believe, sir, that I am right and you are wrong. This is war. We must fight it out. I'm a soldier and a soldier's business is to die."

The tall figure suddenly crossed the space that separated them and grasped his hand:

"You're a brave man, Ned Vaughan, the kind of man that saves this world from hell--the kind that makes this Nation great and worth saving whole! I wish I could keep you here--but I can't. You know that--good-bye----"

"Good-bye, sir," was the firm answer.

The mother began to sob piteously until Betty spoke something softly in her ear.

Ned turned, pressed her to his heart, and held her in silence. He took Betty's hand and bent to kiss it.

"You shall not die," she whispered tensely. "I'm going to save you."

She felt the answering pressure and knew that he understood.

Betty held the mother at the door a moment and spoke in low tones:

"I can get permission from the President to delay the execution until his sister may arrive and say good-bye to him in prison the night before the execution. Wait and I'll get it now."

The mother stood and gazed in a stupor of dull despair while Betty pressed to his desk and begged the last favor. It was granted without hesitation.

The President wrote the order delaying the death for three days and handed her his card on which was written:

"Admit the bearer, the sister of the prisoner, Ned Vaughan, the night before his execution to see him for five minutes.

"A. LINCOLN."

"I'm sorry, little girl, I couldn't do more for *your* sake--but you understand?"

Betty nodded, returned the pressure of his hand and hurriedly left the room.

The hanging was fixed for the following Friday at noon. The pass would admit his sister on Thursday night. Betty had three days in which to work. She drew every dollar of her money and went at her task swiftly, silently, surely, until she reached the guard inside the grim old prison, who held the keys to the death watch.

She couldn't trust the sister with her daring plan. She might lose her nerve. She must impersonate her. It was a dangerous piece of work, but it was not impossible. She had only to pass the inspectors. The guards inside were her friends.

On Thursday night at eight o'clock a carriage drew up at the little red brick house, on whose door flashed the brass plate sign:

ELIZABETH GARLAND, MODISTE

She had made an appointment with Mrs. Lincoln's dressmaker and arranged for it at this late hour. She must not be seen leaving her father's house to-night.

She drove rapidly to the Capitol, stopped her carriage at the north end, entered the building through the Senate wing, quickly passed out again, and in a few minutes had presented her pass to the commandant of the Old Capitol Prison.

The woman inspector made the most thorough search and finding nothing suspicious, allowed her to enter the dimly lighted corridor of the death watch.

The turnkey loudly announced:

"The sister of the prisoner, Ned Vaughan!"

She met him face to face in the large cell in which the condemned were allowed to pass their last night on earth. The keen eyes of a guard from the Inspector's office watched her every act and every movement of her body.

Ned stared at her. His heart beat with mad joy. She was going to play his sister's part! He would take her in his arms for the first time and feel the beat of her heart against his and their lips would meet. He laughed at death as he looked into her eyes with the hunger of eternity gleaming in his own.

There could be no hesitation on her part.

She threw both arms around his neck crying:

"Brave, foolish boy!"

He held her close, crushed her with one mad impulse, and slowly relaxed his arms. She would forgive him for this moment of delirium on the brink of the grave, but he must be reasonable.

"I am ready to die, now, dearest," he murmured.

She slowly lifted her lips to his in a long kiss--a kiss that thrilled body and soul--and pressed into his mouth a tiny piece of tissue paper.

She stood holding both his hands for a moment and hesitated, glancing at the guard from the corner of her eye. He was watching with steady stolid business-like stare. She must play her part to the end carefully and boldly.

"I've only this moment just to say good-bye, Boy," she faltered. "I promised not to stay long." Slowly her arms stole round his neck, and the blood rushed to his face in scarlet waves.

"Love has made death glorious, dearest," he breathed tenderly. "God bless you for coming, for all you have done for me, and for all this holy hour means to my soul--you understand."

The tears were streaming down her cheeks now. The plan might fail after all--the gallows was there in the jail yard lifting its stark arms in the lowering sky. She pressed his hands hysterically:

"Yes, yes, I understand."

She turned and hurried to the guard:

"Take me out quickly. I'm going to faint. I can't endure it."

The guard caught her arm, supporting her as she made her way to the street.

In fifteen minutes she had returned to the dressmaker's and from there called another carriage and went home.

The guard had no sooner turned his back than Ned Vaughan quickly opened and read the precious message which gave the plan of escape.

When the sentinel on his corridor was changed at midnight the blond, blue-eyed boy would be his friend and explain.

When he found the rope ladder concealed on the roof it was raining. He fastened it carefully in the shadow of an offset in the outer wall and waited for the appearance of the guard. As he passed the gas lamp post and the flickering light fell on his face he studied it with care. He was stupid and allowed the rain to dash straight into his fat face. It should be easy to reach the shadows by a quick leap when he turned against the rain and reached the length of his beat.

He calculated to a second the time required to make the descent, threw himself swiftly to the end of his rope and dropped to the pavement.

In his eagerness to strike the ground on the run, his foot slipped and he fell. The guard heard and ran back, blinking his stupid eyes through the rain. He found a young sport who had lost his way in the storm.

"I shay, partner," the fallen drunk blubbered. "What'ell's the matter here? Ain't this Joe Hall's place?"

"Not by a dam sight."

"Ah, g'long with yer, f-foolishness--man--and open the door--I'm an old customer--I ain't no secret service man--I'm all right--open her up----"

"Here, here, get up an' move on now, I can't fool with you," the guard growled good-naturedly. He lifted Ned to his feet and helped him to the end of his beat, waved him a jolly good-night, and turned to his steady tramp. The rope was still dangling next morning ten feet above his head.

The sensation that thrilled the War Department was one that made history for the Nation, as well as the individuals concerned, and for some unfortunately who were not concerned.

CHAPTER XX
THE INSULT

The day General Lee's army turned toward the north for the Maryland shore, the President, with the eagerness of a boy, hurried to McClellan's house to shake his hand, bid him God's speed and assure him of his earnest support and good wishes.

The absurdity of the ruler of a mighty Nation hurrying on foot to the house of one of his generals never occurred to his mind.

The autocratic power over the lives and future of millions to which he had been called had thrown no shadow of vanity or self pride over his simple life. Responsibility had only made clearer his judgment, strengthened his courage, broadened and deepened his love for his fellow man.

He wished to see his Commanding General and bid him God's speed. The General was busy and he wished to take up but a few minutes of his time. And so without a moment's hesitation he walked to his house accompanied only by Hay, his

The Southerner

Assistant Secretary.

On the way he was jubilant with hope:

"We've got them now, Boy--we've got them, and this war must speedily end! Lee will never get into Maryland with fifty thousand effective men. With the river hemming him in on the rear I'll have McClellan on him with a hundred thousand well shod, well fed, well armed and with the finest artillery that ever thundered into battle. We're bound to win."

"If McClellan can whip him, sir?"

"Yes, of course, he's got to do that," was the thoughtful answer. "And you know I believe he'll do it. McClellan's on his mettle now. His army will fight like tigers to show their faith in him. He's vain and ambitious, yes--many great men are. Ambition's a mighty human motive."

"I'm afraid it's bad diplomacy, sir, to go to his house like this--he is vain, you know," the younger man observed with a frown.

"Tut, tut, Boy, it's no time for ceremony. Who cares a copper!"

The clock in the church tower struck ten as Hay sprang up the steps and rang the bell.

"I hope he hasn't gone to bed," the Secretary said.

"At ten o'clock?" the President laughed, "a great general about to march on the most important campaign of his life--hardly."

The straight orderly saluted and ushered them into the elegant reception room--the room so often graced by the Prince de Joinville and the Comte de Paris, of the General's staff.

The orderly sniffed the air in a superior butler style:

"The General has not come in yet, gentlemen."

"We'll wait," was the President's quick response.

They sat in silence and the minutes dragged.

The young Secretary, in rising wrath, looked again and again at the clock.

"Don't be so impatient, John," the quiet, even voice said. "Great bodies move slowly, they say--come here and sit down--I'll tell you a secret. The Cabinet knows it--and you can, too."

He leaned his giant figure forward in his chair and touched an official document which he had drawn from his pocket.

"Great events hang on this battle. I've written out here a challenge to mortal combat for all our foes, North, South, East and West. I'm going to free the slaves if we win this battle and we're sure to win it----"

Hay glanced at the door with a startled look.

"McClellan and I don't agree on this subject and he mightn't fight as well if he knew it. It's a thing of doubtful wisdom at its best to hurl this challenge into the face of my foe. But the time has come and it must be done. We have made no headway in this war, and we must crush the South to end it. If the Copperhead leaders should get control of the Democratic party because of it--well, it means trouble at home. Douglas is dead and the jackal is trying to wear the lion's skin. He may succeed, but then I must risk it. I'll lose some good soldiers from the army but I've got to do it. All I'm waiting for now is a victory on which to launch my thunderbolt----"

A key clicked in the front door and the quick, firm step of McClellan echoed through the hall.

The orderly was reporting his distinguished visitor. They could hear his low words, and the sharp answer.

The General mounted the stairs and entered the front room overhead. He was there, of course, to arrange his toilet. He was a stickler for handsome clothes, spotless linen and the last detail of ceremony.

Again the minutes dragged. The tick of the clock on the mantel rang through the silent room and the face of the younger man grew red with rage.

Unable to endure the insolence of a subordinate toward the great Chieftain, whom he loved with a boy's blind devotion, Hay sprang to his feet:

"Let's go, sir!"

The big hand was quietly raised in a gesture of command and he sank into his seat.

Five minutes more passed and the sound of approaching footsteps were heard quickly, firmly pressed with military precision.

The President nodded:

"You see, my son!"

But instead of the General the handsome figure of his aide, John Vaughan, appeared in the doorway:

"The General begs me to say, Mr. President, that he is too much fatigued to see any one this evening and has retired for the night."

The orderly stepped pompously to the door to usher them out and John Vaughan bowed and returned to his commander.

Hay sprang to his feet livid with rage and spoke to his Chief with boyish indignation.

"You are not going to take this insult from him?"

The tall figure slowly rose and stood in silence.

"Remove him from his command," the younger man pleaded. "For God's sake do it now. Write the order for his removal this minute--give it to me! I'll kick his door open and hand it to him."

The deep set dreamy eyes were turned within as he said in slow intense tones:
"No--I'll hold McClellan's horse for him if he'll give us one victory!"

CHAPTER XXI
THE BLOODIEST DAY

The struggle opened with disaster for the Union army. Though Lee's plan of campaign fell by accident into McClellan's hands, it was too late to frustrate the first master stroke. Relying on Jackson's swift, bewildering marches, Lee, in hostile territory and confronted by twice his numbers, suddenly divided his army and hurled Jackson's corps against Harper's Ferry. The garrison, after a futile struggle of two days, surrendered twelve thousand five hundred and twenty men and their vast stores of war material.

The contrast between General White, the Federal officer in command who surrendered, and Jackson, his conqueror, was strikingly dramatic. The Union General rode a magnificent black horse, was carefully dressed in shining immaculate uniform--gloves, boots and sword spotless. The Confederate General sat carelessly on his little shaggy sorrel, dusty, travel-stained and carelessly dressed.

The curiosity of the Union army which had surrendered was keen to see the famous fighter. The entire twelve thousand prisoners of war lined the road as Jackson silently rode by.

A voice from the crowd expressed the universal feeling as they gazed:

"Boys, he ain't much for looks, but, by God, if we'd had him we wouldn't have been caught in this trap!"

The first shock of Lee's and McClellan's armies was at South Mountain, where the desperate effort was made to break through and save Harper's Ferry. The attempt failed, though the Union forces won the fight. Lee lost twenty-seven hundred men, killed and wounded and prisoners, and the Federal general, twenty-one hundred.

Lee withdrew to Sharpsburg on the banks of the Antietam to meet Jackson's victorious division sweeping toward him from Harper's Ferry.

On the first day the Confederate commander made a display of force only, awaiting the alignment of Jackson's troops. His men were so poorly shod and clothed they could not be brought into line of battle. When the fateful day of September 17th, 1862, dawned, still and clear and beautiful over the hills of Maryland, more than twenty thousand of Lee's men had fallen by the roadside barefooted and exhausted. When the first roar of McClellan's artillery opened fire in the grey dawn, they hurled their shells against less than thirty-seven thousand men in the Confederate lines. The Union commander had massed eighty-seven thousand tried veterans behind his guns.

The President received the first news of the battle with a thrill of exultation. That Lee's ragged, footsore army hemmed in thus with Antietam Creek on one side and the broad, sweeping Potomac on the other would be crushed and destroyed he could not doubt for a moment.

As the sun rose above the eastern hills a gleaming dull-red ball of blood, the Federal infantry under Hooker swept into action and drove the Confederates from the open field into a dense woods, where they rallied, stood and mowed his men down with deadly aim. Hooker called for aid and General Mansfield rushed his corps into action, falling dead at the head of his men as they deployed in line of battle.

For two hours the sullen conflict raged, blue and grey lines surging in death-locked embrace until the field was strewn with the dead, the dying and the wounded.

Hooker was wounded. Sedgwick's corps swept into the field under a sharp artillery fire and reached the shelter of the woods only to find themselves caught in a trap between two Confederate brigades massed at this point. In the slaughter which followed Sedgwick was wounded and his command was saved from annihilation with the loss of two thousand men.

While this desperate struggle raged in the Union right, the centre was the scene of a still bloodier one. French and Richardson charged the Confederate position with reckless valor. A sunken road lay across the field over which they rushed. For four terrible hours the men in grey held this sunken road until it was piled with their bodies, and when the last charge of the resistless blue lines took it, they found but three hundred living men who had been holding it against the assaults of five thousand--and "Bloody Lane" became immortal in American history.

It was now one o'clock and the men had fought almost continuously since the sun rose. The infantry fire slowly slackened and ceased in the Union right and centre.

Burnside, who held the Union left, was ordered to advance by the capture of the stone bridge over the Antietam. But a single brigade under General Toombs guarding this bridge held an army at bay and it was one o'clock before the bridge was captured.

Burnside now pushed his division up the heights against Sharpsburg to cut Lee's line of retreat. The Confederates held their ground with desperate courage, though outnumbered here three to one. At last the grey lines melted and the men in blue swept triumphantly through the village and on its edge suddenly ran into a line of men clad in their own blue uniform.

They paused in wonder. How had their own men gotten in such a position? They were not left long in doubt. The blue line suddenly blazed with long red waves of flame squarely in their faces. It was Hill's division of Jackson's corps from Harper's Ferry. The ragged men had dressed themselves in good blue suits from the captured Federal storehouse. The shock threw the Union men into confusion and a desperate charge of the strange blue Confederates drove them back through the village, and night fell with its streets still held by Lee's army.

For fourteen hours five hundred pieces of artillery and more than one hundred thousand muskets had thundered and hissed their cries of death. On the hills and valleys lay more than twenty thousand men killed and wounded.

Lee's little army of thirty-seven thousand had been cut to pieces, having lost fourteen thousand. He had but twenty-three thousand left. McClellan had lost twelve thousand, but had seventy-five thousand left. And yet so desperate had been the deadly courage with which the grey tattered army had fought that McClellan lay on his arms for three days.

The day's work had been a drawn battle, but the President's heart was broken as he watched in anguish the withdrawal of Lee's army in safety across the river. It was the last straw. McClellan had been weighed and found wanting. He registered a solemn promise with God that if the great Confederate Commanders succeeded in making good their retreat from this desperate situation he would remove McClellan.

The Confederates withdrew, rallied their shattered forces safely in Virginia, and Jeb Stuart once more rode around the Northern army!

The President issued his Emancipation Proclamation, challenging the South to war to the death, and flung down the gauntlet to his rival, the coming leader of Northern Democracy, George Brinton McClellan, by removing him from command.

CHAPTER XXII
BENEATH THE SKIN

John Vaughan saw the blow fall on McClellan's magnificent headquarters in deep amazement. The idol of the army was ordered to turn over his command to General Burnside and the impossible had happened.

Instead of the brilliant *coup d'etat* which he and the entire staff had predicted, the fallen leader obeyed and took an affectionate leave of his men.

McClellan knew, what his staff could not understand, that for the moment the President was master of the situation. He still held the unbounded confidence of his officers, but the rank and file of his soldiers had become his wondering critics. They believed they had crushed Lee's army at Antietam and yet they lay idle until the skillful Southern Commander had crossed the Potomac, made good his retreat, and once more insulted them by riding around their entire lines. The volunteer American soldier was a good fighter and a good critic of the men who led him. He had his own ideas about how an army should be fought and maneuvered. As the idol of fighting men, McClellan had ceased to threaten the supremacy of the civil law. There was no attempt at the long looked for *coup d'etat*. It was too late. No one knew this more clearly than McClellan himself.

But his fall was the bitterness of death to the staff who adored him and the generals who believed in him. Burnside, knowing the condition of practical anarchy he must face, declined the command. The President forced him to accept. He took it reluctantly with grim forebodings of failure.

John received his long leave of absence from his Chief and left for Washington the night before the formal farewell. His rage against the bungler who ruled the Nation with autocratic power was fierce and implacable.

His resentment against the woman he loved was scarcely less bitter. It was her triumph, too. She believed in the divine inspiration of the man who sat in the chair of Washington and Jefferson. Great God, could madness reach sublimer folly! She had written him a letter of good wishes and all but asked for a reconciliation before the battle. Love had fought with pride through a night and pride had won. He hadn't answered the letter.

He avoided his newspaper friends and plunged into a round of dissipation. Beneath the grim tragedy of blood in Washington flowed the ever widening and deepening torrent of sensual revelry--of wine and women, song and dance, gambling and intrigue.

The flash of something cruel in his eye which Betty Winter had seen and feared from the first burned now with a steady blaze. For six days and nights he played in Joe Hall's place a desperate game, drinking, drinking always, and winning. Hour after hour he sat at the roulette table, his chin sunk on his breast, his reddened eyes gleaming beneath his heavy black brows, silent, surly, unapproachable.

A reporter from the *Republican* recognized him and extended his hand:
"Hello, Vaughan!"

John stared at him coldly and resumed his play without a word. At the end of six days he had won more than two thousand dollars from the house, put it in his pocket, and, deaf to the blandishments of smooth, gentlemanly proprietor, pushed his way out into the Avenue.

It was but four o'clock in the afternoon and he was only half drunk. He wandered aimlessly down the street and crossed in the direction of hell's half-acre below the Baltimore depot. His uniform was wrinkled, his boots had not been blacked for a week, his linen was dirty, his hair rumpled, his handsome black moustache stained with drink, but he was hilariously conscious that he had two thousand dollars of Joe Hall's ill-gotten money in his pocket. There was a devil-may-care swing to his walk and a look in his eye that no decent woman would care to see twice.

He ran squarely into Betty Winter in the crowd emerging from the depot. The little bag she was carrying fell from her hands, with a cry of startled anguish:

"John--my God!"

He made no effort to pick up the fallen bag or in any way return the greeting. He merely paused and stared--deliberately stood and stared as if stupefied by the apparition. In fact, he was so startled by her sudden appearance that for a moment he felt the terror of a drunkard's first hallucination. The thought was momentary. He knew better. He was not drunk. The girl was there all right--the real thing--living, beautiful flesh and blood. For one second's anguish the love of her strangled him. The desire to take her in his arms was all but resistless in its fierce madness. He bit his lips and scowled in her face.

"John--John--dearest," she gasped.

The scowl darkened and he spoke with insulting deliberation: "You have made a mistake. I haven't the honor of your acquaintance."

Before Betty could recover from the horror of his answer he had brushed rudely past her and disappeared in the crowd. She picked up her bag in a stupor of dumb rage and started home. She was too weak for the walk she had hoped to take. She called a hack and scarcely had the strength to climb into the high, old-fashioned seat.

Never in all her life had blind anger so possessed her soul and body. In a moment of tenderness she had offered to forgive and forget. It was all over now. The brute was not worth a tear of regret. She would show him!

Two weeks later John Vaughan stared into the ebony face of a negro who had attached himself to his fortune somewhere in the revelry of the night before. Washington was swarming with these foolish black children who had come in thousands. They had no money and it had not occurred to them that they would need any. Their food and clothes had always been provided and they took no thought for the morrow.

John had forgotten the fact that he had taken the negro in his hack for two hours and finally adopted him as his own.

He sat up, pressed his hand over his aching head and stared into the grinning face:

"And what are you doing here, you imp of the devil?"

Julius laughed and rolled his eyes:

"I'se yo' man. Don't you min' takin' me up in de hack wid you las' night?"

"What's your name?"

"Julius Caesar, sah."

"Then it's all right! You're the man I'm looking for. You're the man this country's looking for. You're a born fighter----"

"Na, sah, I'se er cook!"

"Sh! Say not so--we're going back to war!"

"All right, sah, I'se gwine wid you."

"I warn you, Julius Caesar, don't do it unless you're in for a fight! I'm going back to fight--to fight to kill. No more red tape and gold braid for me. I'm going now into the jaws of hell. I'm going into the ranks as a private."

"Don't make no difference ter me, sah, whar yer go. I'se gwine wid yer. I kin look atter yer shoes an' cook yer sumfin' good ter eat."

"I warn you, Julius! When they find your torn and mangled body on the field of Death, don't you sit up and blame me!"

"Don't yer worry, sah. Dey ain't gwine fin' me dar, an' ef dey do, dey ain't gwine ter be nuttin' tore er mangled 'bout me, I see ter dat, sah!"

Three weeks later Burnside's army received a stalwart recruit. Few questions were asked. The ranks were melting.

CHAPTER XXIII
THE USURPER

The answer which the country gave the President's Proclamation of Emancipation was a startling one, even to the patient, careful far-seeing man of the people in the White House. For months he had carried the immortal document in his pocket without even allowing his Cabinet to know it had been written. He had patiently borne the abuse of his party leaders and the fierce assaults of Horace Greeley until he believed the time had come that he must strike this blow--a blow which would rouse the South to desperation and unite his enemies in the North. He had finally issued it with grave fears.

The results were graver than he could foresee. More than once he was compelled to face the issue of its repeal as the only way to forestall a counter revolution in the North.

Desertions from the army became appalling--the number reached frequently as high as two hundred a day and the aggregate over eight thousand a month. His Proclamation had provided for the enlistment of negroes as soldiers. Not only did thousands of men refuse to continue to fight when the issue of Slavery was injected, but other thousands felt that the uniform of the Republic had been dishonored by placing it on the backs of slaves. They refused to wear it longer, and deserted at the risk of their lives.

The Proclamation had united the South and hopelessly divided the North. How serious this Northern division was destined to become was the problem now of a concern as deep as the size and efficiency of General Lee's army.

The election of the new Congress would put his administration to a supreme fight for existence. If the Democratic Party under its new leader, Clay Van Alen of Ohio, should win it meant a hostile majority in power whose edict could end the war and divide the Union. They had already selected in secret George B. McClellan for their coming standard bearer.

For the first time the question of Union or Disunion was squarely up to the North in an election. And it came at an unlucky moment for the President. The army in the West had ceased to win victories. The Southern army under Lee was still defending Richmond as strongly as ever.

There was no evading the issue at the polls. The Proclamation had committed the President to the bold, far-reaching radical and aggressive policy of the utter destruction of Slavery. The people were asked to choose between Slavery on the one hand and nationality on the other. The two together they could not again have.

The President had staked his life on his faith that the people could be trusted on a square issue of right and wrong.

This time he had underestimated the force of blind passions which the hell of war had raised.

Maine voted first and cut down her majority for the administration from nineteen thousand to a bare four thousand. The fact was ominous.

Ohio spoke next and Van Alen's ticket against the administration swept the State, returning fourteen Democrats and only five Republicans to Congress.

Indiana, the State in which the President's mother slept, spoke in thunder tones against him, sending eight Democrats and three Republicans. Even the rockribbed Republican stronghold of Pennsylvania was carried by the opposition by a majority of four thousand, reversing Lincoln's former majority of sixty thousand.

In New York the brilliant Democratic leader, Horatio Seymour, was elected Governor on a platform hostile to the administration by more than ten thousand majority. New Jersey turned against him, Michigan reduced his majority from twenty to six thousand. Wisconsin evenly divided its delegates to Congress.

Illinois, the President's own State, gave the most crushing blow of all. His big majority there was completely reversed and the Democrats carried the State by over seventeen thousand and the Congressional delegates stood eleven to three against him.

And then his Border State Policy, against which the leaders of his party had raged in vain was vindicated in the most startling way. True to his steadfast purpose to hold these States in the Union at all hazards, he had not included them in his Emancipation Proclamation.

One of the reasons for which they had refused his offer of United States bonds in payment for their slaves was they did not believe them worth the paper they were written on. A war costing two million dollars a day was sure to bankrupt the Nation before the end could be seen.

And yet because he had treated them with patience and fairness, with justice and with generosity, the Border States and the new State of West Virginia born of this policy, voted to sustain the President, saved his administration from ruin and gave him another chance to fight for the life of the Union.

It was a close shave. His working majority in Congress was reduced to a narrow margin, the opposition was large, united and fierce in its aggression, but he had been saved from annihilation.

The temper of the men elected to the Legislatures, both State and National, in the great Northern States was astounding.

So serious was the situation in Indiana that Governor Morton hastened to Washington to lay the crisis before the President.

"I'm sorry to have to tell you," the Governor began, "but we must face it. The Democratic politicians of Ohio, Indiana, and Illinois now called to power assume that the rebellion will not be crushed----"

"And therefore?"

"That their interests are antagonistic to New England and in harmony with the South. Another three months like the last six and we are lost, sir--hopelessly lost!"

"Is it as bad as that Governor?" the sad even voice asked.

A smile flickered across the stern, fine face of the war Governor:

"If you think me a pessimist remember that Van Alen their leader, has just presided over a Democratic jubilee meeting in Ohio which was swept again and again by cheers for Jefferson Davis--curses and jeers for the Abolitionists. His speech has been put in the form of a leaflet which is being mailed in thousands to our soldiers at the front----"

"You know that to be a fact?" the President asked sharply.

"The fact is notorious, sir. It will be disputed by no one. The outlook is black. Meeting after meeting is being held in Indiana demanding peace at any price, with the recognition of the Southern Confederacy--and, mark you, what is still more significant the formation of a Northwestern Confederacy with its possible Capital at your home town of Springfield, Illinois----"

"No, no!" the President groaned.

"Your last call for three hundred thousand volunteers," the Governor went on, "as you well know was an utter failure. Only eighty-six thousand men have been raised under it. I was compelled to use a draft to secure the number I did in Indiana. It is useless to call for more volunteers anywhere----"

"Then we'll have to use the draft," was the firm response.

"If we can enforce it!" the Governor warned. "A meeting has just been held in my State in which resolutions were unanimously passed demanding that the war cease, denouncing the attempt to use the power to draft men, declaring that our volunteers had been induced to enter the army under the false declaration that war was waged solely to maintain the Constitution and to restore the Union----"

"And so it is!" the President interrupted.

"Until you issued your Proclamation, freeing the slaves----"

"But only as a war measure to weaken the South, give us the victory and restore the Constitution!"

"They refuse to hear your interpretation; they make their own. Van Alen boldly declares that ninety-nine men out of every hundred whom he represents in Congress breathe no other prayer than to have an end of this hellish war. When news of victory comes, there is no rejoicing. When news of our defeat comes there is no sorrow----"

"Is that statement really true?" the sorrowful lips asked.

"Of the majority who elected him, yes. In the Northwest, distrust and despair are strangling the hearts of the people. More and more we hear the traitorous talk of arraying ourselves against New England and forming a Confederacy of our own. More than two thousand six hundred deserters have been arrested within a few weeks in Indiana. It generally requires an armed detail. Most of the deserters, true to the oath of the order of the Knights of the Golden Circle, desert with their arms----"

"Is it possible?"

"And in one case seventeen of these fortified themselves in a log cabin with outside paling and ditch for protection, and were maintained by their neighbors. Two hundred armed men in Rush County resisted the arrest of deserters. I was compelled to send infantry by special train to take their ringleaders. Southern Indiana is ripe for Revolution.

"I have positive information that the incoming Democratic Legislature of my State is in quick touch with the ones gathering in Illinois and Ohio. In Illinois, your own State, they have already drafted the resolutions demanding an armistice and a convention of all the States to agree to an adjustment of the war. It is certain to pass the Illinois House.

"My own Legislature has put this resolution into a more daring and dangerous form. They propose boldly and at once to acknowledge the Southern Confederacy and demand that the Northwest dissolve all further relations with New England.

When they have passed this measure in Indiana, they expect Ohio and Illinois to follow suit.

"Their secret order which covers my State with a network of lodges, whose purpose is the withdrawal of the Northwestern States from the Union, has obtained a foothold in the army camps inside the city of Washington itself----"

The President rose with quick, nervous energy and paced the floor. He stopped suddenly in front of Morton, his deep set eyes burning a steady flame:

"And what do you propose?"

"I haven't decided yet. I have the best of reasons to believe that the first thing my Legislature will do when it convenes is to pass a resolution refusing to receive any message from me as Governor of the State!"

"Will they dare?"

"I'm sure of it. It will be composed of men sworn to oppose to the bitter end any prosecution of this war. They intend to recognize the Southern Confederacy, and dissolve their own Federal relation with the United States. It may be necessary, sir----" he paused and fixed the President with compelling eyes, "---it may be necessary to suspend the civil government in the North in order to save the Union!"

The President lifted his big hand in a gesture of despair:

"God save us from that!"

"I came here to tell you just this," the Governor gravely concluded. "If the crisis comes and I must use force I expect you to back me----"

Two big rugged hands grasped the one outstretched:

"God bless you, Governor Morton,--we've got to save the Union, and we're going to do it! Since the day I came into this office I have fought to uphold the supremacy of the civil law. My enemies may force me to use despotic powers to crush it for larger ends!----But I hope not. I hope not. God knows I have no vain ambitions. I have no desire to use such power----"

The Governor left him gazing dreamily over the river toward Virginia a great new sorrow clouding his soul.

CHAPTER XXIV
THE CONSPIRACY

Lord Lyons, the British Minister, was using smooth words to the Secretary of State. Mr. Seward, our wily snuff dipper, was fully his equal in expressions of polite friendship. What he meant to say, of course, was that he could plunge a poisoned dagger into the British Lion with the utmost pleasure. What he said was:

"I am pleased to hear from your lordship the expressions of good will from her Gracious Majesty's Government."

"I am sorry to say, however," the Minister hastened to add, "that the Proclamation of Emancipation was not received by the best people of England as favorably as we had hoped."

"And why not?" Seward politely asked.

"Seeing that it could have no effect in really freeing the slaves until the South is conquered it appeared to be merely an attempt to excite a servile insurrection."

The Secretary lifted his eyebrows, took another dip of snuff, and softly inquired:

"And may I ask of your lordship whether this would not have been even more true in the earlier days of the war than now?"

"Undoubtedly."

"And yet I understand that her Gracious Majesty's Government was cold toward us because we had failed to take such high moral grounds at once in the beginning of the war?"

His lordship lifted his hands in polite admission of the facts.

"The trouble you see is," he went on softly, "Europe begins to feel that the division of sentiment in the North will prove a fatal weakness to the administration in so grave a crisis. Unfortunately, from our point of view, of course, your Government is a democracy, the sport of every whim of the demagogue of the hour----"

Seward lifted his eyes with a quick look at his lordship and smiled:

"Allow me to reassure her Gracious Majesty's Government on that point immediately. The administration will find means of preserving the sovereign power the people have entrusted to it. For example, my lord, I can touch the little bell on my right hand and order the arrest without warrant of a citizen of Ohio. I can touch the little bell on my left hand and order the imprisonment of a citizen of New York; and no power on earth except that of the President, can release them. Can the Queen of Great Britain do as much?"

His lordship left apparently reassured.

The tinkle of the little bell on the desk of the Secretary of State which had begun to fill the jails of the North with her leading Democratic citizens did not have the same soothing effect on American lawmakers, however. These arrests were made without warrant and the victim held without charges, the right to bail or trial.

The President had dared to suspend the great ***writ of habeas corpus*** which guaranteed to every freeman the right to meet his accuser in open court and answer the charge against him.

The attitude of the bold aggressive opposition was voiced on the floor of the House of Representatives in Washington in no uncertain language by Daniel Voorhees of Indiana, in a speech whose passionate eloquence was only equalled by its reckless daring.

"The present Executive of the Government," he declared, "has usurped the powers of Law and Justice to an extent subversive of republican institutions, and not to be borne by any free people. He has given access to the vaults of prisons but not to the bar of justice. It is a part of the nature of frail men to sin against laws, both human and divine; but God Himself guarantees him a fair trial before punishment. Tyrants alone repudiate the justice of the Almighty. To deny an accused man the right to be heard in his own defense is an echo from the dark ages of brutal despotism. We have in this the most atrocious tyranny that ever feasted on the groans of a captive or banqueted on the tears of the widow and the orphan.

"And yet on this spectacle of shame and horror American citizens now gaze. The great bulwark of human liberty which generations in bloody toil have built against the wicked exercise of unlawful power has been torn away by a parricidal hand. Every man to-day from the proudest in his mansion to the humblest in his cabin--all stand at the mercy of one man, and the fawning minions who crouch before him for pay.

"We hear on every side the old cry of the courtier and the parasite. At every new aggression, at every additional outrage, new advocates rise to defend the source of patronage, wealth and fame--the department of the Executive! Such assistance has always waited on the malignant efforts of tyranny. Nero had his poet laureate, and Seneca wrote a defense even for the murder of his mother. And this dark hour affords us ample evidence that human nature is the same to-day as two thousand years ago."

Such speeches could not be sent broadcast free of charge through the mails without its effect on the minds of thousands. The great political party in opposition to the administration was now arrayed in solid phalanx against the war itself on whose prosecution the existence of the Nation depended.

Again the Radical wing of his party demanded of the President the impossible.

The Abolitionists had given a tardy and lukewarm support in return for the issue of the Proclamation of Emancipation. Their support lasted but a few days. Through their spokesman, Senator Winter, they demanded now the whole loaf. They had received but half of their real program. They asked for a policy of reconstruction in the parts of Louisiana and Tennessee held by the Union army in accordance with their ideas. They demanded the ballot for every slave, the confiscation of the property of the white people of the South and its bestowment upon negroes and camp-followers as fast as the Union army should penetrate into the States in rebellion.

Senator Winter's argument was based on sound reasoning theoretically whatever might be said of its wisdom as a National policy.

"Your Emancipation Proclamation," he declared to the President, "provides for the arming and drilling of negro soldiers to fight for the Republic. If they are good enough to fight they are good enough to vote. The ballot is only another form of the bayonet which we use in time of peace----"

"Correct, Senator," was the calm reply, "if we are to allow the negro race to remain in America in physical contact with ours. But we are not going to do this. No greater calamity could befall our people. Colonization and separation must go hand in hand with the emancipation of these children of Africa. I incorporated this principle in my act of emancipation. I have set my life on the issue of its success. As a matter of theory and abstract right we may grant the suffrage to a few of the more intelligent negroes and the black soldiers we may enroll until they can be removed----"

"Again we deal with a Southerner, Mr. President!" the Senator sneered.

"So be it," was the quiet answer. "I have never held any other views. They were well known before the war. But two years before my election I said in my debate with Douglas:

"'I am not, nor ever have been, in favor of bringing about in any way, the social and political equality of the white and black races. I am not, nor ever have been, in favor of making voters or jurors of negroes, nor of qualifying them to hold office, nor to inter-marry with white people. I will say in addition to this that there is a physical difference between the white and black races which, I believe, will forever forbid the two living together on terms of social and political equality.'"

"Yet," the Senator sneered, "you can change your mind. You said in your Inaugural that you had no intention or right to interfere with the institution of Slavery. You did so just the same."

"As an act of war to save the Union only. But mark you, I have always hated Slavery from principle for the white man's sake as well as the negro's. I am equally determined **on principle** that the negro race after it is free shall never be absorbed into our social or political life!"

"You'll change your principles or retire to private life!" the old man snapped.

"When I have saved the Union we shall see. Time will indicate the wisdom of my position. I have no longer any ambition except to give the best that's in me to my people."

The breach between the President and the most powerful leaders of his own party was now complete. It was a difference that was fundamental and irreconcilable. They asked him to extend the autocratic power he wielded to preserve the Union in a time of war to a program of revenge and proscription against the South as it should fall before the advancing army. His answer was simple:

"Secession was void from the beginning. The South shall not be laid waste as conquered territory when the Union is restored. They shall return as our brethren to live with us in peace and good will with the curse of Slavery lifted from them and their children. Nor will I permit the absorption of this black blood into our racial stock to degrade our National character. When free, the negro must return to his own."

With fierce, sullen determination the Radical wing of his party organized a secret powerful conspiracy to drive Abraham Lincoln from public life.

Behind this first line of attack stood the Democratic party with its millions of loyal voters now united under George B. McClellan. The Radicals and the Democrats hated each other with a passion second only to their hatred of the President. They agreed to remove him first and then settle their own differences.

CHAPTER XXV
THE TUG OF WAR

Betty Winter, having made up her mind to put John Vaughan out of her life for all time, volunteered for field service as a nurse and by permission of the President joined Burnside's army before Fredericksburg.

The General had brought its effective fighting force to a hundred and thirteen thousand. Lee's army confronted him on the other side of the Rappahannock with seventy-five thousand men. A great battle was impending.

Burnside had reluctantly assumed command. He was a gallant, genial, cultured soldier, a gentleman of the highest type, a pure, unselfish patriot with not a trace of vulgar ambition or self-seeking. He saw the President hounded and badgered by his own party, assaulted and denounced in the bitterest terms by the opposition, and he knew that the remedy could be found only in a fighting, victorious army. A single decisive victory would turn the tide of public opinion, unite the faction-ridden army and thrill the Nation with enthusiasm.

He determined to fight at once and risk his fate as a commander on the issue of victory or defeat. His council of war had voted against an attack on Lee's army in Fredericksburg. Burnside brushed their decision aside as part of the quarrel McClellan has left. Even the men in the ranks were fighting each other daily in these miserable bickerings and intrigues. A victory was the remedy for their troubles, and he made up his mind to fight for it.

The General received Betty with the greatest courtesy:

"You're more than welcome at this moment, Miss Winter. The surgeons won't let you in some of their field hospitals. But there's work to be done preparing our corps for the battle we're going to fight. You'll have plenty to do."

"Thank you, General," she gravely answered.

Burnside read for the second time the gracious letter from the President which Betty presented.

"You're evidently pretty strong with this administration, Miss Betty," he remarked.

"Yes. The patience and wisdom of the President is a hobby of mine."

"Then I'll ask you to review the army with me. You can report to him."

Within an hour they were passing in serried lines before the Commander. Betty watched them march with a thrill of patriotic pride, a hundred and thirteen thousand men, their dark blue uniforms pouring past like the waters of a mighty river, the December sun gleaming on their polished bayonets as on so many icicles flashing on its surface.

Her heart suddenly stood still. There before her marched John Vaughan in the outer line of a regiment, his eyes straight in front, looking neither to the right nor the left. He was a private in the ranks, clean and sober, his face rugged, strong and sun-tanned.

For a moment there was a battle inside that tested her strength. He had not seen her and was oblivious of her existence apparently. But she had noted the regiment under whose flag he marched. It would be easy to find him if she wished.

When the first moment of love-sickness and utter longing passed, she had no desire to see him. The dead could bury its dead. Her love was a thing of the past. The cruel thing in this man's nature she had seen the first day was there still. She saw it with a shudder in his red, half-drunken eyes the day they met in Washington, saw it so plainly, so glaringly, the memory of it could never fade. He was sober and in his right mind now, his cheeks bronzed with the new life of sunshine and open air the army had given. The thing was still there. It spoke in the brute strength of his powerful body as his marching feet struck the ground, in the iron look about his broad shoulders, the careless strength with which he carried his musket as if it were a feather, and above all in the hard cold glint from his shining eyes set straight in front.

She lay awake for hours on the little white cot at the headquarters of the ambulance corps reviewing her life and dropped to sleep at last with a deep sense of gratitude to God that she was free, and could give herself in unselfish devotion to her country. Her last waking thoughts were of Ned Vaughan and the sweet, foolish worship he had laid at her feet. She wondered vaguely if he were in those grey lines beyond the river. Ned Vaughan was there this time--back with his regiment.

Lee, Jackson and Longstreet had known for days that a battle was imminent. Their scouts from over the river had brought positive information. The Confederate leaders had already planned the conflict. Their battle lines circled the hills beyond Fredericksburg, spread out in a crescent, five miles long. Nature had piled these five miles of hills around Fredericksburg as if to build an impregnable fortress. On every crest, concealed behind trees and bushes, the Confederate artillery was in place-- its guns trained to sweep the wide plain with a double cross fire, besides sending a storm of shot and shell straight from the centre. Sixty thousand matchless grey infantry crouched among those bushes and lay beside stone walls, in sunken roadways or newly turned trenches.

The great fan-shaped death-trap had been carefully planned and set by a master mind. Only a handful of sharpshooters and a few pieces of artillery had been left in Fredericksburg to dispute the passage of the river and deceive Burnside with a pretense of defending the town.

The Confederate soldier was ragged and his shoes were tied together with strings. His uniform consisted of an old hat or cap usually without a brim, a shirt of striped bed-ticking so brown it seemed woven of the grass. The buttons were of discolored cow's horn. His coat was the color of Virginia dust and mud, and it was out at the elbow. His socks were home-made, knit by loving hands swift and tender in their endless work of love. The socks were the best things he had.

The one spotless thing about him was his musket and the bayonet he carried at his side. His spirits were high.

A barefooted soldier had managed to get home and secure a pair of boots. He started back to his regiment hurrying to be on time for the fight. The new boots hurt him so terribly he couldn't wear them. He passed Ned's regiment with his precious footgear hanging on his arm.

"Hello, Sonny, what command?" Ned cried.

"Company E, 12th Virginia, Mahone's brigade!" he proudly answered.

"Yes, damn you," a soldier drawled from the grass, "and you've pulled your boots off, holdin' 'em in yer hand, ready to run now!"

The laugh ran along the line and the boy hurried on to escape the chaff.

A well-known chaplain rode along a narrow path on the hillside. He was mounted on an old horse whose hip bones protruded like two deadly fangs. A footsore Confederate was hobbling as fast as he could in front of him, glancing back over his shoulder now and then uneasily.

"You needn't be afraid, my friend," the parson called, "I'm not going to run over you."

"I know you ain't," the soldier laughed, "but ef I wuz ter let you pass me, and that thing wuz ter wobble I'll be doggoned ef I wouldn't be gored ter death!"

The preacher reined his steed in with dignity and spoke with wounded pride:

"My friend, this is a better horse than our Lord rode into Jerusalem on!"

The soldier stepped up quickly, opened the animal's mouth and grinned:

"Parson, that's the very same horse!"

A shout rose from the hill in which the preacher joined.

"Dod bam it, did ye ever hear the beat o' that!" shouted a pious fellow who was inventing cuss words that would pass the charge of profanity.

A distinguished citizen of Fredericksburg passed along the lines wearing a tall new silk hat. He didn't get very far before he changed his line of march. A regular fusillade poured on him from the ranks.

"Say, man, is dat a hat er a bee gum?"

"Come down now!"

"Come down outen that hat an' help us with these Yanks!"

"Come down I say--I know you're up there for I can see your legs!"

When the silk hat vanished, a solemn country boy with slight knowledge of books began to discuss the great mysteries of eternity.

Ned had won his unbounded faith and admiration by spelling at the first trial the name of his native village in the Valley of Virginia--McGaheysville. Tom held this fact to be a marvellous intellectual achievement.

"What I want to know, Ned, is this," he drawled, "who started sin in this world, anyhow? What makes a good thing good and what makes a bad thing bad, and who said so first?"

"That's what I'd like to know myself, Tom," Ned gravely answered.

"An' ye don't know?"

"I certainly do not."

"I don't see why any man that can spell like you don't know everything."

He paused, picked up a pebble and threw it at a comrade's foot and laughed to see him jump as from a Minie ball.

"You know, Ned," he went on slowly, "what I think is the prettiest piece of poetry?"

"No--what?"

"Hit's this:

"'The men of high condition That rule affairs of State;   Their purpose is ambition,   Their practice only hate.'"

"Pretty good, Tom," was the quick reply, "but I think I can beat it with something more hopeful. I got it in Sunday School out in Missouri:

"'The sword and spear, of needless worth, Shall prune the tree and plough the earth;   And Peace shall smile from shore to shore And Nations learn to war no more.'"

The country boy's eyes gleamed with eager approval. He had fought for nearly two years and the glory of war was beginning to lose its glamour.

"Say that again, Ned," he pleaded. "Say it again! That's the prettiest thing I ever heard in my life!"

He was silent a moment:

"Yes, I used to think it would be glorious to hear the thunder of guns and the shriek of shells. I've changed my mind. When I hear one of 'em comin' now, I begin to sing to myself the old-fashioned tune I used to hear in the revivals:

"'Hark from the tomb a doleful sound!   'My thoughts in dreadful subjects roll damnation and the dead----'

"I've an idea we're going to sing some o' them old songs on this field pretty soon."

Again Ned thought of John and offered a silent prayer that he might not be in those blue lines that were going to charge into the jaws which Death had opened for them in the valley below.

John Vaughan in his tent beyond the Rappahannock was wasting no energy worrying about the coming battle. Death had ceased to be a matter of personal concern. He had seen so many dead and wounded men as he had ridden over battlefields he had come to take them as a matter of course. He was going into action now for the first time in the ranks as a private soldier and he would see things happen at closer range--that was all. He wished to see them that way. He had reached the point of utter indifference to personal danger and it brought a new consciousness of strength that was inspiring. He had stopped dreaming of the happiness of love after the exhibition he had made of himself before Betty Winter and the brutal insult with which he met her advances. Some girls might forgive it, but not this proud, sensitive, high strung daughter of the snows of New England and the sunlight of France. And so he had resolutely put the thought out of his heart.

Julius had proven himself a valuable servant. He was the best cook in the regiment, and what was still more important, he was the most skillful thief and the most plausible liar in the army. He could defend himself so nobly from the insinuations of the suspicious that they would apologize for the wrong unwittingly done his character. John had not lived so well since he could remember.

"Julius, you're a handy man in war!" he exclaimed after a hearty supper on fried chicken.

"Yassah--I manage ter git 'long, sah."

Julius took up his banjo and began to tune it for an accompaniment to his songs. He had a mellow rhythmical voice that always brought the crowd. He began with his favorite that never failed to please his master. The way he rolled his eyes and sang with his hands and feet and every muscle of his body was the source of unending interest to his Northern audience.

He ran his fingers lightly over the strings and the men threw down their dirty packs of cards and crowded around John's tent. Julius only sang one line at a time and picked his banjo between them to a low wailing sound of his own invention:

"O! far' you well, my Mary Ann;   Far' you well, my dear!   I've no one left to love me now   And little do I care----"

He paused between the stanzas and picked his banjo to a few prose interpolations of his own.

"Dat's what I'm a tellin' ye now, folks--little do I care!"

He knew his master had been crossed in love and he rolled his eyes and nodded his woolly head in triumphant approval. John smiled wanly as he drifted slowly into his next stanza.

"An' ef I had a scoldin' wife I'd whip her sho's yer born, I'd take her down to New Orleans   An' trade her off fer corn----"

Julius stopped with a sudden snap and whispered to John:

"Lordy, sah, I clean fergit 'bout dat meetin' at de cullud folks' church, sah, dat dey start up. I promise de preacher ter fetch you, sah--An' ef we gwine ter march ter-morrow, dis here's de las' night sho----"

The concert was adjourned to the log house which an old colored preacher had converted into a church. It was filled to its capacity and John stood in the doorway and heard the most remarkable sermon to which he had ever listened.

The grey-haired old negro was tremendously in earnest. He could neither read nor write but he opened the Bible to comply with the formalities of the occasion and pretended to read his text. He had taken it from his master who was a clergyman. Ephraim invariably chose the same texts but gave his people his own interpretation. It never failed in some element of originality.

The text his master had evidently chosen last were the words:

"And he healeth them of divers diseases."

Old Ephraim's version was a free one. From the open Bible he solemnly read:

"An' he healed 'em of all sorts o' diseases an' even er dat wust o' complaints called de Divers!"

He plunged straight into a fervent exhortation to sinners to flee from the Divers.

"I'm gwine ter tell ye now, chillun," he exclaimed with uplifted arms, "ye don't know nuttin' 'bout no terrible diseases till dat wust er all called de Divers git ye! An' hit's a comin' I tell ye. Hit's gwine ter git ye, too. Ye can flee ter the mountain top, an' hit'll dive right up froo de air an' git ye dar. Ye kin go down inter de bowels er de yearth an' hit'll dive right down dar atter ye. Ye kin take de wings er de mornin' an' fly ter de ends er de yearth--an' de Divers is dar. Dey kin dive anywhar!

"An' what ye gwine ter do when dey git ye? I axe ye dat now? What ye gwine ter do when hit's forever an' eternally too late? Dese doctors roun' here kin cure ye o' de whoopin'-cough--mebbe--I hain't nebber seed 'em eben do dat--but I say, mebbe. Dey kin cure ye o' de measles, mebbe. Er de plumbago or de typhoid er de yaller fever sometimes. But I warns ye now ter flee de wrath dat's ter come when dem Divers git ye! Dey ain't no doctor no good fer dat nowhar--exceptin' ye come ter de Lord. For He heal 'em er all sorts er diseases an' de wust er all de complaints called de Divers!

"Come, humble sinners, in whose breast er thousand thoughts revolve!"

John Vaughan turned away with a smile and a tear.

"In God's name," he murmured thoughtfully, "what's to become of these four million black children of the tropic jungles if we win now and set them free! Their fathers and mothers were but yesterday eating human flesh in naked savagery."

He walked slowly back to his tent through the solemn starlit night. The new moon, a silver thread, hung over the tree tops. He thought of that dusky grey-haired child of four thousand years of ignorance and helplessness and the tragic role he had played in the history of our people. And for the first time faced the question of the still more tragic role he might play in the future.

"I'm fighting to free him and the millions like him," he mused. "What am I going to do with him?"

The longer he thought the blacker and more insoluble became this question, and yet he was going into battle to-morrow to fight his own brother to the death on this issue. True the problem of national existence was at stake, but this black problem of the possible degradation of our racial stock and our national character still lay back of it unsolved and possibly insoluble.

The red flash of a picket's gun on the shore of the river and the quick answer from the other side brought his dreaming to a sudden stop before the sterner fact of the swiftly approaching battle.

He snatched but a few hours sleep before his regiment was up and on the march to the water's edge. A dense grey fog hung over the river and obscured the town. The bridge builders swung their pontoons into the water and soon the sound of timbers falling into place could be heard with the splash of the anchors and the low quick commands of the officers.

The grey sharpshooters, concealed on the other shore, began to fire across the water through the fog. The sound was strangely magnified. The single crack of a musket seemed as loud as a cannon.

The work went quickly. The bullets flew wide of the mark. The fog suddenly lifted and a steady fusillade from the men hidden in the hills of Fredericksburg began to pick off the bridge builders with cruel accuracy. At times every man was down. New men were rushed to take their places and they fell.

The signal was given to the artillery and a hundred and forty-seven great guns suddenly began to sweep the doomed town. Houses crumpled like egg-shells and fires began to blaze.

The sharpshooters fell back. The bridges were laid and the grand army of a hundred and thirteen thousand began to pour across. The caissons, with their huge black, rifled-barrel guns rumbling along the resounding boards in a continuous roar like distant thunder.

On the southern shore the deep mud cut hills put every team to the test of its strength and the utmost skill of their drivers. Hundreds of men were in the mud at the wheels and still they would stick.

And then the patient heavens above heard the voices of army teamsters in plain and ornamental swearing! Such profanity was probably never heard on this earth before and it may well be hoped will not be heard again.

The driver whose wheels had stuck, cracked his whip first and yelled. He yelled again and cracked his whip. And then he began to swear, loudly, and angrily at first and then in lower, steadier, more polite terms--but always in an unending nerve-racking torrent.

He cursed his mules individually by name and the whole team collectively, and consigned it to the lowest depth of the deepest hell and then the devil for not providing a deeper one. Each trait of each mule, good and bad, he named without fear or favor and damned each alike with equal emphasis. He named each part of each mule's anatomy and damned it individually and as a whole, with full bill of particulars.

He swore in every key in the whole gamut of sound and last of all he damned himself for his utter inability to express anything he really felt.

The last big gun up the hill and the infantry poured into the town of Fredericksburg, halting in regiments and brigades in its streets. Only a few shots had been exchanged with the men in grey. They had withdrawn to the heights a mile beyond. The assault had been a mere parade. Many of the inhabitants had fled in terror at the approach of the men in blue. Some of the lower types of soldiers in the

Northern army broke into these deserted houses and began to rob and pillage.

Julius "found" many delicacies lying about on lawns and in various unheard-of places. His master never pressed him with rude questions when his zeal bore such good results for their table.

Ned Vaughan had been very much amused at an old woman who had been driven from her home by marauders. She had piled such goods and chattels as she could handle into an ox cart and drove past the grey battle lines, hurrying as fast as she could Southward. Her wrinkled old face beamed with joy at the sight of their burnished muskets and her eyes flashed with the gleam of an Amazon as she shouted:

"Give it to the damned rascals, boys! Give 'em one fer me--one fer me and don't you forget it!"

Far down the line she could be heard delivering her fierce exhortation. The men smiled and answered her good-naturedly. The day of wrath and death had dawned. It was too solemn an hour for boastful words.

For two days the grand army in blue poured across the river and spread out through the town of Fredericksburg. The fateful morning of the 13th of December, 1862, dawned in another heavy fog. Its grey mantle of mystery shrouded the town, clung wet and heavy to the ground in the silent valley before the crescent-shaped hills and veiled the face of their heights.

Under the cover of this fog the long waves of blue spread out in the edge of the valley and took their places in battle line. The grey men in the brown grass on the hills crouched behind their ditches and stone walls, gripped their guns and waited for the foe to walk into the trap their commanders had set.

An unseen hand slowly lifted the misty curtain and the sun burst on the scene. The valley lay like the smooth ground of some vast arena prepared for a pageant and back of it rose the silent hills, tier on tier like the seats of a mighty amphitheatre. But the men crouching on those seats were not spectators--they were the grimmest actors in the tragedy.

For a moment it was a spectacle merely--the grandest display of the pageantry of war ever made on a field of death.

Franklin's division suddenly wheeled into position for its united assault on the right.

Ned Vaughan, from his lair on the hill, could see the officers in their magnificent new uniforms, their swords flashing as they led their men. A hundred thousand bayonets were gleaming in the sparkling December sun. Magnificent horses in rich tasselled trappings were plunging and prancing with the excitement of marching hosts, some of them keeping time to the throb of regimental bands.

The bands were playing now, all of them, a band for every thousand men, the shrill scream of their bugles and the roar of their drums sending a mighty chorus into the heavens that echoed ominously against the silent hills.

And flags, flags, flags, were streaming in billowy waves of red, white and blue, as far as the eye could reach!

"Isn't that pretty, boys!" Ned sighed admiringly.

Tom lifted his solemn eyes from the grass.

"Lord, Lord, look at them new warm clothes, an' my elbows a-freezin' in this cold wind!"

"Ain't it a picture?"

"What a pity to spile it!"

A ripple of admiration ran along the crouching lines as fingers softly felt for the triggers of their guns.

A quick order from John Vaughan's Colonel sent their battery of artillery rattling and bounding into position. The cannoneers sprang to their mounts. A handsome young fellow missed his foothold and fell beneath the wheels. The big iron tire crushed his neck and the blood from his mouth splashed into John's face. The men on the guns didn't turn their heads to look back. Their eyes were searching the brown hills before them.

The long roll beat from a thousand drums, the call of the buglers rang over the valley--and then the strange, solemn silence that comes before the shock--the moment when cowards collapse and the brave falter.

John Vaughan's soul rose in a fierce challenge to fate. If he died it was well; if he lived it was the same. He had ceased to care.

At exactly eight-thirty, General Meade hurled his division, supported by Doubleday and Gibbon, against Jackson's weakest point, the right of the Confederate lines. Their aim was to seize an opposing hill. The curving lines of grey were silent until the charging hosts were well advanced in deadly range and then the brown hills flamed and roared in front and on their flanks.

The blue lines were mowed down in swaths as though the giant figure of Death had suddenly swung his scythe from the fog banks in the sky.

Again and again came those awful volleys of musketry and artillery cross-firing on the rushing lines. The men staggered and recovered, reformed and charged again over the dead bodies of their comrades carrying the crest for a moment. They captured a flag and a handful of prisoners only to be driven back down the hill with losses more frightful in retreat than when they breasted the storm.

In the centre the tragedy was repeated with results even more terrible. As the charging lines fell back, staggering, bleeding and cut to pieces, fresh brigades threw down their knapsacks, fixed their bayonets and charged through their own melting ranks into the jaws of Death to fall back in their turn.

With a mighty shout the blue line swept across the railroad, took the ditches at the point of the bayonet and captured two hundred grey prisoners. But only for a moment. From the supporting line rang the rebel yell and they were hurled back, shattered and cut to pieces. These retreats were veritable shambles of slaughter. The curved lines on the hills raking them with their deadly accurate cross-fire.

John Vaughan's regiment leaped to the support of the falling blue waves.

A wounded soldier had propped himself against a stone and smiled as the cheering men swept by. He could rest a while now.

A battery of artillery suddenly blazed from the hill-crest and his Colonel threw his command flat on their stomachs until the storm should slacken. John heard the shrill deadly swish of the big shots passing two feet above.

He lifted his eyes to the hill and a frightened pigeon suddenly swooped straight down toward his head. He ducked quickly, sure he had escaped a cannon ball until the laugh of the man at his side told of his mistake.

They rose to charge. The knapsack of the man who had laughed was struck by a ball and a deck of cards sent flying ten feet in the air.

"Deal me a winning hand!" John shouted.

A shot cut the sword belt of the first lieutenant, left him uninjured, glanced and killed the captain. The lieutenant picked up his sword, took his captain's place and led the charge.

Men were falling on the right and left and John Vaughan loaded and fired with steady, dogged nerve without a scratch.

Four times the blue billows had dashed against the hills only to fall back in red confusion. The din and roar were indescribable. The color-bearer of the regiment confused by conflicting orders paused and asked for instructions. The Colonel, mistaking his act for retreat, tore the colors from his hand and gave them to another man. The boy burst into tears. The new color-bearer had scarcely lifted the flag above his head when he fell. The disgraced soldier snatched the tottering flagstaff and, lifting it on high, dashed up the hill ahead of his line of battle.

The men were ducking their heads low beneath the fierce hail of lead and staggering blindly.

John saw this boy waving his flag and shaking his fist back at the halting line. He was not a hundred feet from the Confederate trenches.

"Come on there!" he shouted. "Damn it, what's the matter with you?"

Ned Vaughan and his grey men behind the little mound of red dirt were watching this drama with flashing eyes. Beside him crouched a boy whose early piety had marked him for the ministry. But he had wandered from the fold in the stress of army life. Ned heard his voice now in low, eager prayer:

"O Lord, drive 'em back! Drive 'em back, O Lord!"

He fired his musket down the hill and prayed harder:

"Lord, drive 'em back! I've sinned and come short, but drive 'em, O Lord!"

He paused and whispered to Ned as he reached for another cartridge:

"Are they comin' or goin'?"

"Coming!"

Again he prayed with fervor:

"Drive 'em back, Lord Goddermighty, we're weak and you're strong--help us now! Drive 'em--just this time, O Lord, and you can have me--I'll be good!"

He paused for breath and turned to Ned:

"Now look!--Comin' or goin'?"

"That follow with the flag cussin' the men has dropped----"

"Thank God!"

"Another's lifted it----"

"Lord, save us!"

"Why don't you lie down, ye damn fool," Tom shouted. "I'm huggin' the ground so close now I don't want a piece of paper under me, and if there's got to be a piece I don't want no writin' on it!"

"Now look, are they comin'?" the pious boy gasped.

Ned made no answer. His wide set eyes were staring at the man who had caught that color-bearer in his arms and was carrying him to the rear.

It was John Vaughan!

His lips were moving now in silent prayer and his sword hung limp in his hands.

Through chattering teeth he cried:

"Don't shoot that fellow carrying his friend down the hill, boys!"

"They're runnin' now?" the pious one asked.

"It isn't war--it's a massacre!" Ned sighed.

The man of prayer leaped on the ditch bank suddenly and shook his fist defiantly.

"Come back here, you damned cowards!" he yelled. "Come back and we'll whip hell out o' you!"

Slowly the shattered regiment fell back down the bloody slope, stumbling over their dead and wounded. The dim smoke-bound valley was a slaughter pen. Where magnificent lines of blue had marched with flashing bayonets and streaming banners at eight o'clock, the dead lay in mangled heaps, and the wounded huddled among them slowly freezing to death.

John saw a magnificent gun a heap of junk with four dead horses and every cannoneer on the ground dead or freezing where they fell. A single shell had done the work. Riderless horses galloped wildly over the field, shying at the grim piles of dark blue bodies, sniffing the blood and neighing pitifully.

Twelve hundred men in his regiment had charged up that hill. But two hundred and fifty came down.

From the steeple of the Court House in Fredericksburg General Couch, in command of the Second Corps, stood with his glasses on this frightful scene. He whispered to Howard by his side:

"The whole plain is covered with our men fallen and falling--I've never seen anything like it!"

He paused, his lips quivering as he gasped:

"O my God! see them falling--poor fellows, falling--falling!"

He signalled Burnside for reinforcements.

General Sumner's division on the Union right had charged into the deadliest trap of all.

Down the road toward the foot of Marye's Heights his magnificent army swept at double quick. The Confederate batteries had been specially trained to rake this road from three directions, right, and left flank and centre.

Steadily, stoically the men in blue pressed into this narrow way in silence and met the flaming torrent from three directions. Rushing on over the bodies of their fallen comrades the thinning ranks reached the old stone wall at the foot of the hill. General Cobb lay concealed behind it with three thousand infantry. The low quick order ran along his line:

"Fire!"

Straight into the faces of the heroic Union soldiers flashed a level blinding flame from three thousand muskets, slaying, crushing, tearing to pieces the proud army of an hour ago. A thousand men in blue fell in five minutes. The ground was piled with their bodies until it was impossible to charge over them effectively.

For a moment a cloud of smoke pitifully drew a soft grey veil over the awful scene while the men who were left fell back in straggling broken groups.

Five times the Union hosts had charged those terrible brown hills and five times they had been rolled back in red waves of blood.

Late in the day a fierce bitter wind was blowing from the north. There was yet time to turn defeat into victory. The desperate Union Commander ordered the sixth charge.

The men in blue pulled their hats down low as if to shut out the pelting hail of lead and iron and without a murmur charged once more into the mouth of hell. The winds had frozen stiff the bodies of their dead. The advancing blue lines snatched these dead men from the ground, carried them in front, stacked them in long piles for bulwarks, and fought behind them with the desperation of madmen. There was no escape. The keen eyes of the Confederate Commanders had planted their right and left flanking lines to pour death into these ranks no matter how high their corpses were piled. The crescent hill blazed and roared with unceasing fury. Only the darkness was kind at last.

And then the men in blue planted the frozen bodies of their comrades along the outer battle line as dummy sentinels, and under cover of the night began to slip back through Fredericksburg and across the silver mirror of the Rappahannock to their old camp, shattered, broken, crushed.

It was four o'clock in the morning before John Vaughan's regiment would give up the search for their desperately wounded. Only the strongest could endure that bitter cold. Through the long, desolate hours the pitiful cries of the wounded men rang through the black, freezing night, and few hands stirred to save them. A great army was fighting to save its flags and guns and reach the shelter beyond the river.

Amid the few flickering lanterns could be heard the greetings of friends in subdued tones as they clasped hands:

"Is that you, old boy?"

"God bless you--yes--I'm glad to see you!"

A dying man in blue was pitifully calling for water somewhere, in the darkness in front of Ned Vaughan's ditch. He took his canteen, got a lantern and went to find him. It might be John. If not, no matter, he was some other fellow's brother.

As the light fell on his drawn face Ned murmured:

"Thank God!"

He pressed the canteen to his lips and held his head in his lap. It was only too plain from the steel look out of the eyes that his minutes were numbered. He moved and turned his dying face up to Ned:

"Why is it you always whip us, Johnny?"

He paused for breath:

"I wonder--every battle I've been in we've been defeated--why--why--why, O God, why----"

His head drooped and he was still.

Ned wondered if some waiting loved one on the shores of eternity had given him the answer. He wrapped him tenderly in his blanket and left him at rest at last.

As he turned toward his lines the unmistakable wail of a baby came faintly through the darkness--a wee voice, the half smothered cry sounding as if it were nestling in a mother's arms. He followed the sound until his lantern flashed in the wild eyes of a young woman who had fled from her home in terror during the battle and was hugging her baby frantically in her arms.

Ned led her gently to an officer's quarters and made her comfortable.

The glory of war was fast fading from his imagination. A grim spectre was slowly taking its place.

John's shattered regiment lay down on the field with the rear guard at four o'clock to snatch an hour's sleep, their heads pillowed on the bodies of the dead. The cold moderated and a light mantle of snow fell softly just before day and covered the field, the living and the dead. When the reveille sounded at dawn, the bugler looked with awe at the thousands of white shrouded figures and wondered which would stir at his note. The living slowly rose as from the dead and shook their white shrouds. Thousands lay still, cold and immovable to await the archangel's mightier call at the last.

Beyond the river, through the long night, Burnside, wild with anguish, had paced the floor of his tent. Again and again he threw his arms in a gesture of despair toward the freezing blood-stained field:

"Oh, those men--those men over there! I'm thinking of them all the time----"

As the rear guard turned from the field at sunrise, John Vaughan looked back across the valley of Death and saw the ragged brown and grey figures shivering in the cold, as they swarmed down from the hills and began to shake the frost from the new, warm clothes they were stripping from the dead.

CHAPTER XXVI
THE REST HOUR

For two terrible days and nights Betty Winter saw the endless line of ambulances creep from the field of Fredericksburg. Some of these men lay on the frozen ground for forty-eight hours before relief came. Many of the wounded might have lived but for the frightful exposure to cold which followed the battle. They died in hundreds.

Thousands were placed on the train for Washington and so great was the pitiful suffering among them Betty left with the first load. There would be more work in the hospitals there than in Burnside's camp. It would be many a day before his shattered army could be ready again to give battle.

The worst trouble with it was not the bleeding gap torn through its ranks by Lee's shot and shell. Not only was its body wounded, its soul was crushed. Its commanding generals were divided into warring factions, the rank and file of its stern fighting men discouraged.

Again an epidemic of desertions broke out and ten thousand men were lost in a single month.

Burnside assumed the full responsibility for the disaster and asked to be relieved of his command. The third Union General had gone down before Lee--McClellan, Pope and Burnside.

The President, heartsick but undismayed, called to the head of the army the most promising general in sight, Joseph Hooker, popularly known as "Fighting Joe Hooker." There was inspiration to the thoughtless in the name, yet the Chief had misgivings.

On sending him the appointment he wrote his new general a remarkable letter:

"GENERAL:

"I have placed you at the head of the Army of the Potomac. Of course, I have done this upon what appears to me to be sufficient reasons; and yet I think it best for you to know that there are some things in regard to which I am not quite satisfied with you.

"I believe you to be a brave and skillful soldier--which of course I like. I also believe you do not mix politics with your profession--in which you are right. You have confidence in yourself--which is a valuable if not indispensable quality. You are ambitious--which within reasonable bounds does good rather than harm; but I think that during General Burnside's command of the army you have taken counsel of your ambition and thwarted him as much as you could, in which you did a great wrong to the country, and to a most meritorious and honorable brother officer.

"I have heard in such a way as to believe of you recently saying that both the army and the Government needed a dictator. Of course it was not for this, but in spite of it, that I gave you the command. Only those generals who gain successes can set up as dictators.

"What I now ask of you is military success, and I will risk the dictatorship.

"The Government will support you to the utmost of its ability--which is neither more nor less than it has done and will do for all commanders. I much fear that the spirit which you have aided to infuse into the army of criticising their commander and withholding confidence from him, will now turn upon you. I shall assist you as far as I can to put it down. Neither you nor Napoleon, if he were alive again, could get any good out of an army while such a spirit prevails in it.

"And now beware of rashness--but with energy and sleepless vigilance go forward and give us victories."

While Hooker lay in winter quarters reorganizing his army his picket lines in speaking distance with those of his opponent across the river, the President bent his strong shoulders to the task of cheering the fainting spirits of the people. On his shaggy head was heaped the blame of all the sorrows, the failures and the agony of the ever deepening tragedy of war. Deeper and deeper into his rugged kindly face were cut the lines of life and death, and darker grew the shadows through which his sensitive lonely soul was called to walk.
And yet, through it all, there glowed with stronger radiance the charm of his quaint genius and his magnetic personality--tragic, homely, gentle, humorous, honest, merciful, wise, laughable and lovable.
He found time to run down to Hampton Roads with Gideon Welles, his loyal

Secretary of the Navy, to inspect the ships assembled there. He saw a narrow door bound with iron.

"What is that?" he asked sharply.

"Oh, that is the sweat box," the Secretary replied, "used for insubordinate seamen----"

"Oh," the rugged giant exclaimed, "how do you work it?"

"The man to be punished is put inside and steam heat is turned on. It brings him to terms quickly."

The tall figure bent curiously examining the contrivance:

"And we apply this to thousands of brave American seamen every year?"

"Undoubtedly."

"Let me try it and see what it's like."

It was useless to protest. He had already taken off his tall silk hat and there was a look of quiet determination in his hazel-grey eyes.

He stepped quickly into the enclosure, which he found to be about three feet in length and about the same in width. His tall figure of six feet four was practically telescoped.

"Close your door now and turn on the steam," he ordered. "I'll give you the signal when I've had enough."

The door was closed and the steam turned on.

He stood it three minutes and gave the signal of release.

He stepped out, stretched his long legs, and breathed deeply. He mopped his brow and there was fire in his sombre eyes as he turned to Welles:

"Mr. Secretary, I want every one of those things dumped into the sea. Never again allow it to be found on a vessel flying the American flag!"

In an hour every sailor in the harbor had heard the news. The old salts who had felt its shame and agony lifted their caps and stood with bared heads, cheering and crying as he passed.

One by one, every country of Europe heard the news and the sweat box ceased to be an instrument of discipline on every sea of the civilized world.

Seated at his desk in the White House, he received daily the great and the humble, and no man or woman came and left without a patient hearing. There were over thirty thousand cases of trial and condemnations by court-martial every year now--only a small portion with the death penalty attached--but all had the right to appeal. They were not slow in finding the road to the loving heart.

Stanton, worn out by vain protests against his pardons, sent Attorney General Bates at last.

The great lawyer was very stern as he faced his Chief:

"I regret to say it, Mr. President, but you are not fit to be trusted with the pardoning power, sir!"

A smile played about the corner of the big kindly mouth as he glanced over his spectacles at his Attorney General:

"It's my private opinion, Bates, that you're just as pigeon-hearted as I am!"

Judge Advocate General Holt was sent to labor with him and insist that he enforce the law imposing the death penalty.

"Your reasons are good, Holt," he answered kindly, "but I can't promise to do it. You see, so many of my boys have to be shot anyhow. I don't want to add another one to that lot if I can help it----"

He paused and went on whimsically:

"I don't see how it's going to make a man better to shoot him, anyhow--give them another trial."

In spite of all Holt's protests he steadfastly refused to sanction any death warrant against a man for cowardice under fire. "Many a man," he calmly argued, "who honestly tries to do his duty is overcome by fear greater than his will--I'm not at all sure how I'd act if Minie balls were whistling and those big shells shrieking in my ears. How can a poor man help it if his legs just carry him away?"

All these he marked "leg cases," put them in a separate pigeon hole and always suspended their sentence.

He would smile gently as he filed each death warrant away:

"It would frighten that poor devil too terribly to shoot him. They shan't do it."

On one he wrote:

"Let him fight again--maybe the enemy will shoot him--I won't."

Betty Winter came with two cases. The first was a mother to plead for her boy sentenced to die for sleeping at his post on guard.

"You see, sir," the mother pleaded, "he'd been on watch once that night and had done his duty faithfully. He volunteered to take a sick comrade's place. He was so tired he fell asleep. He was always a big-hearted, generous boy--you won't let them shoot him?"

"No, I won't," was the quick response.

The mother laughed aloud through her tears and threw her arms around Betty's neck.

The President bent over the paper and wrote across its back:

"Pardoned. This life is too precious to be lost."

Betty waited until the crowd had passed out and he was alone with Colonel Nicolay. She hurried to his desk with her second case which she had kept outside in the corridor until the time to enter.

A young mother walked timidly in, smiling apologetically. She carried a three-months-old baby in her arms. She was evidently not in mourning, though her eyes were red from weeping.

"What's the matter now?" the President laughed, nodding to Betty.

"Tell him," she whispered.

"If you please, sir," the woman began timidly, "we ain't been married but a little over a year. My husband has never seen the baby. He's in the army. I couldn't stand it any longer, so I come down to Washington to get a pass to take the baby to him. But they wouldn't let me have it. I've been wandering 'round the streets all day crying till I met this sweet young lady and she brought me to you, sir----"

The President turned to his secretary:

"Let's send her down!"

The Colonel smiled and shook his head:

"The strictest orders have been given to allow no more women to go to the front----"

The big gentle hand stroked the shaggy beard.

"Well, I'll tell you what we can do," he cried joyfully, "give her husband a leave of absence and let him come to see them here!"

The secretary left at once for the Adjutant General's office and the President turned to the laughing young mother, who was trying to thank Betty through her tears:

"And where are you stopping, Madam?"

"Nowhere yet, sir. I went straight from the depot to the War Department and then walked about blind with crying eyes until I came here."

"All right then, we'll fix that. I'll give Miss Betty an order to take you and your baby to her hospital and care for you until your husband comes and he can stay there a week with you----"

The mother's voice wouldn't work. She tried to speak her thanks and could only laugh.

The big hand pressed Betty's as she left:

"Thank you for bringing her, little girl, things like that rest me."

The hour was swiftly coming when he was going to need all the strength that rest could bring body and soul. His enemies were sleepless. The press inspired by Senator Winter had begun to strike below the belt.

CHAPTER XXVII
DEEPENING SHADOWS

Again the eyes of the Nation were fixed on the Army of the Potomac and its new General. The President went down to his headquarters at Falmouth Heights opposite Fredericksburg to review his army of a hundred and thirty thousand men.

Riding up to Hooker's headquarters through the beautiful spring morning his weary figure was lifted with new hope as he breathed the perfume of the flowers and blooming hedgerows.

The driver only worried him for the moment. He was swearing eloquently at his team in the pride of his heart at the honor of hauling the Chief Magistrate of the Nation. He swore both plain and ornamental oaths with equal unction.

The President endured it a while in amused silence. He was deeply annoyed, but too much of a gentleman to hurt his patriotic driver's feelings.

At last he observed:

"I see you are an Episcopalian, driver."

The man turned in surprise:

"Oh, no, sir, I'm Methodist."

"Is it possible?"

"Yes, sir, Methodist--why, sir?"

A whimsical smile played about the big kindly mouth:

"I thought you must be an Episcopalian because you swear exactly like Mr. Seward, and he's a churchwarden!"

A deep silence fell on the sweet spring air. The driver glanced over his shoulder with a sheepish grin, and cracked his whip without an oath:

"G'long there, boys!"

As the serried lines of blue, with bayonets flashing in the warming sun of April, marched past the tall giant on horseback, they were in fine spirits. They cheered the President with rousing enthusiasm.

John Vaughan did not join. He marched past with eyes straight in front.

The President hurried back to Washington to keep his vigil from his window overlooking the Potomac, and Hooker began the execution of his skillful plan of attack. On the day his advance began he had one hundred and thirty thousand men and four hundred and forty-eight great guns in seven grand divisions. Lee, still lying on the crescent hills behind Fredericksburg, had sixty-two thousand men and one hundred and seventy guns. He had detached Longstreet's corps for service in Tennessee.

The Federal Commander was absolutely sure that he could throw the flower of this magnificent army across the river seven miles above Fredericksburg, get into Lee's rear, hurl the remainder of his forces across the river as Burnside had done, and crush the grey army like an egg shell. It was well planned, but in war the unexpected often happens.

Again the unexpected thing turned up in the shape of the strange, dusty figure on his little sorrel horse.

The night before Hooker moved, Julius met with an accident which delayed John's supper. He was just approaching the camp after a successful stroll over the surrounding territory, carrying on his back a sheep he meant to cook for the coming march. A rude and unsympathetic guard arrested him. Julius was greatly grieved at his unkind remarks.

"Lordy, man, you ought not ter say things lak dat ter me! I nebber steal nutting in my life. I wasn't even foragin' dis time----"

"The hell you weren't!"

"Na, sah. I wasn't even foragin'. I know dat de General done issue dem orders agin hit, an' I quit long ergo----"

"This sheep looks like it----"

"Dat sheep?"

"That's what I said, you black thief!"

"Say, man, don't talk lak dat ter me--you sho hurts my feelin's. I nebber stole dat sheep. I nebber go atter de sheep, an' I weren't studyin' 'bout no animals. I was des walkin' long de road past a man's house whar dis here big, devilish-lookin' old sheep come er runnin' right at me wid his head down--an' I lammed him wid er stick ter save my life, sah. An' den when he fell, I knowed hit wuz er pity ter leave him dar ter spile, an' so I des nachelly had ter fetch him inter de camp ter save him. Man, you sho is rude ter talk dat way."

The guard was obdurate until Julius began to describe how he cooked roast mutton. He finally agreed to accept his version of the battle with the sheep as authentic if he would bring him a ten pound roast to test the truth of his conversation.

Julius was still harping on the rudeness of this guard as he fanned the flies off John's table with a sassafras brush at supper.

"I don't know what dey ebber let sech poor white trash ez dat man git in er army for, anyhow!" he exclaimed indignantly.

"We have to take 'em as they come now, Julius. There's going to be a draft this summer. No more volunteers now. Wait till you see the conscripts."

"Dey can't be no wus dan dat man. He warn't no gemman 'tall, sah."

John rose from his hearty supper and strolled along the line of his regiment, recruited again to its full strength of twelve hundred men.

Two fellows who were messmates were scrapping about a question of gravy. One wanted lots of gravy and his meat done brown. The other insisted on having his meat decently cooked, but not swimming in grease. The man in favor of gravy was on duty as cook at this meal and stuck to his own ideas. They suddenly clinched, fell to the ground, rolled over, knocked the pan in the fire and lost both meat and gravy.

John smiled and passed on.

A lieutenant was sitting on a stump holding a letter from his sweetheart to the flickering camp fire. He bent and kissed the signature--the fool! For a moment the old longing surged back through his soul. He wondered if she ever thought of him now. She had loved him once.

He started back to his tent to write her a letter before they broke camp tomorrow morning. Nature was calling in the balmy spring night wind that floated over the waters of the river.

Nature knew naught of war. She was pouring out her heart in budding leaf and blossom in the joy of living.

And then the bitterness of shame and stubborn pride welled up to kill the tender impulse. There were slumbering forces beneath the skin the scenes through which he was passing had called into new life. They were bringing new powers both of mind and body. They added nothing to the gentler, sweeter sources of character. He began to understand how men could feed their ambitions on the bodies of fallen hosts and still smile.

He had felt the brutalizing touch of war. With a cynical laugh he threw off his impulse to write and turned into his blanket dreaming of the red carnival toward which they would march at dawn.

As the sun rose over the new sparkling fields of the South on the morning of the 27th of April, 1863, the great movement began.

The Federal commander ordered Sedgwick's division to cross the Rappahannock below Fredericksburg and deploy in line of battle to deceive Lee as to his real purpose while he secretly marched his main army through the woods seven miles above to throw them on his rear.

As the men stood, thousands banked on thousands, awaiting the order to march, John Vaughan saw, for the first time, the grim procession pass along the lines carrying a condemned deserter, to be shot to death before his former comrades. His hands were tied across his breast with rough knotted rope and he was seated on his coffin.

The War Department had gotten around the tender heart in the White House at last. The desertions had become so terrible in their frequency it was absolutely necessary to make examples of some of these men. The poor devil who sat forlornly on his grim throne riding through the sweet spring morning had no mother or sister or sweetheart to plead his cause.

The men stared in silence as the death cart rumbled along the lines. It halted and the man took his place before the firing squad but a few feet away.

A white cloth was bound over his eyes. The sergeant dealt out the specially prepared round of cartridges--all blank save one, that no soldier might know who did the murder.

In low tones they were ordered to fire straight at the heart of the blindfolded figure. The muskets flashed and the man crumpled in a heap on the soft young grass, the blood pouring from his breast in a bright red pool beside the quivering form.

And then the army moved.

The stratagem of the Commander was executed with skill. But there was an eagle eye back of those hills of Fredericksburg. Lee was not only a great stark fighter, he was a past master in the arts of war. He had divined his opponent's plan from the moment of his first movement.

By April the 30th, Hooker had effected his crossing and slipped into the rear of Lee's left wing. The Southerner had paid little attention to Sedgwick's menace on his front. He left but nine thousand men on Marye's Heights to hold in check this forty thousand, and by a rapid night march suddenly confronted Hooker in the Wilderness before Chancellorsville.

So strong was the Union General's position he issued an exultant order to his army in which he declared:

"The enemy must now flee shamefully or come out of his defences to accept battle on our own ground, to his certain destruction."

The enemy had already slipped out of his defenses before Fredericksburg and at that moment was feeling his way through the tangled vines and undergrowth with sure ominous tread.

The soul of the Confederate leader rose with elation at the prospect before him. In this tangle called the Wilderness, broken only here and there by small, scattered farm houses and fields, the Grand Army of the Republic had more than twice his numbers, and nearly three times as many big guns, but his artillery would be practically useless. It was utterly impossible to use four hundred great guns in such woods. Lee's one hundred and seventy were more than he could handle. It would be a fight between infantry at close range. The Southerner knew that no army of men ever walked the earth who would be the equal, man for man, with these grey veteran dead shots, who were now silently creeping through the undergrowth of their native woods.

On May the 1st, their two lines came into touch and Lee felt of his opponent by driving in his skirmishers in a desultory fire of artillery.

On the morning of May the 2nd, the two armies faced each other at close range.

With Sedgwick's division of forty thousand men now threatening Lee's rear from Fredericksburg, his army thus caught between two mighty lines of blue, Hooker was absolutely sure of victory. The one thing of which he never dreamed was that Lee would dare, in the face of such a death trap, to divide his own small army. And yet this is exactly what the Southerner decided to do contrary to all the rules of military science or the advice of the strange, silent figure on the little sorrel horse.

When Lee, Jackson and Stuart rode along the lines of Hooker's front that fatal May morning, Jackson suddenly reined in his little sorrel and turned his keen blue eyes on his grey-haired Chief:

"There's just one way, General Lee. The front and left are too strong. I can swing my corps in a quick movement to the rear while you attack the front. They will think it a retreat. Out of sight, I'll turn, march for ten miles around their right wing, and smash it from the rear before sundown."

Lee quickly approved the amazing plan of his lieutenant, though it involved the necessity of his holding Hooker's centre and left in check and that his nine thousand men behind the stone wall on Marye's Heights should hold Sedgwick's forty thousand. He believed it could be done until Jackson had completed his march.

He immediately ordered his attack on the centre and left of his enemy. The artillery horses were cropping the tender dew-laden grass with eagerness. They had had no breakfast. The riders sprang to their backs at seven o'clock and they dashed into position.

Lee's guns opened the fateful day. For hours his lines blazed with the steady sullen boom of artillery and rattle of musketry. Hooker's hosts replied in kind.

At noon a shout swept the Federal lines that Lee's army was in retreat. Sickles' division could see the long grey waves hurrying to the rear. They were close enough to note the ragged, dirty, nondescript clothes Jackson's men wore. No man in all the Union hosts doubted for a moment that Lee had seen the hopelessness of his position and was hurrying to save his little army of sixty-two thousand men from being crushed into pulp by the jaws of a hundred and thirty thousand in two grand divisions closing in on him. It was a reasonable supposition--always barring the utterly unexpected--another name for Stonewall Jackson, whom they seemed to have forgotten for the moment.

Sickles, seeing the "retreat," sent a courier flying to Hooker, asking for permission to follow the fugitives with his twenty thousand men. Hooker consented, and Sickles leaped from his entrenchments and set out in mad haste to overtake the flying columns. He got nearly ten miles in the woods away from the battle lines before he realized that the ghostly men in grey had made good their escape. Certainly they had disappeared from view.

It was five o'clock in the afternoon when Jackson's swift, silent marchers began to draw near to the unsuspecting right wing of Hooker's army under the command of General Howard.

Ned Vaughan was in Jackson's skirmish line feeling the way through the tender green foliage of the spring. The days were warm and the leaves far advanced--the woods so dense it was impossible for picket or skirmisher to see more than a hundred yards ahead--at some points not a hundred feet.

The thin, silent line suddenly swept into the little opening of a negro cabin with garden and patch of corn. A kindly old colored woman was standing in the doorway.

She looked into the faces of these eager, slender Southern boys and they were her "children." The meaning of war was real to her only when it meant danger to those she loved.

She ran quickly up to Ned, her eyes dancing with excitement:

"For de Lawd's sake, honey, don't you boys go up dat road no fudder!"

"Why, Mammy?" he asked with a smile.

"Lordy, chile, dey's thousan's, an' thousan's er Yankees des over dat little hill dar--dey'll kill every one er you all!"

"I reckon not, Mammy," Ned called, hurrying on.

She ran after him, still crying:

"For Gawd's sake, come back here, honey--dey kill ye sho!"

She was calling still as Ned disappeared beyond the cabin into the woods redolent now with the blossoms of chinquepin bushes and the rich odors of sweet shrub.

They climbed the little ridge on whose further slope lay an open field, and caught their first view of Howard's unsuspecting division. They halted and sent their couriers flying with the news to Jackson.

Ned looked on the scene with a thrill of exultation and then a sense of deepening pity. The boys in blue had begun to bivouac for the night, their camp fires curling through the young green leaves. The men were seated in groups laughing, talking, joking and playing cards. The horses were busy cropping the young grass.

"God have mercy on them!" Ned exclaimed.

It was nearly six o'clock before Jackson's men had all slipped silently into position behind the dense woods on this little slope--in two long grim battle lines, one behind the other, with columns in support, his horse artillery with their big guns shotted and ready.

Ned saw a slight stir in the doomed camp of blue. The men were standing up now and looking curiously toward those dense woods. A startled flock of quail had swept over their heads flying straight down from the lull crest. A rabbit came scurrying from the same direction--and then another. And then another flock of quail swirled past and pitched among the camp fires, running and darting in terror on the ground.

An officer drew his revolver and potted one for his supper.

The men glanced uneasily toward the woods but could see nothing.

"What'ell ye reckon that means?"

"What ails the poor birds?"

"And the rabbits?"

They were not long in doubt. The sudden shrill note of a bugle rang from the woods and Jackson's yelling grey lines of death swept down on their unprotected rear.

The first regiments in sight were blown into atoms and driven as chaff before a whirlwind. Behind them lay twenty regiments in their trenches pointed the wrong way. The men leaped to their guns and fought desperately to stay the rushing torrent. Beyond them was a ragged gap of a whole mile without a man, left bare by the chase of Sickles' division now ten miles away. Without support the shattered lines were crushed and crumpled and rolled back in confusion. Every regiment was cut to pieces and pushed on top of one another, men, horses, mules, cattle, guns, in a tangled mass of blood and death.

Ned was sent to bring the supporting column to drive them on and on. He mounted a horse and dashed back to the reserve line yelling his call:

"Hurry! Hurry up, men!"

"What's the hurry?" growled a grey coat.

"Hurry! Hurry!" Ned shouted. "We've captured fifty pieces of artillery and ten thousand prisoners!"

"Then what'ell's the use er hurryin' us on er empty stomach--but we're a-comin', honey--we're a-comin'!"

The colonel of a regiment snatched his hat off and was getting his men ready for the charge. He waved his hand toward Ned:

"Make that damn-fool get out of the way. I'm going to charge. Now you men listen--listen to me, I say! not to that fellow--listen to me!"

Ned could hear him still talking excitedly to his eager men as he dashed back to the battle line.

General Hooker sat on the porch of the Chancellor House, his headquarters. On the east there was heavy firing where his men were attempting to carry out his orders to flank Lee's retreating army. Sickles' and Pleasanton's cavalry were already in pursuit. By some curious trick of the breeze or atmospheric conditions not a sound had reached him from the direction of his right wing. A staff officer suddenly turned his glasses to the west.

"My God, here they come!"

Before the astounded Commander could leap from the porch to his horse the flying stragglers of his shattered right were pouring into view--men, wagons, ambulances, in utter confusion. Hooker swung his old division under General Berry into line and shouted to his veterans:

"Forward with the bayonet!"

The sturdy division plowed its way through the receding blue waves of panic-stricken men and dashed into the face of the overwhelming hosts.

Major Keenan, in command of the 8th Pennsylvania Cavalry, charged with his gallant five hundred into the face of almost certain death and held the grey lines in check until the artillery of the Third Corps was saved and turned on the advancing Confederates. He fell at the head of his men.

The fighting now became a battle. It was no longer a rout.

Ned saw a lone deaf man in blue standing bareheaded, fighting a whole army so intent on his work he hadn't noticed that his regiment had retreated and left him.

Two men in grey raised their muskets and fired point blank at this man at the same instant. The unconscious hero fell.

"I hit him!" cried one.

"No, I hit him!" said the other.

And they both rushed up and tenderly offered him help.

A grey soldier came hurrying by taking two prisoners to the rear. A cannon ball from the rescued battery cut off his leg and he dropped beside Ned shouting hysterically:

"Pick me up! Pick me up! Why don't you pick me up?"

The blue prisoner looked back in terror at the battery and started to run. A grey soldier stopped them:

"Here! Here! What'ell's the matter with you? Them's your own guns. What are ye tryin' to get away from 'em for?"

Men were falling now at every step.

Ned had advanced a hundred yards further when the boy on his right suddenly threw his hands over his head and his leg full to the ground, cut off by a cannon ball, Ned leaped to his side and caught him in his arms. A look of anguish swept his strong young face as he gasped:

"My poor old mother! O my God, what'll she do now?"

Ned tied his handkerchief around the mangled leg, twisted the knot, and stayed the blood gushing from the severed arteries, and rushed back to his desperate work.

Four horses dashed by his side dragging through the woods a big gun to train on the battery that was plowing through their lines. A solid shot crashed straight through a horse's head, blinding Ned with blood and brains.

He threw his hand to his face and buried it in the hot quivering mass, exclaiming:

"My God, boys, my brains are out!"

"You've got the biggest set I ever saw then!" the Captain said, helping him to clear his eyes.

A shell exploded squarely against the gun carriage, hurling it into junk and piling all four horses on the ground. Their dying cries rang pitifully through the smoke-wreathed woods. One horse lifted his head, placed both fore feet on the ground and tried to rise. His hind legs were only shreds of torn flesh. He neighed a long, quivering, soul-piercing shriek of agony and a merciful officer drew his revolver and killed him.

A cannoneer lay by this horse's side with both his legs hopelessly crushed so high in the thick flesh of the thighs there was no hope. He was moaning horribly. He turned his eyes in agony to the officer who had shot the horse:

"Please, Captain--for the love of God--shoot me, too, I can't live----"

The Captain shook his head.

"Have mercy on me--for Jesus' sake--kill me--you were kind to my horse--can't you do as much for me?"

The Captain turned away in anguish. He couldn't even send for morphine. The South had no more morphine. The blockade's iron hand was on her hospitals now.

Ned fought for half an hour behind a tree. Twice the bullets striking the hark knocked pieces into his eyes. He was sure at least fifty Minie balls struck it.

A bald-headed Colonel rushed by at double quick leading a fresh regiment into action to support them. The hell of battle was not so hot the Southern soldier had lost his sense of humor. They were glad to see this dashing old fighter and they told him so in no uncertain way.

"Hurrah for Baldy!"

"Sick 'em, Baldy--sick 'em----"

"I'll bet on old man Baldy every time----"

"Hurrah for the bald-headed man!"

The Colonel paid no attention to their shouts. The flash of his muskets in the deepening twilight turned the tide in their favor. The big guns had been unlimbered and pulled back deeper into the blue lines.

John Vaughan's line was swung to support the charge of Hooker's old division which first halted the rush of Jackson's men. In the field beyond the Chancellor

House stood a huge straw stack. As the regiment rushed by at double quick the Colonel spied a panic-stricken officer crouching in terror behind the pile.

The Colonel slapped him across the shoulders with his sword:

"What sort of a place is this for you, sir?"

Through chattering teeth came the trembling response:

"W-w-hy, m-my God, do you think the bullets can come through?"

The Colonel threw up his hands in rage and pressed on with his men.

A wagon loaded with entrenching tools, on which sat half a dozen negroes rattled by on its way to the rear. A solid shot plumped squarely into the load.

John saw picks, spades, shovels and negroes suddenly fill the air. Every negro lit on his feet and his legs were running when he struck the ground. They reached the tall timber before the last pick fell.

The regiments were going into battle double quick, but they were not going so fast they couldn't laugh.

"Hurry up men!" the Colonel called. "Hurry up, let's get in there and help 'em!"

A moment more and they were in it.

The man beside John threw up both hands and dropped with the dull, unmistakable thud of death--the soldier who has been in battle knows the sickening sound.

They were thrown around the Third Corps battery to protect their guns which had been dragged to a place more securely within the lines. Still their gunners kept falling one by one--falling ominously at the crack of a single gun in the woods. A Confederate sharpshooter had climbed a tree and was picking them off.

A tall Westerner spoke to the Colonel:

"Let me go huntin' for him!"

The Commander nodded and John went with him--why? He asked himself the question before he had taken ten steps through the shadowy underbrush. The answer was plain. He knew the truth at once. The elemental brutal instinct of the hunter had kindled at the flash in that Westerner's eye. It would be a hunt worth while--the game was human.

For five minutes they crept through the bushes hiding from tree to tree in the open spaces. They searched the tops in vain, when suddenly a piece of white oak bark fluttered down from the sky and struck the ground at their feet.

The Westerner smiled at John and stood motionless:

"Well, I'm damned!"

They waited breathlessly, afraid to look up into the boughs of the towering oak beneath which they were standing.

"Don't move now!" the man from the West cried, "and I'll pot him."

Slowly he stepped backward, softly, noiselessly, his eye fixed in the treetop, his gun raised and finger on the trigger.

He stopped, aimed, and fired.

John looked up and saw the grey figure fall back from the tree trunk and plunge downward, bounding from limb to limb and striking the ground within ten feet of where he stood with heavy thud. The blood was gushing in red streams from his nose and mouth.

They turned and hurried back to their lines--another fierce attack was being made on those guns. The men in grey charged and drove them a hundred feet before they rallied and pushed them back with frightful loss on both sides.

John's Captain fell, dangerously wounded, and lay fifty feet beyond their battle line. The dry leaves in the woods had taken fire from a shell and the blaze was nearing the wounded men. The Westerner coolly leaped from his position behind a tree, walked out in a hail of lead, picked up his wounded Commander, and carried him safely to the rear. He had just stepped back to take his stand in line by John's side when a flying piece of shrapnel tore a hole in his side. He dropped to his knees, sank lower to his elbow, turned his blue eyes to the darkening sky and slowly muttered as if to himself:

"Poor--little--wife--and--babies!"

The night was drawing her merciful veil over the scene at last. Jackson having crushed and mangled Hooker's right wing and rolled it back in red defeat over five miles in two hours, was slowly feeling his way on his last reconnaissance for the day to make his plans for the next. Through a fatal misunderstanding he was fired on by his own men and borne from the field fatally wounded.

A shiver of horror thrilled the Southerners when the news of Jackson's fall was whispered through the darkness.

At midnight Sickles led his division back into the dense woods and for three terrible hours the men on both sides fought as demons in the shadows. The long lines of blazing muskets in the darkness looked like the onward rush of a forest fire. At times two solid walls of flame seemed to leap through the tree tops into the starlit heavens. A small portion of the captured ground was recovered at a frightful loss--and no man knows to this day how many gallant men in blue were shot down by their own comrades in the darkness and confusion of that mad assault.

Hooker sent a desperate call to Sedgwick to hurry to his relief by carrying out his plan of sweeping Marye's Heights and falling on Lee's rear.

At dawn Stuart in command of Jackson's corps led the new charge on Hooker's lines, his grey veterans shouting:

"Remember Jackson!"

Through the long hours of the terrible third day of May the fierce combat of giants raged. During the morning Hooker's headquarters were reached by the Confederate artillery and the old Chancellor House, filled with the wounded, was knocked to pieces and set on fire. The women and children and slaves of the Chancellor family were shivering in its cellar while the shells were hurling its bricks and timbers in murderous fury on the helpless wounded who lay in hundreds in the yard. The men from both armies rushed into this hell and carried the wounded to a place of safety.

General Hooker was wounded and the report flew over the Federal army that he had been killed. To allay their fears the General had himself lifted into the saddle and rode down his lines and out of sight, when he was taken unconscious from his horse.

Sedgwick was fighting his way with desperation now to force Marye's Heights and strike Lee's rear.

Once more the stone wall blazed with death for the gallant men in blue. They dashed themselves against it wave on wave, only to fall back in confusion. They tried to flank it and failed. Hour after hour the mad charges rolled against this hill and broke in deep red pools at its base. There were but nine thousand men holding it against forty thousand, but it was afternoon before the grey lines slowly gave way and Sedgwick's victorious troops poured over the hill toward Lee's lines. Hooker had asked him to appear at daylight. The long rows and mangled heaps of the dead left on Marye's bloody slopes was sufficient answer to all inquiries as to his delay.

But the way was still blocked. The receding line of grey was suddenly supported by Early's division detached from Lee's reserves. Again Sedgwick was stopped and fought until dark.

As the sun was sinking over the smoke-wreathed spring-clothed trees of the wilderness, Stuart gathered Jackson's corps for a desperate assault on Hooker's last line of defense. Waving his plumed hat high above his handsome bearded face, he put himself at the head of his troops and charged, chanting with boyish enthusiasm his improvised battle song:

"Old--Joe--Hooker,
Won't you come out o' the Wilderness!
Come out o' the Wilderness!
Come out o' the Wilderness!

Old--Joe--Hooker--
Come out o' the Wilderness--
Come--come--I say!"

The cheering grey waves swept all before them and left Lee in full possession of Chancellorsville and the whole position the Federal army had originally held.

As the Confederates rolled on, driving the fiercely fighting men in blue before them, Lee himself rode forward to encourage his men and then it happened--the thing for which the great have fought, and longed, and dreamed since time dawned--the spontaneous tribute of the brave to a trusted leader.

His victorious troops went wild at the sight of him. Above the crash and roar of battle rose the shouts of the Southerners:

"Hurrah for Lee!"

"Lee!"

"Lee!"

From lip to lip the thrilling name leaped until the wounded and the dying turned their eyes to see and raised their feeble voices:

"Lee!--Lee!--Lee!"

It was at this moment that he received the note from Jackson announcing that he was badly wounded. With the shouts of his men ringing in his ears, he drew his pencil and wrote across the pommel of his saddle:

> "GENERAL: I have just received your note informing me that you are wounded. I cannot express my regret at the occurrence. Could I have directed events, I should have chosen, for the good of the country, to be disabled in your stead.
>
> "I congratulate you upon the victory which is due to your skill and energy.
>
> "Very respectfully, your obedient servant,
>
> "R. E. LEE,
> "GENERAL."

It was quick, bloody work next day for the Southerner to turn and spring on Sedgwick with the ferocity of a tiger, crush and hurl his battered and bleeding corps back on the river.

Under cover of a storm General Couch, in command of Hooker's army, retreated across the Rappahannock. The blue and grey picket lines that night were so close to each other the men could talk freely. The Southern boys were chaffing the Northerners over their oft repeated defeats. Through the darkness a Yankee voice drawled:

"Ah, Johnnie, shut up--you make us tired! You're not so much as you think you are. Swap Generals with us and we'll come over and lick hell out of you!"

A silence fell over the boasting ones and then the listening Yankee heard a low voice chuckle to his comrade:

"I'm damned if they wouldn't, too!"

When the grey dawn broke through the storm they began to bury the dead and care for the wounded. The awful struggle had ended at last.

The Northern army had lost seventeen thousand men, the Southerners thirteen thousand.

It was a great victory for the South, but a few more such victories and there would be none of her brave boys left to tell the story.

John Vaughan's company had been detailed to help in cleaning the field. The day before, on Sunday morning, they had eaten their breakfast seated on the ground among hundreds of dead bodies whose odor poisoned the air. It is needless to say, Julius was not present. He had kept the river between him and the roar of contending hosts.

The suffering of the wounded had been terrible. Some of them had fallen on Friday, thousands on Saturday, and it was now Monday. All through the blood-soaked tangled woods they lay groaning and dying. And everywhere the flap of black wings. The keen-eyed vultures had seen from the sky where they fell.

John found a brave old farmer from Northern New York lying beside his son. He had met them in the fight at Fredericksburg in December.

"Well, here we are, Vaughan," the father cried feebly. "My boy's dead, and I'll be with him soon--but it's all right--it's all right--my country's worth it!"

They were lying in a bright open space, where the warm sun of May had pushed the wood violets into blossom in rich profusion. The dead boy's head lay in a bed of blue flowers.

Some of the bodies further on were black and charred by the flames that had swept the woods again and again during the battles. Some of them had been wounded men and they had been burned to death. Their twisted bodies and the agony on their cold faces told the hideous story more plainly than words. The odor of burning flesh still filled the air in these black spots.

With a start John suddenly came on the crouching figure of a Confederate soldier kneeling behind a stump, the paper end of the cartridge was in his teeth and his fingers still grasped the ball. He was just in the act of tearing the paper as a bullet crashed straight through his forehead. A dark streak of blood marked his face and clothes. His gun was in his other hand, the muzzle in place to receive the cartridge, the body cold and rigid in exactly the position death had called him.

A broad-shouldered, bearded man in blue had just fallen asleep nearby. The body was still warm, the blue eyes wide open, staring into the leaden sky. On his breast lay an open Bible with a bloody finger mark on the lines:

"The Lord is my shepherd,
I shall not want
He maketh me to lie down in green pastures--
He restoreth my soul."

A hundred yards further lay a dead boy from his own company. The stiff hands were still holding a picture of his sweetheart before the staring eyes. Near him lay a boy in grey with a sweetheart's letter clasped in his hand. They had talked and tried to cheer one another, these dying boys--talked of those they loved in far off villages as the mists of eternity had gathered about them.

It was late that night before the wounded had all been moved. Through every hour of its black watches the surgeons, with their sleeves rolled high, their arms red, bent over their tasks, until legs and arms were piled in ghastly heaps ten feet high.

As John Vaughan turned from the scene where he had laid a wounded man to wait his turn, his eye caught the look of terror on the face of a wounded Southern boy. He was a slender little dark-haired fellow, under sixteen, a miniature of Ned. The surgeon had just taken up his knife to cut into the deep flesh wound for the Minie ball embedded there. John saw the slender face go white and the terror-stricken young eyes search the room for help. His breath came in quick gasps and he was about to faint.

John slipped his arm around him:

"Just a minute, Doctor----"

He pressed his hand and whispered:

"Come now, little man, you're among your enemies. You've got to be brave. Show your grit for the South. I've got a brother in your army who looks like you. No white feather now when these Yankees can see you."

The slender figure stiffened and his eyes flashed:

"All right!" the sturdy lips cried. "Let him go ahead--I'm ready now!"

John held his hand, while the knife cut through the soft young flesh and found the lead. The grip of the slim fingers tightened, but he gave no cry. John handed him the bullet to put in his pocket and left him smiling his thanks.

He began to wonder vaguely if he had lost his cook forever. Julius should have found the regiment before this. It was just before day that he came on him working with might and main at a job that was the last one on earth he would have selected.

He had been seized by a burying squad and put to work dragging corpses to the trenches from the great piles where the wagons had dumped them.

The black man rolled his eyes in piteous appeal to his master:

"For Gawd's sake, Marse John, save me--dese here men won't lemme go. I been er throwin' corpses inter dem trenches since dark. I'se most dead frum work, let 'lone bein' scared ter death."

"Sorry, Julius," was the quick answer, "we've all got to work at a time like this. There's no help for it."

Julius bent again to his horrible task. The thing that appalled him was the way the dead men kept looking at him out of their eyes wide and staring in the flickering light of the lanterns.

John stood watching him thoughtfully. He had finished one pile of bodies, dragging them by the heels one by one, and throwing them into the trenches. He was just about to begin on the last stack when he saw that he had left one lying a little further back in the shadows.

Julius looked at it dubiously and scratched his head. He didn't like the idea of going so far back in the dark, away from the light, but there was no help for it. The guard stood with his musket scowling:

"Get a move on you--damn you, don't stand there!" he growled.

Julius walled his eyes at his tormentor and ran for the body. It happened to be the sleeping form of a tired guard who had been up three nights. The negro grabbed his legs and rushed toward the lights and the trenches.

He had almost reached the grave when the corpse gave a vicious kick and yelled:

"Here--what'ell!"

Julius didn't stop to look or to answer. What he felt in his hands was enough. With a yell of terror he dropped the thing and plunged straight ahead.

"Gawd, save me!" he gasped.

His foot slipped on the edge of the trench and he rolled in the dark hole. With the leap of a frightened panther he reached the solid earth and flew, each leap a muttered prayer:

"Save me! Lawd, save me!"

Standing there beside the grim piles of his dead comrades John Vaughan joined the guard in uncontrollable laughter. It was many a day before he saw his cook again.

The laughter suddenly stopped, and he turned from the scene with a shudder.

"I wonder," he muttered, "if I live through this war, whether I'll come out of it with a soul!"

The report from Chancellorsville drifted slowly, ominously, appallingly, over Washington with the clouds and mists of the storm which swept up the Potomac and shrouded the city in a grey mantle of mourning. The White House was still. The dead were walking through its great rooms of state. The anguished heart who watched by the window toward the hills of Virginia saw and heard each muffled footfall.

He walked to the table with stumbling, uncertain step at last, his face ghastly and rigid, its color grey ashes, his deep set eyes streaming with tears, sank helplessly into a chair, and for the first time gave way to despair:

"O my God! My God! what will the country say!"

CHAPTER XXVIII
THE MOONLIT RIVER

Betty Winter was quick to answer the hurry call for more nurses in the field hospital at Chancellorsville. The results at the end of three days' carnage had paralyzed the service.

She left the Carver Hospital on receipt of the first cry for help and hurried to her home to complete her preparations to leave for the front.

Her father was at breakfast alone.

She called her greeting from the hall, rushed to her room, packed a bag, and quickly came down.

The Southerner

She slipped her arm around his neck, bent and kissed him good-bye. He held her a moment:

"You must leave so early, dear?"

"I must catch the first bout for Aquia. The news from the front is hideous. The force there is utterly inadequate. They've asked for every nurse that can be spared for a week. The wounded lay on the ground for three days and nights, and hundreds of them can't be moved to Washington. The woods took fire dozens of times and many of the poor boys were terribly burned. The suffering, they say, is indescribable."

The old man suddenly rose, with a fierce light flashing in his eyes:

"Oh, the miserable blunderer in the White House--this war has been one grim and awful succession of his mistakes!"

Betty placed her hand on his arm in tender protest:

"Father, dear, how can you be so unreasonable--so insanely unjust? Your hatred of the President is a positive mania----"

"I'm not alone in my affliction, child; Arnold is his only friend in Congress to-day----"

"Then it's a shame--a disgrace to the Nation. Every disaster is laid at his door. In his big heart he is carrying the burden of millions--their suffering, their sorrows, their despair. You blamed him at first for trifling with the war. Now you blame him for the bloody results when the army really fights. You ask for an effective campaign and when you get these tragic battles you heap on his head greater curses. It isn't right. It isn't fair. I can't understand how a man with your deep sense of justice can be so cruelly inconsistent----"

The Senator shook his grey head in protest:

"There! there! dear--we won't discuss it. You're a woman and you can't understand my point of view. We'll just agree to disagree. You like the man in the White House. God knows he's lonely--I shouldn't begrudge him that little consolation. His whole attitude in this war is loathsome to me. To him the Southerners are erring brethren to be brought back as prodigal sons in the end. To me they are criminal outlaws to be hanged and quartered--their property confiscated, the foundations of their society destroyed, and every trace of their States blotted from the map----"

"Father!"

"Until we understand that such is the purpose of the war we can get nowhere--accomplish nothing. But there, dear--I didn't mean to say so much. There is always one thing about which there can be no dispute--I love my little girl----"

He slipped his arm about her tenderly again.

"I'm proud of the work you're doing for our soldiers. They tell me in the big hospital that you're an angel. I've always known it, but I'm glad other people are beginning to find it out. In all the horrors of this tragedy there's one ray of sunshine for me--the light that shines from your eyes!"

He bent and kissed her again:

"Run now, and don't miss your boat."

In the five swift days of tender service which followed, Betty Winter forgot her own heartache and loneliness in the pity, pathos, and horror of the scenes she witnessed--the drawn white faces--the charred flesh, the scream of pain from the young, the sigh of brave men, the last messages of love--the gasp and the solemn silences of eternity.

When the strain of the first rush had ended and the time to follow the lines of ambulance wagons back to Washington drew near, the old anguish returned to torture her soul. She told herself it was all over, and yet she knew that somewhere in that vast city of tents, stretching for miles over the hills and valleys about Falmouth Heights, was John Vaughan. She had put him resolutely out of her life. She said this a hundred times--yet she was quietly rejoicing that his name was not on that black roll of seventeen thousand. All doubt had been removed by the announcement in the ***Republican*** of his promotion to the rank of Captain for gallantry on the field of Chancellorsville.

She hoped that he had freed himself at last from evil associates. She couldn't be sure--there were ugly rumors flying about the hospital of the use of whiskey in the army. These rumors were particularly busy with Hooker's name.

Seated alone in the quiet moonlight before the field hospital, the balmy air of the South which she drew in deep breaths was bringing back the memory of another now. The pickets had been at their usual friendly tricks of trading tobacco and coffee and exchanging newspapers. From a Richmond paper she had just learned that Ned Vaughan had fought in Lee's army at Chancellorsville. Somewhere beyond the silver mirror of the Rappahannock he was with the men in grey to-night.

Her heart in its loneliness went out to him in a wave of tender sympathy. Again she lived over the tragic hours when she had fought the battle for his life and won at last at the risk of her own.

A soldier saluted and handed her a piece of brown wrapping paper, neatly folded. Its corner was turned down in the old-fashioned way of a schoolboy's note to his sweetheart.

She went to the light and saw with a start it was in Ned Vaughan's handwriting. She read, with eager, sparkling eyes.

"DEAREST: I've just seen in a Washington paper which our boys traded for that you are here. I must see you, and to-night. I can't wait. There will be no danger to either of us. Our pickets are on friendly terms. I've arranged everything with some good tobacco for your fellows. Follow the man who hands you this note to the river. A boat will be ready for you there with one of my men to row you across. I will be waiting for you at the old mill beside the burned pier of the railroad bridge.

"NED."

Betty's heart gave a bound of joy, and in half an hour she was standing on the shining shore of the river before the old mill. Its great wheel was slowly turning, the water falling in broken crystals sparkling in the moonlight. Through the windows of the brick walls peered the black-mouthed guns trained across the water.

She looked about timidly for a moment while the man in grey who had rowed her over made fast his boat.

He tipped his old slouch hat:

"This way, Miss."

He led her down close, to the big wheel, crossed the stream of water which poured from its moss-covered buckets, and there, beneath an apple tree in bloom, stood a straight, soldierly figure in the full blue uniform of a Federal Captain, exactly as she had seen Ned Vaughan that night in the Old Capitol Prison.

The soldier saluted and Ned said:

"Wait, Sergeant, at the water's edge with your boat."

He was gone and Ned grasped both Betty's hands and kissed them tenderly:

"My glorious little heroine! I just had to tell you again that the life you saved is all, all yours. You are glad to see me--aren't you?"

"I can't tell you how glad, Boy! How brown and well you look!"

"Yes, the hard life somehow agrees with me. It's a queer thing, this army business. It makes some men strong and clean, and others into beasts."

"And why did you wear that dangerous uniform, sir?" she asked, with a smile.

"In honor of a beautiful Yankee girl, my guest. I've not worn it since that night, Betty, until now----"

His voice dropped to a whisper:

"It has been a holy thing to me, this blue uniform that cost me the life which you gave back at the risk of your own----"

"I was in no danger. I had powerful friends."

"They might not have been powerful enough--but it's sacred for another reason--as precious to me as the seamless robe for which the Roman soldiers cast lots on Calvary--I wore it in the one glorious moment in which I held you in my arms, dearest."

"O Ned, Boy, you shouldn't be so foolish!"

"I'm not. I'm sensible. I've done no more scout work since. I said that my life was yours and I had no right to place it again in such mad danger----"

"And so you face death on the field!"

"Yes, come sit here, dearest, I've made a seat for you of the broken timbers from the bridge. We can see the moonlit river and the lazy turn of the old wheel while we talk."

He led her to the seat in the edge of the moonlight and Betty drew a deep breath of joy as she drank in the beauty of the entrancing scene. The shadows of night had hidden the scars of war. Only the tall stone piers standing, lone sentinels in the river, marked its ravages where the bridge had fallen. The moon had flung her sparkling silver veil over the blood-stained world.

"You know," Ned went on eagerly, "those big pillars won't stand there naked long. We'll put the timbers back on them soon and run our trains through to Washington----"

"Sh, Ned," Betty whispered, touching his arm lightly, "be still a moment, I want to feel this wonderful scene!"

The air was sweet with the perfume of apple blossoms, the water from the old wheel fell with silvery echo and ran rippling over the stones into the river. Somewhere above the cliff a negro was playing a banjo and far down the river, beside a little cottage torn with shot and shell, but still standing, a mocking-bird was singing in the lilac bushes.

The girl looked at Ned with curious tenderness, and wondered if she had known her own heart after all--wondered if the fierce blinding passion she had once felt for his brother had been the divine thing that links the soul to the eternal? A strange spiritual beauty enveloped this younger man and drew her to-night with new power. There was something restful in its mystery. She wondered vaguely if it were possible to love two men at the same moment. She could almost swear it were. If she had never really loved John Vaughan at all! Why had his powerful, brutal personality drawn her with such terrible power? Was such a force love? It was something different from the tender charm which enveloped the slender straight young figure by her side now. She felt this with increasing certainty.

Ned took her hand and kissed the tips of her fingers.

The touch of his lips sent a thrill through her heart. It was sweet to be worshipped in this old-fashioned, foolish way. Whatever her own feeling's might be, this was love--in its divinest flowering. It drew her to-night with all but resistless tug.

"May I break the silence now, dearest, to ask you something?" he said softly.

"Yes."

"Haven't you realized yet that you are going to be mine?"

"Not in the way you mean----"

"But you are, dearest, you are!" he whispered rapturously. "You love me. You just haven't really faced the thing yet and put it to the test in your heart. War has separated us, that's all. But there's never been a moment's doubt in my soul since I looked into your eyes that night in the old prison. Their light made the cell shine with the glory of heaven! And when you kissed me, dearest----"

"You know why I did that, Ned," she murmured.

"You're fooling yourself, darling! You couldn't have done what you did, if you hadn't loved me. It came to me in a flash as I held you in my arms and pressed you to my heart. There can be no other woman on earth for me after that moment. I lived a life time with it. Say you'll be mine, dearest?"

"But I don't love you, Ned, as you love me----"

"I don't ask it now. I can wait. The revelation will come to you at last in the fullness of time--promise me, dearest--promise me!"

For an hour he poured into her ears his passionate tender plea, until the rapture of his love, the perfumed air of the spring night, and the shimmer of moonlit waters stole into her lonely heart with resistless charm.

She lifted her lips to his at last and whispered:

"Yes."

CHAPTER XXIX
THE PANIC

The morning after Betty returned to Carver Hospital from the front, a mother was pouring out her heart in a burst of patriotic joy over a wounded boy.

She thought of the lonely figure in the White House treading the wine press of a Nation's sorrow alone and asked the mother to go with her to the President, meet him and repeat what she had said. She consented at once.

For the first time Betty failed to gain admission promptly. Mr. Stoddard, his third Secretary, was at the door.

"We must let him eat something, Miss Winter," he whispered. "All night the muffled sound of his footfall came from his room. I heard it at nine, at ten, at eleven. At midnight Stanton left his door ajar and his steady tramp, tramp, tramp, came with heavier sound. The last thing I heard as I left at three was the muffled beat upstairs. The guard told me it never stopped for a moment all night."

Betty was surprised to see his face illumined by a cheerful smile as she entered. She gazed with awe into the deep eyes of the man whose single word could stop the war and divide the Union. She wondered if he had fought the Nation's battle alone with God through the night until his prophetic vision had seen through cloud and darkness the dawn of a new and more wonderful life.

She spoke softly:

"I've brought you a good mother who lost a son at Fredericksburg. She has a message for you."

The tall form bent reverently and pressed her hand. A wonderful smile transfigured his rugged face as he listened:

"God help you in your trials, Mr. President, as he has helped me in mine----"

"And you lost your son at Fredericksburg?"

"Yes. It was long before I could feel reconciled. But I've been praying for you day and night since----"

"For me?"

"You must be strong and courageous, and God will bring the Nation through!"

"You say that to me, standing beside the grave of your son?"

"Yes, and beside the cot of my other boy who is here wounded from Chancellorsville. I'm proud that God gave me such sons to lay on the altar of my country. Remember, I am praying for you day and night!"

Both big hands closed over hers and he was silent a moment.

"It's all right then. I'll get new strength when I remember that such mothers are praying for me."

He pressed Betty's hand at the door:

"Thank you, child. You bring medicine that reaches soul and body!"

The hour of despair had passed and the President returned to his task patient, watchful, strong.

Daily the shadows deepened over the Nation's life. Blacker and denser rose the clouds. Four Northern Generals had now gone down before Lee's apparently invincible genius--McClellan, Pope, Burnside, and Hooker, and with each fall the corpses of young men were piled higher.

Again the clamor rose for the return of McClellan to command. This cry was not only heard in the crushed Army of the Potomac, it was backed by the voice of two million Democrats who had chosen the man on horseback as their leader.

It was for precisely this reason that McClellan could not be considered again for command. His party had fallen under the complete control of its Copperhead leaders who demanded the ending of the war at once and at any sacrifice of principle or of the Union.

The only way the President could stop desertions and prevent the actual secession of the great Northern States of the Middle West, now under the control of these men, was to use his arbitrary power to suspend the civil law and put them in prison. Through the State and War Departments he did this sorrowfully, but promptly.

His answer to his critics was the soundest reasoning and it justified him in the judgment of thinking men.

"I make such arrests," he declared, "because these men are laboring to prevent the raising of troops and encouraging desertion. Armies cannot be maintained unless desertion shall be punished by the penalty of death.

"I will not shoot a simple-minded soldier boy who deserts, and refuse to touch a wily agitator who induces him to commit the crime. To silence the agitator and save the boy is not only Constitutional, but withal a great mercy."

Volunteers were no longer to be had and a draft of five hundred thousand men had been ordered for the summer. The Democratic leaders in solid array were threatening to resist this draft by every means in their power, even to riot and revolution.

The masses of the North were profoundly discouraged at the unhappy results of the war. In thousands of patriotic loyal homes, men and women had begun to ask themselves whether it were not cruel folly to send their brave boys to be slaughtered.

The prestige of the Southern army was at its highest point and its terrible power was nowhere more gravely realized than in the North, whose thousands of mourning homes attested its valor.

Europe at last seemed ready to spring on the throat of America. Distinct reports were in circulation in the Old World that the Emperor of France, Napoleon III, intended to interfere in our affairs. On the 9th of January, the French Government denied this. The Emperor himself, however, sent to the President an offer of mediation so blunt and surprising it could not be doubted that it was a veiled hint of his purpose to intervene. Beyond a doubt he expected the Union to be dismembered and he proposed to form an alliance between the Latin Empire which he was founding in Mexico and the triumphant Confederate States.

Great Britain was behind this Napoleonic adventure. Outwitted by the President in the affair of the ***Trent***, the British Government was eager for the chance to strike the Republic.

To cap the climax of disasters Lee was preparing to invade the North with his victorious army. The announcement struck terror to the Northern cities and produced a condition among them little short of panic.

The move would be the height of audacity and yet Lee had good reasons for believing its success possible and probable. His grey veterans were still ragged and poorly shod. With Southern ports blockaded and no manufacturing this was inevitable, but they had proven in two years' test of fire Lee's proud boast:

"There never were such men in an army before. They will go anywhere and do anything if properly led."

This opinion was confirmed to the President by Charles Francis Adams, a veteran of his own Army of the Potomac, whom he summoned to the White House for a conference.

"I do not believe," said Adams gravely, "that any more formidable or better organized and animated force was ever set in motion than that which Lee is now leading toward the North. It is essentially an army of fighters--men who individually, or in the mass, can be depended on for any feat of arms in the power of mere mortals to accomplish. They will blanch at no danger. Lee knows this from experience and they have full confidence in him."

He could not hope to enter Pennsylvania with more than sixty-five thousand men, but his plan was reasonable. With such an army he had hurled McClellan's hundred and ten thousand soldiers back from the gates of Richmond and scattered them to the winds. With a less number he had all but annihilated Pope's men and flung them back into Washington a disorganized rabble. With thirty-seven thousand grey soldiers he had repelled in a welter of blood McClellan's eighty-six thousand at Antietam and retired at his leisure. With seventy thousand men he had crushed Burnside's host of one hundred and thirteen thousand at Fredericksburg. With sixty thousand he had just struck Hooker's grand army of a hundred and thirty thousand men and four hundred and thirty-eight guns, rolled it up as a scroll and thrown it across the Rappahannock in blinding, bewildering defeat.

From every prisoner taken at Fredericksburg and Chancellorsville he knew the Northern army was discouraged and heartsick. That he could march his ragged men, the flower of Southern manhood, into Pennsylvania and clothe and feed them on her boundless resources he couldn't doubt. Virginia was swept bare, and the demoralization of Hooker's army with the profound depression of the North left his way open.

To say that Lee's invasion, as it rapidly developed under such conditions, struck terror to the Capital of the Republic is to mildly express it. The movement of his army from Culpepper in June indicated clearly that his objective point was Harrisburg, Pennsylvania. If the Capital of the State fell, nothing could withstand the onward triumphant rush of his army into Philadelphia, Baltimore and Washington.

To meet the extraordinary danger the President called for one hundred thousand militia for six months' emergency service from the five States clustering around Pennsylvania. And yet as the two armies drew near to each other, General George Meade, the new Union Commander who had succeeded Hooker, had but one hundred and five thousand against Lee's sixty-two thousand. So terrible had been the depression following Chancellorsville, so rapid the desertions, so numerous the leaves of absence, that the combined forces of the Army of the Potomac with the State troops under the new call reached only this pitiful total.

Lee's swift column penetrated almost to the gates of Harrisburg before Meade's advance division of twenty-five thousand men had caught up with his rear at Gettysburg on July 1st.

Seeing that a battle was inevitable, Lee drew in his advance lines and made ready for the clash. The Northern army was going into this fight with the smallest number of men relatively which he had ever met--though outnumbering him nearly two to one. The difference was that here the North was defending her own soil.

It was not surprising that on the eve of such a battle in the light of the frightful experiences of the past two years that Washington should be in a condition of panic. A single defeat now with Lee's victorious army north of the Capital meant its fall, the inevitable dismemberment of the Union, and the bankruptcy and ruin of the remaining Northern States.

Brave men in Congress who had fought heroically with their mouths inveighing with bitter invective against the weak and vacillating policy of the President in temporizing with the South were busy packing their goods and chattels to fly at a moment's notice.

The President realized, as no other man could, the deep tragedy of the crisis. He sat by his window for hours, his face a grey mask, his sorrowful eyes turned within, the deep-cut lines furrowed into his cheeks as though burned with red hot irons.

He was struggling desperately now to forestall the possible panic which would follow defeat.

He had sent once more for McClellan and in painful silence, all others excluded from the Executive Chamber, awaited his coming.

"You are doubtless aware, General," the President began, "that a defeat at Gettysburg might involve the fall of the Capital and the dismemberment of the Union?"

"I am, sir."

"First, I wish to speak to you with perfect frankness about some ugly matters which have come to my ears--may I?"

The compelling blue eyes flashed and the General spoke with an accent of impatience:

"Certainly."

"A number of Secret Societies have overspread the North and Northwest, whose purpose is to end the war at once and on any terms. I have the best of reasons for believing that the men back of these Orders are now in touch with the Davis Government in Richmond. I am informed that a coterie of these conspirators, a sort of governing board, have gotten control or may get control of the organization of your Party. I have heard the ugly rumor that they are counting on you----"

"Stop!" McClellan shouted.

The General sprang to his feet, the President rose and the two men confronted each other in a moment of tense silence.

The compact figure of McClellan was trembling with rage--the tall man's sombre eyes holding his with steady purpose.

"No man can couple the word treason with my name, sir!" the General hissed.

"Have I done so?"

"You are insinuating it--and I demand a retraction!"

The President smiled genially:

"Then I apologize for my carelessness of expression. I have never believed you a traitor to the Union."

"Thank you!"

"I don't believe it now, General. That's why I've sent for you."

"Then I suggest that you employ more caution in the use of words if this conversation is to continue."

"Again I apologize, General, with admiration for your manner of meeting the ugly subject. I'm glad you feel that way--and now if you will be seated we can talk business."

McClellan resumed his seat with a frown and the President went on:

"I have sent for you to ask an amazing thing----"

"Hence the secrecy with which I am summoned?"

"Exactly. I'm going to ask you to take my place and save the Union."

McClellan's handsome face went white:

"What do you mean?"

"Exactly what I've said."

"And your conditions?" the General asked, with a quiver in his voice.

"They are very simple: Preside to-morrow night at a great Democratic Union Mass Meeting in New York and boldly put yourself at the head of the Union Democracy----"

"And you?"

"I will withdraw from the race."

"What race?"

"For the next term of the Presidency."

"Oh----"

"My convention is but ten months off. Yours can meet a day earlier. I will withdraw in your favor and force my Party to endorse you. Your election will be a certainty."

The General lifted his hand with a curious smile:

"You're in earnest?"

"I was never more so. It is needless for me to say that I came into this office with high ambitions to serve my country. My dream of glory has gone--I have left only agony and tears----" He paused and drew a deep breath.

"I did want the chance," he went on wistfully, "to stay here another term to see the sun shine again, to heal my country's wounds, and show all my people, North, South, East, and West, that I love them! But I can't risk this new battle, if you will agree to take my place and save the Union. Will you preside over such a meeting?"

"No," was the sharp, clear answer.

"I am sorry--why?"

"Perhaps I am already certain of that election without your assistance?"

"Oh--I see."

"Besides, what right have you to ask anything of me?"

"Only the right of one who sinks all thought of himself in what he believes to be the greater good."

"You who, with victory in my grasp before Richmond, snatched it away! You, who nailed me to the cross on the bloody field of Antietam with your accursed Proclamation of Emancipation and removed me from my command before I could win my campaign!"

The big hand rose in kindly protest:

"Can't you believe me, General, when I tell you, with God as my witness, that I have never allowed a personal motive or feeling to enter into a single appointment or removal I have made? What I've done has always been exactly what I believed was for the best interests of the country. Can't you believe this?"

"No."

"In spite of the fact that I risked the dissolution of my Cabinet and the united opposition of my party when I restored you to command?"

"No--you had to do it."

"Grant then," the persuasive voice went on, "that I have treated you unfairly, that I had personal feelings. Surely you should in this hour of my reckoning, this hour of my Golgotha, when I climb the hill alone and ask the man I have wronged to take my place--surely you should be content with my humiliation? I shall not hesitate to proclaim it from the housetop when I ask for your election. If I have wronged you, my anguish could not be more pitifully complete! Will you do as I ask, and assure the safety of our country?"

"I'll do my best to save my country," was the slow, firm answer, "but in my own way."

The General rose, bowed stiffly and left the President standing in sorrowful silence, his deep eyes staring into space and seeing nothing.

On the morning of July 1st the two armies were rapidly approaching each other, marching in parallel lines stretched over a vast distance--the extreme wings more than forty miles apart.

Buford, commanding the advance guard of the Union army, struck Hill's division of the Confederates before the town of Gettysburg and the first gun of the great battle echoed over the green hills and valleys of Pennsylvania.

The President caught the flash of the shock from the telegraph wires with a sense of sickening dread. The rear guard of his army was yet forty miles away. What might happen before they were in line God alone could tell. He could not know, of course, that but twenty-two thousand Confederates had reached the field and stood confronting twenty-four thousand under John F. Reynolds, one of the ablest and bravest generals of the Union army.

Through every hour of this awful day he sat in the telegraph office of the War Department and read with bated breath the news.

The brief reports were not reassuring. The battle was raging with unparalleled fury. At ten o'clock General Reynolds fell dead from his horse in front of his men, and when the news was flashed to Meade he sent Hancock forward riding at full speed to take command.

The President read the message announcing Reynolds' death with quivering lip. He put his big hand blindly over his heart as if about to faint.

At three o'clock the smoke which had enveloped the battle line was lifted by a breeze as Hancock dashed on the field. He had not arrived a moment too soon. His superb bearing on his magnificent horse, his shouts of confidence, his promise of heavy reinforcements, stayed the tide of retreat and brought order out of chaos.

The day had been won again by Lee's apparently invincible men. They had driven the Union army from their line a mile in front of Gettysburg back through the town and beyond it, captured the town, taken five thousand men in blue prisoners with two generals, besides inflicting a loss of three thousand killed and wounded, including among the dead the gallant and popular commander, John F. Reynolds.

When this message reached the President late at night he had eaten nothing since breakfast. He rose from his seat in the telegraph office and walked from the building alone in silence. His step was slow, trance-like, and uncertain as if he were only half awake or had risen walking in his sleep.

He went to his bedroom, locked the door and fell on his knees in prayer. Hour after hour he wrestled alone with God in the darkness, while his tired army rushed

The Southerner

through the night to plant themselves on the Heights beyond Gettysburg, before Lee's men could be concentrated to forestall them.

Over and over again, through sombre eyes that streamed with tears, the passionate cry was wrung from his heart:

"Lord God of our fathers, have mercy on us! I have tried to make this war yours--our cause yours--if I have sinned and come short, forgive! We cannot endure another Fredericksburg or Chancellorsville. Into thy hands, O Lord, I give our men and our country this night--save them!"

CHAPTER XXX
SUNSHINE AND STORM

When the sun rose over Gettysburg on the second day of July, the Union army, rushing breathlessly through the night to the rescue of its defeated advance corps, had reached the heights beyond the town. Before Longstreet had attempted to obey Lee's command to take these hills, General Meade's blue host had reached them and were entrenching themselves.

The Confederate Commander discovered that in the death of Jackson, he had lost his right arm.

It was one o'clock before Longstreet moved to the attack, hurling his columns in reckless daring against these bristling heights. When darkness drew its kindly veil over the scene, Lee's army had driven General Sickles from his chosen position to his second line of defense on the hill behind, gained a foothold in the famous Devil's Den at the base of the Round Tops, broken the lines of the Union right and held their fortifications on Culp's Hill.

The day had been one of frightful slaughter.

The Union losses in the two days had reached the appalling total of more than twenty thousand men. Lee had lost fifteen thousand.

The brilliant July moon rose and flooded this field of blood and death with silent glory. From every nook and corner, from every shadow and across every open space, through the hot breath of the night, came the moans of thousands, and louder than all the long agonizing cries for water. Many a man in grey crawled over the ragged rocks to press his canteen to the lips of his dying enemy in blue, and many a boy in blue did as much for the man in grey.

Fifteen thousand wounded men lay there through the long black hours.

At ten o'clock a wounded Christian soldier began to sing one of the old, sweet hymns of faith, whose words have come ringing down the ages wet with tears and winged with human hopes. In five minutes ten thousand voices of blue and grey, some of them quivering with the agony of death, had joined. For two hours the woods and hills rang with the songs of these wounded men.

All through this pitiful music the Confederates were massing their artillery on Seminary Ridge, replacing their wounded horses and refilling their ammunition chests.

The Union army were burrowing like moles and planting their terrible batteries on the brows of the hills beyond the town.

At Lee's council of war that night Longstreet advised his withdrawal from Gettysburg into a more favorable position in the mountains. But the Confederate Commander, reinforced now by the arrival of Pickett's division of fifteen thousand men and Stuart's cavalry, determined to renew the battle.

At the first grey streak of dawn on the 3rd the Federal guns roared their challenge to the Confederate forces which had captured their entrenchments on Culp's Hill. Seven terrible hours of bombardment, charge and counter charge followed until every foot of space had claimed its toll of dead, before the Confederates yielded the Hill.

At noon there was an ominous lull in the battle. At one o'clock a puff of smoke from Seminary Ridge was followed by a dull roar. The signal gun had pealed its call of death to thousands. For two miles along the crest of this Ridge the Confederates had planted one hundred and fifty guns. Two miles of smoke-wreathed flame suddenly leaped from those hills in a single fiery breath.

The longer line of big Federal guns on Seminary Ridge were silent for a few minutes and then answered gun for gun until the heavens were transformed into a roaring hell of bursting, screaming, flaming shells. For two hours the earth trembled beneath the shock of these volcanoes, and then the two storms died slowly away and the smoke began to lift.

An ominous sign. The grey infantry were deploying in line under Pickett to charge the heights of Cemetery Ridge. Fifteen thousand gallant men against an impregnable hill held by seventy thousand intrenched soldiers, backed by the deadliest and most powerful artillery.

They swept now into the field before the Heights, their bands playing as if on parade--their grey ranks dressed on their colors. Down the slope across the plain and up the hill the waves rolled, their thinning ranks closing the wide gaps torn each moment by the fiery sleet of iron and lead.

A handful of them lived to reach the Union lines on those heights. Armistead, with a hundred men, broke through and lifted his battle flag for a moment over a Federal battery, and fell mortally wounded.

And then the shattered grey wave broke into a spray of blood and slowly ebbed down the hill. The battle of Gettysburg had ended.

For the first time the blue Army of the Potomac had won a genuine victory. It had been gained at a frightful cost, but no price was too high to pay for such a victory. It had saved the Capital of the Nation. The Union army had lost twenty-three thousand men, the Confederate twenty thousand. Meade had lost seventeen of his generals, and Lee, fourteen.

When the thrilling news from the front reached Washington on July 4th, the President lifted his big hands above his head and cried to the crowd of excited men who thronged the Executive office:

"Unto God we give all the praise!"

None of those present knew the soul significance of that sentence as it fell from his trembling lips. He seated himself at his desk and quickly wrote a brief proclamation of thanks to Almighty God, which he telegraphed to the Governor of each Union State, requesting them to repeat it to their people.

While the North was still quivering with joy over the turn of the tide at Gettysburg, Gideon Welles, the Secretary of the Navy, hurried into the President's office and handed him a dispatch from the gunboat under Admiral Porter cooeperating with General Grant announcing the fall of Vicksburg, the surrender of thirty-five thousand Confederate soldiers of its garrison, and the opening of the Mississippi River to the Gulf of Mexico.

The President seized his hat, his dark face shining with joy:

"I will telegraph the news to General Meade myself!"

He stopped suddenly and threw his long arms around Welles:

"What can we do for the Secretary of the Navy for this glorious intelligence? He is always giving us good news. I cannot tell you my joy over this result. It is great, Mr. Welles, it is great!"

With the eagerness of a boy he rushed to the telegraph office and sent the message to Meade over his own signature.

For the first time in dreary months the sun had burst for a moment through the clouds that had hung in endless gloom over the White House. The sorrowful eyes were shining with new hope. The President felt sure that General Lee could never succeed in leading his shattered army back into Virginia. He had lost twenty thousand men out of his sixty-two thousand--while Meade was still in command of a grand army of eighty-two thousand soldiers flushed with victory. The Potomac River was in flood and the Confederate army was on its banks unable to recross.

It was a moral certainty that the heroic Commander who had saved the Capital at Gettysburg could, with his eighty-two thousand men, capture or crush Lee's remaining force, caught in this trap by the swollen river, and end the war.

The men who crowded into the Executive office the day after the news of Vicksburg, found the Chief Magistrate in high spirits. Among the cases of deserters, court-martialed and ordered to be shot, he was surprised to find a negro soldier bearing the remarkable name of Julius Caesar Thornton. John Vaughan had telegraphed the President asking his interference with the execution of this cruel edict.

The President was deeply interested. It was the beginning of the use of negro troops. He had consented to their employment with reluctance, but they were proving their worth to the army, both in battle and in the work of garrisons.

Julius was brought from prison for an interview with the Chief Magistrate.

Stanton had sternly demanded the enforcement of the strictest military discipline as the only way to make these black troops of any real service to the Government. He asked that an example be made of Julius by sending him back to the army to be publicly shot before the assembled men of his race. He was convicted of two capital offenses. He had been caught in Washington shamelessly flaunting the uniform he had disgraced.

Julius faced the President with an humble salute and a broad grin. The black man liked the looks of his judge and he threw off all embarrassment his situation had produced with the first glance at the kindly eyes gazing at him over the rims of those spectacles.

"Well, Julius Caesar Thornton, this is a serious charge they have lodged against you?"

"Yassah, dat's what dey say."

"You went forth like a man to fight for your country, didn't you?"

"Na, sah!"

"How'd you get there?"

"Dey volunteered me, sah."

"Volunteered you, did they?" the President laughed.

"Yassah--dat dey did. Dey sho' volunteered me whether er no----"

"And how did it happen?"

"Dey done hit so quick, sah, I scacely know how dey did do hit. I was in de war down in Virginia wid Marse John Vaughan--an' er low-lifed Irishman on guard dar put me ter wuk er buryin' corpses. I hain't nebber had no taste for corpses nohow, an' I didn't like de job--mo' specially, sah, when one ob 'em come to ez I was pullin' him froo de dark ter de grave----"

"Come to, did he?" the President smiled.

"Yassah--he come to all of er sudden an' kicked me! An' hit scared me near 'bout ter death. I lit out fum dar purty quick, sah, an' go West. An' I ain't mor'n got out dar 'fore two fellers drawed dere muskets on me an' persuaded me ter volunteer, sah. Dey put dese here cloze on me an' tell me dat I wuz er hero. I tell 'em dey must be some mistake 'bout dat, but dey say no--dey know what dey wuz er doin'. Dey keep on tellin' me dat I wuz er hero an', by golly, I 'gin ter b'lieve hit myself till dey git me into trouble, sah."

"You were in a battle?"

Julius scratched his head and walled his eyes:

"I had er little taste ob it, sah,----"

"Well, you tried to fight, didn't you?"

"No, sah,--I run."

"Ran at the first fire?"

"Yas, *sah*! An' I'd a ran sooner ef I'd er known hit wuz comin'----"

Julius paused and broke into a jolly laugh:

"Dey git one pop at me, sah, 'fore I seed what dey wuz doin'!"

The President suppressed a laugh and gazed at Julius with severity:

"That wasn't very creditable to your courage."

"Dat ain't in my line, sah,--I'se er cook."

"Have you no regard for your reputation?"

"Dat ain't nuttin' ter me, sah, 'side er life!"

"And your life is worth more than other people's?"

"Worth er lot mo' ter me, sah."

"I'm afraid they wouldn't have missed you, Julius, if you'd been killed."

"Na, sah, but I'd a sho missed myself an' dat's de pint wid me."

The President fixed him with a comical frown:

"It's sweet and honorable to die for one's country, Julius!"

"Yassah--dat's what I hear--but I ain't fond er sweet things--I ain't nebber hab no taste fer 'em, sah!"

"Well, it looks like I'll have to let 'em have you, Julius, for an example. I've tried to save you--but there doesn't seem to be any thing to take hold of. Every time I grab you, you slip right through my fingers. I reckon they'll have to shoot you----"

The negro broke into a hearty laugh:

"G'way fum here, Mr. President! You can't fool me, sah. I sees yer laughin' right now way back dar in yo' eyes. You ain't gwine let 'em shoot me. I'se too vallable a nigger fer dat. I wuz worth er thousan' dollars 'fore de war. I sho' oughter be wuth two thousan' now. What's de use er 'stroyin' er good piece er property lak dat? I won't be no good ter nobody ef dey shoots me!"

The President broke down at last, leaned back in his chair and laughed with every muscle of his long body. Julius joined him with unction.

When the laughter died away the tall figure bent over his desk and wrote an order for the negro's release, and discharge from the army.

One of the things which had brought the President his deepest joy in the victory of Vicksburg was not the importance of the capture of the city and the opening of the Mississippi so much as the saving of U. S. Grant as a commanding General.

From the capture of Fort Donelson, the eyes of the Chief Magistrate had been fixed on this quiet fighter. And then came the disaster to his army at Shiloh--the first day's fight a bloody and overwhelming defeat--the second the recovery of the ground lost and the death of Albert Sydney Johnston, his brilliant Confederate opponent.

As a matter of fact, in its results, the battle had been a crushing disaster to the South. But Grant had lost fourteen thousand men in the two days' carnage and it was the first great field of death the war had produced. McClellan had not yet met Lee before Richmond. The cry against Grant was furious and practically universal.

Senator Winter, representing the demands of Congress, literally stormed the White House for weeks with the persistent and fierce demand for Grant's removal.

The President shook his head doggedly:

"I can't spare this man--he fights!"

The Senator submitted the proofs that Grant was addicted to the use of strong drink and that he was under the influence of whiskey on the first day of the battle of Shiloh.

In vain Winter stormed and threatened for an hour. The President was adamant.

He didn't know Grant personally. But he had felt the grip of his big personality on the men under his command and he refused to let him go.

He turned to his tormentor at last with a quizzical look in his eye:

"You know, Winter, that reminds me of a little story----"

The Senator threw up both hands with a gesture of rage. He knew what the wily diplomat was up to.

"I won't hear it, sir," he growled. "I won't hear it. You and your stories are sending this country to hell--it's not more than a mile from there now!"

The sombre eyes smiled as he slowly said:

"I believe it *is* just a mile from here to the Senate Chamber!"

The Senator faced him a moment and the two men looked at each other tense, erect, unyielding.

"There may or may not be a grain of truth in your statements, Winter," the quiet voice continued, "but your personal animus against Grant is deeper. He is a Democrat married to a Southern woman, and is a slave-holder. You can't be fair to him. I can, I must and I will. I am the President of all the people. The Nation needs this man. I will not allow him to be crushed. You have my last word."

The Senator strode to the door in silence and paused:

"But you haven't mine, sir!"

The tall figure bowed and smiled.

The President found the task a greater one than he had dreamed. So furious was the popular outcry against Grant, so dogged and persistent was the demand for his removal he was compelled to place General Halleck in nominal command of the district in which his army was operating until the popular furor should subside. In this way he had kept Grant as Second in Command at the head of his army, and Vicksburg with thirty-five thousand prisoners was the answer the silent man in the West had sent to his champion and protector in the White House.

The thrilling message had come at an opportune moment. The new commander of the army of the Potomac had defeated General Lee at Gettysburg and for an hour his name was on every lip. The President and the Nation had taken it for granted that he would hurl his eighty-two thousand men on Lee's army hemmed in by the impassable Potomac.

So sure of this was Stanton that he declared to the President:

"If a single regiment of Lee's army ever gets back into Virginia in an organized condition it will prove that I am totally unfit to be Secretary of War."

Once more the impossible happened. Lee did get back into Virginia, his army marching with quick step and undaunted spirit, ready to fight at any moment his rear guard came in touch with Meade's advancing hosts. He not only crossed the Potomac with his army in perfect fighting form with every gun he carried, but with thousands of fat cattle and four thousand prisoners of war captured on the field of Gettysburg.

The President's day of rejoicing was brief. As Lee withdrew to his old battle ground with his still unconquered lines of grey, the man in the White House saw with aching heart his dream of peace fade into the mists of even a darker night than the one through which his soul had just passed.

Slowly but surely the desperate South began to recover from the shock of Gettysburg and Vicksburg and filled once more her thinning battle lines. General Lee, sorely dissatisfied with himself for his failure to win in Pennsylvania, tendered his resignation to the Richmond Government, asking to be relieved by a younger and abler man. As no such man lived, Jefferson Davis declined his resignation, and he continued his leadership with renewed faith in his genius by every man, woman and child in the South.

General Meade, stung to desperation by the bitter disappointment of the President and the people of the North, also tendered his resignation.

For the moment the President refused to consider it, though his eyes were fixed with growing faith on the silent figure of Grant. One more victory from this stolid fighter and he had found the great commander for which he had sought in vain through blood and tears for more than two years.

The first task to which he must turn his immediate attention was the filling of the depleted ranks of the Northern armies. Volunteering had ceased, the terms of the enlisted men would soon expire, and it was absolutely necessary to enforce a draft for five hundred thousand soldiers.

The President had been warned by the Democratic Party, at present a powerful and aggressive minority in Congress, that such an act of despotism would not be tolerated by a free people.

The President's answer was simple and to the point:

"The South has long since adopted force to fill her ranks. If we are to continue this war and save the Union it is absolutely necessary, and therefore it shall be done."

The great city of New York was the danger point. The Government had been warned of the possibility of a revolution in the metropolis, whose representatives in Congress had demanded the right to secede in the beginning of the war. And yet the warning had not been taken seriously by the War Department. No effort had been made to garrison the city against the possibility of an armed uprising to resist the draft. Demagogues had been haranguing the people for months, inflaming their minds to the point of madness on the subject of this draft.

On the night before the drawing was ordered in New York the leading speaker had swept the crowd off their feet by the daring words with which he closed his appeal:

"We will resist this attempt of Black Republicans and Abolitionists to force the children of the poor into the ranks they dare not enter. Will you give any more of your sons to be food for vultures on the hills of Virginia? Will you allow them to be torn from your firesides and driven as dumb cattle into the mouths of Southern cannon? If you are slaves, yes,----if you are freemen, no!"

When the lottery wheel began to turn off its fatal names at the Government Draft Office at the corner of Forty-sixth Street and Third Avenue on the morning of July 14th, a sullen, determined mob packed the streets in front of the building. Among them stood hundreds of women whose husbands, sons and brothers were listed on the spinning wheel of black fortune.

Their voices were higher and angrier than the men's:

"This is a rich man's war--but a poor man's fight----"

"Yes, if you've got three hundred dollars you can hire a substitute from the slums----"

"But if you happen to be a working man, you can stand up and be shot for these cowards and sneaks!"

"Down with the draft!"

"To hell with the hirelings and their wheel!"

"Smash it----"

"Burn the building!"

A tough from the East Side waved his hand to the crowd of frenzied men and women:

"Come on, boys,----"

With a single mighty impulse the mob surged toward the doors, and through them. A sound of smashing glass, blows, curses. A man rushed into the street holding the enrollment books above his head:

"Here are your names, men--the list of white slaves!"

The mob tore the sheets from his grasp and fell on them like hungry wolves. In ten minutes the books were only scraps of paper trampled into the filth of Third Avenue. Wherever a piece could be seen men and women stamped and spit on it.

They smashed the wheel and furniture into kindling wood, piled it in the middle of the room and set fire to it. No policemen or firemen were allowed to approach. Every officer of the law, both civil and military, had been chased and beaten and disappeared.

Half the block was in flames before the firemen could break through and reach the burning buildings.

Down the Avenue, the maddened mob swept with resistless impulse, jelling, cursing, shouting its defiance.

"Down with the Abolitionists!"

"Hang Horace Greeley on a sour apple tree!"

"To the *Tribune* Office!"

Howard, a reporter of the *Tribune*, was recognized:

"Kill him!"

"Hang him!"

The mob seized the reporter, dragged him to a lamp post and were about to put the rope around his neck when a blow from a cobblestone felled him to the sidewalk, the blood trickling down his neck.

A man bending over his body, shouted to the crowd:

"He's dead--we'll take the body away!"

A friend helped and they carried him into a store and saved his life.

For three days and nights this mob burned and killed at will and fought every officer of the law until the streets ran red with blood. They burned the Negro Orphan Asylum, beat, killed or hanged every negro who showed his face, sacked the home of Mayor Opdyke, at 79 Fifth Avenue, and attempted to burn it. They smashed in the *Tribune* building, gutted part of it and would have reduced it to ashes but for the brave defense put up by some of its men.

On the third day the announcement was made that the draft was suspended. Five thousand troops reached the city and partly succeeded in restoring order.

More than a thousand men had been killed and three thousand wounded-- among them many women.

The Democratic papers now boldly demanded that the draft should be officially suspended until its constitutionality could be tested by the courts. The State and Municipal authorities of New York appealed to the President to suspend the draft.

He answered:

"If I suspend the draft there can be no army to continue the war and the days of the Republic are numbered. The life of the Nation is at stake."

They begged for time, and he hesitated for a day. The victories of Gettysburg and Vicksburg were forgotten in the grim shadow of a possible repetition of the French Revolution on a vast scale throughout the North. The mob had already sacked the office of the *Times* in Troy, broken out in Boston, and threatened Cincinnati.

The President gave the Governor of New York his final answer by sending an army of ten thousand veterans into the city. He planted his artillery to sweep the streets with grape and cannister, and ordered the draft to be immediately enforced.

The new wheel was set up, and turned with bayonets. The mobs were overawed and the ranks of the army were refilled.

CHAPTER XXXI
BETWEEN THE LINES

Betty Winter found to her sorrow that the memory of a dead love could be a troublesome thing. Ned Vaughan's tender and compelling passion had been resistless in the moonlight beneath a fragrant apple tree with the old mill wheel splashing its music at their feet. She had returned to her cot in the hospital that night in a glow of quiet, peaceful joy. Life's problem had been solved at last in the sweet peace of a tender and beautiful spiritual love--the only love that could be real.

All this was plain, while the glow of Ned's words were in her heart and the memory of his nearness alive in the fingers and lips he had kissed. And then to her terror came stealing back the torturing vision of his brother. Why, why, why could she never shut out the memory of this man!

Over and over again she repeated the angry final word:

"He isn't worth a moment's thought!"

And yet she kept on thinking, thinking, always in the same blind circle. At last came the new resolution,

"Worthy or unworthy, I've given my word to a better man and that settles it."

The fight had become in her inflamed imagination the struggle between good and evil. The younger man with his chivalrous boyish ideals was God, Love, Light. The older with his iron will, his fierce ungovernable passion, was the Devil, Lust and Darkness. She trembled with new terror at the discovery that there was something elemental deep within her own life that answered the challenge of this older voice with a strange joyous daring.

She had just risen from her knees where she had prayed for strength to fight and win this battle when the maid knocked on her door. She had left the hospital and returned home for a week's rest, tottering on the verge of a nervous collapse since her return from the meeting with Ned.

"A letter, Miss Betty," the maid said with a smile.

She tore the envelope with nervous dread. It bore no postmark and was addressed in a strange hand.

Inside was another envelope in Ned's handwriting, and around it a sheet of paper on which was scrawled,

"DEAR MISS WINTER: The bearer of this letter is a trusted spy of both Governments. I have friends in Washington and in Richmond. In Richmond I am supposed to betray the Washington Government. In Washington it is known that I am at heart loyal to the Union, and all my correspondence from Richmond to the Confederate agents in Canada and the North I deliver to the President and Stanton. This one is an exception. I happened to have met Mr. Ned. Vaughan and like him. I deliver this letter to you unopened by any hand. I've a sweetheart myself."

With a cry of joy, Betty broke the seal and read Ned's message. It was written just after the battle of Gettysburg.

"DEAREST: I am writing to you to-night because I must--though this may never reach you. The whole look of war has changed for me since that wonderful hour we spent in the moonlight beside the river and you promised me your life. It's all a pitiful tragedy now, and love, love, love seems the only thing in all God's universe worth while! I don't wish to kill any more. It hurts the big something inside that's divine. I'm surprised at myself that I can't see the issues of National life as I saw them at first. Somehow they have become dwarfed beside the new wonder and glory that fills my heart. And now like a poor traitor, I am praying for peace, peace at any price. Oh, dearest, you have brought me to this. I love you so utterly with every breath I breathe, every thought of mind and every impulse of soul and body, how can I see aught else in the world?

"In every scene of these three days of horror through which we've just passed, my thought was of you. The signal gun that called the men to die boomed your name for me. I heard it in the din and roar and crash of armies. The louder came the call of death, the sweeter life seemed because life meant you. Life has taken on a new and wonderful meaning. I love it as I never loved it before and I've grown to hate death and I whisper it to you, my love, my own--to hate war! I want to live now, and I'm praying, praying, praying for peace. My mind is yet clear in its conviction of right or I could not stay here a moment longer. But I'm longing and hoping and wondering whether God will not show us the way out of your tragic dilemma.

"During the battle I found a handsome young Federal officer who had fallen inside out lines. With his last strength he was trying to write a message to his bride who was waiting for him behind the Union lines. I couldn't pass by. I stopped and got his name, gave him water and made him as comfortable as possible. I got permission from my General while the battle raged and sent his message with a flag of truce to his wife. She came flying to his side at the risk of her life, got to the rear and saved him. Perhaps I wasn't an ideal soldier in that pause in my fight. But I had to do it, dearest. It was your sweet spirit that stopped me and sent the white flag of love and mercy.

"And the strangest of all the things of the war happened that night. I spent six hours among the wounded, helping the poor boys all I could--both blue and grey--and I suddenly ran into John at the same pitiful work. It's curious how all the bitterness is gone out of my heart.

"I grabbed him and hugged him, and we both cried like two fools. We sat down between the lines in the brilliant moonlight and talked for an hour. I told him of you, dearest, and he wished me all the happiness life could give, but with a queer hitch in his voice, and after a long silence, which made me wonder if he, too, had not been loving you in secret. I shouldn't wonder if every man who sees you loves you. The wonder to me is they don't.

"Our band is playing an old-fashioned Southern song that sets my heart to beating with joyous madness again. I'm dreaming through that song of the home I'm going to build for you somewhere in the land of sunshine. Don't worry about me. I'm not going to die. I know I'm immortal now. I had faith once. Now I know--because I love you and time is too short to tell and all too short to live my love.

"NED."

She read it over twice through eyes that grew dim with each foolish, sweet extravagance. And then she went back and read for the third time the line about John, threw herself across her bed and burst into tears.

CHAPTER XXXII
THE WHIRLWIND

The draft of half a million men was scarcely completed when Rosecrans' Western army, advancing into Georgia, met with crushing defeat at Chickamauga, "The River of Death." His shattered hosts were driven back into Chattanooga with the loss of eighteen thousand men in a rout so complete and stunning that Charles A. Dana, the Assistant Secretary of War, telegraphed the President from the front that it was another "Bull Run."

Rosecrans himself wired that he had met with a terrible disaster. The White House sent him words of cheer. The Confederate Commander, General Bragg, rapidly closed in and began to lay siege to Chattanooga, and the defeated Federal army were put on short rations.

The President turned his eyes now from Meade and his army of the Potomac which Lee's strategy had completely baffled and gave his first thought to the armies of the West. He sent Sherman hurrying from the Mississippi to Rosecrans' relief and Hooker from the East. In the place of Rosecrans he promoted George H. Thomas, whose gallant stand had saved the army from annihilation and won the title, "The Rock of Chickamauga." And most important of all he placed in supreme command of the forces in Tennessee the silent man whom his patience and faith had saved to the Nation, the conqueror of Vicksburg--Ulysses S. Grant.

On November the 24th and 25th, the new Commander raised the siege of Chattanooga, and drove Bragg's army from Missionary Ridge and Lookout Mountain back into Georgia.

At last the President had found the man of genius for whom he had long searched. Grant was summoned to Washington and given command of all the armies of the United States East and West.

The new General at once placed William Tecumseh Sherman at the head of an army of a hundred thousand men at Chattanooga for the purpose of reinvading Georgia, sent General Butler with forty thousand up the Peninsula against Richmond along the line of McClellan's old march, raised the Army of the Potomac to one hundred and forty thousand effective fighters, took command in person and faced General Lee on the banks of the Rapidan but a few miles from the old ground in the Wilderness around Chancellorsville where Hooker's men had baptized the earth in heroic blood the year before.

Grant's army was the flower of Northern manhood and with its three hundred and eighteen great field guns the best equipped body of fighting men ever brought together on our continent. His baggage train was over sixty miles long and would have stretched the entire distance to Richmond.

By the spring of 1864 when he reached the Rapidan Lee's army had been recruited again to its normal strength of sixty-two thousand.

A great religious revival swept the Southern camps during the winter and its meetings lasted into the spring almost to the hour of the opening guns of the Wilderness campaign. Had whispers from the Infinite reached the souls of the ragged men in grey and told them of coming Gethsemane and Calvary?

Certain it is that though Lee's army were ragged and poorly fed their courage was never higher, their faith in their Commander never more sublime than in those beautiful spring mornings in April when they burnished their bayonets to receive Grant's overwhelming host.

The Chaplain of Ned Vaughan's regiment was leading a prayer meeting in the moonlight. An earnest brother was praying fervently for more manhood, and more courage.

A ragged Confederate kneeling nearby didn't like the drift of his petition and his patience gave out. He raised his head and called.

"Say, hold on there, brother! You're getting that prayer all wrong. We don't need no more courage--got so much now we're skeered of ourselves sometimes. What we need is provisions. Ask the Lord to send us something to eat. That's what we want now----"

The leader took the interruption in good spirit and added an eloquent request for at least one good meal a day if the Lord in his goodness and mercy could spare it.

No persimmon tree was ever stripped without the repetition of their old joke. They all knew the words by heart,

"Don't eat those persimmons--they're not good for you!"

"I know it, man, I'm just doin' it to pucker my stomach to fit my rations!"

Ned was passing the door of a cabin in which a prayer meeting of officers was being held. He was walking with his Colonel who was fond of a sip of corn whiskey at times. He was slightly deaf.

The leader of the meeting called from the door:

"Won't you join us in prayer, Colonel?"

"Thank you, no, I've just had a little!" he answered innocently.

Ned roared and the brethren inside the cabin joined the laugh.

No body of men of any race ever marched to death with calmer faith than those ragged lines of grey now girding their loins for the fiercest, bloodiest struggle in the annals of the world.

Lee allowed Grant to cross the Rapidan unopposed and penetrate the tangled wilds of the Wilderness. The Southerner knew that in these dense woods the effectiveness of his opponent's superior numbers would be vastly reduced. Longstreet's corps had not yet arrived from Gordonsville where he had been sent to obtain food, and he must concentrate his forces.

The days were oppressively hot, as the men in blue tramped through the forest aisles of the vast Virginia jungle--a maze of trees, underbrush and dense foliage. A pall of ominous silence hung over this labyrinth of desolation, broken only by the chirp of bluebird or the distant call of the yellowhammer.

Not waiting for the arrival of Longstreet on his forced march from Gordonsville, Lee suddenly threw the half of his army on Grant's advancing men with savage energy. Their march was halted and through every hour of the day and far into the night the fierce conflict raged. As darkness fell the Confederates had pushed the blue lines back, captured four guns and a number of prisoners.

But Longstreet had not come and Lee's army of barely forty thousand men were in a dangerous position before Grant's legions.

Both Generals renewed the fight at daylight. The Federals attacked Lee's entire line with terrific force. Just as the Confederate right wing was being crushed and rolled back in disorder, Longstreet reached the field and threw his men into the breach. Lee himself rode to the front to lead the charge and reestablish his yielding lines.

From a thousand throats rose the cry:

"Lee to the rear!"

"Go back, General Lee!"

"This is no place for you!"

"We'll settle this!"

The men refused to move until their Commander had withdrawn. And then with their fierce yell they charged and swept the field.

Lee repeated the brilliant achievement of Jackson at Chancellorsville. Longstreet was sent around Hancock's left to turn and assail his flank. The movement was a complete success. Hancock's line was smashed and driven back a mile to his second defenses.

General Wadsworth at the head of his division was mortally wounded and fell into the hands of the on-sweeping Confederates. Just as the movement had reached the moments of its triumph which would have crumpled Grant's army in confusion back on the banks of the river, Longstreet fell dangerously wounded, struck down by a volley from his own men in exactly the same way and almost in the same spot where Jackson had fallen. General Jenkins, who was with him, was instantly killed.

The charging hosts were halted by the change of Commanders and the movement failed of its big purpose, though at sunset General John B. Gordon broke through Sedgwick's Union lines, rolled back his right flank, drove him a mile from his entrenchments and captured six hundred prisoners with two brigadier generals.

The mysterious fate which had pursued the South had once more stricken down a great commander in the moment of victory, and snatched it from his grasp--at Shiloh, Albert Sydney Johnston; at Seven Pines, Joseph E. Johnston; at Chancellorsville, Jackson, and now Longstreet.

Grant in two days lost seventeen thousand six hundred and sixty-six men, a larger number than fell under Hooker when he had retreated in despair. Any other General than Grant, the stolid bulldog fighter, would have retreated across the Rapidan to reorganize his bleeding lines.

As one of his Generals rode up the following morning out of the confusion and horror of the night, Grant, chewing on his cigar, waved his right arm with a quick movement:

"It's all right, Wilson; we'll fight again!"

Next day the two armies lay in their trenches facing each other in grim silence. Grant determined again to turn Lee's right flank and get between him and Richmond.

Lee divined his purpose before a single regiment had begun to march. Spottsylvania Court House lay on his right. The Confederate Commander hurried his advance guard to the spot and lay in wait for his opponent.

The day of the 19th was spent by both armies in adjusting lines and constructing breastworks. These fortifications were made by digging huge ditches and on the top of their banks fastening heavy logs. In front of these, abatis were made by filling the trees and cutting their limbs in such a way that the sharp spikes projected toward the breasts of the advancing foe.

While placing his guns in position General Sedgwick was killed by a sharpshooter's bullet--a commander of high character and fearless courage and loved by every man in his army.

On the morning of the 10th Hancock attempted to turn Lee's rear by crossing the Po. The movement failed and he was recalled with heavy losses under Early's assault as he recrossed the river.

Warren led his division in a determined charge on the Confederate front and they were mowed down in hundreds by Longstreet's men behind their entrenchments. They reached the abatis and one man leaped on the breastworks before they fell back in bloody confusion. General Rice was mortally wounded in this charge.

On the left of Warren, Colonel Emory Upton charged and broke through the Confederate lines capturing twelve hundred prisoners, but was driven back at last with the loss of a thousand of his men. Grant made him a Brigadier General on the field.

The first day at Spottsylvania ended with a loss of four thousand Union men. Lee's losses were less than half that number.

The 11th they paused for breath, and Grant sent his famous dispatch to Washington:

"I propose to fight it out on this line if it takes all summer."

On the morning of the 12th Hancock was ordered to charge at daylight. Lee's lines were spread out in the shape of an enormous letter V. Hancock's task was to capture the angle which formed the key to this position.

In pitch darkness under pouring rain his four divisions under Birney, Mott, Barlow and Gibbon slipped through the mud and crept into position within a few hundred yards of the Confederate breastworks.

As the first streaks of dawn pierced the murky clouds, without a shot, the solid, silent lines of blue rushed this angle and leaped into the entrenchments before the astounded men in grey knew what had happened.

So swift was the blow, so surprising, so overwhelming in numbers, the angle was captured practically without a struggle and the three thousand men within it were forced to surrender with every cannon, their muskets, colors and two Generals. It was the most brilliant single achievement of "Hancock the Superb."

Pressing on, Hancock's men advanced against the second series of trenches a half mile beyond. Here the fight really began.

Into their faces poured a terrific volley of musketry and General John B. Gordon led his men in a desperate charge to drive the invaders back.

Lee, seeing the dangerous situation, rode to the front with the evident intention of joining in this charge.

Again the cry rang from the hearts of the men who loved him:

"Lee to the rear!"

They refused to move until he was led out of range of the fire. Gordon's men charged and drove the Federal hosts back until at last they stood against the entrenchments they had captured. Reinforcements now poured in from both sides and the fighting became indescribable in its mad desperation. Thousands of men in blue and men in grey fought face to face and hand to hand. Muskets blazed in one another's eyes and blew heads off. The dead were piled in rows four and five deep, blue and grey locked in each other's arms. The trenches were filled with the dead and cleared of bodies again and again to make room for the living until they in turn were thrown out.

Ned Vaughan saw a grey color-bearer's arm shot away at the shoulder, the quivering flesh smeared with mud, stained with powder and filled with the shreds of his grey sleeve--and yet, without blenching, he grasped his colors with the other hand and swept on into the jaws of this flaming hell at the head of his men. The rain of musketry fire against the trees came to Ned's ears in low undertone like the rattle of myriads of hail stones on the roof of a house.

A grey soldier was fighting a duel to the death with a magnificently dressed officer in blue, bare bayonet against bare sword. The soldier, with a sudden plunge, ran his opponent through. With a shudder, Ned looked to see if it were John.

A company of men in blue were caught and cut off by a grey wave and were trying to surrender. Their officers with drawn revolvers refused to let them.

"Shoot your officers!" a grey man shouted. In a moment every Commander dropped and the men were marched to the rear.

Hour after hour the flames of hell swirled in an endless whirlwind around this "Bloody Angle." Battle line after battle line rushed in never to return. Ned saw an oak tree two feet in diameter gnawed down by musket balls. It fell with a crash, killing and wounding a number of men.

Color-bearers waved their flags in each other's faces, clinched and fought like demons. Two soldiers, their ammunition spent, choked each other to death on top of the entrenchment and rolled down its banks among the torn and mangled bodies that filled the ditch.

In the edge of this red whirlwind Ned Vaughan saw a grim man in grey standing beside a tree using two guns. His wounded comrade loaded one while he took deliberate aim and fired the other. With each crack of his musket a man in blue was falling.

In the centre of this mass of struggling maniacs the men were fighting with gun swabs, handspikes, clubbed muskets, stones and fists.

The night brought no rest, no pause to succor the wounded or bury the dead. Through the black murk of the darkness they fought on and on until at last the men who were living sank in their tracks at three o'clock before day and neither line had given from this "Bloody Angle."

The rain ceased to fall, the clouds lifted and the waning moon came out.

Ned Vaughan passing over the outer field saw a long line of men lying in regular ranks in an odd position. He turned to the Commander.

"Why don't you move that line of battle now to make it conform to your own?"

"They're all dead men," was the quiet answer. "They are Georgia soldiers."

John Vaughan, on the other side, crossing an open space, came on a blue battle line asleep rank on rank, skirmishers in front and battle line behind, all asleep on their arms. There was no one near to answer a question. They were all dead.

The blue and grey men were talking to one another now.

"Well, Johnnie," a Yankee called through the shadows, "I can't admit that you're inspired of God, but after to-day I must say that you are possessed of the devil."

"Same to you, Yank! Your papers say we're all demoralized anyhow--so to-morrow you oughtn't have no trouble finishin' us!"

"Ah, shut up now, Johnnie, and go to sleep!"

"All right, good-night, Yank, hope ye'll rest well. We'll give ye hell at daylight!"

For five days Grant swung his blue lines in circles of blood trying in vain to break Lee's ranks and gave it up. He had lost at Spottsylvania eighteen thousand more men. The stolid, silent man of iron nerves was terribly moved by the frightful losses his gallant army had sustained. He watched with anguish the endless lines of wagons bearing his stricken men from the field. Lee's forces had been handled with such consummate and terrible skill, his crushing numbers had made little impression.

Grant was facing a new force in the world. The ordinary methods of war which he had used with success in the West went here for nothing. The devotion of Lee's men was a mania. Small as his army was the bulldog fighter saw with amazement that it was practically unconquerable in a square, hand-to-hand struggle.

Once more he was forced to maneuver for advantage in position. He ordered a new flank movement by the North Anna River.

He had opened his fight with Lee on the 5th, and in two weeks he had lost thirty-six thousand men, without gaining an inch in the execution of his original plan of thrusting himself between the Confederate leader and his Capital. Lee's army was apparently as terrible a fighting machine as on the day they had met.

A truce now followed to bury the dead and care for the wounded. So sure had Grant been of crushing his opponent he had refused to agree to this during the struggle.

They found them piled six layers deep in the trenches, blue and grey, blue and grey. Black wings were spread over the top with red beaks tearing at eyes and lips while deep down below, yet groaned and moved the living wounded.

God of Love and Pity, draw the veil over the scene! No pen can tell its story--no heart endure to hear it.

The stop was brief. Already the cavalry were skirmishing for the next position.

Again the keen eye of Lee had divined his enemy's purpose. By a shorter road his men had reached the North Anna before Grant. When the Union leader arrived on the scene he found the position of his advance division dangerous and quickly withdrew with the loss of two thousand men.

Once more he determined to turn Lee's flank and hurled his army toward Cold Harbor. This time he reached his chosen ground before his opponent and on the

31st, Sheridan's cavalry took possession of the place. The two armies had rushed for this point in waving parallel lines, flashing at each other death-dealing volleys as they touched.

Both armies immediately began to entrench in their chosen positions. Lee, familiar with his ground, had chosen his position with consummate skill. On June the 1st, the preliminary attack was made at six o'clock in the afternoon. It was short and bloody. The Northern division under Smith and Wright charged and lost two thousand two hundred men in an hour.

Again Lee had placed his guns and infantry in a fiery crescent on the hills arranged to catch both flanks and front of an advancing army.

Grant's soldiers knew that grim work had been cut out for them on that fatal morning the third day of June. As John Vaughan walked along the lines the night before he saw thousands of silent men busy with their needle and thread sewing their names on their underclothing.

The hot, close weather of the preceding days had ended in a grateful rain at five o'clock, which continued through the night and brought the tired, suffering men gracious relief.

Grant decided to assault the whole Confederate front and gave his orders for the attack at the first streak of dawn at four-thirty.

The charging blue hosts literally walked into the crater of a volcano flaming in their faces and pouring tons of steel and lead into their stricken flanks. Nothing like it had ever before been seen in the history of war.

Ten thousand men in blue fell in twenty minutes!

The battle was practically over at half past seven o'clock.

General Smith received an order from Meade to renew the assault and flatly refused.

The scene which followed has no parallel in the records of human suffering. Its horror is inconceivable and unthinkable. Through the summer nights the shrieks and groans of the wounded and dying rose in pitiful endless waves. And no hand was lifted to save. For three days they lay begging for water, groaning and dying where they had fallen. It was certain death to venture in that storm-swept space. Only a few brave men fought their way through to rescue a fallen comrade.

It was not until the 7th that a truce was arranged to clear this shamble and then every man in blue was dead save two. Everywhere blood, blood, blood in dark slippery pools--dead horses--dead men--smashed guns, legs, arms, torn and mangled pieces of bodies--the earth plowed with shot and shell.

Thirty days had passed since Grant met Lee in the tangled Wilderness and the Northern army had lost sixty thousand men, two thousand a day.

It is small wonder that he decided not to try longer "to fight it out on that line."

Lee had put out of combat as many men for his opponent as he had under his command at any time and his army with the reinforcements he had received was now as strong as the day he met Grant.

For twelve days the two armies lay in their entrenchments on this field of death while the Federal Commander arranged a new plan of campaign. The sharpshooting was incessant. No man in all the line of blue could stand erect and live an instant. Soldiers whose time of service had expired and were ordered home, had to crawl on their hands and knees through the trenches to the rear.

The new Commander, on whose genius the President and the people had planted their brightest hopes, had just reached the spot where McClellan stood in June, 1862. And he might have gotten there by the James under cover of his gunboats without the loss of a single life.

Again John Vaughan's memory turned to McClellan with desperate bitterness. The longer he brooded over the hideous scenes of the past month, the higher rose his blind rage against the President.

CHAPTER XXXIII
THE BROTHERS MEET

When Julius, who had returned to John Vaughan's service, saw those piles of dead men on the field of Cold Harbor he lost faith in the Union Cause. He made up his mind that the past month's work had more than paid for that letter to the President and he took to the woods on his own hook.

He lay down to sleep the night he deserted in a clump of trees near the Confederate outposts and rested his head on a pillow of pine straw. When he waked in the morning at dawn he felt something tickle his nose. He cautiously reached one hand up to see what it was and felt a lock of hair. He rose slowly, fearing to look till he had gained his feet. He turned his eyes at last and saw that he had been sleeping on a dead man's head protruding through the shallow dirt and pine straw that had been hastily thrown over it the first day of the battle.

With a yell of terror he started on a run for his life.

He never stopped until he had flanked Lee's army by a wide swing, made his way to the rear and joined the Confederacy.

Grant had now changed his plan of campaign. He determined to capture Petersburg by a *coup* and cut the communication of Lee and Richmond with the South. The *coup* failed. The ragged remnants of Lee's army which had been left there to defend it, held the trenches until reinforcements arrived.

He determined to take it by a resistless concerted assault. On the 16th he threw three of his army corps on Beauregard's thin lines before Petersburg, capturing four redoubts. At daylight, on the 17th, he again hurled his men on Beauregard and drove his men out of his first line of defense. All day the defenders held their second line, though Grant's crack divisions poured out their blood like water. As night fell the dead were once more piled high on the Federal front and the Confederate dead filled the trenches.

As the third day dawned the fierce, assault was renewed, but Lee had brought up Anderson's Corps with Kershaw and Field's division and the blue waves broke against the impregnable grey ranks and rolled back, leaving the dead in dark heaps.

As the shadows of night fell, Grant withdrew his shattered lines to their trenches.

He had lost ten thousand five hundred more men and had failed.

He began to burrow his fortifications into the earth around Petersburg and try by siege what had been found impossible by assault. Further and further crept his blue lines with pick and axe and spade and shovel, digging, burrowing, piling their dirt and timbers. Before each blue rampart silently grew one in grey until the two siege lines stretched for thirty-seven miles in bristling, flaming semicircle covering both Richmond and Petersburg.

Again Grant planned a *coup*. He chose the role of the fox this time instead of the lion. He selected the key of Lee's long lines of defense and set a regiment of Pennsylvania miners to work digging a tunnel under the Confederate fort known as "Elliot's Salient," which stood but two hundred yards in front of Burnside's corps.

The tunnel was finished, the mine ready, the fuses set, and eight thousand pounds of powder planted in the earth beneath the unsuspecting Confederates.

Hancock's division with Sheridan's cavalry were sent to make a demonstration against Richmond and draw Lee's main army to its defense. The ruse was partly successful. There were but eighteen thousand behind the defenses of Petersburg on the dark night when Grant massed fifty thousand picked men before the doomed fort. The pioneers with their axes cleared the abatis and opened the way for the charging hosts. Heavy guns and mortars were planted to sweep the open space beyond the Salient and beat back any attempted counter charge.

The time set for the explosion was just before dawn. The fuse was lit and fifty thousand men stood gripping their guns, waiting for the shock. A quarter of an hour passed and nothing happened. An ominous silence brooded over the dawning sky. The only sounds heard were the twitter of waking birds in the trees and hedgerows. The fuse had failed. Two heroic men crawled into the tunnel and found it had spluttered out in a damp spot but fifty feet from the powder. It required an hour to secure and plant a new fuse. Day had dawned. Just in front of John Vaughan's regiment a Confederate spy was caught. He could hear every word of the pitiful tragedy.

He was a handsome, brown-eyed youngster of eighteen.

He glanced pathetically toward the doomed fort, and shook his head:

"Fifteen minutes more and I'd have saved you, boys!"

He turned then to the executioners:

"May I have just a minute to pray?"

"Yes."

He knelt and lifted his head, the fine young lips moving in silence as the first rays of the rising sun flooded the scene with splendor.

"May I write just a word to my mother and to my sweetheart?" he asked with a smile. "They're just over there in Petersburg."

"Yes."

They gave him a piece of paper and he wrote his last words of love, and in a moment was swinging from the limb of a tree. Only a few of the more thoughtful men paid any attention. It was nothing. Such things happened every day. God only kept the records.

The new fuse was set and lighted. The minutes seemed hours as the men waited breathlessly. With a dull muffled roar from the centre of the earth beneath their very feet the fort rose two hundred feet straight into the sky, driven by a tower of flame that stood stark and red in the heavens. And then with blinding crash the mighty column of earth, guns, timbers and three hundred grey bodies sank into the yawning crater. The pit was sixty-five feet wide and three hundred feet long.

The explosion had been a complete success. The undermined fort had been wiped from the landscape. A great gap opened in Lee's lines marked by the grave of three hundred of his men.

Burnside's division rushed into the crater and climbed through the breach. His men were met promptly by Ransom's brigade of North Carolinians and held. The Union support became entangled in the hole, stumbled and fell in confusion.

General Mahone's brigades hastily called, rushed into position, and a general Confederate charge was ordered. In silence, their arms trailing by their sides, they quickly crossed the open space and fell like demons on the confused blue lines which were driven back into the crater and slaughtered like sheep. The Confederate guns were trained on this yawning pit whose edges now bristled with flaming muskets. Regiment after regiment of blue were hurled into this hell hole to be torn and cut to pieces.

A division of negro troops were hurried in and the sight of them drove the Southerners to desperation. It took but a moment's grim charge to hurl these black regiments back into the pit on the bodies of their fallen white comrades. The crater became a butcher's shambles.

When the smoke cleared four thousand more of Grant's men lay dead and wounded in the grave in which had been buried three hundred grey defenders.

Lee's losses were less than one third as many. Grant asked for a truce to bury his dead and from five until nine next morning there was no firing along the grim lines of siege for the first time since the day Petersburg had been invested.

So confident now was Lee that he could hold his position against any assault his powerful opponent could make, he detached Jubal Early with twenty thousand men and sent him through the Shenandoah Valley to strike Washington.

The Southerner

Grant was compelled to send Sheridan after him. In the meantime he determined to take advantage of Lee's reduced strength and cut the Weldon railroad over which were coming all supplies from the South.

Warren's corps was sent on this important mission. His attack failed and he was driven back with a loss of three thousand men. He entrenched himself and called for reinforcements. Hancock's famous corps was hurried to the assistance of Warren.

John Vaughan's regiment was now attached to Hancock's army. As they were strapping on their knapsacks for this march, to his amazement Julius suddenly appeared, grinning and bustling about as if he had never strayed from the fold. His clothes were in shreds and tatters.

"Where have you been all this time, nigger?" John asked.

"Who, me?"

"And where'd you get that new suit of clothes?"

"Well, I'm gwine tell ye Gawd's truf, Marse John. Atter dat Cold Harbor business I lit out fur de odder side. I wuz gittin' 'long very well dar wid General Elliot in de Confederacy when all of er sudden somfin' busted an' blowed me clean back inter de Union. An' here I is--yassah. An' I'se gwine ter stick by you now. 'Pears lak de ain't no res' fur de weary no whar."

John was glad to have his enterprising cook once more and received the traitor philosophically.

Lee threw A. P. Hill's corps between Warren and Hancock's advancing division. Hancock entrenched himself along-the railroad which he was destroying.

Hill trained his artillery on these trenches and charged them with swift desperation late in the afternoon. The Union lines were broken and crushed and the men fled in panic. In vain "Hancock the Superb," who had seen his soldiers fall but never fail, tried to rally them. In agony he witnessed their utter rout. His trenches were taken, his guns captured and turned in a storm of death on his fleeing men. He lost twelve stands of colors, nine big guns and twenty-five hundred men.

As the darkness fell General Nelson A. Miles succeeded in rallying a new line and stayed the panic by a desperate countercharge.

Once more the grapple was hand to hand, man to man, in the darkness. John Vaughan had fired the last load, save one, from his revolver, and sword in hand, was cheering his men in a mad effort to regain their lost entrenchments. Blue and grey were mixed in black confusion. Only by the light of flashing guns could friend be distinguished from foe. A musket flamed near his face and through the deep darkness which followed a sword thrust pierced his side. He sprang back with an oath and clinched with his antagonist, feeling for his throat in silence. For a minute they wheeled struggled and fought in desperation, stumbling over underbrush, slipping to their knees and rising. Every instinct of the fighting brute in man was up now and the battle was to the death for one--perhaps both.

John succeeded at last in releasing his right hand and drawing his revolver. His enemy sprang back at the same moment and through the darkness again came the sword into his breast. He felt the blood following the blade as it was snatched away, raised his revolver and fired his last shot squarely at his foe. The muzzle was less than two feet from his face and in the flash he saw Ned's look of horror, both brothers recognizing each other in the same instant.

"John--my God, it's you!"

"Yes--yes--and it's you--God have mercy if I've killed you!"

In a moment the older brother had caught Ned's sinking body and lowered it gently on the leaves.

"It's all right, John, old man," he gasped. "If I had to die it's just as well by your hand. It's war--it's hell--all hell--anyhow--what's the difference----"

"But you mustn't die, Boy!" John whispered fiercely. "You mustn't, I tell you!"

"I didn't want to die," Ned sighed. "Life was--just--becoming--real--beautiful--wonderful----"

He stopped and drew a deep breath.

John bent lower and Ned's arm slipped toward his neck and his fingers touched the warm blood soaking his clothes.

"I'm--afraid--I--got--you,--too,--John----"

"No, I'm all right--brace up, Boy. Pull that devil will of yours together--we've both got it--and live!"

The younger man's head had sunk on his brother's blood-stained breast.

"Now, look here, Ned, old man--this'll never do--don't--don't--give up!"

The answer came faint and low:

"Tell--Betty--when--you--see--her--that--with--my--last--breath--I--spoke

--her--name--her--face--lights--the--dark--way----"

"You're going, Ned?"

"Yes----"

"Say you forgive me!"

"There's--nothing--to--forgive--it's--all--right--John--good-bye----"

The voice stopped. The battle had ceased. The woods were still. The older brother could feel the slow rising and falling of the strong young chest as if the muscles in the glory of their perfect life refused to hear the call of Death.

He bent in the darkness and kissed the trembling lips and they, too, were still. He drew himself against the trunk of a tree and through the beautiful summer night held the body of his dead brother in his arms.

His fevered eyes were opened at last and he saw war as it is for the first time. It had meant nothing before this reckoning of the dead and wounded after battle--sixty thousand men from the Rapidan to Cold Harbor in thirty days--ten thousand five hundred in the futile dash against Petersburg--four thousand in the crater--five thousand five hundred more now on this torn, twisted railroad, and all a failure--not an inch of ground gained.

These torn and mangled bundles of red rags he had watched the men dump into trenches and cover with dirt had meant nothing real. They were only loathsome things to be hidden from sight before the bugles called the army to move.

Now he saw a vision. Over every dark bundle on those blood-soaked fields bent a brother, a father, a mother, a sister or sweetheart. He heard their cries of anguish until all other sounds were dumb.

The heaps of amputated legs and arms he had seen so often without a sigh were bathed now in tears. The surgeons with their hands and arms and clothes soaked with red--he saw them with the eyes of love--scene on scene in hideous review--the young officer at Cold Harbor whose leg they were cutting off without the use of chloroform, his face convulsed, his jaws locked as the knife crashed through nerve and sinew, muscle and artery. And those saws gnawing through bones--God in heaven, he could hear them all now--they were cutting and tearing those he loved.

He heard their terrible orders with new ears. For the first time he realized what they meant.

"Give them the bayonet now----"

The low, savage, subdued tones of the officer had once thrilled his soul. The memory sickened him.

He could hear the impassioned speech of the Colonel as the men lay flat on their faces in the grass--the click of bayonets in their places--the look on the faces of the men eager, fierce, intense, as they sprang to their feet at the call:

"Charge!"

And the fight. A big, broad-shouldered brute is trying to bayonet a boy of fifteen. The boy's slim hand grips the steel with an expression of mingled rage and terror. He holds on with grim fury. A comrade rushes to his rescue. His bayonet misses the upper body of the strong man and crashes hard against his hip bone. The man with his strength seizes the gun, snatches it from his bleeding thigh and swings it over his head to brain his new antagonist, when the first boy, with a savage laugh, plunges his bayonet through the strong man's heart and he falls with a dull crash, breaking the steel from the musket's muzzle and lies quivering, with the blood-spouting point protruding from his side. He understood now--these were not soldiers obeying orders--they were fathers and brothers and playmates, killing and maiming and tearing each other to pieces.

Lord God of Love and Mercy, the pity and horror of it all!

It was one o'clock before Julius, searching the field with a lantern, came on him huddled against the tree with Ned's body still in his arms, staring into the dead face.

CHAPTER XXXIV
LOVE'S PLEDGE

Again Betty Winter found in her work relief from despair. She had hoped for peace in the beauty and tenderness of Ned's chivalrous devotion. Yet his one letter reporting the meeting had revealed her mistake. The moment she had read his confession the impulse to scream her protest to John was all but resistless. She had tried in vain to find a way of writing to Ned to tell him that she had deceived him and herself, and ask his forgiveness.

It was impossible to write to John under such conditions and she had suffered in silence. And then the wounded began to pour into Washington from Grant's front. The like of that procession of ambulances from the landing on Sixth Street to the hospitals on the hills back of the city had never been seen. The wounded men were brought on swift steamers from Aquia Creek. Floors and decks were covered with mattresses on which they lay as thickly as they could be placed. As the wounded died on the way they were moved to the bow and their faces covered.

At the landing tender hands were lifting them into the ambulances which slowly moved out in one line to the hospitals and back in a circle by another. These ambulances stretched in tragic, unbroken procession for three miles and never ceased to move on and on in an endless circle for three days and nights.

In an agony of anxiety Betty asked to be transferred to the landing that she might watch them fill the wagons. Her soul was oppressed with the certainty that John Vaughan would be found in one of them.

On the morning of the third day they were still coming in never-ending streams from the steamer decks. She wrung her hands in a moment of despair:

"Merciful God! Are they bringing back Grant's whole army?"

The patience of these suffering men was sublime. Only a sigh from one who would rise no more. Only a groan here and there from parched lips that asked for water.

At last came the ominous news for which she had watched and waited with sickening forebodings. The **Republican** printed the name of Captain John Vaughan among the wounded in the fight of Warren and Hancock's corps over the Weldon Railroad. There were only two thousand wounded men sent in on the steamers from the front after this battle, and they arrived at night.

Betty hurried to the landing and found that the ambulances had begun to move. She searched every face in vain, and when the last stretcher had passed out walked with trembling steps and scanned each silent covered face in the bow.

"Thank God," she murmured, "he's not there!"

She must begin now the patient search among the eighty thousand sick and wounded men in the city of sorrows on the hills.

She secured a hack and tried to reach the head of the procession and find the destination of the first wagons that had left before her arrival.

It was after midnight. A thunder storm suddenly rolled its dense clouds over the city and smothered the street lamps in a pall of darkness. The rain burst with a flash of lightning and poured in torrents. The electric display was awe-inspiring. The horses in one of the ambulances in the long line stampeded and smashed the vehicle in front. The procession was stopped in the height of the storm. The vivid flame was now continuous and Betty could see the wagons standing in a mud-splashed row for a mile, the lightning play bringing out in startling outline each horse and vehicle.

From every ambulance was hanging a fringe of curious objects shining white against the shadows when suddenly illumined. Betty looked in pity and awe. They were the burning fevered arms and legs and heads of the suffering wounded men eager to feel the splash of the cooling rain.

A full week passed before her search ended and she located him in one of the big new buildings hastily constructed of boards.

With trembling step she started to go straight to his cot. The memory of his brutal stare that day stopped her and she scribbled a line and sent it to him:

"John, dear, may I see you a moment?

"BETTY."

The doctor assured her that he was rapidly recovering, though restless and depressed. She caught her breath in a little gasp of surprise at the sight of his white face, pale and spiritual looking now from the loss of blood.

Her eyes were shining with intense excitement as she swiftly crossed the room, dropped on her knees beside his cot and seized his hands:

"O John, John, can you ever forgive me!"

He slipped his arm around her neck and held her a long time in silence.

The men in the room paid no attention to the little drama. It was happening every day around them.

"Oh, dearest," she went on eagerly, "I tried to put you out of my heart, but I couldn't. I am yours, all yours, body and soul. Love asks but one question--do you love me?"

"Forever!" he whispered.

"In my loneliness and despair I tried to give myself to Ned, but I couldn't, dear. I would have told him so had I been able to reach him--though I dreaded to hurt him."

John drew her hands down and looked at her with a strange expression.

"He's beyond the reach of pain and disappointment now, dear----"

"Dead?" she gasped.

The man only nodded, and clung desperately to her hands while her head sank in a flood of tears.

"We'll cherish his memory," he said in a curiously quiet voice, "as one of the sweetest bonds between us, my love----"

"Yes--always!" was the low answer.

For the life of him John Vaughan couldn't tell the terrible fact that his hand had struck him down. God alone should know that.

When she had recovered from the shock of the announcement Betty caressed his hand gently:

"We just love whom we love, dearest, and we can't help it. I am yours and you are mine. It's not a question of good or bad, right or wrong. We love--that's all."

"Yes, we love--that's all and it's everything. There's no more doubt, dear?"

"Not one," she cried. "I'm going to bring back the red blood to your cheeks now and take that fevered look out of your eyes----"

The weeks of convalescence were swift and beautiful to Betty--her ministry to his slightest whim a continuous joy. The only cloud in her sky was the strange, feverish, unquiet look in his eyes. On the day of his discharge he received a letter from his mother which deepened this expression to the verge of mania.

"What is it, dear?" Betty asked in alarm.

"One of those unfortunate things that have been happening somewhere every day for the past year--an arrest and imprisonment for treasonable utterances----"

"Who has been arrested?"

"This time my father in Missouri."

"Your father?" she gasped.

"Yes. He has been a bitter critic of the war. He seems to have gone too far. There was a riot of some sort in the village and he took the wrong side."

There was an ominous quiet in the way he talked.

"I'll take you to see the President, dearest," she said soothingly. "We'll ask for his release. It's sure to be granted."

John's eyes suddenly flashed.

"You think so?"

"Absolutely sure of it."

"We'll try it then," he said, with a cold ring in his voice that chilled Betty's heart, and sent her home wondering at its meaning.

CHAPTER XXXV
THE DARKEST HOUR

In the summer of 1864 the President saw the darkest hours of his life. The change in his appearance was startling and pitiful. His sombre eyes seemed to have sunk into their caverns beneath the bushy brows and all but disappeared. Their gaze was more and more detached from earth and set on some dim, invisible shore. Deeper and deeper sank the furrows in his ashen face. The shoulders drooped beneath a weight too great for any human soul to bear.

To Betty Winter's expression of loyalty and sympathy he answered sadly:

"It's success I need, child,--not sympathy. My own burdens of cares are as nothing to my soul. It's our cause--our cause--the Union must live or I shall die!"

He sat sometimes by his window for hours immovable as a marble statue, his deep, hungry eyes gazing, gazing forever over the shining river toward the Southern hills. His Secretaries stepped softly about the room in silent sympathy with the Chief they loved with passionate devotion.

Grant had crossed the Rapidan on that glorious spring morning in May with his magnificent army accompanied by the highest hopes of millions. And there had followed those awful sickening battles, one after another, until he had fallen back in failure before the impassable trenches around Petersburg.

The star of Grant, the conquering hero of the West, had apparently set in a sea of blood.

Lee, with inferior numbers, alert, resourceful, vigilant, had checked and baffled him at every turn, and Richmond's fall was no nearer to human eye than in 1862.

The miles and miles of hospital barracks in Washington, crowded to their doors with wounded, dying men, were the living witnesses of the Nation's mortal agony.

Every city, town, village, hamlet and county in the North was in mourning. Death had literally flung its pall over the world.

From these thousands of stricken homes there had slowly risen a storm of protest against the new leader of the Army. The word "Butcher" was on every lip. General Grant, they said, possessed merely the qualities of the bulldog fighter--tenacity and persistence. He held what he had won so long as men were poured into his ranks by tens of thousands to take the place of the dead. They declared that he possessed no genius, no strategic skill, no power to originate plans and devise means to overcome his skillful and brilliant antagonist. The demand was pressed on the President for his removal.

His refusal had brought on him the blame for all the blood and all the suffering and all the failures of the past bitter year.

His answer to his critics was remorseless in its common sense, but added nothing to his hold on the people.

"We must fight to win," he firmly declared. "Grant is the ablest general we have yet developed. His losses have been appalling--but the struggle is now to the bitter end. Our resources are exhaustless. The South can not replace her fallen soldiers--her losses are fatal, ours are not."

In the face of a political campaign he prepared a call by draft for five hundred thousand more men and issued a proclamation appointing a day of Humiliation, Fasting and Prayer.

The spirits of the people touched the lowest tide ebb of despair.

The war debt had reached the appalling total of two thousand millions of dollars and its daily cost was four millions. The paper of the Treasury was rapidly depreciating and the premium on gold rising until the value of a one dollar greenback note was less than fifty cents in real money. The bankers, fearing the total bankruptcy of the Nation, had begun to refuse further loans on bonds at any rate of interest.

The bounty offered to men for reenlistment in the army when their terms expired amounted to the unheard of sum of one thousand five hundred dollars cash on signing for the new term. Bounty jumping had become the favorite sport of adventurous scoundrels. Millions of dollars were being stolen by these men without the addition of a musket to the fighting force. Grant was hanging them daily, but the traitor's work continued. The enlisted man deserted in three weeks and reappeared at the next post and reenlisted again, collecting his bounty with each enrollment.

The enemies of the President in his own party, led by Senator Winter, to make sure of his defeat before the convention, which was about to meet in Baltimore, held a National convention of Radical Republicans in Cleveland and nominated John C. Fremont for the Presidency. Their purpose was by this party division to make Lincoln's nomination an impossibility. Fremont's withdrawal was the weapon with which they would fight the President before the regular Republican convention and after. Senator Winter voiced the feeling of this convention in a speech of bitter and vindictive eloquence.

"I denounce the administration of Abraham Lincoln," he declared, "as imbecile and vacillating. We demand not only the crushing of Lee's army, but a program of vengeance against the rebels, which will mean their annihilation when conquered. We demand the confiscation of their property, the overthrow of every trace of local government and the reduction of their States to conquered provinces under the control of Congress. The milk and water policy of Lincoln is both a civil and a military failure, and his renomination would be the greatest calamity which could befall our Nation!"

A week later the regular party convention met at Baltimore. On the night before this meeting the President's renomination was not certain.

On every hand his enemies were assailing him with unabated fury. Every check to the National arms was laid at his door--every mistake of civil or military management. The ravages of the Confederate cruisers which were built in England and had swept the seas of our commerce were blamed on him. He should have called Great Britain to account for these outrages and had two wars instead of one!

The cost of the great struggle mounting and mounting into billions was his fault. The draft might have been avoided with the Government in abler hands. The emancipation policy had not freed a single negro and driven the whole Democratic Party into opposition to the war. His Border State policy had held four Slave States in the Union, but crippled the moral power of his position as anti-Slavery man. Every lie, every slander of four years were now repeated and magnified.

A competent man must be put into the White House. The Rail-splitter must go!

The real test of strength would come in the secret meeting of the Grand Council of the Union League--the Secret Society which had been organized to defeat the schemes of the Knights of the Golden Circle. In this meeting men will say exactly what they think. In the big convention to-morrow all will be harmony and peace. The convention will do what these powerful leaders from every State in the North tell them to do.

The assembly is dignified and orderly. The men who compose it are the eyes and ears and brains of the party they represent. They are the real rulers of the Nation. The party will obey their orders. These are the men who do the executive thinking for millions. The millions can only reject or ratify their wills. We are a democracy in theory, but in reality here is assembled the aristocracy of brains which constitutes our government.

The Grand President Edmunds raps for order and faces a crowd of keen, intelligent leaders of men his equal in culture and will.

The meeting is called for but one purpose. With swift, direct action the battle begins. A friend of the President offers a resolution endorsing his administration, preceded by a preamble which declares it to be unwise to swap horses while crossing a stream.

The big guns open on this battle line without a moment's hesitation. Senator Winter has not thought it wise to make this opening speech. The prominent part he took in organizing and launching the Fremont convention has put him in the position of an avowed bolter. He has already put forward a colleague from the Senate who is supposed to be friendly to the administration.

The Senator is a man of blunt speech and dominating personality. He speaks with earnestness, conviction and eloquence. He does not mince words. All the petty grievances and mistakes and disappointments of his four years under the tall, quiet man's strong hand are firing his soul now with burning passion.

He boldly accuses the President of tyranny, usurpation, illegal acts, of abused power, of misused advantages, of favoritism, stupidity, frauds in administration, timidity, sluggish inaction, oppression, the willful neglect of suffering and the willful refusal to hear the cry of the down-trodden slave.

He turns the battery of his scorn now on his personal peculiarities, his drawn and haggard and sorrow marked face, his heartlessness in reading and telling funny stories, and last of all his selfish ambition which asks a second term at the sacrifice of his party and his country.

A Congressman of unusual brilliance and power follows this assault with one of even greater eloquence and bitterness.

Two more in quick succession and all demand with one accord the same thing:

"Down with Lincoln!"

Not a voice has been lifted in his favor. If he has a friend he is apparently afraid to open his mouth.

And then the giant form of Jim Lane slowly rises. He looks quietly over the crowd as if passing in review the tragic events of four years. Is he going to add his voice to this chorus of rage? A year ago in the same Grand Council he had a bitter grievance against the President and assailed him furiously. Yesterday he was at the White House and came away with a shadow on his strong face.

He stood for a long time in silence and seemed to be scanning each individual in the crowd of tense listeners.

And then his deep voice broke the stillness. His words rang like the boom of cannon and their penetrating power seemed to pierce the brick walls of the room.

"Mr. President and Gentlemen of the Grand Council:

"To stir up sore and wounded hearts to bitterness requires no skill or power of oratory. To address the minds of men sickened by disaster, wearied by long trial, heated by passion, bewildered by uncertainty, heavy with grief, and cunningly to turn them into one vindictive channel, into one blind rush of senseless fury requires no great power of oratory and no great mastery of the truth. It may be the trick of a charlatan!"

He paused and gazed with deliberate and offensive insolence into the faces of the men who had spoken. Their eyes blazed with wrath, and a fierce thrill of excitement swept the crowd.

"For a man to address himself to an assembly like this, however, goaded to madness by suffering, sorrow, humiliation, perplexity--and now roused by venomous arts to an almost unanimous condemnation of the innocent--I say to address you, turn you in your tracks and force you to go the other way--that would indeed be a feat of transcendent oratorical power. I am no orator--but I am going to tell you the truth and the truth will make you do that thing!"

Men began to lean forward in their seats now as with impassioned faith he told the story of the matchless work the great lonely spirit had wrought for his people in the White House during the past passion-torn years. His last sentence rang like the clarion peal of a trumpet:

"Desert him now and the election of **George B. McClellan** on a 'Peace-at-any-Price' platform is a certainty--the Union is dissevered, the Confederacy established, the slaves reshackled, the dead dishonored and the living disgraced!"

His last sentence was an angry shout whose passion swept the crowd to its feet. The resolution was passed and Lincoln's nomination became a mere formality.

But Senator Winter had only begun to fight. His whole life as an Abolitionist had been spent in opposition to majorities. He had no constructive power and no constructive imagination. His genius was purely destructive, but it was genius. Without a moment's delay he began his plans to force the President to withdraw from his own ticket in the midst of his campaign.

The one ominous sign which the man in the White House saw with dread was the rapid growth through these dark days of a "Peace-at-any-Price" sentiment within his own party lines in the heart of the loyal North. Again Horace Greeley and his great paper voiced this cry of despair.

The mischief he was doing was incalculable because he persisted in teaching the millions who read his paper that peace was at any time possible if Abraham Lincoln would only agree to accept it. As a Southern-born man, the President knew the workings of the mind of Jefferson Davis as clearly as he understood his own. Both these men were born in Kentucky within a few miles of each other on almost the same day. The President knew that Jefferson Davis would never consider any settlement of the war except on the basis of the division of the Union and the recognition of the Confederacy. When Greeley declared that the Confederate Commissioners were in Canada with offers of peace, the President sent Greeley himself immediately to meet them and confer on the basis of a restored Union with compensation for the slaves. The Conference failed and Greeley returned from Canada angrier with the President than ever for making a fool of him.

In utter disregard for the facts he continued to demand that the Government bring the war to an end. The thing which made his attack deadly was that he was rousing the bitterness of hopeless sorrow in thousands of homes whose loved ones had fallen.

Thoughtful men and women had begun to ask themselves new questions:

"Is not the price we are paying too great?"

"Can any cause be worth this ocean of tears, this endless deluge of blood?"

The President must answer this bitter cry with the positive assurance that he would make peace at any moment on terms consistent with the Nation's preservation or both he and his party must perish.

He determined to draw from Mr. Davis a positive declaration of the terms on which the South would accept peace. He dared not do this openly, as it would be a confession to Europe of defeat and would lead to the recognition of the Confederacy.

He accordingly sent Colonel Jaquess, a distinguished Methodist clergyman in the army, and J. R. Gilmore, of the *Tribune*, on a secret mission to Richmond for this purpose. They must go without credentials or authority, as private individuals and risk life and liberty in the undertaking.

Both men promptly accepted the mission and left for Grant's headquarters to ask General Lee for a pass through his lines.

The Democratic Party was now a militant united force inspired by the Copperhead leaders, who had determined to defeat the President squarely on a peace platform and put General McClellan into the White House. Behind them in serried lines stood the powerful Secret Orders clustered around the Knights of the Golden Circle.

Positive proofs were finally laid before the President that these Societies had planned an uprising on the night of the election and the establishment of a Western Confederacy.

Edmunds, the President of the Union League, handed him the names of the leaders.

"Now, sir, you can strike!" he urged.

The tall, sorrowful man slowly shook his head.

"You doubt the truth of these statements?" Edmunds asked.

"No. They are too true. Let sleeping dogs lie. One revolution at a time. We have all we can manage at present. If we win the election they won't dare rise. If we lose, it's all over anyhow--and it makes no difference what they do."

With patient wisdom he refused to stir the dangerous hornet's nest.

And to cap the climax of darkness, Jubal Early's army suddenly withdrew from Lee's lines, swept through the Shenandoah Valley and invaded Maryland and Pennsylvania.

With three-quarters of a million blue soldiers under arms, the daring men in grey were once more threatening the Capital. They seized and cut the Northern railroads, burning their bridges and capturing trains; they threatened Baltimore, captured Chambersburg, Pennsylvania, burned it, spread terror throughout the State and surrounding territory, and brushing past Lew Wallace's six thousand men at Monocacy, were bearing down on Washington with swift ominous tread.

It was incredible! It was unthinkable, and yet the reveille of Early's drums could be heard from the White House window.

John Bigelow, our **Charge d'Affaires** at Paris, had sent warning of a conversation with the Emperor of France, at which the President had only smiled.

"Lee will take Washington," the Emperor had declared, "and then I shall recognize the Confederacy. I have just received news that Lee is certain to take the Capital."

The message was flashed to Grant for help. The city was practically at Early's mercy if he should strike. He couldn't hold the Capital, of course, but if he took it even for twenty-four hours the Government would lose all prestige and standing in the Courts of Europe.

For twenty-four hours the panic in Washington was complete. The Government clerks were rushed into the trenches and hastily armed.

Early threw one shell into the city, which crashed through a house, his cavalry dashed into the corporate limits and took a prisoner and later burned the house of Blair, a member of the Cabinet.

The Sixth Corps arrived from Petersburg; a thousand men were killed and wounded in the skirmishing of two days, but the Capital escaped by the skin of its teeth.

Grant laconically remarked:

"If Early had been one day earlier he would have entered the Capital."

While he had not actually taken Washington, Lee's strategy was a masterly stroke. He had cleared the Shenandoah Valley, which was his granary, and enabled the farmers to reap their crops. He had showed the world that his army was still so terrible a weapon that with it he could hold Grant at bay, drive his enemy from the Valley, invade two Northern States, burn their cities and destroy their railroads, and throw his shells into Washington.

A wave of incredulous sickening despair swept the North. If this could be done after three and a half years of blood and tears and two billions of dollars spent, where could the end be?

Early had done in Washington what neither McDowell, McClellan, Pope, Burnside, Hooker, Meade nor Grant had yet succeeded in doing for Richmond--thrown shells into the city and taken a prisoner from its very streets. Had he arrived a day earlier--in other words, had not Lew Wallace's gallant little army of six thousand delayed him twenty-four hours--he could have entered the city, raided the Treasury and burned the Capitol.

Senator Winter was not slow to strike the blow for which he had been eagerly waiting a favorable moment. He succeeded in detaching from the President in this moment of panic a group of men who had stood squarely for his nomination at Baltimore. He agreed to withdraw Fremont's name if they would induce the President to withdraw and a new convention be called.

So deep was the depression, so black the outlook, so certain was McClellan's election, that the members of the National Republican Executive Committee met and conferred with this Committee of traitors to their Chief.

No more cowardly and contemptible proposition was ever submitted to the chosen leader of a great party. It was not to be wondered at that Winter and his Radical associates could stoop to it. They were theorists. To them success was secondary. They would have gladly and joyfully damned not only the Union--they would have damned the world to save their theories. But that his own party leaders should come to him in such an hour and ask him to withdraw cut the great patient heart to the quick.

He agreed to consider their humiliating proposition and give them an answer in two weeks. Nicolay, his first Secretary, wrote to John Hay, who was in Illinois:

"DEAR MAJOR: Hell is to pay. The politicians have a stampede on that is about to swamp everything. The National Committee are here to-day. Raymond thinks a commission to Richmond is the only salt to save us. The President sees and says it would be utter ruin. The matter is now undergoing consultation. Weak-kneed damned fools are on the move for a new candidate to supplant the President. Everything is darkness and doubt and discouragement. Our men see giants in the airy and unsubstantial shadows of the opposition, and are about to surrender without a blow. Come to Washington on the first train. Every man who loves the Chief must lay off his coat now and fight to the last ditch. He's too big and generous to be trusted alone with these wolves. He is the only man who can save this Nation, and we must make them see it."

Worn and angry after the long discussion with his cowardly advisers, the President retired to his bedroom, locked the door, laid down, and tried to rest. Opposite the lounge on which he lay was a bureau with a swinging mirror. He gazed for a moment at his long figure, which showed full length, his eye resting at last on the deep cut lines of the haggard face. Gradually two separate and distinct images grew--one behind the other, pale and death-like but distinct. He looked in wonder, and the longer he looked the clearer stood this pale second reflection.

"That's funny!" he exclaimed.

He rose, rubbed his eyes, and walked to the mirror, examining it curiously. He had always been a man of visions--this child of the woods and open fields.

"I wonder if it's an illusion?" he muttered. "I'll try again."

He returned to the couch and lay down. Again it grew a second time plainer than before, if possible. He watched for a long time with a feeling of awe.

"I wonder if I'm looking into the face of my own soul?" he mused.

He studied this second image with keen interest. It was five shades paler than the first. The thing had happened to him once before and his wife had declared it a sign that he would be elected to a second term, but the paleness of the second image meant that he would not live through it. It was uncanny. He rose and paced the floor, laid down again, and the image vanished. What did it mean?

Only that day a secret service man had come to warn him of a new plot of assassination and beg him to double the guard.

"What is the use, my dear boy, in setting up the gap when the fence is down all around?"

"Remember, sir, they shot a hole through your hat one night last week on your way to the Soldiers' Home."

"Well, what of it? If a man really makes up his mind to kill me he can do it----"

"You can take precautions."

"But I can't shut myself up in an iron box--now, can I? If I am killed I can die but once. To live in constant dread of it is to die over and over again. I decline to die until the time comes--away with your extra guards! I've got too many now. They bother me."

He threw off his depression and took up a volume of Artemus Ward's funny sayings to refresh his soul with their quaint humor. He must laugh or die. He had promised to see Betty Winter with a friend who had a petition to present at ten o'clock. He would rest until she came.

John Vaughan had insisted on her coming at this unusual hour. She protested, but he declared the chances of success in asking for his father's release would be infinitely better if she took advantage of the President's good nature and saw him alone at night when they would not be interrupted.

As they neared the White House grounds, crossing the little park on the north side, Betty's nervousness became unbearable. She stopped and put her hand on John's arm.

"Let's wait until to-morrow?" she pleaded.

"The President is expecting us----"

"I'll send him word we couldn't come."

"But, why?"

She hesitated and glanced at him uneasily:

"I don't know. I'm just nervous. I don't feel equal to the strain of such an interview to-night. It means so much to you. It means so much to me now that love rules my life----"

He took her hands in his and drew her into the friendly shadows beside the walk.

"Love does rule life, doesn't it?"

"Absolutely. I'm frightened when I realize it," she sighed.

"You are all mine now? In life, in death, through evil report and good report?"

"In life, in death, through evil report and good report----yours forever, dearest!"

He took her in his arms and held her in silence. She could feel him trembling with deep emotion.

"There's nothing to be nervous about then," he said, reassuringly, as his arms relaxed. "Come, we'll hurry. I want to send a message to my father to-night announcing his release."

At the entrance to the White House grounds they passed a man who shot a quick glance at John, and Betty thought his head moved in a nod of approval or recognition.

"You know him?" she asked nervously.

"One of Baker's men, I think--attempt on the President's life last week. They've doubled the guard, no doubt."

They passed another, strolling carelessly from the shadows of the white pillars of the portico.

"They seem to be everywhere to-night," John laughed carelessly.

The White House door was open and they passed into the hall and ascended the stairs to the Executive Chamber without challenge. Little Tad, the President's son, who ran the House to suit himself at times, was in his full dress suit of a lieutenant of the army and had ordered the guard to attend a minstrel show he was giving in the attic.

The President had agreed to meet Betty in his office at ten o'clock and told her to bring her friend right upstairs and wait if he were not on time.

They sat down and waited five minutes in awkward silence. Betty was watching the strange glittering expression in John Vaughan's eyes with increasing alarm.

She heard a muffled footfall in the hall, stepped quickly to the door, and saw the man they had passed at the entrance to the grounds.

She returned trembling.

"The man we passed at the gate is in that hall," she whispered.

"What of it?" was the careless answer. "Baker's secret service men come and go when they please here----"

He paused and glanced at the door.

"He has his eye on us maybe," he added, with a little laugh.

He studied Betty's flushed face for a moment, curiously hesitated as if about to speak, changed his mind, and was silent. He drew his watch from his pocket and looked at it.

"I've ordered a carriage to wait for you at the gate at a quarter past ten," he said quickly. "I forgot to tell you."

"Why--it may take us longer than half an hour?"

"That's just it. We may be talking two hours. Such things can't be threshed out in a minute. You can introduce me, say a good word, and leave us to fight it out----"

"I want to stay," she interrupted.

"Nonsense, dear, it may take hours. Besides, I may have some things to say to the President, and he some things to say to me that it were better a sweet girl's ears should not hear----"

"That's exactly what I wish to prevent, John, dear," she pleaded. "You must be careful and say nothing to offend the President. It means too much. We must win."

"I'll be wise in the choice of words. But you mustn't stay, dear. I'm not a child. I don't need a chaperone."

"But you may need a friend----"

"He does wield the power of kings--doesn't he?"

"With the tenderness and love of a father, yes."

"And yet I've wondered," he went on in a curious cold tone, "why he hasn't been killed--when the death of one man would end this carnival of murder----"

"John, how can you say such things?" Betty gasped.

"It's true, dear," he answered calmly. "This man's will alone has prevented peace and prevents it now. The soldiers on both sides joke with one another across the picket lines. They get together and play cards at night. Before the battle begins, our boys call out:

"'Get into your holes, now, Johnnie, we've got to shoot.'

"Left to themselves, the soldiers would end this war in thirty minutes. It's the one man at the top who won't let them. It's hellish--it's hellish----"

"And you would justify an assassin?" Betty asked breathlessly.

"Who is an assassin, dear?" he demanded tensely. "The man who wields a knife or the tyrant who calls the fanatic into being? Brutus or Caesar, William Tell or Gessler? Resistance to tyrants is obedience to God----"

"John, John--how can you say such things--you don't believe in murder----"

"No!" he breathed fiercely. "I don't now. I used to until I had a revelation----"

He stopped short as if strangled.

"Revelation--what do you mean?" Betty whispered, watching his every movement, with growing terror.

He looked at her with eyes glittering.

"I didn't want to tell you this," he began slowly. "I meant to keep the black thing hidden in my own soul. But you'll understand better if I speak. I killed Ned Vaughan with my own hands----"

"You're mad----" Betty shivered.

"I wish I were--no--I was never sane before that flash of red from hell showed me the truth--showed me what I was doing. We fought in the darkness of a night attack, hand to hand, like two maddened beasts. He ran me through with his sword and I sent the last ball left in my revolver crashing through his breast. In the glare of that shot I saw his face--the face of my brother! I caught him in my arms as he fell and held him while the life blood ebbed away through the hole I had torn near his heart. And then I saw what I'd been doing, saw it all as it is--war--brother murdering his brother--the shout and the tumult, the drums and bugles, the daring and heroism of it all, just that and nothing more--brother cutting his brother's throat----"

His head sank into his hands in a sob that strangled speech.

Betty slipped her arm tenderly around his shoulder and stroked the heavy black hair.

"But you didn't know, dear--you wouldn't have fired that shot if you had----"

He lifted himself suddenly and recovered his self-control.

"No. That's just it," he answered bitterly. "I wouldn't have done it had I known-

-nor would he, had he known. But I should have seen before that every torn and mangled body I had counted in the reckoning of the glory of battle was some other man's brother, some other mother's boy----"

He paused and drew himself suddenly erect:

"Well I'm awake now--I know and see things as they are!"

His hand unconsciously felt for his revolver, and Betty threw her arms around his neck with a smothered cry of horror:

"Merciful God--John--my darling--you are mad--what are you going to do?"

"Why nothing, dear," he protested, "nothing! I'm simply going to ask the President whose power is supreme to give my father a fair trial or release him--that's all--you needn't stay longer--the carriage is waiting. I can introduce myself and plead my own cause. If he's the fair, great-hearted man you believe, he'll see that justice is done----"

"You are going to kill the President!" Betty gasped.

"Nonsense--but if I were--what is the death of one man if thousands live? I saw sixty thousand men in blue fall in thirty days--two thousand a day--besides those who wore the grey. At Cold Harbor I saw ten thousand of my brethren fall in twenty minutes. Why should you gasp over the idea that one man may die whose death would stop this slaughter?"

"John, you're mad!" she cried, clinging to him desperately. "You're mad, I tell you. You've lost your reason. Come with me, dear--come at once----"

"No. I was never more sane than now," he answered firmly.

"Then I'll warn the President----"

He held her with cruel force:

"You understand that if it's true, my arrest, court-martial and death follow?"

"No. I'll warn him not to come. I alone know----"

She broke his grip on her arm and started toward the door. He lifted his hand in quick commanding gesture:

"Wait! my men are in that hall--it's his life or mine now. You can take your choice----"

The girl's figure suddenly straightened:

"Take your men out and go with them at once!"

"No. If he does justice, I may spare his life. If he does not----"

"You shall not see him----"

"It's my life or his--I warn you----"

"Then it's yours--I choose my country!"

She walked with quick, firm step to the door leading into the family apartments of the President. On the threshold her feet faltered. She grasped the door facing, turned, and saw him standing with folded arms watching her--with the eyes of a madman. Her face went white. She lifted her hand to her heart and slowly stumbled back into his arms.

"God have mercy!" she sobbed. "I'm just a woman--my love--my darling--I--I--can't--kill you----"

Her arms relaxed and she would have fallen to the floor had he not caught the fainting form and carried her into the hall.

Two men were at his side instantly.

"Take Miss Winter downstairs," he whispered. "There's a carriage at the gate. Bring it quietly to the door--one of you take her to the Senator's home. The other must return here immediately and wait my orders. There's no guard in this outer hall at night. The one inside is with the boy. Keep out of sight if any one passes."

The men obeyed without a word and John Vaughan stepped quickly back into the Executive office, drew the short curtains across the window, turned the lights on full, examined his revolver, and sat down in careless attitude beside the President's desk. He could hear his heavy step already approaching the door.

CHAPTER XXXVI
THE ASSASSIN

John Vaughan's face paled with the sudden realization of the tremendous deed he was about to do. It had seemed the only solution of the Nation's life and his own, an hour ago. The air of Washington reeked with deadly hatred of the President. Every politician who could not control his big, straightforward, honest mind was his enemy. The gloom which shrouded the country over Grant's losses and the failure of his campaign had set every hound yelping at his heels in full cry. He spent much of his time in the hospitals visiting and cheering the wounded soldiers. These men were his friends. They believed in his honesty, his gentleness and his humanity, and yet so deadly had grown the passions of war and so bitter the madness of political prejudice that the majority of the wounded men were going to vote against him in the approaching election.

An informal vote taken in Carver Hospital had shown the amazing result of three to one in favor of McClellan!

John Vaughan, in his fevered imagination, had felt that he was rendering a heroic service to the people in removing the one obstacle to peace. The President was the only man who could possibly defeat McClellan and continue the war. He was denounced by the opposition as usurper, tyrant, and dictator. He was denounced by thousands of men in his own party as utterly unfit to wield the power he possessed.

And yet, as he heard the slow, heavy footfall approaching the door, a moment of agonizing doubt gripped his will and weakened his arm. His eye rested on a worn thumbed copy of the Bible which lay open on the desk. This man, who was not a church member, in the loneliness of his awful responsibilities, had been searching there for guidance and inspiration. There was a pathos in the thought that found his inner conscience through the mania that possessed him.

Well, he'd test him. He would try this tyrant here alone before the judgment bar of his soul--condemn him to death or permit him to live, as he should prove true or false to his mighty trust.

His hand touched his revolver again and he set his square jaws firmly.

The tall figure entered and closed the door.

A flash of blind rage came from the depths of John Vaughan's dark eyes at the first sight of him. He moved forward a step and his hand trembled in a desperate instinctive desire to kill. He was a soldier. His enemy was before him advancing. To kill had become a habit. It seemed the one natural thing to do.

He stopped with a shock of surprise as the President turned his haggard eyes in a dazed way and looked about the room.

The light fell full on his face increasing its ghost-like pathetic expression. The story of anxiety and suffering was burnt in letters of fire that left his features a wrinkled mask of grey ashes. The drooping eyelids were swollen, and dark bags hung beneath them. The muscles of his massive jaws were flaccid, the lines about his large expressive mouth terrible in their eloquence. His sombre eyes seemed to gaze on the world with the anguish of millions in their depths.

For a moment John Vaughan was held in a spell by the unexpected apparition.

"You are alone, sir?" the quiet voice slowly asked.

"Yes."

"I had expected Miss Winter----"

"She came with me and was compelled to leave."

"Oh--will you pull up a chair."

The tall form dropped wearily at his desk. His voice had a far-away expression in its tones.

"And what can I do for you, sir?" he asked.

"My name is Vaughan--John Vaughan----"

The dark head was lifted with interest:

"The brother of Ned Vaughan, who escaped from prison?"

John nodded:

"The son of Dr. Richard Vaughan, of Palmyra, Missouri."

"Then you're our boy, fighting with Grant's army--yes, I heard of you when your brother was in trouble. You've been ill, I see--wounded, of course?"

"Yes."

The President rose and took his visitor's hand, clasping it with both his own:

"There's nothing I won't do for one of our wounded boys if I can--what is it?"

"My mother writes me that my father has been arrested without warrant, is held in prison without bail and denied the right to trial----"

He paused and leaned on the desk, trembling with excitement which had increased as he spoke.

"I have come to ask you for justice--that he shall be confronted by his accusers in open court and given a fair trial----"

A frown deepened the shadows in the dark, kindly face:

"And for what was he arrested?"

"For exercising the right of free speech. In a public address he denounced the war----"

The President shook his head sorrowfully:

"You see, my boy, your house is divided against itself--the symbol in the family group of our unhappy country. Of course, I didn't know of this arrest. Such things hurt me, so I refuse to know of them unless I must. They tell me that Seward and Stanton have arrested without warrant thirty-five thousand men. I hope this is an exaggeration. Still it may be true----"

He stopped, sighed, and shook his head again:

"But come, now, my son, and put yourself in my place. What can I do? I've armed two million men and spend four millions a day to fight the South because they try to secede and disrupt the Union. My opponents in the North, taking advantage of our sorrows, harangue the people and elect a hostile legislature in Indiana, Ohio, and Illinois. They are about to pass an ordinance of secession and strike the Union in the back. If secession is wrong in the South it is surely wrong in the North. Shall I fight secession in the South and merely argue politely with it here? Instead of shooting these men, I've consented to a more merciful thing, I just let Seward and Stanton lock them up until the war is over and then I'll turn them all loose.

"Understand, my boy, I don't shirk responsibility. No Cabinet or Congress could conduct a successful war. There must be a one man power. I have been made that power by the people. I am using it reverently but firmly. And I am backed by the prayers, the good will and the confidence of the people--the silent millions whom I don't see, but love and trust.

"This war was not of my choosing. Once begun, it must be fought to the end and the Nation saved. It will then be proved that among free men there can be no successful appeal from the ballot to the bullet, and that they who take such appeal are sure to lose their case and pay the cost. To preserve the life of the Constitution I must strain some of its provisions in time of war----"

"And you will not interfere to give these accused men a trial?" John Vaughan interrupted in hard tones.

"I cannot, my boy, I dare not interfere. The civil law must be suspended temporarily in such cases. I cannot shoot a soldier for desertion and allow the man to go free who, by denouncing the war, causes him to desert. It cuts to the very heart of the Nation--its life is involved----"

He rose again and paced the floor, turning his back on his visitor in utter unconsciousness of the dangerous glitter in his eyes.

He paused and placed his big hand gently on John's arm:

"I know in doing this I am wielding a dangerous power--the power of kings--not because I love it, but because I must save my country. And I'm the humblest man who walks God's earth to-night!"

In spite of his bitterness, the simplicity and honesty of the President found John Vaughan's heart. No vain or cruel or selfish man could talk or feel like that. In the glow of his eager thought the ashen look of his face disappeared and it became radiant with warmth and tenderness. In dreamy, passionate tones he went on as if talking to convince himself he must not despair. The younger man for the moment was swept resistlessly on by the spell of his eloquence.

"They are always asking of me impossible things. Now that I shall remove Grant from command. I know that his battles have been bloody. Yet how else can we win? The gallant, desperate South has only a handful of men, ragged and half starved, yet they are standing against a million and I have exhaustless millions behind these. With Lee they seem invincible and every move of his ragged men sends a shiver of horror and of admiration through the North. Yet, if Grant fights on he must win. He will wear Lee out--and that is the only way he can beat him.

"Besides, his plan is bigger than the single campaign against Richmond. There's a grim figure at the head of a hundred thousand men fighting his way inch by inch toward Atlanta. If Sherman should win and take Atlanta, Lee's army will starve and the end is sure. I can't listen to this clamor. I will not remove Grant--though I've reasons for believing at this moment that he may vote for McClellan for President.

"Don't think, my son, that all this blood and suffering is not mine. It is. Every shell that screams from those big guns crashes through my heart. The groans of the wounded, the sighs of the dying, the tears of widows and orphans, of sisters and mothers--all--blue and grey--they are mine. I see and hear it all, feel all, suffer all.

"No man who lives to-day is responsible for this war. I could not have prevented it, nor could Jefferson Davis. We are in the grip of mighty forces sweeping on from the centuries. We are fighting the battle of the ages.

"But our country's worth it if we can only save it. Out of this agony and tears will be born a united people. We have always been cursed with the impossible contradiction of negro slavery.

"There has never been a real Democracy in the world because there has never been one without the shadow of slavery. We must build here a real government of the people, by the people, for the people. It's not a question merely of the fate of four millions of black slaves. It's a question of the destiny of millions of freemen. I hear the tread of coming generations of their children on this continent. Their destiny is in your hand and mine--a free Nation without a slave--the hope, refuge and inspiration of the world.

"This Union that we must save will be a beacon light on the shores of time for mankind. It will be worth all the blood and all the tears we shall give for it. The grandeur of our sacrifice will be the birthright of our children's children. It will be the end of sectionalism. We can never again curse and revile one another, as we have in the past. We've written our character in blood for all time. We've met in battle. The Northern man knows the Southerner is not a braggart. The Southerner knows the Yankee is not a coward.

"There can be but one tragedy, my boy, that can have no ray of light--and that is that all this blood should have flowed in vain, all these brave men died for nought, that the old curse shall remain, the Union be dismembered into broken sections and on future bloody fields their battles be fought over again----"

He paused and drew a deep breath:

"This is the fear that's strangling me! For as surely as George B. McClellan is elected President, surrounded by the men who at present control his party, just so surely will the war end in compromise, failure and hopeless tragedy----"

"Why do you say that?" John asked sharply.

"Because standing here on this very spot, before the battle of Gettysburg I offered him the Presidency if he would preside at a great mass meeting of his party and guarantee to save the Union. I offered to efface myself and give up the dearest ambition of my soul to heal the wounds of my people--and he refused----"

"Refused?" John gasped.

"Yes."

The younger man gazed at the haggard face for a moment through dimmed eyes, sank slowly to a seat and covered his face in his hands in a cry of despair!

The reaction was complete and his collapse utter.

The President gazed at the bent figure with sorrowful amazement, and touched his head gently with the big friendly hand:

"Why, what's the matter, my boy? I'm the only man to despair. You're just a captain in the army. If to be the head of hell is as hard as what I've had to undergo here I could find it in my heart to pity Satan himself. And if there's a man out of hell who suffers more than I do, I pity him. But it's my burden and I try to bear it. I wish I had only yours!"

John Vaughan sprang to his feet and threw his hands above his head in a gesture of anguish:

"O my God, you don't understand!"

He quickly crossed the space that separated them and faced the President with grim determination:

"But I'm going to tell you the truth now and you can do what you think's right. In the last fight before Petersburg I killed my brother in a night attack and held his dying body in my arms. I think I must have gone mad that night. Anyhow, when I lay in the hospital recovering from my wounds, I got the letter about my father and made up my mind to kill you----"

He paused, but the sombre eyes gave no sign--they seemed to be gazing on the shores of eternity.

"And I came here to-night for that purpose--my men are in that hall now!"

He stopped and folded his hands deliberately, waiting for his judge to speak.

A long silence fell between them. The tall, sorrowful man was looking at him with a curious expression of wonder and self pity.

"So you came here to-night to kill me?"

"Yes."

Again a long silence--the deep eyes looking, looking with their strange questioning gaze.

"Well," the younger man burst out at last, "what is my fate? I deserve it. Even generosity and gentleness have their limit. I've passed it. And I've no desire to escape."

The kindly hand was lifted to John Vaughan's shoulder:

"Why didn't you do it?"

"Because for the first time you made me see things as you see them--I got a glimpse of the inside----"

"Then I won you--didn't I?" the President cried with elation. "I've been talking to you just to keep my courage up--just to save my own soul from the hell of despair. But you've lifted me up. If I can win you I can win the others if I could only get their ear. All I need is a little time. And I'm going to fight for it. Every act of my life in this great office will stand the test of time because I've put my immortal soul into the struggle without one thought of saving myself.

"I've told you the truth, and the truth has turned a murderer into my friend. If only the people can know--can have time to think, I'll win. You thought me an ambitious tyrant--now, didn't you?"

"Yes."

"Great God!--I had my ambitions, yes--as every American boy worth his salt has. And I dared to dream this vision of the White House--I, the humblest of the humble, born in a lowly pioneer's cabin in the woods of Kentucky. My dream came true, and where is its glory? Ashes and blood. And I, to whom the sight of blood is an agony unendurable, have lived with aching heart through it all and envied the dead their rest on your battlefields----"

He stopped suddenly and fixed John with a keen look:

"You'll stand by me, now, boy, through thick and thin?"

"I'd count it an honor to die for you----"

"All right. I give you the chance. I'm going to send you on a dangerous mission. I need but two things to sweep the country in this election and preserve the Union--a single big victory in the field to lift the people out of the dumps and make them see things as they are, and a declaration from Mr. Davis that there can be no peace save in division. I know that he holds that position, but the people in the North doubt it. I've sent Jaquess and Gilmore there to obtain his declaration. Technically they are spies. They may be executed or imprisoned and held to the end of the war. They go as private citizens of the North who desire peace.

"I want another man in Richmond whose identity will be unknown to report the results of that meeting in case they are imprisoned. You must go as a spy at the double risk of your life----"

"I'm ready, sir," was the quick response.

The big hand fumbled the black beard a moment:

"You doubtless said bitter things in Washington when you returned?"

"Many of them."

"Then you were approached by the leaders of Knights of the Golden Circle?"

"Yes."

"Good! You're the man I want without a doubt. You can use their signs and pass words in Richmond. Besides, you have a Southern accent. Your chances of success are great. I want you to leave here in an hour. Go straight through as a scout and spy in Confederate uniform. If Jaquess and Gilmore are allowed to return and tell their story--all right, your work with them is done. If they are imprisoned, get through the lines to Grant's headquarters, report this fact and Mr. Davis' answer, and it will be doubly effective--you understand?"

"Perfectly, sir."

"That's your first job. But I want you to go to Richmond for a double purpose--to take the train for Atlanta, get through the lines and give a message to a man down South I've been thinking about for the past month. The world has forgotten Sherman in the roar of the great battles Grant has fought. I haven't. Slowly but surely his grim figure has been growing taller on the horizon as the smoke lifts from each of his fights. Grant says he is our biggest general. Only a great man could say that about a subordinate commander. That's another reason I won't listen to people who demand Grant's removal.

"Sherman is now a hundred and fifty miles in Georgia before Atlanta. His road is being cut behind him every other day. You might be weeks trying to get to him by Chattanooga. The trains run through from Richmond. I want you to reach him quick, and give him a message from me. I can't send a written order. It wouldn't be fair to Grant. I'll give you credentials that he'll accept that will cost you your life in Richmond if their meaning is discovered.

"Tell General Sherman that if he can take Atlanta the blow will thrill the Nation, carry the election, and save the Union. Grant is deadlocked at Petersburg and may be there all winter. If he can fight at once and give us a victory, it's all that's needed. I'll send him an order to strike. Tell him to destroy it if he wins. If he loses--I'll publish it and take the blame on myself. Can you do this?"

"I will or die in the effort," was the quick reply.

"All right. Take this card at once to Stanton's office. Ask him to send you by boat to Aquia--by horse from there. Return here for your papers."

In ten minutes John had dispatched a note to Betty:

"DEAREST: God saved me from an act of madness. He sent His message through your sweet spirit. I am leaving for the South on a dangerous mission for the President. If I live to return I am all yours--if I die, I shall still live through eternity if only to love you.

"JOHN."

Within an hour he had communicated with the commander of the Knights, his arrangements were complete, and he was steaming down the river on his perilous journey.

CHAPTER XXXVII
MR. DAVIS SPEAKS

John Vaughan arrived in Richmond a day before Jaquess and Gilmore. His genial Southern manner, his perfect accent and his possession of the signs and pass words of the Knights of the Golden Circle made his mission a comparatively easy one.

He had brought a message from the Washington Knights to Judah P. Benjamin, which won the confidence of Mr. Davis' Secretary of State and gained his ready consent to his presence on the occasion of the interview.

The Commissioners left Butler's headquarters with some misgivings. Gilmore took the doughty General by the hand and said: "Good-bye, if you don't see us in ten days you may know we have 'gone up.'"

"If I don't see you in less time," he replied, "I'll demand you, and if they don't produce you, I'll take two for one. My hand on that."

Under a flag of truce they found Judge Ould, the Exchange Commissioner, who conducted them into Richmond under cover of darkness.

They stopped at the Spottswood House and the next morning saw Mr. Benjamin, who agreed to arrange an interview with Jefferson Davis.

Mr. Benjamin was polite, but inquisitive.

The Southerner

"Do you bring any overtures from your Government, gentlemen?"

"No, sir," answered Colonel Jaquess. "We bring no overtures and have no authority from our Government. As private citizens we simply wish to know what terms will be acceptable to Mr. Davis."

"Are you acquainted with Mr. Lincoln's views?"

"One of us is fully," said Colonel Jaquess.

"Did Mr. Lincoln in any way authorize you to come here?"

"No, sir," said Gilmore. "We came with his pass, but not by his request. We came as men and Christians, not as diplomats, hoping, in a frank talk with Mr. Davis, to discover some way by which this war may be stopped."

"Well, gentlemen," said Benjamin, "I will repeat what you say to the President, and if he follows my advice, he will meet you."

At nine o'clock the two men had entered the State Department and found Jefferson Davis seated at the long table on the right of his Secretary of State.

John Vaughan was given a seat at the other end of the table to report the interview for Mr. Benjamin.

He studied the distinguished President of the Confederate States with interest. He had never seen him before. His figure was extremely thin, his features typically Southern in their angular cheeks and high cheek bones. His iron-grey hair was long and thick and inclined to curl at the ends. His whiskers were small and trimmed farmer fashion--on the lower end of his strong chin. The clear grey eyes were full of vitality. His broad forehead, strong mouth and chin denoted an iron will. He wore a suit of greyish brown, of foreign manufacture, and as he rose, seemed about five feet ten inches. His shoulders slightly stooped.

His manner was easy and graceful, his voice cultured and charming.

"I am glad to see you, gentlemen," he said. "You are very welcome to Richmond."

"We thank you, Mr. Davis," Gilmore replied.

"Mr. Benjamin tells me that you have asked to see me to----"

He paused that the visitors might finish the sentence.

"Yes, sir," Jaquess answered. "Our people want peace, your people do. We have come to ask how it may be brought about?"

"Withdraw your armies, let us alone and peace will come at once."

"But we cannot let you alone so long as you repudiate the Union----"

"I know. You would deny us what you exact for yourselves--the right of self-government."

"Even so," said Colonel Jaquess, "we can not fight forever. The war must end sometime. We must finally agree on something. Can we not agree now and stop this frightful carnage?"

"I wish peace as much as you do," replied Mr. Davis. "I deplore bloodshed. But I feel that not one drop of this blood is on my hands. I can look up to God and say this. I tried all in my power to avert this war. I saw it coming and for twelve years I worked day and night to prevent it. The North was mad and blind, and would not let us govern ourselves and now it must go on until the last man of this generation falls in his tracks and his children seize his musket and fight our battle, ***unless you acknowledge our right to self-government***. We are not fighting for slavery. We are fighting for independence, and that or extermination we *will* have."

"We have no wish to exterminate you," protested the Colonel. "But we must crush your armies. Is it not already nearly done? Grant has shut you up in Richmond. Sherman is before Atlanta."

"You don't seem to understand the situation," Mr. Davis laughed. "We're not exactly shut up in Richmond yet. If your papers tell the truth it is your Capital that is in danger, not ours. Lee, whose front has never been broken, holds Grant in check and has men enough to spare to invade Maryland and Pennsylvania and threaten Washington. Sherman, to be sure, is before Atlanta. But suppose he is, the further he goes from his base of supplies, the more disastrous defeat must be. And defeat may come."

"But you cannot expect," Gilmore said, "with only four and one half millions to hold out forever against twenty?"

Mr. Davis smiled:

"Do you think there are twenty millions at the North determined to crush us? I do not so read the returns of your elections or the temper of your people."

"If I understand you, then," Jaquess continued, "the dispute with your government is narrowed to this, union or disunion?"

"Or, in other words, independence or subjugation. We will be free. We will govern ourselves. We will do it if we have to see every Southern plantation sacked and every Southern city in flames."

The visitors rose, and after a few pleasant remarks, took their leave. Mr. Davis was particularly cordial to Colonel Jaquess, whom he knew to have been a clergyman.

John was surprised to see him repeat the habit of Abraham Lincoln, of taking the hand of his visitor in both his in exactly the same cordial way.

He had forgotten for the moment that both Lincoln and Davis were Southerners, born in the same State and reared in precisely the same school of thought and social usage.

"Colonel," the thin Southerner said in his musical voice, "I respect your character and your motives and I wish you well--every good wish possible consistent with the interests of the Confederacy."

As they were passing through the door, he added:

"Say to Mr. Lincoln that I shall at any time be pleased to receive proposals for peace on the basis of our independence. It will be useless to approach me with any other."

Next morning the visitors waited in vain for the appearance of Judge Ould to convey them once more into the Union lines. Visions of a long term in prison, to say nothing of a possible hang-man's noose, began to float before their excited fancy. They had expected the Judge at eight o'clock. It was three in the afternoon when he entered with the laconic remark:

"Well, gentlemen, if you are ready, we'll walk around to Libby Prison."

Certain of their doom, the two men rose and spoke in concert:

"We are ready."

They followed the Judge downstairs and found the same coal black driver with the rickety team that had brought them into Richmond.

Gilmore smiled into the Judge's face:

"Why were you so long coming?"

Ould hesitated and laughed:

"I'll tell you when the war's over. Now I'll take you through the Libby and the hospitals, if you'd like to go."

When they had visited the prison and hospitals, Gilmore again turned to the Judge:

"Now, explain to us, please, your delay this morning--we're curious."

Ould smiled:

"I suppose I'd as well tell you. When I called on Mr. Davis for your permit, Mr. Benjamin was there impressing on the President of the Confederate States the absolute necessity of placing you two gentlemen in Castle Thunder until the Northern elections are over. Mr. Benjamin is a very eloquent advocate, and Mr. Davis hesitated. I took issue with the Secretary of State and we had a very exciting argument. The President finally reserved decision until two o'clock and asked me to call and get it. He handed me your pass with this remark:

"It's probably a bad business for us, but it would alienate many of our Northern friends if we should hold on to these gentlemen."

In two hours the visitors had reached the Union lines, John Vaughan had obtained his passes and was on his way to Atlanta.

CHAPTER XXXVIII
THE STOLEN MARCH

John Vaughan's entrance into Atlanta was simple. His credentials from Richmond were perfect. His exit proved to be a supreme test of his nerve.

The two lines of siege and battle stretched in wide semicircle for miles over the ragged wood tangled hills about the little Gate City of the South.

Sherman had fought his way from Chattanooga one hundred and fifty miles since May with consummate skill. His march had been practically a continuous series of battles, and yet his losses had been small compared to General Grant's. In killed, wounded and prisoners he had only lost thirty-two thousand men in four months. The Confederate losses had been greater--at least thirty-five thousand.

Hood, the new Southern Commander, had given him battle a month before and suffered an overwhelming defeat, losing eight thousand men, Sherman but thirty-seven hundred. The Confederate forces had retired behind the impregnable fortifications of Atlanta and Sherman lay behind his trenches watching in grim silence.

The pickets at many places were so close together they could talk. John Vaughan attempted to slip through at night while they were chaffing one another.

He lay for an hour in the woods near the Southern picket line watching his chance. The men were talking continuously.

"Why the devil don't you all fight?" a grey man called.

"Uncle Billy says it's cheaper to flank you and make you Johnnies run to catch up with us."

"Yes--damn you, and we've got ye now where ye can't do no more flankin'. Ye got ter fight!"

"Trust Uncle Billy for that when the time comes----"

"Yes, and we've got Billy Sherman whar we want him now. We're goin' to blow up every bridge behind ye and ye'll never see home no more----"

"Uncle Billy's got duplicates of all your bridges fast as ye blow 'em up."

"All right, we're goin' ter blow up the tunnels through the mountains----"

"That's nothin'--we got duplicates to all the tunnels, too!"

John Vaughan began to creep toward the Federal lines and muskets blazed from both sides. He dropped flat on the ground and it took two hours to crawl to a place of safety.

He felt these lines next morning where they were wider apart and found them too dangerous to attempt. The pickets, at the point he approached, were in an ugly mood and a desultory fire was kept up all day. The men had bunched up two together and entrenched themselves, keeping a deadly watch for the men in blue. He stood for half an hour close enough to see every movement of two young pickets who evidently had some score to pay and were hunting for their foe with quiet, deadly purpose.

"There's a Yank behind that clump," said one.

"Na--nothin' but a huckleberry bush," the other replied.

"Yes there is, too. We'll decoy and pot him. I'll get ready now and you raise your cap on a ramrod above the hole. He'll lift his head to fire and I'll get him."

The speaker cautiously slipped his musket in place and drew a bead on the spot. His partner placed his hat on his ramrod and slowly lifted it a foot above their hiding place.

The hat had scarcely cleared the pile of dirt before the musket flashed.

"I got him! I told you he was there!"

John turned from the scene with a sense of sickening horror. He would die for his country, but he hoped he would not be called on to kill again.

He made a wide detour and attempted to cross the lines five miles further from the city and walked suddenly into a squad of grey soldiers in command of a lieutenant.

The officer eyed him with suspicion.

"What's your business here, sir?" he asked sharply.

"Looking over the lines," John replied casually.

"So I see. That's why I asked you. Show your pass."

"Why, I haven't one."

"I thought not. You're a damned spy and you'd just as well say your prayers. I'm going to hang you."

The men pressed near. Among them was a second lieutenant, a big, strapping, quiet-looking fellow.

"You've made a mistake, gentlemen," John protested.

"I'm a newspaper man from Atlanta. The chief sent me out to look over the lines and report."

"It's a lie. We've forbidden every paper in town to dare such a thing----"

John smiled:

"That's just why my office sent me, I reckon."

"Well, he sent you once too often----"

He turned to his orderly:

"Get me a bridle rein off my horse."

In vain John protested. The Commander shook his head:

"It's no use talking. You've passed the deadline here to-day. This is a favorite spot for scouts to cross. I'm not going to take any chances; I'm going to hang you."

"Why don't you search me first?"

He was sure that his dangerous message was so skillfully sewed in the soles of his shoes they would not be discovered.

"I can search you afterwards," was the laconic reply.

He quickly tied the leather strap around his neck and threw the end of it over a limb. The touch of his hand and the rough way in which he had tied the leather stirred John Vaughan's rage to boiling point. All sense of danger was lost for the moment in blind anger. He turned suddenly and faced his executioner:

"This is a damned outrage, sir! Even a spy is entitled to a trial by drumhead court-martial!"

"Yes, that's what I say," the big, quiet fellow broke in.

"I'm in command of this squad!" thundered the lieutenant.

"I know you are," was the cool answer, "that's why this outrage is going to be committed."

The executioner dropped the rein and faced his subordinate:

"You're going to question my authority?"

"I've already done it, haven't I?"

A quick blow followed. The quiet man, in response, knocked his commander down and the men sprang on them as they drew their revolvers.

John Vaughan, with a sudden leap, reached the dense woods and in five minutes was inside Sherman's lines.

The bridle rein was still around his neck and the blue picket helped him untie the ugly knot.

"I've had a close call," he panted, with a glance toward the woods.

"You look it, partner. You'll be wantin' to see General Sherman, I guess?"

"Yes--to headquarters quick--you can't get there too quick to suit me."

He had recovered his composure before reaching the farm house where General Sherman and his staff were quartered.

The day was one of terrific heat--the first of September. The President's description of the famous fighter and the tremendous responsibility which was now being placed on his shoulders had roused John's curiosity to the highest pitch.

The General was seated in an arm chair in the yard under a great oak. His coat was unbuttoned and he had tilted back against the tree in a comfortable position reading a newspaper. His black slouch hat was pulled far down over his face.

John saluted:

"This is General Sherman?"

"Yes," was the quick, pleasant answer as the tall, gaunt form slowly rose.

John noted his striking and powerful personality--the large frame, restless hazel eyes, fine aquiline nose, bronzed features and cropped beard. His every movement was instinct with the power of perfect physical manhood, forty-four years old, the incarnation of health and wiry strength.

"I come from Washington, General," John continued, "and bear a special message from the President."

"From the President! Oh, come inside then."

The tall figure moved with quick, nervous energy. In ten minutes couriers were dashing from his headquarters in every direction.

At one o'clock that night the big movement of his withdrawal from the siege lines began. He had no intention of hurling his men against those deadly trenches. He believed that with a sure, swift start undiscovered by the Confederates he could by a single battle turn their lines at Jonesboro, destroy the railroad and force General Hood to evacuate Atlanta.

His sleeping men were carefully waked. Not a single note from bugle or drum sounded. The wheels of the artillery and wagons were wrapped with cloth and every sound muffled.

Through pitch darkness in dead silence the men were swung into marching lines. The moving columns could be felt but not seen. Each soldier followed blindly the man before. Somewhere in the black night there must be a leader--God knew--they didn't. They walked by faith. The wet grounds, soaked by recent rains, made their exit easier. The sound of horses' hoofs and tramping thousands could scarcely be heard.

The ranks were strung out in long, ragged lines, each man going as he pleased. Something blocked the way ahead and the columns butted into one another and pinched the heels of the men in front.

In their anger the fellows smarting with pain forgot the orders for silence. A storm of low muttering and growling rumbled through the darkness.

"What 'ell here!"

"What's the matter with you----"

"Keep off my heels!"

"What 'ell are ye runnin' over me for?"

"Hold up your damned gun----"

"Keep it out of my eye, won't you?"

"Damn your eye!"

They start again and run into a bog of mud knee deep cut into mush by the artillery and wagons which have passed on.

The first men in line were in to their knees and stuck fast before they could stop the lines surging on in the dark. They collide with the bogged ones and fall over them. The ranks behind stumble in on top of the fallen before word can be passed to halt.

The night reeks with oaths. The patient heavens reverberate with them. The mud-soaked soldiers damned with equal unction all things visible and invisible on the earth, under it and above it. They cursed the United States of America and they damned the Confederate States with equal emphasis and wished them both at the bottom of the lowest depths of the deepest pit of perdition.

As one fellow blew the mud from his mouth and nose he bawled:

"I wish Sherman and Hood were both in hell this minute!"

"Yes, and fightin' it out to suit themselves!" his comrade answered.

On through the black night the long blue lines crept under lowering skies toward their foe, the stern face of William Tecumseh Sherman grimly set on his desperate purpose.

CHAPTER XXXIX
VICTORY

Betty had found the President at the War Telegraph office in the old Army and Navy building. He was seated at the desk by the window where in 1862 he had written his first draft of his Emancipation Proclamation on pieces of pasteboard.

"You have heard nothing yet from General Sherman?" she asked pathetically.

"Nothing, child."

"And no message of any kind from John Vaughan since he left!" she exclaimed hopelessly.

"But I'm sure, remember, sure to a moral certainty--that he reached Richmond safely and left there safely."

"How do you know?"

"Gilmore has just arrived with his reply from Jefferson Davis. It will be worth a half million votes for us. From his description of the 'reporter' with Benjamin I am sure it was our messenger."

"But you don't know--you don't know!" Betty sighed.

The President bent and touched her shoulder gently:

"Come, dear, it's not like you to despair----"

The girl smiled wanly.

"How long since any message arrived from General Sherman?"

"Three days, my child. I know the hole he went in at, but I can't tell where he's going to come out----"

"If he ever comes out," Betty broke in bitterly.

"Oh, he'll come out somewhere!" the President laughed. "It's a habit of his. I've watched him for months--sometimes I can't hear from him for a week--but he always bobs up again and comes out with a whoop, too----"

"But we've no news!" she interrupted.

"No news has always been good news from Sherman----"

He paused and looked at his watch:

"Wait here. I'll be back in a few moments. We're bound to hear something to-day. I've an engagement with my Committee of Undertakers. They are waiting for me to deliver my corpse to them--and they are very restless about it because I haven't given up sooner, I'm full of foolish hopes. I'm going to adjourn them until we can get a message of some kind----"

He returned in half an hour and sat in silence for a long time listening to the steady, sharp click of the telegraph keys.

Betty was too blue to talk--too heartsick to move.

At last the tall figure rose and walked back among the operators. They knew that he was waiting for the magic call, "Atlanta, Georgia." It had been three years and more since that heading for a message had flashed over their wires. Every ear was keen to catch it.

The President bent over the table of Southern wires and silently watched:

"You can't strain a little message through for me, can you, my boy?"

The operator smiled:

"I wish I could, sir."

The President returned to the front room and shook his head to Betty:

"Nothing."

"He entered Atlanta a spy, didn't he?" she said despairingly.

"Yes--of course."

"They couldn't execute him without our knowing it, could they?"

"If they trap him--yes--but he's a very intelligent young man. He'll be too smart for them. I feel it. I know it----"

He stopped and looked at her quizzically:

"I've a sort of second sight that tells me such things. I saw General Sickles in the hospital after Gettysburg. They said he couldn't live. I told him he would get well and he did."

Again the President returned restlessly to the operator's room and Betty followed him to the door. He waited a long time in silence, shook his head and turned away. He had almost reached the door when suddenly the operator sprang to his feet livid with excitement:

"Wait--Mr. President!--It's come--my God, it's here!"

Every operator was on his feet listening in breathless excitement to the click of that Southern wire.

The President had rushed back to the table.

"It's for you, sir!"

"Read it then--out with it as you take it!" he cried.

"Atlanta, Georgia, September 3rd, 1864."

"Glory to God!" the President shouted.

"Atlanta is ours and fairly won. W. T. Sherman."

"O my soul, lift up thy head!" the sorrowful lips shouted. "Unto thee, O God, we give all the praise now and forever more!"

He seated himself and quickly wrote his thanks and congratulations:

"EXECUTIVE MANSION,
"WASHINGTON, D. C.
"September 3, 1864.

"The National thanks are rendered by the President to Major General W. T. Sherman and the gallant officers and soldiers of his command before Atlanta, for the distinguished ability and perseverance displayed in the campaign in Georgia, which under Divine favor has resulted in the capture of Atlanta. The marches, battles and sieges that have signalized this campaign must render it famous in the annals of war, and have entitled you to the applause and thanks of the Nation.

"ABRAHAM LINCOLN,
"*President of the United States*."

His sombre eyes flamed with a new light. He took the copy of his message from Sherman and started to the White House with long, swift strides.

Betty greeted him outside with tearful joy still mixed with deep anxiety.

"You have no word from him, of course?"

"Not yet, child, but it will come--cheer up--it's sure to come. You see that he reached Atlanta and delivered my message!"

"We are not sure. The city may have fallen, anyhow----"

"Yes, yes, but it didn't just fall, anyhow. Sherman took it. He got my message. I know it. I felt it flash through the air from his soul to mine!"

His faith and enthusiasm were contagious and Betty returned home with new hope.

In half an hour the Committee who were waiting for his resignation from the National Republican ticket filed into his office to receive as they supposed his final surrender.

The Chairman rose with doleful countenance:

"Since leaving you, Mr. President, we have just heard a most painful and startling announcement from the War Department. We begged you to withhold the new draft for five hundred thousand men until after the election. Halleck informs us of the discovery of a great combination to resist it by armed force and General Grant must detach a part of his army from Lee's front in order to put down this counter revolution. This is the blackest news yet. We trust that you realize the impossibility of your administration asking for indorsement at the polls----"

With a sign of final resignation he sat down and the tall, dark figure rose with quick, nervous energy.

"I, too, have received important news since I saw you an hour ago."

He held the telegram above his head:

"I'll read it to you without my glasses. I know it by heart. I have just learned that my administration will be indorsed by an overwhelming majority, that the defeat of George B. McClellan and his platform of failure is a certainty. The war to preserve the Union is a success. The sword has been driven into the heart of the Confederacy. Sherman has captured Atlanta--the Union is saved!"

The Committee leaped to their feet with a shout of applause and crowded around him to congratulate and praise the man they came to bury. There was no longer a question of his resignation. The fall of Atlanta would thrill the North. A wave of wild enthusiasm would sweep into the sea the last trace of gloom and despair. They were practical men--else, as rats, they would never have tried to desert their own ship. They knew that the tide was going to turn, but it was a swift tide that could turn before they could!

They wrung the President's hands, they shouted his praise, they had always gloried in his administration, but foolish grumblers hadn't been able to see things as they saw them--hence this hue and cry! They congratulated him on his certain triumph and the President watched them go with a quiet smile. He was too big to cherish resentments. He only pitied small men, he never hated them.

CHAPTER XL
WITH MALICE TOWARD NONE

General Grant fired a salute in honor of the Atlanta victory with shotted guns from every battery on his siege lines of thirty-seven miles before Richmond and Petersburg. To Sherman he sent a remarkable message--the kind which great men know how to pen:

"You have accomplished the most gigantic undertaking given to any General in this war, with a skill and ability which will be acknowledged in history as unsurpassed if not unequaled."

From the depths of despair the North swung to the wildest enthusiasm and in the election which followed Abraham Lincoln was swept into power again on a tidal wave. He received in round numbers two million five hundred thousand votes, McClellan two millions. His majority by States in the electoral college was overwhelming--two hundred and twelve to his opponent's twenty-one.

The closing words of his second Inaugural rang clear and quivering with emotion over the vast crowd:

"With malice toward none; with charity for all; with firmness in the right, as God gives us to see the right, let us strive on to finish the work we are in; to bind up the nation's wounds; to care for him who shall have borne the battle, and for his widow and his orphan--to do all which may achieve and cherish a just and lasting peace among ourselves and with all nations."

As the last echo died away among the marble pillars above, the sun burst through the clouds and flooded the scene. A mighty cheer swept the throng and the guns boomed their second salute. The war was closing in lasting peace and the sun shining on the finished dome of the Capitol of a new nation.

Betty Winter, leaning on John Vaughan's arm, was among the first to grasp his big, outstretched hand:

"A glorious day for us, sir," she cried, "a proud one for you!"

With a far-away look the President slowly answered:

"And all that I am in this world, Miss Betty, I owe to a woman--my angel mother--blessings on her memory!"

"I trust her spirit heard that beautiful speech," the girl responded tenderly.

She paused, looked up at John, blushed and added:

"We are to be married next week, Mr. President----"

"Is it so?" he said joyfully. "I wish I could be there, my children--but I'm afraid 'Old Grizzly' might bite me. So I'll say it now--God bless you!"

He took their hands in his and pressed them heartily. His eyes suddenly rested on a shining black face grinning behind John Vaughan.

"My, my, can this be Julius Caesar Thornton?" he laughed.

"Yassah," the black man grinned. "Hit's me--ole reliable, sah, right here--I'se gwine ter cook fur 'em!"

* * * * *

From the moment of Abraham Lincoln's election the end of the war with a restored Union was a foregone conclusion.

In the fall of Atlanta the heart of the Confederacy was pierced, and it ceased to beat. Lee's army, cut off from their supplies, slowly but surely began to starve behind their impregnable breastworks. Sherman's march to the sea and through the Carolinas was merely a torchlight parade. The fighting was done.

When Lee's emaciated men, living on a handful of parched corn a day, staggered out of their trenches in the spring and tried to join Johnston's army they marched a few miles to Appomattox, dropping from exhaustion, and surrendered.

When the news of this tremendous event reached Washington, the Cabinet was in session. Led by the President, in silence and tears, they fell on their knees in a prayer of solemn thanks to Almighty God.

General Grant won the gratitude of the South by his generous treatment of Lee and his ragged men. He had received instructions from the loving heart in the White House.

Long before the surrender in April, 1865, the end was sure. The President knowing this, proposed to his Cabinet to give the South four hundred millions of dollars, the cost of the war for a hundred days, in payment for their slaves, if they would lay down their arms at once. His ministers unanimously voted against his offer and he sadly withdrew it. Among all his councillors there was not one whose soul was big enough to understand the far-seeing wisdom of his generous plan. He would heal at once one of the Nation's ugliest wounds by soothing the bitterness of defeat. He knew that despair would send the older men of the South to their graves.

Edmund Ruffin, who had fired the first shot against Sumter and returned to his Virginia farm when his State seceded, was a type of these ruined, desperate men. On the day that Lee surrendered he placed the muzzle of his gun in his mouth, pulled the trigger with his foot, and blew his own head into fragments.

When Senator Winter demanded proscription and vengeance against the leaders of the Confederacy, the President shook his head:

"No--let down the bars--let them all go--scare them off!"

He threw up his big hands in a vivid gesture as if he were shooing a flock of troublesome sheep out of his garden.

"Triumphant now, you will receive our enemies with open arms?" the Senator sneered.

"Enemies? There are no such things. The Southern States have never really been out of the Union. Their Acts of Secession were null and void. They know now that the issue is forever settled. The restored Union will be a real one. The Southern people at heart are law-abiding. It was their reverence for the letter of the old law which led them to ignore progress and claim the right to secede under the Constitution. They will be true to Lee's pledge of surrender. I'm going to trust them as my brethren. Let us fold up our banners now and smelt the guns--Love rules--let her mightier purpose run!"

So big and generous, so broad and statesmanlike was his spirit that in this hour of victory his personality became in a day the soul of the New Republic. The South had already unconsciously grown to respect the man who had loved yet fought her for what he believed to be her highest good.

He was entering now a new phase of power. His influence over the people was supreme. No man or set of men in Congress, or outside of it, could defeat his policies. Even through the years of stunning defeats and measureless despair his enemies had never successfully opposed a measure on which he had set his heart.

His first great work accomplished in destroying slavery and restoring the Union, there remained but two tasks on which his soul was set--to heal the bitterness of the war and remove the negro race from physical contact with the white.

He at once addressed himself to this work with enthusiasm. That he could do it he never doubted for a moment.

His first care was to remove the negro soldiers from the country as quickly as possible. He summoned General Butler and set him to work on his scheme to use these one hundred and eighty thousand black troops to dig the Panama Canal. He summoned Bradley, the Vermont contractor, and put him to work on estimates for moving the negroes by ship to Africa or by train to an undeveloped Western Territory.

His prophetic soul had pierced the future and seen with remorseless logic that two such races as the Negro and Caucasian could not live side by side in a free democracy. The Radical theorists of Congress were demanding that these black men, emerging from four thousand years of slavery and savagery should receive the ballot and the right to claim the white man's daughter in marriage. They could only pass these measures over the dead body of Abraham Lincoln.

The assassin came at last--a vain, foolish dreamer who had long breathed the poisoned air of hatred. It needed but the flash of this madman's pistol on the night of the 14th of April to reveal the grandeur of Lincoln's character, the marvel of his patience and his wisdom.

The curtains of the box in Ford's theatre were softly drawn apart by an unseen hand. The Angel of Death entered, paused at the sight of the smile on his rugged, kindly face, touched the drooping shoulders, called him to take the place he had won among earth's immortals and left to us "the gentlest memory of our world."

THE END

www.bookjungle.com *email: sales@bookjungle.com fax: 630-214-0564 mail: Book Jungle PO Box 2226 Champaign, IL 61825*

The Codes Of Hammurabi And Moses
W. W. Davies

QTY

The discovery of the Hammurabi Code is one of the greatest achievements of archaeology, and is of paramount interest, not only to the student of the Bible, but also to all those interested in ancient history...

Religion   **ISBN:** *1-59462-338-4*   **Pages:**132   *MSRP $12.95*

The Theory of Moral Sentiments
Adam Smith

QTY

This work from 1749. contains original theories of conscience amd moral judgment and it is the foundation for systemof morals.

Philosophy   **ISBN:** *1-59462-777-0*   **Pages:**536   *MSRP $19.95*

Jessica's First Prayer
Hesba Stretton

QTY

In a screened and secluded corner of one of the many railway-bridges which span the streets of London there could be seen a few years ago, from five o'clock every morning until half past eight, a tidily set-out coffee-stall, consisting of a trestle and board, upon which stood two large tin cans, with a small fire of charcoal burning under each so as to keep the coffee boiling during the early hours of the morning when the work-people were thronging into the city on their way to their daily toil...

Childrens   **ISBN:** *1-59462-373-2*   **Pages:**84   *MSRP $9.95*

My Life and Work
Henry Ford

QTY

Henry Ford revolutionized the world with his implementation of mass production for the Model T automobile. Gain valuable business insight into his life and work with his own auto-biography... "We have only started on our development of our country we have not as yet, with all our talk of wonderful progress, done more than scratch the surface. The progress has been wonderful enough but..."

Biographies/   **ISBN:** *1-59462-198-5*   **Pages:**300   *MSRP $21.95* www.bookjungle.com email: sales@bookjungle.com fax: 630-214-0564 mail: Book Jungle PO Box 2226 Champaign, IL 61825

The Art of Cross-Examination
Francis Wellman

QTY

I presume it is the experience of every author, after his first book is published upon an important subject, to be almost overwhelmed with a wealth of ideas and illustrations which could readily have been included in his book, and which to his own mind, at least, seem to make a second edition inevitable. Such certainly was the case with me; and when the first edition had reached its sixth impression in five months, I rejoiced to learn that it seemed to my publishers that the book had met with a sufficiently favorable reception to justify a second and considerably enlarged edition. ..

Reference   ISBN: *1-59462-647-2*

Pages:412
MSRP *$19.95*

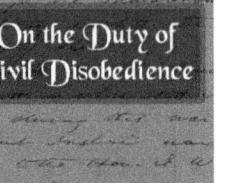

On the Duty of Civil Disobedience
Henry David Thoreau

QTY

Thoreau wrote his famous essay, On the Duty of Civil Disobedience, as a protest against an unjust but popular war and the immoral but popular institution of slave-owning. He did more than write—he declined to pay his taxes, and was hauled off to gaol in consequence. Who can say how much this refusal of his hastened the end of the war and of slavery ?

Law   ISBN: *1-59462-747-9*

Pages:48
MSRP *$7.45*

Dream Psychology Psychoanalysis for Beginners
Sigmund Freud

QTY

Sigmund Freud, born Sigismund Schlomo Freud (May 6, 1856 - September 23, 1939), was a Jewish-Austrian neurologist and psychiatrist who co-founded the psychoanalytic school of psychology. Freud is best known for his theories of the unconscious mind, especially involving the mechanism of repression; his redefinition of sexual desire as mobile and directed towards a wide variety of objects; and his therapeutic techniques, especially his understanding of transference in the therapeutic relationship and the presumed value of dreams as sources of insight into unconscious desires.

Psychology   ISBN: *1-59462-905-6*

Pages:196
MSRP *$15.45*

The Miracle of Right Thought
Orison Swett Marden

QTY

Believe with all of your heart that you will do what you were made to do. When the mind has once formed the habit of holding cheerful, happy, prosperous pictures, it will not be easy to form the opposite habit. It does not matter how improbable or how far away this realization may see, or how dark the prospects may be, if we visualize them as best we can, as vividly as possible, hold tenaciously to them and vigorously struggle to attain them, they will gradually become actualized, realized in the life. But a desire, a longing without endeavor, a yearning abandoned or held indifferently will vanish without realization.

Self Help   ISBN: *1-59462-644-8*

Pages:360
MSRP *$25.45*

www.bookjungle.com email: sales@bookjungle.com fax: 630-214-0564 mail: Book Jungle PO Box 2226 Champaign, IL 61825

QTY

☐ **The Rosicrucian Cosmo-Conception Mystic Christianity** by *Max Heindel* ISBN: *1-59462-188-8* **$38.95**
The Rosicrucian Cosmo-conception is not dogmatic, neither does it appeal to any other authority than the reason of the student. It is: not controversial, but is: sent forth in the, hope that it may help to clear... *New Age/Religion Pages 646*

☐ **Abandonment To Divine Providence** by *Jean-Pierre de Caussade* ISBN: *1-59462-228-0* **$25.95**
"The Rev. Jean Pierre de Caussade was one of the most remarkable spiritual writers of the Society of Jesus in France in the 18th Century. His death took place at Toulouse in 1751. His works have gone through many editions and have been republished... *Inspirational/Religion Pages 400*

☐ **Mental Chemistry** by *Charles Haanel* ISBN: *1-59462-192-6* **$23.95**
Mental Chemistry allows the change of material conditions by combining and appropriately utilizing the power of the mind. Much like applied chemistry creates something new and unique out of careful combinations of chemicals the mastery of mental chemistry... *New Age/Business Pages 354*

☐ **The Letters of Robert Browning and Elizabeth Barret Barrett 1845-1846 vol II** ISBN: *1-59462-193-4* **$35.95**
by *Robert Browning* and *Elizabeth Barrett* *Biographies Pages 596*

☐ **Gleanings In Genesis (volume I)** by *Arthur W. Pink* ISBN: *1-59462-130-6* **$27.45**
Appropriately has Genesis been termed "the seed plot of the Bible" for in it we have, in germ form, almost all of the great doctrines which are afterwards fully developed in the books of Scripture which follow... *Religion/Inspirational Pages 420*

☐ **The Master Key** by *L. W. de Laurence* ISBN: *1-59462-001-6* **$30.95**
In no branch of human knowledge has there been a more lively increase of the spirit of research during the past few years than in the study of Psychology, Concentration and Mental Discipline. The requests for authentic lessons in Thought Control, Mental Discipline and... *New Age/Business Pages 422*

☐ **The Lesser Key Of Solomon Goetia** by *L. W. de Laurence* ISBN: *1-59462-092-X* **$9.95**
This translation of the first book of the "Lernegton" which is now for the first time made accessible to students of Talismanic Magic was done, after careful collation and edition, from numerous Ancient Manuscripts in Hebrew, Latin, and French... *New Age/Occult Pages 92*

☐ **Rubaiyat Of Omar Khayyam** by *Edward Fitzgerald* ISBN:*1-59462-332-5* **$13.95**
Edward Fitzgerald, whom the world has already learned, in spite of his own efforts to remain within the shadow of anonymity, to look upon as one of the rarest poets of the century, was born at Bredfield, in Suffolk, on the 31st of March, 1809. He was the third son of John Purcell... *Music Pages 172*

☐ **Ancient Law** by *Henry Maine* ISBN: *1-59462-128-4* **$29.95**
The chief object of the following pages is to indicate some of the earliest ideas of mankind, as they are reflected in Ancient Law, and to point out the relation of those ideas to modern thought. *Religiom/History Pages 452*

☐ **Far-Away Stories** by *William J. Locke* ISBN: *1-59462-129-2* **$19.45**
"Good wine needs no bush, but a collection of mixed vintages does. And this book is just such a collection. Some of the stories I do not want to remain buried for ever in the museum files of dead magazine-numbers an author's not unpardonable vanity..." *Fiction Pages 272*

☐ **Life of David Crockett** by *David Crockett* ISBN: *1-59462-250-7* **$27.45**
"Colonel David Crockett was one of the most remarkable men of the times in which he lived. Born in humble life, but gifted with a strong will, an indomitable courage, and unremitting perseverance... *Biographies/New Age Pages 424*

☐ **Lip-Reading** by *Edward Nitchie* ISBN: *1-59462-206-X* **$25.95**
Edward B. Nitchie, founder of the New York School for the Hard of Hearing, now the Nitchie School of Lip-Reading, Inc, wrote "LIP-READING Principles and Practice". The development and perfecting of this meritorious work on lip-reading was an undertaking... *How-to Pages 400*

☐ **A Handbook of Suggestive Therapeutics, Applied Hypnotism, Psychic Science** ISBN: *1-59462-214-0* **$24.95**
by *Henry Munro* *Health/New Age/Health/Self-help Pages 376*

☐ **A Doll's House: and Two Other Plays** by *Henrik Ibsen* ISBN: *1-59462-112-8* **$19.95**
Henrik Ibsen created this classic when in revolutionary 1848 Rome. Introducing some striking concepts in playwriting for the realist genre, this play has been studied the world over. *Fiction/Classics/Plays 308*

☐ **The Light of Asia** by *sir Edwin Arnold* ISBN: *1-59462-204-3* **$13.95**
In this poetic masterpiece, Edwin Arnold describes the life and teachings of Buddha. The man who was to become known as Buddha to the world was born as Prince Gautama of India but he rejected the worldly riches and abandoned the reigns of power when... *Religion/History/Biographies Pages 170*

☐ **The Complete Works of Guy de Maupassant** by *Guy de Maupassant* ISBN: *1-59462-157-8* **$16.95**
"For days and days, nights and nights, I had dreamed of that first kiss which was to consecrate our engagement, and I knew not on what spot I should put my lips..." *Fiction/Classics Pages 240*

☐ **The Art of Cross-Examination** by *Francis L. Wellman* ISBN: *1-59462-309-0* **$26.95**
Written by a renowned trial lawyer, Wellman imparts his experience and uses case studies to explain how to use psychology to extract desired information through questioning. *How-to/Science/Reference Pages 408*

☐ **Answered or Unanswered?** by *Louisa Vaughan* ISBN: *1-59462-248-5* **$10.95**
Miracles of Faith in China *Religion Pages 112*

☐ **The Edinburgh Lectures on Mental Science (1909)** by *Thomas* ISBN: *1-59462-008-3* **$11.95**
This book contains the substance of a course of lectures recently given by the writer in the Queen Street Hall, Edinburgh. Its purpose is to indicate the Natural Principles governing the relation between Mental Action and Material Conditions... *New Age/Psychology Pages 148*

☐ **Ayesha** by *H. Rider Haggard* ISBN: *1-59462-301-5* **$24.95**
Verily and indeed it is the unexpected that happens! Probably if there was one person upon the earth from whom the Editor of this, and of a certain previous history, did not expect to hear again... *Classics Pages 380*

☐ **Ayala's Angel** by *Anthony Trollope* ISBN: *1-59462-352-X* **$29.95**
The two girls were both pretty, but Lucy who was twenty-one who supposed to be simple and comparatively unattractive, whereas Ayala was credited, as her Bombwhat romantic name might show, with poetic charm and a taste for romance. Ayala when her father died was nineteen... *Fiction Pages 484*

☐ **The American Commonwealth** by *James Bryce* ISBN: *1-59462-286-8* **$34.45**
An interpretation of American democratic political theory. It examines political mechanics and society from the perspective of Scotsman James Bryce *Politics Pages 572*

☐ **Stories of the Pilgrims** by *Margaret P. Pumphrey* ISBN: *1-59462-116-0* **$17.95**
This book explores pilgrims religious oppression in England as well as their escape to Holland and eventual crossing to America on the Mayflower, and their early days in New England... *History Pages 268*

www.bookjungle.com *email: sales@bookjungle.com fax: 630-214-0564 mail: Book Jungle PO Box 2226 Champaign, IL 61825*

Title	ISBN	Price	QTY
The Fasting Cure by Sinclair Upton — *In the Cosmopolitan Magazine for May, 1910, and in the Contemporary Review (London) for April, 1910, I published an article dealing with my experiences in fasting. I have written a great many magazine articles, but never one which attracted so much attention...* New Age/Self Help/Health Pages 164	1-59462-222-1	$13.95	
Hebrew Astrology by Sepharial — *In these days of advanced thinking it is a matter of common observation that we have left many of the old landmarks behind and that we are now pressing forward to greater heights and to a wider horizon than that which represented the mind-content of our progenitors...* Astrology Pages 144	1-59462-308-2	$13.45	
Thought Vibration or The Law of Attraction in the Thought World by William Walker Atkinson — Psychology/Religion Pages 144	1-59462-127-6	$12.95	
Optimism by Helen Keller — *Helen Keller was blind, deaf, and mute since 19 months old, yet famously learned how to overcome these handicaps, communicate with the world, and spread her lectures promoting optimism. An inspiring read for everyone...* Biographies/Inspirational Pages 84	1-59462-108-X	$15.95	
Sara Crewe by Frances Burnett — *In the first place, Miss Minchin lived in London. Her home was a large, dull, tall one, in a large, dull square, where all the houses were alike, and all the sparrows were alike, and where all the door-knockers made the same heavy sound...* Childrens/Classic Pages 88	1-59462-360-0	$9.45	
The Autobiography of Benjamin Franklin by Benjamin Franklin — *The Autobiography of Benjamin Franklin has probably been more extensively read than any other American historical work, and no other book of its kind has had such ups and downs of fortune. Franklin lived for many years in England, where he was agent...* Biographies/History Pages 332	1-59462-135-7	$24.95	

Name	
Email	
Telephone	
Address	
City, State ZIP	

☐ Credit Card   ☐ Check / Money Order

Credit Card Number	
Expiration Date	
Signature	

Please Mail to: Book Jungle
　　　　　　　　　PO Box 2226
　　　　　　　　　Champaign, IL 61825
or Fax to:　　　 630-214-0564

ORDERING INFORMATION

web: *www.bookjungle.com*
email: *sales@bookjungle.com*
fax: *630-214-0564*
mail: *Book Jungle PO Box 2226 Champaign, IL 61825*
or PayPal *to sales@bookjungle.com*

Please contact us for bulk discounts

DIRECT-ORDER TERMS

**20% Discount if You Order
Two or More Books**
Free Domestic Shipping!
Accepted: Master Card, Visa,
Discover, American Express

ncontent.com/pod-product-compliance
ource LLC
rg PA
034230426
300016B/2648